SAGE PUBLISHING: OUR STORY

We believe in creating fresh, cutting-edge content that helps you prepare your students to make an impact in today's ever-changing business world. Founded in 1965 by 24-year-old entrepreneur Sara Miller McCune, SAGE continues its legacy of equipping instructors with the tools and resources necessary to develop the next generation of business leaders.

- We invest in the right **authors** who distill the best available research into practical applications.

- We offer intuitive **digital solutions** at student-friendly prices.

- We remain permanently independent and fiercely committed to **quality, innovation, and learning.**

Business Writing Today

Third Edition

For Allan Rosenheck, my big brother, always.

Sara Miller McCune founded SAGE Publishing in 1965 to support the dissemination of usable knowledge and educate a global community. SAGE publishes more than 1000 journals and over 800 new books each year, spanning a wide range of subject areas. Our growing selection of library products includes archives, data, case studies and video. SAGE remains majority owned by our founder and after her lifetime will become owned by a charitable trust that secures the company's continued independence.

Los Angeles | London | New Delhi | Singapore | Washington DC | Melbourne

Business Writing Today

A Practical Guide

Third Edition

Natalie Canavor

Los Angeles | London | New Delhi
Singapore | Washington DC | Melbourne

FOR INFORMATION:

SAGE Publications, Inc.
2455 Teller Road
Thousand Oaks, California 91320
E-mail: order@sagepub.com

SAGE Publications Ltd.
1 Oliver's Yard
55 City Road
London EC1Y 1SP
United Kingdom

SAGE Publications India Pvt. Ltd.
B 1/I 1 Mohan Cooperative Industrial Area
Mathura Road, New Delhi 110 044
India

SAGE Publications Asia-Pacific Pte. Ltd.
3 Church Street
#10-04 Samsung Hub
Singapore 049483

Acquisitions Editor: Maggie Stanley
Editorial Assistant: Alissa Nance
Production Editor: Bennie Clark Allen
Copy Editor: Sarah J. Duffy
Typesetter: C&M Digitals (P) Ltd.
Proofreader: Eleni-Maria Georgiou
Indexer: Jeanne Busemeyer
Cover Designer: Glenn Vogel
Marketing Manager: Amy Lammers

Printed in the United States of America

Library of Congress Cataloging-in-Publication Data

Names: Canavor, Natalie, author.

Title: Business writing today : a practical guide / Natalie Canavor.

Description: Third edition. | Los Angeles : SAGE, [2019] | Includes index.

Identifiers: LCCN 2017057082 | ISBN 9781506388328 (pbk. : alk. paper)

Subjects: LCSH: Business writing.

Classification: LCC HF5718.3 .C3655 2019 | DDC 808.06/665—dc23
LC record available at https://lccn.loc.gov/2017057082

This book is printed on acid-free paper.

SFI label applies to text stock

18 19 20 21 22 10 9 8 7 6 5 4 3 2 1

BRIEF CONTENTS

DETAILED CONTENTS

PREFACE

This book has a simple but ambitious goal: to help give college students—people like you—a powerful edge in today's workplace.

During my own successive careers as a magazine editor, journalist and public relations manager, I've watched far too many talented people sabotage their success through bad writing. I learned on the job, like most professional writers, and I took endless workshops from writing specialists. In turn I began sharing my discoveries and helped businesspeople, professionals and communicators skip all that trial and error and write better. It was rewarding: I found that once people understood what works, they could dramatically improve their writing and reap surprising rewards.

So I wondered: What if young people started out with a more positive model of business writing—one ruled by clarity, simplicity and natural language? And what if they knew how to write for results with practical, down-to-earth techniques, right from the beginning?

A chance to find out materialized through NYU, which had recently founded a master's program in public relations and corporate communications. As an instructor I was able to experiment with my own version of an advanced writing seminar, which led to the first edition of this book and six years of teaching. Success! Students learned to write better!

Yet . . . I realized that even these grad students, preparing for communication careers, began as reluctant learners. Most signed on for the program's writing seminar series only because the courses were required. My feelings weren't hurt: I had already learned that few businesspeople choose a writing workshop if given a choice. A seminar on speaking skills sounds so much sexier!

That's why I'd like to say to each one of you: Don't miss this chance. You own the opportunity to transform your writing. This will help you accomplish your future goals and become a more successful person with a happier life. This is a lot to promise, I know. But I believe this can happen *when you learn to communicate strategically.*

To open up your thinking, let me name the most likely negative assumptions that stand in your path.

"I didn't learn to write well yet, so I know I can't learn now." If you're convinced that writing is some kind of inborn mystical talent, think again. Writing for business purposes—which encompasses everything from e-mail to blogging, social media, proposals, résumés and reports—is better seen as a strategic thinking process: You figure out what you want to accomplish and then how to do so in the simplest, most effective way. You can learn to do this every time, given a helpful structure and a little practice.

"Learning to write is boring." That assumes you need to memorize rules. Not so. Do you think people are boring? Do you think *you're* boring? Writing is the ultimate people skill. Every message is an "ask." Whatever you want—an appointment, an approval, a referral, a reward—you must find its value in the other person's eyes. In this book, learning to write centers on how to understand other people better—and yourself.

"My career path won't require it." Ready or not, in today's practical world, you are what you write. Whether you aim for a career as an engineer or business executive, nonprofit leader or entrepreneur, expect to be constantly judged by the effectiveness of your writing. It's how most opportunities are won or lost. And everything you write contributes to the perception of who you are and what you can do, today and tomorrow. Moreover, thanks to the amazing digital universe, you can connect with almost anybody—if you write well.

"I can bypass the need to write." Sorry, but you can't. Today everybody writes. If you want to polish your speaking skills, great—you'll need them—but don't forget that every good presentation starts with writing. Even a 15-second elevator speech or sales pitch. It's also a mistake to think you can say it all with visuals. You still need words—and you need the right ones. Language is how we think, exercise our imagination and relate to other people. These truths will not change, and what you learn will apply even to media channels not yet invented.

A NOTE TO INSTRUCTORS

Business Writing Today is designed for the classroom, with a wide range of assignments, activities, discussions and project ideas. However, it can also be deployed as a self-help book that students can use on their own.

This third edition makes it easier to use the book in both ways. The learning sequence is more logically organized, progressing from core ideas about goals, audiences and the tools of persuasion to practical techniques for writing and editing. The chapters then demonstrate how to apply the strategies to everyday messaging, more formal business documents and materials, online writing and presentations. A job application chapter focuses on résumés and cover letters. An appendix pulls it all together with additional sentence practice, big-picture activities and self-improvement planning.

Throughout, this third edition is enlivened with new examples and demonstrations that engage young people in ways that tie closely to their lives and perceptions. More emphasis is given to relationship-building and the use of writing techniques to support person-to-person communication.

The principles of good business writing hold rock steady, no matter how the media landscape shifts. The thinking structure at the heart of this book equips students to handle even newly emerging channels with confidence. However, the way writing is perceived in the workplace has changed since the first edition appeared in 2012.

Writing is no longer a hidden asset. New studies pinpoint business communication and writing in particular as the top in-demand skill across virtually every career field. Notably, a growing number of organizations require writing tests as the only tangible way to assess what candidates can do and how they think.

The entrepreneur mindset has come front and center. Many young people entering college are already engaged in the gig economy and, sooner rather than later, plan to run their own businesses. At the same time, today's valued employees are those who take charge of their own growth, find opportunities, represent their interests well and contribute to the common mission.

The data dump challenge is upon us. We are overwhelmed by information of every kind. We need people who know how to cut through it all to identify what is relevant, important and interesting. Strategic writers know how to identify and communicate what matters, whatever the subject or enterprise.

The generation gap needs negotiation. We all know thoughtful and considerate young people, and senior people who empathize with and support younger ones. But today's diverse workplace is increasingly the scene of misconceptions and misinterpretations. We need to understand each other better, recognize how we are different, and connect beyond what appears to divide us. Better communication is the *only* way to accomplish this.

In sum, the need for good writing becomes more urgent every day. Your contribution to your students' future could not be more important. I hope this book helps you create more effective communicators and writers who are motivated to keep learning and growing.

ACKNOWLEDGMENTS

This new edition was gracefully supported by editor Maggie Stanley, whose enthusiasm for the project has sustained through three editions—thank you! And much appreciation is due to the SAGE team: Bennie Clark Allen, who shepherded the book through production so efficiently and tactfully; Sarah J. Duffy, the very model of a modern copy editor/proofreader; and editorial assistant Alissa Nance for all her support.

And I am more than grateful to all my colleagues who generously shared their professional insights and techniques in the three dozen-plus View From the Field features that amplify my own experience. I feel privileged to know every one of you.

And special thanks to the reviewers who provided thoughtful critiques, ideas and suggestions to make *Business Writing Today* an even more effective tool for teaching and learning:

Janel Bloch, *Northern Kentucky University*

Rod Carveth, *Morgan State University*

Michelle M. Davidson, *University of Toledo*

Mary Lynn Engel, *Saint Joseph's College*

Steven Engel, *Marygrove College*

Renee Nelms King, *Eastern Illinois University*

Geoffrey Luurs, *North Carolina State University*

Astrid Sheil, *California State University San Bernardino*

Elizabeth Weiser, *Ohio State University*

Alyssa Wertz, *Merrimack College*

ABOUT THE AUTHOR

 **Natalie Canavor** is a business writer, author and journalist. Throughout her successive careers as a magazine editor and public relations manager, she originated programs to help people communicate more effectively. Today she focuses on this work with practical programs for business and professional audiences, college students and writing instructors.

As an adjunct professor at NYU for six years, Natalie taught advanced writing seminars for the MS program in public relations and corporate communication, and created courses on strategic messaging for professionals and entrepreneurs.

Her byline as a journalist has appeared on hundreds of features and columns in the *New York Times, Newsday, Communication World* and a host of business and technical publications. For six years, she wrote a column on better writing for the International Association of Business Communicators, read by 15,000 professionals worldwide. Currently she writes and edits the award-winning magazine *Impact* for Ben-Gurion University of the Negev, which shares faculty research.

As a national magazine editor, Natalie created a series of successful start-ups including *Today's Filmmaker, Videography* and *Technical Photography.* As an organizational communicator, Natalie built a 14-person PR department for New York State's largest educational agency and counseled management on communication strategy; directed print, video, and e-media; and created communications skills training programs for school leaders.

Natalie is also the author of *Business Writing for Dummies,* currently in its second edition, and coauthor of *Workplace Genie: An Unorthodox Toolkit to Help Transform Your Work Relationships and Get the Most From Your Career,* with psychotherapist Susan Dowell. She also coauthored *The Truth About the New Rules of Business Writing,* a popular guide for businesspeople.

Natalie's work has earned dozens of national and international awards for feature articles, video scripts, websites and publications. She served two terms as president of an International Association of Business Communicators (IABC) chapter, which recognized her as Communicator of the Year, and was a founding officer of IABC's Heritage Region. Natalie is a member of the Author's Guild, the American Society of Journalists and Authors, the Association of Business Communicators and the Plain Language Center.

HOW TO COMMUNICATE IN WRITING

1 BUSINESS WRITING TODAY—AND YOU

How do you see your future:

Growing, learning and progressing in a business career you love?

Leading a nonprofit enterprise that contributes to a better world?

Running your own independent business or service?

Practicing as an engineer, technologist, scientist, lawyer, teacher, accountant or other professional?

LEARN...

- How good communication helps your career
- Why writing matters in the workplace
- How to define good business writing
- How to use this book

Your path may be unclear at this point. And it's predicted that if you are now of college age, you will probably migrate among these possibilities during your work life and fulfill roles not yet envisioned in ways that may differ widely from today's.

Despite all the adaptability this suggests, one skillset will remain constant: Good communication. Media and platforms morph, but communication only grows more important. And writing is the heart of communication. Today everybody writes, and tomorrow too, we will keep writing: everyday messages to get the job done. Reports and proposals and articles and white papers. Résumés and letters and networking messages. Speeches and presentations and videos. Websites and blogs and social media posts.

Business writing connects us, informs us, entertains us, persuades us. It encompasses spoken forms of communication as well as the visual, because all are built on words. Good writing bestows many gifts:

Reach: A dazzling universe awaits you—contacts and networks and potential employers, clients, customers and readers with whom you can connect.

Opportunity: Good writing enables you to win the job and do it better, or score the projects and assignments you want as an independent worker.

Growth: Once you're established, effective communication enables you to expand your horizons, become more valuable and move forward.

Authority: In today's world you are what you write. Good writers are granted credibility and respect in every field of endeavor.

Content: Everyone wants it. The Internet consumes infinite material, and many organizations struggle to feed it. But the competition is fierce: Good writers make the grade.

Good relationships: Today, we depend on writing to connect us and foster positive work relationships. Doing it consciously reaps big rewards.

This book's goal is to equip you with the central communication skills you need to gain your opportunities and use them well. While the focus is on writing, the same strategies help you succeed in person, whether you're handling an important conversation with the boss, pitching a client or presenting more formally. Writing is the best way to prepare for the challenges you expect—and the ones that surprise.

To start, you learn a structure that guides you to reason out *what to say,* whatever the medium and particular challenge.

Next you're furnished with a toolkit of ideas, guidelines and techniques for sharpening *how you say it.* Rather than trying to memorize grammar-based rules, absorb practical tools that are based on common sense and the techniques professionals use to write and improve their work. You'll find alternative methods for identifying what to fix and how to fix it, and tools to monitor your success. With this foundation in place, the book focuses on specific areas of writing: everyday messaging, business documents, online platforms, video, speeches and presentations.

Do you expect that learning to write better will bore you?

Consider that, essentially, good writing is good thinking. It's also a people skill. One of this book's premises is that every business message is in some form an "ask." Therefore effective writing requires that you understand the person or group that you're writing to and think systematically about how to connect with their perspective rather than solely your own. How can you decipher another person's viewpoint and frame your requests so you are heard and understood? Reach agreement? Persuade? You'll find a range of practical ideas drawn from psychology and systems that bring out your inner detective.

Seeing through another person's eyes enables you to communicate strategically—meaning you are able to accomplish your goals on many levels. In addition to immediate gains, your rewards are many. You become a more interesting, trustworthy, likeable, valued you. A you perceived as more intelligent, thoughtful and capable. Someone who enjoys better relationships with those you work with and for . . . relates to customers and clients more effectively . . . knows how to solve problems and, better yet, how to prevent them. You become a better collaborator—and a better leader. You'll enjoy a better sense of your own individuality and how to present it. And did I mention you get what you want more often?

To promise that you'll achieve all this by reading a book is pretty ambitious. But the intent is to introduce you to techniques and lead you to actively practice them. I don't guarantee any overnight transformations. I won't kid you—it takes time. You may not want to know that professional writers never stop learning and honing their craft! But even with some of the first steps, you'll discover immediate rewards. I know that if you try the strategies, you'll give yourself a solid head start on standing out from the crowd and move closer to your personal dreams.

> *The ability to communicate well, both verbally and in writing, is a real discriminator and critical to success, yet relatively rare among engineers. Excellent writing skills are often undervalued by engineers when, in fact, the writing process is an important aspect of not only getting work, but the design and development process as well. Everyone understands the importance of writing clear and compelling engineering proposals. Less appreciated, however, is the fact that documenting a design or a process almost always identifies gaps, oversights and areas that need additional thought, definition, investigation and design.*

> —Jean Logan, consulting engineer

WHY WORKPLACE WRITING MATTERS

Some perspective on business communication may help you notice opportunities in your environment and understand why you may at first find the workplace less than perfect. We human beings are inherently resistant to change, and our institutions reflect that. And the world we function in has in fact changed profoundly with mind-blowing speed.

Once upon a time, only a few decades ago, few people needed to write. They frequently interacted face to face, and professional specialists handled important communication. Managers typically depended on support staff to correct and improve their documents.

The digital revolution changed all this. Once computers replaced typewriters, people on even the highest levels found themselves writing their own everyday messages. As communication channels grew from e-mail to websites to blogs and social media, more and more people were called on to write. There seems to be an ever-increasing mountain of material that needs writing. Today's media offer companies, groups and individuals infinite ways to be heard and known—but all demand writing.

It's taken the business world a while to catch up to this reality. But the realization is now dawning.

> *Good business writing saves time and money. It prevents mistakes and helps solve problems. It connects people, leaps across geographic and time zones, and bridges culture gaps. It empowers individuals and organizations to succeed in new ways.*

Unfortunately, the general quality of writing in the business, government and nonprofit worlds is dismal. The evidence for this is not just anecdotal. Recent research studies demonstrate that bad writing is a significant challenge to American industry. Writing that comes from government agencies, for its part, has been so bad that a federal law was passed—the Plain Writing Act of 2010—which mandates that all documents aimed at the public be clearly written.

Until recently, business gave writing relatively little attention. But whatever the reason that writing skills have become so inadequate, the impact on the bottom line is now an acknowledged fact of life. Everything we do from business planning to marketing, educating to collaborating, depends at pivotal stages on how we write. Even media we think of as visual or oral start with writing.

Technology has revolutionized how we communicate, and by enabling us to reach people anywhere, bring them to us and directly interact, it's reversing centuries of one-way, top-down communication. We haven't caught up with this major shift. Some of the impact: We now live in an opt-in world. Possibly excepting political despots or rulers of multibillion-dollar empires, no one any longer owns a captive audience. No one is obliged to read what you write—they must choose to. Readers' attention must be earned.

Further, the digital revolution affects how we relate to one another in basic ways. It enables a growing number of people to work at home or in remote locations and rely on virtual teaming. Through online media, we can collaborate with people we may never see across national boundaries—and across the corridor. In many an office, people come to work each day and text or e-mail each other instead of talking to people across the hall.

Across the generations we're using the telephone less, too, and moving steadily toward written, voice-free exchanges.

The bottom line: The new range of communication options doesn't just supplement the traditional varieties or speed up delivery. It is transforming how we relate. We talk less and meet less. The channels we rely on all demand one thing—writing. But just as this huge need to write well becomes understood, the skill proves hard to come by. Take this personally: *See it as opportunity.*

GOOD WRITING GETS THE JOB: HERE'S PROOF

Burning Glass Technologies, a company that helps employers strategize their talent resources, scanned 25 million job postings to identify the most valued non-technical skills sought by American business. This big-data analysis revealed that in the 13 industries studied—ranging from finance and healthcare to manufacturing, hospitality, information technology, management and marketing—*11 rank communication skills as the number 1 most sought skill.* The other two industries rank it second. Further, *writing is number 3 in overall ranking across the industries* (number 2 is organizational skills). The 28 skills listed include computer capabilities, problem solving, creativity, leadership, analytic and teamwork.

An excerpt:

Writing, communication skills and organizational skills are scarce everywhere.

These skills are in demand across nearly every occupation—and in nearly every occupation they're being requested far more than you'd expect based on standard job profiles. Even fields like IT and Engineering want people who can write. . . . Clear communication, particularly writing, is at a premium in nearly every occupation.

Knowing which skill gaps employers seek to fill, the authors note, gives job seekers the opportunity to stand out.

—Burning Glass Technologies. 2015. *The Human Factor: The Hard Time Employers Have Finding Soft Skills.* http://burning-glass.com/wp-content/uploads/Human_Factor_Baseline Skills_FINAL.pdf.

HOW EMPLOYERS SEE WRITING

As one business communication specialist concludes, "the fuzzy, terrible writing we slog through every day at work" costs American business $4 billion every year (Josh Bernoff, *Daily Beast*, October 16, 2016). Add to that the $3 billion companies spend annually to remediate bad writing, according to a national study back in 2004, and you can see why managers feel increasingly desperate to fill the writing gap.

Day to day, poor communication impairs every organization's efficiency. When everyday messages are unclear, incomplete or even irrelevant—as many are—mistakes and misunderstandings abound. Major investment of time and fortune are required to remedy errors and bad feelings.

Smart leaders know that poor proposals don't win projects, indifferent reports don't provide useful platforms for decision making and stale websites don't accomplish their goals. Careless communication can capsize the most expensive efforts to keep customers, employees, stockholders and donors happy. It also prevents organizations from demonstrating transparency and building trust, which is so important to today's corporations, nonprofits and government agencies alike.

Moreover, most businesses and government offices must maintain expensive customer support functions to handle consumer complaints resulting from poor instructions—the primary reason people contact companies. And some industries, notably aerospace, consumer electronics and automotive, find that most accidents and disasters trace to poorly described problems, inadequate records, and muddy cross-departmental memos.

All organizations share an imperative: to engage and motivate employees. Practicing good communication is an essential way to accomplish this. Leaders need to encourage people on all levels to understand the company mission, stay informed, learn new ways of working and contribute their best efforts to the community.

Leaders "listen" to employees and respond most often in writing, too. Change management—the art of adapting organizations to function better in a shifting environment—wholly depends on good communication.

Then there's the new media spawned by the digital revolution. Businesses, nonprofits and government offices alike must meet the endless demand for new material to draw people to websites, sell something—whether a product, service or idea—and build their goodwill. They also face an unrelenting need to monitor what customers, clients and the media are sharing and address problems quickly in well-strategized responses.

Even the art of selling, traditionally a face-to-face endeavor, depends on producing the right written message somewhere along the way. Most organizations today center their marketing, customer relations and publicity efforts on their Internet presence. More and more employees are called on to contribute to this enterprise.

No wonder so many employers prefer to hire and promote good writers. And no wonder a growing number of them give their job candidates a writing test, no matter what level job they're competing for.

Writing and the Private Sector

For a long time writing has been devalued in the private sector—it was the redheaded stepchild in the communications food chain. But the shift to a knowledge based economy meant it was only a matter of time before people recognized that writing matters a lot, that strong clear compelling content affects the bottom line. But now they do. The realization is dawning at a time when even in communication firms, the number of people who can write is actually dwindling. As the millennials rise, their skills are very poor.

—Dan Gerstein, president of Gotham Ghostwriters
and political consultant

DEFINING BUSINESS WRITING FOR TODAY

So what *is* good business writing?

When I give workshops for business and professional people, I ask them to describe the writing they like to read. Invariably, they offer a list of attributes such as this:

- clear

- concise

- easy to understand

- conversational

- to the point

- obvious in purpose

- reader oriented

- jargon free

These characteristics add up to a pretty good definition of contemporary, reader-friendly business writing that achieves its goals.

So if everyone intuitively knows how to describe good writing, why do so few people write that way?

Common experience tells us that most business writing is exactly the opposite: unclear, wordy, stilted, unfocused, full of jargon and not geared to reader self-interest.

Here are a few speculations about why we're surrounded by so much counterproductive business writing.

First, practical writing is rarely taught in school. Unless we major in communications or another practical subject area, most of us learn academic writing, which aims to demonstrate what we know and advance knowledge for its own sake. Often the only audience is the instructor. In general, academic writing values erudite language, abstract thought and precision grammar. All of this is contrary to the principles of good business writing.

Second, because most people don't learn to write well during their school years, they conclude that they lack natural talent and can't learn. This book is here to tell you that's not true: I promise you can write infinitely better, once you understand what good business writing looks like and sounds like and absorb some easy step-by-step processes to guide your decisions on content, style and language.

A third reason so many people don't develop their abilities is because they think learning to write isn't much fun. But that's based on the school model. In the business world, it's not about rules. Good writing is about understanding other people and what motivates them, clarifying your own goals and strategizing your messages to achieve those goals.

Good writing is not "a way with words"—ultimately, it's good thinking. This book gives you techniques and tools that help you think more clearly and therefore write better.

That's not to say that correctness doesn't count: We need other people to understand our messages and read them quickly. Bogging them down with mistakes annoys them and clouds comprehension. But grammar and punctuation are the servants of ideas, not the masters.

The time you invest in improving how you write will reward you well.

When someone is interviewing for a job, representing another organization or coming from a consulting firm, I judge them on their writing because it will affect me. It's one of the biggest things—I care less about people's interpersonal skills; I don't need to be friends with them. But if they can't write well I'm stuck. In my job and others I work with, writing is so much of what you do that if you can't do it well you can't do your job well.

—Alicia Phillips Mandaville, vice president for
global development policy and learning at InterAction
(alliance of international development and relief organizations)

NOW, BACK TO YOU

If you are currently preparing for your career, you need writing to win opportunities and communicate who you are. Your résumé, cover letters, networking messages and social media presence must be first rate for you to make the first cut. When you do make the cut, advance planning based on writing helps you ace Round 2: the interview. If you do well in person, you may well encounter a Round 3: a writing test. This happens increasingly even when the role isn't described as "writing."

To see why, try looking at it from the employers' perspective. When they have an attractive opportunity to offer, especially if the job is entry-level or early-career in nature, hundreds, maybe thousands of applications come in. Typically many of the candidates who make it to Round 2 look beautifully qualified: Their education, internships, community volunteer work, school activities and references are all right on target. They come for interviews well prepared to speak glowingly about their skills. So how to distinguish among these applicants for the most promising match?

A growing number of employers solve this dilemma with a writing test. They use it to assess the actual capabilities of each applicant. For some jobs, the test may take the form of a grammar quiz. But more often you may be asked to come up with a good relevant idea and write it up on the spot; or write an effective e-mail with a given goal; or solve a problem and explain it in writing. Asking for all of the above is not uncommon. This is the organization's way of practicing former president Ronald Reagan's credo: "Trust but verify." Whether you're applying to a company, nonprofit or government agency, the hiring manager wants to see *how you think and strategize through your writing.*

> *When I'm interviewing people, I like to give them a writing test. . . . I find that you can tell a lot more about a person's personality from a few paragraphs of their writing than from a lengthy verbal interview. Many people can pretend to be something they're not in person, but very few people can do so in writing.*
>
> —Phil Libin, CEO of Evernote, in *Inc.*

Once you're employed, writing well helps you make the most of the opportunity. And/or it equips you to take advantage of the level playing field the Internet creates and establish your own business or part-time gig. Today virtually anyone with an idea can compete with long-established enterprises and directly connect with customers, media, investors and collaborators—if they know how to create and deliver a strong message.

In sum, whatever your immediate and future career aspirations, writing gives you the chance to outmatch your competition.

Develop your writing skills and you become more valuable, and better able to prove your value. If you question this claim, think about people you've worked with who were identified as rising stars. Was good communication, written and spoken, one of the abilities that distinguished them? Communication is an indispensable leadership asset.

And the vistas can only expand: Every day, technology develops more powerful ways to access people you want to reach and accomplish your goals.

Writing and Nongovernmental Organizations

> *The organizations I've worked with have made writing a much bigger part of their focus and screening process, because if people can't learn to write they're relegated to a lesser role. As an NGO department head I gave a writing test asking candidates to distill down the ideas from a batch of documents as if they were writing a quick policy brief with a limited number of words. We assessed the clarity of their communication and also how they were able to take in, understand and express various ideas.*
>
> —Erin Mathews, consultant, international relations

THE IMPACT OF THE DIGITAL AGE

All this doesn't mean that writing skills must be mastered in the traditional way. While many principles of good writing hold steady—and give you a foundation to depend on—the academic, literary style most of us learn in school doesn't work in business.

To give you a glimpse of the chapters that follow, here are some of the essentials of how to write for the digital age:

- Visualize an overscheduled, information-loaded, low-attention-span, impatient and skeptical audience—which is all of them.

- Strategize every message to accomplish immediate and long-range goals, both your own and the organization's.

- Engage your reader with a strong lead that instantly communicates why they should care and should keep reading.

- Use clear, simple, conversational language for optimal readability.

- Frame every message and document in terms of *you*, not *I*.

- Employ techniques of persuasion to state your case and represent your interests.

- Build in tactics to foster dialogue and interaction.

- Clarify exactly what you want the reader to do.

- Write, consciously, in ways that build and maintain relationships.

The last point is especially important. An environment that leads us to interact through writing rather than face to face is depersonalizing, even dehumanizing. It starves us for warmth and authenticity. We need to purposely counter this drift by writing more caringly. The curt, abrupt style that texting and instant messaging foster does not contribute to relationship building and requires awareness.

Writing and Nonprofits

A nonprofit's messaging is critical to success. You need support from the community, donors, funders—and the only way you can get that word out is through writing: websites, brochures, appeal letters, reports to funders. Writing is even more important today because everyone is seeking the same amount of money from a more limited pool. Someone who can communicate powerfully and effectively will always go straight to the top. When we do executive searches we don't even pass a letter with an error on to the next level.

—Ann Marie Thigpen, director of the Center
for Nonprofit Leadership at Adelphi University

Especially with ever-faster delivery speed, we've become careless of how our messages make other people feel. A live interaction offers a wealth of clues we sense automatically. Beyond what someone else says or questions while talking to us, we hear tone of voice, inflection, hesitation, emphasis. And we process what we see—facial expression, posture, body language, gestures. We react to all this by adapting what we say, in conversation and when giving a presentation. Writing, of course, lacks these cues. So we may easily produce chilly impersonal messages that don't serve us as well as they could. Even worse, we may fail to make the points that matter most to the audience.

GOVERNMENT-SPEAK MEETS THE PLAIN LANGUAGE MOVEMENT

Two Washington, D.C.–based groups advocate for clarity in government communications: the government group Plain Language Action and Information Network (www.plainlanguage.gov) and the non-profit Center for Plain Language (www.center forplainlanguage.org). The movement's most notable achievement to date is passage of the Plain Writing Act of 2010, which requires government agencies to use clear language in documents directed to the public and to train their employees accordingly (the act is posted at www.plainlanguage.gov).

The Plain Language movement is also international—check out the Plain Language Association International (plainlanguagenetwork .org) and Clarity (www.clarity-international.net); these organizations' websites have helpful resources and examples. The Center for Plain Language presents awards annually for the best and the worst. Here's how the center's co-founder and former board chair, Dr. Annetta Cheek, describes plain language goals and obstacles:

We define plain language as something your intended readers can understand and use the first time they read it. Given that, I don't believe there's any material that cannot be put in plain language. In fact, if

it's very technical there's an even greater responsibility to put it into plain language.

We understand the Plain Language Act is not a silver bullet, but its passage has brought the writing problem more to the forefront and hopefully agencies will really start to take notice. It's important that Congress made a statement that this is important. It will affect what the government produces that goes out to the public, and we believe that if government writes better, it will leak into the business world.

We believe that communicating clearly improves an organization's bottom line and helps it give better customer service. A lot of people think that using all those big words leads people to respect them more—but studies show this is just not true. People who write clearly are thought to be better educated or smarter.

Why don't people complain more? I think they take it for granted that the government puts out stuff they can't understand and that's the way the world is. It's very frustrating.

HOW TO USE THIS BOOK

Preferably, work with this book in the sequence presented. The chapters lead you through a natural learning progression. After considering the strategic nature of writing, the practical skills of clear expression are addressed. Subsequent chapters cover the various major areas of writing with a focus on how to apply the basic process you're mastering and the differences involved in producing the various materials.

The premise is that by starting with everyday messages, you build the capacity to handle more complex documents. Knowing how to write an e-mail that achieves its goal brings you a long way toward writing a powerful proposal because the strategies are essentially the same.

View From the Field insets offer practical tips and guidance from a wide range of specialists including professional communicators, psychologists, negotiators, nonprofit leaders, businesspeople, graphic designers and experts on specific kinds of writing from different arenas.

Success Tip features offer practical, useful ideas to help you stand out from the crowd.

You'll find that sometimes one contributor's insights seem to somewhat contradict another's—or not to completely align with my viewpoint. Writing is not a science. There is always another way to write a message and different ideas about what works. Plus, we differ from one another. A technique that's successful for one person may not help someone else.

So read with an open mind and consider all the ideas and strategies. Adopt those that resonate for you. Engage in the **Practice Opportunities** at each chapter's end. Many of the examples and activities are drawn from real-world situations like those you may encounter on the job.

I hope that in addition to assembling your own repertoire of concepts, techniques and tricks of the trade to make you a better communicator, you emerge from this book with a new energy for writing and find it more enjoyable. And that beyond improving your ability to express yourself more clearly and forcefully, in all media, you'll absorb this book's central ideas—that writing is a strategic tool and that everything you write matters.

Business writing is part craft, part psychology, part negotiation, part management strategy and part detective work. Build your practical skills and also exercise your imagination. You'll find yourself well compensated, because when your writing succeeds, you succeed.

PRACTICE OPPORTUNITIES

I. Write a Memo to Yourself

Think about the career path you're preparing for. What written materials do you anticipate being called on to write? List them, including both the everyday kinds of communication (perhaps e-mails, tweets and social media posts) and formal business documents (such as reports, proposals and website material). For each entry on your list, think about what a well-written message might gain you and write that down.

II. Check Out the Plain Language Movement Websites

Read these sites to find different angles on the value of clarity, brevity and effectiveness. Identify some resources that will be useful to you personally in working toward better writing. Read the latest report on the government's progress in plain writing, and write a report about it.

III. Start a Personal Reference Resource of Strong Writing

Collect at least three examples of writing you like from any arena such as newspapers, magazines, online articles, blogs and book excerpts. For each one, write a paragraph explaining why you chose it. Start a file, organized however you like, to keep the examples in.

Include examples from this book if you wish. Plan to add at least one example per week on an ongoing basis. The goal is to own a resource for your own inspiration.

IV. Hold a Group Discussion

In small groups, share one or more of the examples you collected for Activity III. Discuss: Does everyone agree on the quality of each example? If not, what are the reasons for disagreement? What generalizations can you make as a group about the characteristics of good writing? Does this give you any ideas about the ways you'd like to improve your own writing and what you want to learn from this book?

V. Begin a Personal Improvement Plan for Writing

Collect some of your recent writing, for any purpose, including messages from your personal life. Also recollect any writing challenges you've found difficult to handle, whether at school or work or personally. Based on both considerations, can you identify specific ways you'd like to improve your writing? Pinpoint your challenges with grammar, content, presentation and anything else. Write down your ideas as a starting point for what you want to learn from this book.

VI. Write About Your Needs as an Oral Communicator

Identify any elements of your in-person speaking skills that create uncertainty and worry. Many people find it difficult to handle confrontational conversations as well as presentations. Think through the value of gaining more confidence and what would help. *Business Writing Today* includes specific guidance for preparing speeches and personal interactions, and many of the writing techniques throughout also apply. Write down what you'd like to accomplish in advancing your oral skills to help use the book's ideas.

2 WRITE TO ACCOMPLISH GOALS

Communication is a skill you can learn. It's like riding a bicycle or typing. If you're willing to work at it, you can rapidly improve the quality of every part of your life.

—Richard Branson, founder, Virgin Group

Yes, it's how to get things done, open doors and connect with people and immediate opportunities. But effective writing does far more than accomplish the goal of the moment: It's a powerful tool for achieving your long-range ambitions, a tool to use consciously.

From e-mails to proposals to blogs to résumés, every message offers a chance to build toward your future. The better your writing, the more you succeed. Writing gives you one of the best ways to showcase your strengths and demonstrate your value. In the digital age it's a key tool for building and sustaining good relationships.

This chapter gives you a framework for planning all your documents and making the right decisions about content, structure and style.

HOW AND WHY TO PLAN YOUR MESSAGES

Successful writers don't just plunge into any written communication—first, they plan. And always, they begin with two questions that guide them through every decision.

Question 1: What's my goal? What do I want?

Question 2: Who—exactly—is the audience: the person or group I'm writing to?

When you define your goal and consider your reader, it becomes much easier to figure out the content—the facts, ideas or arguments that will produce the results you want. And when you systematically determine content, organizing your message becomes a more natural process. So does choosing the right language and tone.

Whether writing an e-mail, profile, report or speech, professional writers base their approach on how the factors of goal and audience intersect. Thinking this way may mean spending more time up front than you're used to. However, you save the time that you might otherwise spend floundering around for what to say and how to say it. Moreover, if you plan first, your results are so much better—immediately—that you won't begrudge the thinking time.

But why does even a "simple" e-mail merit such thought?

Perhaps you've wished you could un-click Send after delivering one of these:

- a carelessly written message to a superior or colleague that is forwarded right up the company ladder

- an embarrassing private e-mail to a friend that was widely circulated

- a badly executed cover letter that showed up on the Internet as a laughable example

- a message meant for one person that mistakenly reached a whole group, or someone who particularly should not have seen it, like a competitor

The consequences can be dire. Remember the long run, too. E-mails never go away. As we see in scandal after scandal in the corporate and political worlds, they can usually be retrieved to disgrace or, in worst-case scenario, indict you. Social media platforms also encourage us to be careless because they too are so easy to use and value spontaneity. But the instant delivery feature of digital media does not mean you should communicate without thought. Ever.

Building a great reputation in any setting is a step-by-step, sustained process. *Every message is an opportunity to present yourself in the way you want to be seen.* In fact, because everyday channels are so important to the constant communication flow in nearly every organization, they offer a stellar chance to showcase your skills and create a good impression.

Let's look at our two basic questions in more depth.

STEP 1: IDENTIFY YOUR SHORT- AND LONG-RANGE GOALS

Before everything else, getting ready is the secret of success.

—Henry Ford

Look Past the Obvious

In our early education, most of us had the same goal for a writing assignment, whether a term paper, book review, report or essay: Please the teacher and get a good grade. But in the business world, you need to know your goal for every piece of writing. What do you want to accomplish with the document? What's the desired outcome? What do you want the person to do as a result of your message?

This can be trickier than it looks at first glance. Suppose, for example, you're coordinating a department workshop on a new software system. It will be held at lunch time, and it's a must-attend, so you might just write:

Subject: Mandatory IT workshop March 7

On Thursday, March 7, noon to 1 p.m., plan on attending IT's workshop on the new Mannerly System software, which will be rolled out company-wide May 1. All staff members are expected to attend. Please acknowledge receipt of this message.

You may have received similar notices. How did you react? Were you enthusiastic? Happy to give up your lunch time? Probably not. So when you're the writer, you can easily predict how people who receive such a message will feel. They'll show up because they must, but is that really the outcome you want? The session will be much more productive if people come in a positive frame of mind and motivated to learn. So your message might better say:

Subject: For everyone: IT Workshop, March 7

This Thursday at 2:00 p.m., IT will show us everything we need to know about the Mannerly System software we'll all use starting May 1. The experts will demonstrate how Mannerly can cut your report prep time by 20% and give you instant access to backup data on demand. In addition to giving you a general grounding, the demo will show you how to apply this cutting-edge system to your own needs. All hands on deck for this one—please confirm you'll be there.

This version presents the meeting enthusiastically—enthusiasm is contagious!—and energizes the readers: The event is framed as a good opportunity with clear benefit to them. The topic sounds relevant rather than boring. The message sets a team feeling in the first sentence instead of a dictatorial one, and it personalizes what follows by writing in terms of "you" instead of the indifferent third person language of the first version.

But if you're addressing people with whom you have different relationships, or who work on different levels, there's more to consider. Their status, stake in the subject and expected contribution to the meeting should be taken into account. Version 2 sounds like it's addressed to subordinates. If you're writing to people over whom you have no authority, an invitational tone rather than a command, no matter how team oriented, is more appropriate.

A message to the department head might begin like this:

Dear Joan: I've set up the training on the Mannerly system for Thursday at 2:00 p.m., in line with your schedule. The whole department will participate. I've put your intro first on the agenda, which is attached. OK?

On the job, you want even a simple message to reinforce your professional image with superiors, colleagues, collaborators, suppliers and everyone else you're writing to. It should contribute to your relationships in a positive way. Well-written messages advance your organization's interests—and your own long-range goals.

In the meeting announcement example, then, the goal includes bringing people to the event in the frame of mind you want so it produces the best results. If defining "goal" appears more complex than you expected, and sounds like a lot of weight for an ordinary e-mail to carry, how much thought should go into a complex document like a proposal or report?

Often, quite a lot. But fortunately, the process you're learning applies to every kind of document, both digital and print, and can soon be applied intuitively. Practice with everyday materials pays off with the "important" documents. At heart, good writing is good thinking, so developing your writing skills helps you in many ways. You're better able to define and solve problems, understand and engage others, manage their perceptions and influence their actions. And as will emerge later in this book, skill with writing provides the best basis for successful oral and visual communication.

Define Goals to Shift Your Vision

When you closely identify a document's purpose—or the role it plays to accomplish a purpose—you gain surprisingly helpful insights. The cover letter you write for a proposal, for example, need not bear the burden of selling your product or service. It just needs to set the stage for the reader to view the proposal itself in a favorable light and demonstrate that you've read the specs carefully and understand the problem.

Similarly, cover letters for résumés needn't summarize your credentials. Aim to promote the reviewer's interest in reading the résumé by highlighting what a good match you are with the job (and by showing that you write well). The résumé's job, in turn, is to gain entree to the next step, usually an interview.

Clear goals give you clear guidelines, whatever the medium. And articulating your set of goals can save you from falling into a lot of common traps and unnecessary mistakes.

Put Your Goals Analysis to Work

Here's how to begin your new systematic writing strategy: Practice defining the goal of every message you write on as many levels that apply. Write them down. Writing sharpens our thinking and pushes us to be more specific.

Here are some examples of goals for the meeting invitation:

1. Move people to show up: This is the basic action or response you want from readers.

2. Motivate people: You want them to recognize the subject's importance and approach it enthusiastically, ready to learn. This is the below-surface response you need.

3. Produce a successful event: Preparing everyone to use a new system and work more efficiently is the organization's goal and your responsibility.

4. Create a positive impression on your superiors, peers and subordinates: Building this is your personal long-range goal.

Goal 4 is always important because when you're conscious of your personal goals, you automatically act in line with them.

You recognize opportunities you might otherwise overlook for a productive contact or an extra assignment. And you see ways to build toward your goals in almost every message you write, whether an e-mail or a report or a presentation.

Consider this example:

Bill has been elected a board member of his professional association. No one ran against him, so he doesn't take it seriously at first. He dashes off a memo to his boss:

Mark, guess what? I'm now on the WBEL board. LOL?

Then he thinks some more and realizes he has an opportunity to

- raise his profile in the department,

- strengthen his relationship with the person he reports to, and

- perhaps bring himself to the attention of higher-ups in a positive light.

He rewrites it this way:

Mark, I'm happy to report that I am now a WBEL board member. I was elected last night. As of June, I'll be involved in all the decision making about programs and venues and, of course, look forward to contributing our company perspective and making new contacts for us.

The inauguration lunch is on May 1, and I'd be honored if you would come as my personal guest. Can you attend?

This message is likely to accomplish all three of Bill's goals.

Note, of course, that the goals you make evident in a piece of writing must not be at odds with those of your employer––unless you're aiming to lose your job. Let's assume for now that your goals and those of your employer are basically aligned (though the more aware you are of your own long-term goals, the more selective you'll feel about where you want to work and what you want to work at).

Aim in all your messages to pursue both your employer's goals and your own. That doesn't suggest you should work in self-promotional statements. It means, in all your communications, take the trouble to write as you want to be perceived. Write thoughtfully, using techniques demonstrated in this book, and you own the power to build your image over time as someone who's valuable, resourceful, reliable, creative, responsive . . . whatever—you fill in the blanks.

If you plan to run your own business, either as a side gig or full-time, your degree of success depends largely on how well you communicate. Messages must be even more consistent and agile than when you work for someone else—you simply don't win the jobs otherwise. Nor can you collaborate or lead without good communication. The principles and thinking process apply equally to every kind of enterprise and industry.

So far, it's been all about "you." Now let's move on to "the other"—the person or group you're writing to.

STEP 2: ANALYZE YOUR AUDIENCE SYSTEMATICALLY

Always try to lift yourself out of your parochial mind-set and find out how other people think and feel. It may not make you a better person in all spheres of life, but it will be a source of continuing kindness to your readers.

—Steven Pinker, professor of psychology at Harvard and chair of the *American Heritage Dictionary* Usage Panel

Why Audience Analysis Is Key

When it comes down to it, most messages ask for something. The request may be basic:

Please send me technical specs for your Model G.

A request may be implicit rather than stated:

Please read this message and absorb the information in it.

Or a request can be overt, asking for agreement or action:

Let's get together next Tuesday to plan the agenda.

or

Can we delay the project deadline so we can collect more bids?

If you're asking anyone for something—even if it's only to pay attention to the content—you want your message to be properly received and hopefully acted upon. So you must communicate in terms the reader can hear, understand and relate to. Moreover, you must usually give the reader something he wants, or considers desirable, for your request to succeed.

If, for example, you want your supervisor to move you to a better office, you need to match your message to who she is and what argument will make sense to her. Will she care that the move makes the office workflow more efficient? That it better reflects the staff hierarchy? That you'll be able to concentrate better or be closer to her office? Does she show concern for staff members' well-being and happiness? To succeed, you must take account of such factors and more.

People are different—in how they perceive, what they value, what they care about and how they make decisions. But there is one universal to count on: self-interest. We react to things and make decisions based on "what's in it for me" (marketers call this WIIFM). This doesn't suggest that people are selfish and ungenerous; they may be motivated by a humanitarian cause, an ideal or belief, or a commitment to what's good for other people or the organization they serve or the world at large, above everything else.

In the practical world, even charities and government offices run on business thinking. They must operate efficiently, be well perceived by their stakeholders, use resources well. However, decisions are made by individuals who interpret matters differently. If your department head cares about the quarterly profit and loss statement, it isn't smart to suggest a workplace improvement because it would make people happy and expect to succeed—unless you could prove that happy people are more productive. If you want to persuade employees that a new benefit is as good as the one it replaced, telling them how much the company saves gets you nowhere. They want to know how their lives will improve—or at least not suffer—in real-world terms.

The bottom line is that in addition to defining "what do I want" for each message you write, you need to systematically analyze "who is the person I want it from"—your audience. It's the only way to determine your best content: the facts and ideas that will achieve your goal with the individual or group you're addressing; what to emphasize; and what language, structure and tone will help this message succeed.

SUCCESS TIP

How to Deliver a Message: in Person? In Writing?

This book is about writing, but remember that a written message is not always your best option. A conversation is often better, in person or by telephone or online as practical. Especially if the subject is personal, or requires some give and take—such as negotiating for a raise or opportunity—you'll achieve more if you can read and respond to the other person's questions and subtle reactions. If you have a problem with a coworker, resolving it in person is far better than a written complaint. Especially when you start a new job or role in an organization, resist over-relying on written messages. Build a person-to-person pattern of interaction. Walk down the hall, introduce yourself and look for chances to hold one-on-one conversations. You'll gain a reputation as a people person. Colleagues will react more positively to your ideas and requests. You'll collaborate with them more effectively and learn more. And you'll find it easier to write good materials and messages because knowing your readers enables you to frame your communication within their perspective.

Understanding your audience also tells you what communication channel to use. If your boss doesn't like texting, obviously don't make a request that way. But you probably will send a text if you want advice on the best new smartphone from your 16-year-old cousin.

While we instinctively make such decisions all the time, you succeed more often on the job when you approach a writing challenge methodically. Scan the list of personal characteristics in the sidebar "Some Factors That Determine Who We Are." Do you wonder how you can know so much about someone you only see in the office or connect with formally as a client or business contact?

How to Understand People

The best way to know someone is to thoughtfully interact and observe.

As a trial attorney will tell you, the clues about who someone "is" abound: in what the person says and does, his voice, what he wears and how he wears it, what he reads, how he walks, what he laughs at, how he shakes hands, what his office looks like. If you spend time with people or are familiar with their work environments, observe. And always listen. Active listening with your whole attention is the best way to understand another person. Open up your perceptions to notice what people in your life talk about, what triggers positive and negative reactions, what guides their decision making, what matters to them, how they communicate and more.

If the person is important to you—a boss or significant connection—*back your observation up with research*, so easily done for everyone in the business world. What people choose to say about themselves on a professional site like LinkedIn, and choose to show on social media sites, tells you a lot beyond the facts. You can also ask other people for context and even advice on how to get along with someone to whom they relate well, but be tactful.

And ask questions! Provided your questions are appropriate and don't exceed the relationship's boundaries, most people welcome the chance to talk about themselves, explain things and tell you what they think.

The best salespeople customarily ask open-ended questions like this: "I'm curious—how did you achieve your position here?" Then they listen carefully and interact according to their on-the-spot analysis. This approach isn't devious. It respects the premise that we have individual perspectives and patterns. A good saleswoman may conclude from such a conversation that her product or service is not what the prospect needs, and may even suggest another avenue. But if it looks like a match, she knows how to frame the pitch. In a workplace context, understanding other peoples' frameworks helps you know how to talk their language.

SOME FACTORS THAT DETERMINE WHO WE ARE

Innumerable factors influence how individuals receive and react to messages. Understanding people from this perspective is infinitely rewarding. To develop your awareness of differences, it is useful to consider factors that make us unique, such as the following:

- age and generation
- economic status
- cultural, ethnic or religious background
- gender
- educational level
- where the person grew up and now lives

- career background
- role or status in the organization
- personal values

Beyond such overt factors, when the person is important to you—like a supervisor—consider:

- What does he care about?
- What interests her?
- What are his strengths, weaknesses?
- Problems and challenges: What keeps her up at night?

- Leadership style: Top-down, collaborative or somewhere in between?
- Management style: Fair, consistent? Or plays favorites?
- Decision-making style: Slowly or quickly? Based on what?
- Open to new ideas? Willing to take risks?
- Likes confrontation or avoids it?
- General confidence level and apparent insecurities?
- Sensitive to people's concerns?
- What makes him happy? Angry? Frustrated? Bored?
- Does she have a sense of humor? (Assume not)
- Is he comfortable with emotions? (Assume not)
- Any apparent pro or con feelings toward people your age? Either gender?

Think also about factors that affect how to communicate with this individual.

- What is her relationship to you, both by position and inclination?

- How does he prefer to receive information: e-mail, in person, letter, phone, text, social media channel? PowerPoint? Formal or informal reports?
- What kind of explanations does she prefer: Big-picture? Detailed? Logical? Statistical?
- What is the best time of day to approach him? (Salespeople often aim for after lunch.)
- What are her hot buttons?

The nature of what you're communicating about may suggest that you also pay attention to factors such as these:

- What the supervisor already knows about the subject. What more might he need to know? Any prior experience with the subject?
- How she feels about the subject and her comfort level with it
- Attitude toward innovation and change
- Preference for ideas that he originates (or thinks he originates)

Communicating Across Personal Filters

If audience analysis sounds like a lot of trouble, consider that a primary purpose of every message is to maintain or establish good relationships. You can't do that without taking account of the individual you're writing to. Further, to achieve your goal, you must choose the right strategy for your document. Putting yourself in someone's mindset empowers you to answer this all-important question: What's in it for me? You can't give people what they need if you don't know who they are.

> *We don't see things as they are; we see them as we are.*
>
> —Anais Nin, writer and diarist

Every one of us comes to work (and to life) with a built-in filter that evolves over time through the interplay of genetic traits and everything that makes up our life experience. We interpret everything we encounter and that happens to us through this filter, which also determines our expectations, reactions, assumptions and fears.

Don't ever doubt that you see the world through your own filter. The more conscious you become of your filter's characteristics, as well as those of people with whom you communicate, the better you'll succeed. *Treat communication as a bridge between different worldviews, and you'll be way ahead in your personal life as well as business life.*

The good news is that once you start thinking about your audience analytically, doing so becomes second nature. Of course, the higher the stakes, the more thought it's worth. An e-mail or text message asking a friend to meet for lunch won't require a review of her comfort level with new ideas. But if you want to get project approvals from your supervisor, convince a client prospect that you're worth 20 minutes of his time or close a sale, audience analysis is your friend.

Take account of different personal factors according to the nature of your request. If you want the recipient to understand and follow your instructions on how to file for reimbursement, then education level is important. If you need to know how formal to make your message to a client, then her position matters, as does personal communication and management style.

Here's another major reason why you want to know your audience: *Written communication lacks all the cues we depend on in face-to-face interaction.* When we are in the presence of other people, we unconsciously adapt what we say—and how we say it—to their reaction. If we move the conversation in the wrong direction, their facial expression or body language signals us to switch focus. Otherwise they may interrupt us or stop listening.

With written communication, we can't gauge reader response. Therefore, provided you want more than a random hit-or-miss success ratio, you need to target the message properly and *anticipate* response. In a way, you can hold the conversation in your head and write on that basis.

SUCCESS TIP

Tap Into Your Intuition

Intuition is knowing something without knowing how we know it. An interesting way to tap into it, and put together your impressions of someone and the facts you've marshalled, is to completely imagine the person mentally. If you're working on an important communication, whether through writing or face to face, relax for a few minutes and bring her alive in your mind: Picture her in detail—carriage, dress, manner, expression, gestures, body language; hear her speak, laugh. Visualize her office or other environment she created in full detail. You might hold an imaginary conversation—ask for what you want, observe her reaction, hear her questions and answer them. Then write from this awareness and see how it shapes your content choices, language and tone. If you're preparing for an important conversation, use the insights you gain this way—even if they're hard to rationally explain—to plan a productive conversation. This technique works because we always know a lot more than we think.

Profiling People You've Never Met

In many instances, you're writing to people you haven't met yet and may never meet. This is increasingly common as more enterprises operate with virtual teams in scattered locations. How do you analyze supervisors and coworkers then? Or prospective clients and partners?

Online research plays a bigger role. Scout especially for opportunities to connect visually. If you're writing, or preparing to meet with someone you've not met for an interview, or to pitch a service, look for video of the person. This gives you a good feel for being in his presence.

Phone conversations also tell you a lot. Listen for the individual's conversational pace—what provokes enthusiasm, any repeated words or phrases that indicate a focus or concern or a way of thinking. One individual may cite numbers often and another may show an interest in people. And, of course, ask direct questions if the context allows, such as "What kind of data would you like to see and at what level of detail?" or "How will we communicate to coordinate our tasks?"

VIEW FROM THE FIELD: A PSYCHOLOGIST ON COMMUNICATION

To build rapport and communicate effectively, look past your own perspective and try to understand how someone else sees things. Remember, people are more open to your viewpoint when you make the effort to understand theirs. People have genuinely different ways of looking at things and interacting, and you need to respect this right.

Read their cues. Pay attention to how they talk about things, and talk in frames of reference they will understand. This helps them make sense of what you're saying and opens up your own capacity for real rapport.

When you write, draw on what you know about the person. See her in your mind's eye and use your intuition to reverse roles with her. This will help you better understand how she sees things and, if she is not getting your point, can show you in what way you are not attuned to how she sees things and what she needs.

If you're writing to someone you haven't met, do some research: Talk to colleagues, gather information. The more you understand a person's frames of reference, language, values and priorities, the more you can develop the rapport for a working relationship. Review his written communications. Look for clues in how he responds to written messages, too. Notice whether he uses personal language, technical terms, generalizations. Consider what kind of data he needs to make decisions and whether he decides fast or slowly. Take serious account of that in deciding how to proceed next.

—Susan H. Dowell, psychotherapist and co-author, *Workplace Genie: An Unorthodox Toolkit to Help Transform Your Work Relationships and Get the Most From Your Career*

Reading Between the Lines

Are someone's written messages formal or informal? Carefully written or careless? Is the language old-fashioned, contemporary or breezy? Is the thinking clear and well organized? Moreover, it's startling how much "attitude" is often revealed in even a short, simple e-mail or post. In a large communications department I managed, at least one other person reviewed every significant piece of writing that went out of the office, even internal memos. The feedback rarely concerned technical issues like grammar. Instead, comments focused on observations such as "I gather you don't like this person" or "You're recommending this course of action but it doesn't sound like you believe in it."

It can be extremely hard to keep your own feelings out of your writing, so be aware of that challenge (and have a friend check out your message when it matters). Almost always, it's against your interests to betray negative emotions such as anger, frustration, impatience. In writing they make you look childish, self-centered and small-picture focused. The impact on others may be indelible—that's the power and risk of the written message.

Also beneficial: Practice the reverse awareness. Keep your antennae up for clues to other people's feelings when you're on the receiving end.

Reading between the lines is a particularly useful technique when you're applying for a job or responding to a request for proposals (RFP). Read the ad, posting or RFP a dozen times or more, and pick up its language, hot buttons and rhythm.

You can also pick up the subtext of a message by close attention to what is *not* said and general "atmosphere." A good way to do this is to ask questions and imagine the answers. For example, why did this job ad specify "attention to detail," "detail oriented" and "meticulous follow-through" so many times? Perhaps the last person in the job fell through in this area, so marshal your evidence of this strength.

Inventing an Audience

Another useful strategy when you're writing to someone you don't know is to invent a construct of what that person is most probably like. If it's a human resources (HR) director, for example, visualize others you've known who held that job and consider what would interest and impress them. Or just take a few minutes to see through their eyes and figure out what—if your positions were reversed—the HR director would care about and want to know. Ask yourself, what's in the other person's self-interest in this situation? Assume her role for a few minutes and you'll have helpful answers.

It's always easier to write to an individual than to an anonymous abstract person. But if you can't conjure one appropriate to the situation, then write to a Standard Modern Businessperson—SMB. You can safely assume your SMB wants your written message to be

- respectful but friendly,

- clear on your reason for writing,

- well planned and written,

- logical in its progression of facts or ideas,

- targeted to his self-interest (the what's-in-it-for-me factor),

- self-contained—doesn't require looking up other documents or doing research,

- as brief as possible to get the message across,

- objective, nonemotional and positive in spirit,

- oriented to solving a problem rather than posing one,

- good for the bottom line (you score lots of points when you can show this, even in a minor way).

You can also assume that your SMB is a human being and put the old Golden Rule to work on your behalf. All (or nearly all) of us want to feel

- liked,

- valued,

- treated with courtesy and respect,

- part of the team.

When a message doesn't convey these things implicitly, our reaction is negative, whether or not the message itself has merit. And we especially do not like anything that actively makes us feel

- overlooked or left out,

- disrespected,

- disliked,

- uncomfortable,

- depressed,

- inadequate,

- laughable or ridiculous.

Never criticize anyone in writing, whatever her relationship to you. This applies to informal situations and most formal ones, with the exception of performance reviews and documentation. A careless written remark can easily torpedo a relationship and create a permanent enemy. Similarly, irony and sarcasm are risky ingredients in business writing. When you criticize someone in person, you can establish a supportive atmosphere and listen responsively. And when you say something sarcastically or ironically, your tone of voice conveys "I don't really mean it."

But the critical or sarcastic memo is delivered without face-to-face cues and can devastate your audience and boomerang badly. This applies 110% to online media. If you don't want a viral reputation as a nasty human being, refrain from posting negative personal comments anywhere.

Here is the flip side: It is a rare individual who doesn't want to look good to colleagues and staff—and especially superiors. And we relish good news, including any about a staff member or the department. So make the most of every opportunity to bring good tidings, and craft those messages well. These are the documents most likely to ascend the corporate ladder and help pave your own way.

Always practice a generous spirit in praising other people's accomplishments and share that news. It takes confidence to honor others, and people intrinsically respect those able to do so. Not to mention how well disposed the other person will feel. In every organization, and outside it too, connecting with allies and building a network is essential, so make the most of chances to do this.

VIEW FROM THE FIELD: PRACTICE SOCIAL SKILLS AT WORK

Everyone knows the Golden Rule—treat other people the way you want to be treated—but try the Platinum Rule: Treat others the way they want to be treated. This is harder because not everyone wants to be treated the same way. Beware the false consensus: believing that your own values and ideas are "normal" and that most people share these thoughts. Pay attention to the hints. Here are some guidelines:

1. Assess the environment and don't start out too casually. In case of doubt, begin more formally. Once you've said, "Hey Mandy, what's happening?" it's hard to go back to "How are you, Ms. Davis?"

2. Respect other people's religious, political and cultural feelings without anger or impatience. Make an effort to understand—you don't have to agree.

3. Ask questions—you can't be an interesting person unless you are interested in the thoughts of others. Ask the other person's opinion before stating your own—"What do you think about . . . ?"; or add the question after giving your own. But don't ask a question you would not want to answer.

4. Embrace diversity in all directions. This includes people older and younger than ourselves.

Practicing good manners—which communicate that we care about other people—is the heart of social skills and basic to civilization. Manners are the great equalizer. They apply to everyone and are the opposite of being elitist, arbitrary and artificial. Social skills expressed as beautiful manners are in your best interest. People who can handle any situation with grace, humor and poise will always be valued in the workplace and everywhere else.

—Margery Sinclair, CEO of Good Manners Are Good Business and author, *A Year of Good Manners*

Assessing Corporate Culture

Rather like people, every enterprise—corporate, nonprofit, government—has its own culture. It develops over time according to the industry, company history, leadership and many other factors. You do your best work, and are most valued, when you understand a company and the industry it's part of. Don't expect to comment on corporate strategy (though a growing number of organizations are consulting young people to understand them better and access their skills). But whatever your job level, a solid grasp of the big picture enables you to recognize opportunities and contribute to company priorities. You'll interact more effectively and write better messages, too.

However, you'll seldom get good answers if you ask anyone, "What's the culture here?" Most employees, even those at the top, take the daily culture they work in for granted and seem unaware of its ramifications. A huge percentage of executive hires fail because neither the organization nor the incoming leader considers that a culture clash is involved. So it's up to you to observe. Consider the obvious: how people dress, what their offices look like, how they interact. Is the atmosphere competitive or collegial? Formal or friendly? Do people mostly work alone or is teaming important? Check out how the organization presents itself in written materials and online, and what current and past employees say about it on sharing sites.

Further, identify good sources of information right next to you and ask specific questions. As elaborated on later in this chapter, experienced colleagues are likely to welcome your interest and asking their advice actually helps you find common ground. Most supervisors are glad to encourage your interest in becoming a useful member of the team.

Here are some of the big-picture elements worth knowing:

- How does the enterprise frame its mission? Express its values?

- How are decisions made—and by whom?

- What is rewarded? Who is valued?

- What behaviors are discouraged?

- What are the organization's immediate and long-range goals?

- What challenges does it face? Who are the competitors?

- What are the company's strengths and competitive advantages?

- What is its communication style and the preferred channels?

BRIDGING GENERATIONAL DIFFERENCES

If you were born in 1995 or later, you are part of a cohort identified as Generation Z, post-Millennials. If you began your work experience after 2000, you probably identify most closely with the Millennial generation. Your supervisors are probably Baby Boomers and members of Generation X, perhaps even the older cohort of Millennials. What does this differentiation mean for how you understand people and communicate?

Marketers, advertisers, businesspeople, politicians, university leaders and many others are interested in understanding generational differences for practical purposes. Such analysis is in itself big business! But results must be taken with many grains of salt. They may be speculative in assuming how a group of people will behave and, invariably, are expressed as generalizations that don't consider people's individuality. It's foolish to assume, for example, that someone over 60 is technology averse and out of date. Or that a Millennial sees older people that way. Clearly, in many cases neither judgment is true.

Nevertheless, the research-based generalizations affect how the generations perceive each other and what they expect, so they are important to understand. They also offer useful insights if you remember those grains of salt. Scanning them might illuminate some of the experiences you've already had. When people grew up, how they were raised and what was happening at the time undeniably shape their individual perspectives. Plus, people care about different things at different times in their lives.

Every method you use to see past your own views potentially saves you pain and gives you ways to gain. Most organizations consist of a generational mix. Millennials and Generation X people may be most visible on a daily basis, but many Baby Boomers are still on the job and may run the show on the higher levels. It's an unusual board of directors that doesn't include plenty of Boomers. Understanding the perspectives of people who are older (or younger) than you enables you to interact better in authentic ways—and helps other people understand you better and value you more.

UNDERSTAND YOUR GENERATIONS

Generation is only one factor that influences us, so never characterize anyone primarily by when they were born. But the broad strokes of how the generations are commonly characterized helps clarify how other people see you and keeps you open to what makes other people tick. Keep in mind that the dates with which different generations are identified are fluid and variously interpreted.

Generation Z

Born 1995 or Later

It's too early to characterize this generation, which is just beginning to enter the workplace, but here's how career and marketing professionals describe this group. Its members are the truest digital natives and technology, a constant of their lives, plays a big role in shaping their outlook and social life. Many engage with social media platforms almost constantly and prefer quick-moving formats, especially those that disappear quickly and preserve anonymity, like Whisper and Snapchat. Gen Zs want to be active in the community and in their work. Coming of age during a recession and worldwide tensions, many feel cautious about life and their own work future. A number of them expect to create their own businesses. They appear to be relatively risk-averse, pragmatic and financially conservative. Their thinking tends toward the global and they want to create a better world. This generation is large, so members can expect opportunities to be competitive throughout their careers.

Millennial Generation (Generation Y)

Born 1981 to 1995

Brought up, generally speaking, with devoted support, Millennials are strong users of digital technologies and instant communication media: Facebook, YouTube, and online gaming are natural environments. They are culturally tolerant and liberal in views as well as civic minded. They come to the workplace with high expectations and desire to shape their jobs to fit their lives. They dislike following orders blindly and do not automatically grant respect to the more experienced. Millennials like to know *why* and want to work on their own without being micromanaged. They have short attention spans, want opportunities to learn, like challenge and change. They dislike repetitive work and want the workplace to be fun. Many are creative and optimistic but not company loyal. They like to participate rather than watch, and they desire frequent feedback and encouragement. Many prefer text messaging and social media networking to face-to-face communication or telephone. This is a large and therefore competitive generation.

Generation X

Born 1965 to 1980

This is a relatively small cohort. Many members now occupy middle-management jobs. Brought up in the first period of two-income households, rising divorce rate and latchkey environment, Gen Xers value independence, self-sufficiency, freedom, responsibility and resourcefulness. They are comfortable with computers and technology. While ambitious and hardworking, they want work–life balance. Gen Xers possess entrepreneurial spirit, like flexible hours and in many cases a chance to work at home part of the time. They favor diversity, challenge, creative input, autonomy and independent work, though most team well. They tend to be adaptable and highly responsible. Their communication preferences bridge between old media and new, but many Gen Xers are less comfortable than the younger people with sharing personal life details in social platforms.

Baby Boomers

Born 1946 to 1964

This is a large group whose members often retain power in corporations, law firms, consultancies, nonprofits and most other organizations (except startups and dot-coms). Baby Boomers are loyal, work-centric and cynical; value office face time; and are motivated by perks, prestige, position, high levels of responsibility, praise and challenges. Boomers define themselves by professional accomplishment and are sometimes charged with being workaholics. They are very competitive, generally confident and comfortable with confrontation and hierarchical structure; they don't always like change but will challenge established practice. Though of retirement age, many continue working and believe that Generations X and Y should "pay their dues"—like they did. For example: fulfilling assignments without complaint, showing respect and writing well-structured, well-expressed, well-edited messages. Most Boomers like e-mail, often present themselves on LinkedIn and similar business sites, but may find the fast moving social landscape an unwelcome challenge.

To learn more, enter "generation gaps" or "generational differences" in your search engine. Thousands of articles, blogs and research reports will come up written from business management, HR, marketing and other angles. Check out "creating personas," too, which brings up audience analysis templates favored by online marketers. Here are a few aspects of generational analysis that affect communication.

Communicating Cross-Generation

Generally speaking, different age groups are comfortable with different ways of interacting. Note that many Boomers like face-to-face meetings and telephone contact. Sending them important messages in text format or using its shortcuts in your e-mails may boomerang. And hesitate to friend a Boomer colleague. Many prefer to keep their business lives separate from the personal. And they prefer that you do, too: If you post an unduly revealing page, comment, photo or video, prepare to face negative consequences from your company executives and those at other companies where you want to work.

VIEW FROM THE FIELD: INTERACTING SUCCESSFULLY ACROSS GENERATIONS

If you are a Generation Y/Millennial working with Boomers or Gen Xers, develop rapport by showing initiative. Convey confidence but don't let it come across as arrogance. Ask questions about how you can best contribute to serving the client better and help the organization. Recognize older people's achievements, which they tend to be proud of, and don't instantly dismiss their ideas even if you think you have a new and

(Continued)

(Continued)

better way. You might tactfully suggest reciprocal or mutual learning so you both benefit, remembering that some Boomers may not be happy to be told they must learn from younger people.

Know that older people may find your text-influenced communication style abrupt and short and impersonal. Slow down, think about what you're saying, proof the message. Missing words, bad grammar and typos don't impress others and may hold you back from promotions. Learn good writing skills and practice them.

—Phyllis Weiss Haserot, president of Practice Development Counsel and owner–manager of the LinkedIn Cross-Generational Conversation group

An important aspect of communicating that may involve generational differences is the quality of *tone*, the voice built into a message. When business executives are asked to identify the biggest problem with employee writing, "wrong tone" is usually the first complaint, particularly when they talk about younger staff members.

We can see from our generalized characteristics why this happens. People born after 1980 or so tend to be antihierarchical and more skeptical of authority. In their view, age does not automatically make someone worthy of respect. But older people, who often feel that they worked their tails off to get where they are, want respect with a capital R.

The intergenerational writing problem is further complicated by Millennials' immersion in a digital world where communication is telegraphic. Thus, a careless 25-year-old might e-mail a client this way:

Jen—Here's the report you wanted. Still waiting for you to give me the projects specs. I'm at a standstill. When will you send???

—Mel

This would be more effective:

Dear Jen:

To follow up on our phone conversation, I'm attaching a report on the Black acquisition. I've marked the relevant areas. If this doesn't provide all the information you need, please let me know and I'll dig further.

As soon as we have the new specs, we'll move ahead on preparing the agreement. Thanks.

Best regards, Mel

If you think the second version is a bootlicking waste of time, think again. Mel's credibility and professional image are very much at stake here. Jen may not visibly react to what she perceives as rudeness, but she's likely to register it, remember it and may even talk to Mel's higher-up about it.

VIEW FROM THE FIELD: AN "OLDER FOLKS" WARNING

One of my gripes with younger people is that with e-mail and all the other business communication tools we have today, they don't get back to you in a timely manner. That's a subliminal message and makes you think: Wasn't my message important? Aren't I important? It's so appalling that anyone who does respond within 24 hours, or a business that does so, has a real point of differentiation. And be aware of generational nuances. People who text shouldn't use that jargon in e-mail—we older folks don't understand it.

—Paul Facella, president/CEO of Inside Management Ltd. and former corporate vice president of McDonald's

---

Look at it as necessary business protocol to write in a respectful—no, not obsequious—tone. And do so whenever you're in doubt about the relative status of your audience or where your e-mail might end up.

The guidelines apply equally when you report to a young boss or client. He may in fact be especially sensitive to signs of respect and disrespect. And so are clients and customers, by definition. They do not want to be addressed as a peer or feel ordered around by a junior associate.

HOW UNDERSTANDING OTHER PEOPLE HELPS YOU

Taking a minute to think through other people's perspective helps you handle a host of difficult situations. One example: when you feel you are not treated as you'd like to be. Older people at times react based on their expectations of younger people. And if you're a Millennial or Gen Z, they may have had experience with other members of your cohort that led them to believe that everyone in this group feels entitled to privileges and opportunities, for example, rather than expecting to work for them. This idea is bolstered by the generalizations circulated in every kind of media. The remedy is simple: Take all opportunities to say thank you. It's a good idea anyway.

In other situations, older people may react or act in the framework of their own perspective. If a Gen X supervisor doesn't give you the encouragement you'd like, for example, remember that the broad-strokes generational description suggests that Gen X members prize an independent workstyle and a resourceful, problem-solving spirit. So it's smart to adapt your expectations and demonstrate your talents in ways she values. Do you feel you're being given insufficient time and guidance? Instead of demanding more attention, ask for brief check-in meetings to help you prioritize or make good decisions on your own.

If a Boomer supervisor appears to resist according you value or doesn't acknowledge your contributions—or potential—consider that his own advancement required years of proving himself at each career step. Here, demonstrating your sincere interest in performing every task well goes a long way.

In many cases, extending yourself to understand viewpoints different from your own enables you to field problems creatively. Remember too that perspective depends on role: At each step up an organization's ladder, responsibilities require bigger-picture thinking. A manager charged with running a department or unit always feels pressured to get the work done efficiently by a group of different personalities with different priorities and perspectives. Often not so easy! So what if instead of complaining that you want better opportunities to learn—or just leaving the job without explanation—you asked a question such as "How can I contribute more to the team?" Now you're talking the boss's language!

It's important to represent your own interests well and speak up or write as appropriate. More often than you suspect, it's within your power to create a more satisfying situation for yourself by communicating well. When you practice empathy and strategic thinking, solutions to difficult problems magically materialize. And you give yourself a special gift: Knowing that you were able to handle a challenge well builds your confidence like nothing else.

If you are a Millennial or Gen Z, take comfort in knowing that adapting to intergenerational differences isn't a one-way street. Those who run professional service firms, nonprofits, corporations and all the rest try ever harder to understand the younger generations, because they know that the future (and maybe their retirement income) depends on it. They want to attract the best talent and retain it, and they realize that most younger people do not feel the long-term loyalty that was once common. But few companies have been structured to meet Millennial priorities. Perks like flexible hours, the chance to work at home and a fun workplace are hard to graft onto an old organizational stalk.

Marketing people spend endless time analyzing generational characteristics to calculate how to sell to each group, especially Millennials and younger, recognizing their enormous buying power. And nonprofits from orchestras to museums to charitable causes stress about appealing to younger donors for both time and money. If they fail, their revenue streams will literally age out. So they want to know what makes you happy both as an employee and as a buyer—how people your age think, what they want, how to appeal to them, what communication channels to use and how to use them.

Therefore, if you're just entering the career place, you have a lot to offer. But other people have a lot to give you too, like insight into the organization's culture, the way things work, how to get things done. One of the best strategies to practice everywhere you go is to seek informal partnerships with people of different ages and specializations. Stay alert to people you can learn from. Does one person run great meetings? Does someone else give magnetic presentations? Or know how to get her decisions approved? Or talk to the big boss?

Ask for advice. Most people will be flattered. And where you see ways you can be helpful, take the initiative. Reach out and offer, cheerfully and respectfully. You'll like the people better and your job, too.

WRITING TO GROUPS

Writing to groups is usually harder and more complicated than writing to individuals. Professionals who design communications for big groups, like mass markets, customarily segment the audience and tailor different messages to each because the same one will not succeed with all. Similarly, a large company sends different information to employee groups about subjects like a change in benefits, because their concerns are different.

There are times when you should do this, too. If you're sending a résumé or inquiry to prospective employers, for example, you'll need to take a different tack for consulting firms and marketing departments.

Often, however, one message must be effective for a wide range of people with different educational levels and interests. Good presenters often pick one person at a time to focus on while speaking. Similarly, many good writers think about one individual, or imagine one, and write to that person.

VIEW FROM THE FIELD: THE WORD FROM SUPER PRO WARREN BUFFETT

Here's how the financier, known for his remarkably clear writing on complex financial subjects, pulls it off:

Write with a specific person in mind. When writing Berkshire Hathaway's annual report, I pretend that I'm talking to my sisters. I have no trouble picturing them: Though highly intelligent, they are not experts in accounting or finance. They will understand plain English, but jargon may puzzle them. My goal is simply to give them the information I would wish them to supply me if our positions were reversed. To succeed, I don't need to be Shakespeare; I must, though, have a sincere desire to inform.

No siblings to write to? Borrow mine: Just begin with "Dear Doris and Bertie."

—Warren Buffett, from *A Plain English Handbook: How to Create Clear SEC Disclosure Documents*

Rather than writing to a faceless group, then, try picking a typical representative of the audience to think about, and assemble a list of characteristics from the audience analysis outlined earlier in this chapter. Different factors count depending on your subject and goal. If you're presenting a new companywide data entry program, for example, it's important to consider education, probable degree of knowledge, possible resistance and the audience's view of what's in it for them (which encompasses "how much trouble will this cause me"). Search "developing a persona" in your web browser for useful guidelines as mentioned earlier, but interpret them to your needs.

Gatekeepers and "Serial Audiences"

Often a document needs to be read by different people or groups in succession. There may be a gatekeeper—for example, a manager's assistant—who vets incoming messages and may choose not to pass some of them on to the boss. And with nearly every job application you send, there's probably an entire spectrum of people with the power to short-circuit you.

In other situations, you can anticipate that a message is likely to ascend the company ladder. You deliver a project report to your boss, for example, and see a good possibility that she'll send it to her boss, and the chain might continue to some unknown point. Or you submit your consulting proposal to the executive who invited it, and you count on his passing it on to the relevant department head.

Here are ways to handle this:

- Be very conscious that you're writing to a serial audience when preparing the message.

- Avoid anything that could annoy the immediate recipient and anything not suitable to the audience that may lie beyond.

- Use all the principles of good writing, and proof carefully.

- Err on the side of formality when unsure of the tone to take.

- Keep your eye on the ultimate target—the primary audience—the person or group that will ultimately make the decision to hire you or deliver whatever you're asking for.

- Befriend gatekeepers. It's best to have your supervisor's personal assistant regard you favorably, for example. Public relations people and politicians court editors and reporters for the same reason: They are gatekeepers, or mediators, whose approval is essential for reaching their target audiences.

Remember that today gatekeepers also include machines. A résumé that lacks industry keywords has a good chance of being screened out. A blog or website that doesn't incorporate the right search terms may be ignored by search engines and won't bring them to your audience's attention. Don't write for algorithms—always write for people—but don't ignore their gatekeeper function.

Messages to the Universe: Digital Media

Digital media give us something that never existed before: a way for just about anyone to reach millions, even billions, of people across the country and around the world, with a click, every day, any hour. All the rules of marketing and advertising are morphing into new "truths" as a result.

Anyone can now get her message out via a website, blog, or social media post, for example. But when an audience is so vast and indefinable, how can you understand it to shape a better message?

The premise of goal and audience now works this way: Instead of knowing to whom you're writing and tailoring the message, create a message that your ideal audience will want to find. Through search engine optimization and global networking, this potential audience has the means to find you, rather than the other way around. And if you give it something it wants or needs, leverage that interest intelligently and stay persistent, your audience will come.

So it's even more important to think about your goals and intended recipients in depth and figure out their age range, education, interests, values, worries, hot buttons and all the rest. This will be covered in depth in Chapter 10, "Craft Your Writing for the Interactive World."

Here's the takeaway right now: Don't throw out the basics of good communication because the technology is new and the media channels behave differently. The principles remain as important as ever, and I promise they won't change. But they may need reinterpretation.

In the next chapter, we'll explore how the groundwork of understanding goals and audience pays off by showing you what to say, how to say it, what *not* to say and options for organizing your message or document.

PRACTICE OPPORTUNITIES

I. Chart Your Own Goals

If you're now a student, based on this chapter's discussion of goals and your personal agenda, write down your essential goals for

- this year of study,

- the entire degree program you'll be completing,

- the first year of the job you hope to get after completing your program.

Write in as much detail as you can. Consider whether this effort gives you a different perspective on what you want to achieve—and what difference that might make in what you do, how you spend your time and how you prioritize.

If you're already engaged with your career, think about what you want to accomplish this year and longer term, the opportunities that will help and ways you can envision gaining those opportunities on the job and outside. Write it all down. Writing is a terrific tool for helping yourself—the best way to reason out big life questions as well as small ones. It challenges you to figure out what you want and how to get it by revealing gaps of logic and alerting you to opportunities you'd otherwise overlook.

II. Strategize a Challenging Message

In a way similar to how the Standard Modern Businessperson is outlined earlier in the chapter, construct a Standard Modern Supervisor. What characteristics are people in supervisory roles likely to share? What are their probable needs and expectations from employees? Their goals, pressures, sensitivities? Does the generation a supervisor belongs to suggest additional characteristics?

State a problem you anticipate on the job you'd like to have. For example: Your supervisor isn't giving you the learning opportunities you want. In small groups, see how many ways you can come up with to frame a productive conversation, taking account of the supervisor's probable perspective and responses. Prepare for a face-to-face discussion in writing: your opening line, expected response, major points to make. (For guidance with preparing for a spoken exchange, see "Prepare Talking Points for In-Person Occasions" in Chapter 11.)

III. Review an Earlier Message

Select a substantial e-mail or letter you wrote recently, and review it from the perspective of this chapter. If it yielded disappointing results, all the better. Analyze: Did you define your goals well, including those beyond the obvious? Would considering your goals more analytically have affected your content choices? Did the message make your immediate goal clear? Did you pitch the message well to the specific audience? Did you give the reader a clear what's-in-it-for-me element? How would you evaluate how well the message served your personal goals? How might you write the document differently now? Try it.

IV. Group Project: Define Your Generation

In class or as an assignment:

Work with others in your general age group (preferably in a group of three to five) to review the description of the generation you belong to by virtue of when you were born.

Discuss

Which described qualities do you agree with?

Which do you disagree with?

What else should have been included?

If you come from different countries and cultures, can you find differences? Similarities?

Write

Collaborate on writing a better description of your generation, in at least 250 words. Include cultural comparisons. Share with the class, and talk about the results.

V. Discuss Communication Differences

Contribute to a class discussion one personal experience that demonstrates a difference between your generation and another. As a group, come up with additional factors beyond those outlined in this chapter that can improve cross-generational communication.

VI. Read Between the Lines

Identify a job posting in your field that you'd like to apply for someday—if not now. Clip it or print it out. In writing, analyze:

1. How would you describe the person they're looking for? Be as specific as you can.

2. What are the most important qualifications? Personal qualities?

3. What kind of problems do you think the hired person is likely to face?

4. What can you tell about the company—is it formal and highly structured? Does it value innovation and new thinking? What kind of "personality" does it have?

5. What clues does this give you about how to present yourself in a résumé in terms of the following:

   - qualifications and experience

   - personal qualities

   - any less obvious factors you can cite to suggest you're a great match

6. Does it list any qualifications or qualities you don't have? Can you think of ways to cover for these missing attributes or bridge to proven capabilities you do have?

7. Can you figure out who will read your application initially?

8. And who will probably make the actual hiring decision?

9. How can you accommodate the need to address at least two different audiences?

10. What keywords and terms should you build into your response?

VII. Profile Your Supervisor

If you're currently working, your supervisor is your best candidate for this. If not, choose someone you've reported to in the past at any kind of job.

1. Build a written profile of the person, considering the various factors described in this chapter. Take into account age and generation, communication style, personality, status in the organization, office appearance and as many of the other factors as possible. (If this sounds challenging, think about what you'd tell your younger sister who would take over the job when you leave or are promoted.) Write up the profile (should be at least 500 words).

2. Review the profile and write down everything your analysis tells you about how to best communicate with this individual and achieve the results you want. Include clues and intuitions as well as clear indicators.

3. Write an e-mail to the person requesting something you anticipate will be a hard sell: for example, approval to attend an expensive professional development workshop, buy a costly new piece of technology or work from home on Fridays

VIII. Profile an Organization

If you're currently working, choose that organization. If not, pick one you've worked for in the past, perhaps as an intern or summer employee. Write a detailed profile based on the ideas in this chapter, as if a close friend asked you for insights on how it works and what it's like.

3 PUT THE PLANNING STRUCTURE TO WORK

A problem well put is half solved.

—John Dewey, American philosopher,
psychologist and educator

This chapter builds on the "what to say" part of communication: how to determine the best content for your goal and audience. First let's take a closer look at the spirit from which you write or speak: tone. The tone of a written message communicates how you feel—about both the subject and the other person—and, just like tone of voice and body language, determines how the other person understands and reacts to your message. People are often unconscious of this below-the-surface impact. But it's a top complaint when executives talk about their staff's writing: "It reads too abruptly," "It doesn't seem courteous," "Clients (or donors or customers) feel they're being disrespected."

Recently I presented a business writing workshop to a group of young accounting professionals who'd just been promoted to management roles. We talked about how to apply *goal* and *audience* concepts to everyday messages and I used this example of an e-mail request:

Subject: Need Black analysis Friday!

Hi Garry—I'm afraid the deadline for the April report has been moved up to next Wednesday, the 23rd. So I need your breakdown by the end of the week. I know this may mean putting in extra time—I'll appreciate it very much. Please confirm you can handle this. Thanks, Nina

A participant, "Amy," burst out: "Wait a minute. I'm a very direct person and a very busy one. If I want something from my staff, I write, 'I need you to have the Green report on my desk tomorrow by 2:00.' You're telling me I have to take the time to personalize what I write and care about their feelings? You're saying I have to . . . *sugarcoat* it?"

My answer: Yes. But it's a mistake to label it "sugarcoating." Think of it as expressing courtesy and consideration. And realize that it's also a self-serving strategy. People are much more likely to respond the way you want when you write (and talk) from their perspective and pay attention to how the message will make them feel.

The fact that Amy would be writing to someone who reports to her, rather than a client or supervisor, makes no difference. As explained in Chapter 2, relationship building is always an important underlying goal, though an unstated one. We depend on writing to build bridges between people in a business environment that steadily grows more impersonal. How coworkers and subordinates feel about you is in large part determined by how you communicate with them. These interactions are just as critical to success as how you write and speak to a supervisor or client. Many good business leaders are inspired by the principle "build a team around you." These leaders also notice how staff members treat those around them. Remember that respect engenders respect.

Another basic lesson Amy needed to learn is the power of *why*. Her message didn't include a reason for her demand. Whatever assignment she's meting out, phrasing it as an abrupt demand loses her a free opportunity to foster team spirit and help her assistant feel good about contributing to something important. Her approach creates a negative emotional field rather than a positive one.

Another universal magic bullet is *appreciation*. Resist the take-it-for-granted syndrome. It's hard to say thank you too often. If your supervisor grants you a privilege, like participating in an important meeting, or takes time to advise you, it's smart to express appreciation—even if you don't agree with or like the advice. If a coworker pitches in on your project for which she has no responsibility, appreciate it. If someone who reports to you goes above and beyond, let him know you noticed and value the contribution.

Now that we have some basics about tone in place, let's practice putting the ideas of goal and audience to work. Illustrating with e-mail, the everyday medium, is convenient. But the strategies work for all messages, including long-form documents, blogs, social media, video and oral presentations.

DECIDE WHAT RESPONSE YOU WANT

Suppose you are president of the Entrepreneur Group and must plan 10 guest appearances by prominent local businesspeople. Here is how the structure explained in Chapter 2 helps you determine what to say and how to say it.

Your goals:

- Immediate: Find good speakers and draw them to participate in the program.

- Longer range/personal: Establish contact with business leaders who could prove valuable for your future job hunt.

- Practical: Accomplish these things without killing yourself. This means recruiting enough people from the group to share the burden.

The first challenge is to recruit the volunteers. The folder you received from the outgoing president includes this e-mail from last year:

To: *All Entrepreneur Group Members*

From: *Bunnie White*

Subject: *Need help—important!*

As this year's president, I'm responsible for assembling the next 10-month roster of speakers. Please help! Participate in the planning, organizing the logistics, taking care of speaker needs and general follow-up. This is the most important aspect of our club's work and we should all want to get good results. ***If enough people volunteer, the shared workload will be a lot lighter.*** Our first meeting will be on April 10 at 7:00 p.m. in Room A.

—Bunnie

Does this make participating sound like much fun? Satisfying? Hardly. Nor does it help to know that the writer will probably take all the credit for good outcomes. The benefits are all hers. Even worse, volunteering sounds like a risky business that could sop up an open-ended amount of time. The message is unlikely to attract a lot of volunteers.

APPLY YOUR AUDIENCE ANALYSIS

Let's see how considering audience can help. What do you know about the people to whom you're writing?

That's easy—despite differences in gender, background, national origins and so on, they're much like you. They want to

- look good, get a good résumé credit, be recognized and appreciated;

- establish good contacts for finding jobs;

- achieve all this by doing as little as possible;

- contribute in a collegial atmosphere (which doesn't characterize many ventures run by inexperienced managers).

How to accomplish your goals? Always look through your readers' eyes and ask, "What's in it for me?" (WIIFM).

In this case, it means finding an offer that will appeal to your classmates and overcome their natural resistance to committing their time. Some simple private brainstorming, or conversation with a friend, can provide a set of selling points in line with the list of audience needs or characteristics.

Take a minute to think about how you would approach this e-mail. Good thinking always precedes good writing, but there is always more than one way to achieve what you want. Here's a version based on WIIFM.

To: Entrepreneur Group

From: Jane Green, President

Subject: Meet successful businesspeople and contribute

Dear Colleague:

You are invited to join this year's Speaker's Program Taskforce.

There is room for 10 members who are ready to capitalize on a chance to become personally acquainted with the region's leading businesspeople in a range of industries.

If you become part of the team expect to do the following:

- *Participate in a brainstorming session to come up with a shortlist of the people we'd most like to meet and hear speak.*

- *Maintain telephone and e-mail contact as needed and attend two checkpoint group meetings.*

- *Contact one or more people on the A list to recruit them and plan logistics (we'll try to match you up with people you'd most like to know).*

- *Welcome "your" speaker to campus and introduce him or her.*

This year, all Taskforce members will be listed in every program.

If you want to be part of the best-ever Speaker's Program, drop me a return e-mail by this Friday telling me about yourself in a few lines. I'll assemble the team by the end of next week and set a convenient meeting time for kickoff.

Thanks, Jane

Will this version succeed? It provides a lot more incentive to participate. It uses a little reverse psychology, too—remember how Tom Sawyer got Huck Finn to paint the fence? Jane presents the work as a privilege rather than a burden—and a chance to be part of a winning team, which appeals to everyone.

Notice that because Jane was able to structure the project as she wished, she was able to present it more attractively. Often, the writing process—whether you're using it for a memo or invitation or press release or promotion—reveals weakness in the event itself, or at least room for improvement. If you don't have enough to construct a good message, think about what you'd like to have and whether you can recast the event or project. As in Jane's case, it may cost nothing to do this. Public relations specialists often participate in planning important events because they provide valuable input on how the audience will react. It's hard to promote an event that doesn't interest the targets, no matter how clever the language!

Further, writing a well-planned message oriented to reader viewpoint instantly brands Jane as a good leader. The recipients may not consciously say so to themselves, but they do notice that she's made an attractive offer, spelled out the benefits and limited the time commitment. It's natural to assume she will run a smart and successful operation. *The ability to create such an impression is one reason why good writing is a leadership asset—and another reason to practice it.*

If you think that Jane's original e-mail basically delivered the same message and that readers would work out the reasons to participate on their own, that's a mistake. It leads us to consider this guiding principle:

> *Never assume your reader will make a deductive leap—especially one that helps your cause.*
> It's always up to you, the writer, to spell things out and draw the right conclusions.

It's the writer's job to do the reasoning, and doing it always pays off.

Observe also that when Jane made the effort to see the invitation from her audience's perspective, the message's general spirit—its tone—shifted. It conveys more positive energy, frames the work as a team effort and suggests that the person in charge is nice as well as effective. This is not trivial: Beyond enticing people to join the team, the message sets a good atmosphere for the project from the start.

When you thoroughly consider what you want from your readers' viewpoint, you're guided to choose the right content and to adopt the right tone. This contributes to achieving your immediate goal and the wider ones, like building relationships for the long term.

BRAINSTORM YOUR CONTENT POINTS

Once you take stock of your goal and your audience, you're ready to brainstorm your best message points: the ideas or information that will make your case most effectively *for the reader.* Assembling a simple list often works well. Say you want to ask your colleague Sam to cover for you for a few days while you travel. The following facts and thoughts occur to you:

> *Need to take three days off from June 1 to 4*
>
> *Going to my sister's wedding 400 miles away*
>
> *I'll be grateful for his help*
>
> *Probably I can repay the favor in the future*
>
> *I'll make sure not to leave a lot of loose ends*

It's a slow time of year

I'll stay available by phone or text

I'll leave a comprehensive to-do list

The work will be routine—check that the project materials come in on time, maybe field some phone calls

If you're writing a lengthy document like a competitive proposal, the process is the same but you begin by identifying sections rather than single thoughts. For example: who we are, how we see the project and will handle it, expected happy outcomes, fees. Then brainstorm each section for the content that belongs there. You might, for example, outline the "who we are" section this way:

About the company

Team members

Experience

Proof of performance: track record, awards, testimonials, photographs

Why we're the best match

With the content points spelled out, the next step is to find your opening.

LEAD WITH STRENGTH

It's useful to think about everything you write as three parts:

1. The lead

2. The end

3. The middle: everything that goes between the first two elements

Don't Bury the Lead!

That's the journalist's mantra. Figuring out how to capsulize the story, engage the reader and focus on what's most interesting or important often spells the difference between success and failure. To find the best opening (or as journalists call it, the "lede") for an e-mail, letter, presentation or Executive Summary, scan your content list and identify your strongest or most relevant point. All professional communicators spend a lot of time on this upfront statement. They know that whether they're developing an article, press release, marketing piece or e-mail, the lead captures readers—or not so much. A bonus: Once the opening crystallizes, the rest often falls into place naturally. The content of

Jane's Entrepreneur Group invitation was based on a simple brainstorming list. Leading with strength meant the "meet successful businesspeople" carrot, which immediately gives recipients a reason to care.

To ask a coworker to cover for you during a three-day absence, your lead consists of the subject line and first sentence or paragraph. Perhaps:

Subject: Away June 1–4. Please cover my desk?

Dear Sam:

My sister's wedding is happening on June 2, and of course I want to be there. The location is Las Vegas so I'll need to travel. I'll appreciate it very much if you can cover my work for three days.

Logically, the note would then move on to spell out

- the nature of the work,

- how you will make it easy,

- how much you'll appreciate the favor, and

- ultimately confirm the ask: *"Please let me know ASAP if this is OK."*

MIDDLE WELL

The middle of a letter might consist of a paragraph; the middle of a report might occupy 50 pages. Either way, the middle typically contains the bulk of informational content. For example, a memo explaining how to fill out a form would lead with a statement about why an employee is getting these instructions (*"On March 3, we will all begin using a new system for vacation time requests"*). The middle explains the procedures in the detail judged necessary. A longer document like a project report would similarly lead with the subject, typically the reason for doing the project, or the problem to solve (*In order to determine which new software will best help us analyze costs, we tested four systems newly available in the last six months: Red, Blue, Green and Tan*).

The middle section might spell out the criteria, the evaluation process and the results.

Whatever your document length, your content list guides you. You don't necessarily need to include every point on it. On the other hand, in pulling the message together pay attention to additional ideas that bolster your case—and any omissions you notice. For example, the message points listed for the "please cover my work" request are given in the order that they occurred to me. I didn't think to include "what the work will consist of"—an essential—until later. And in framing the message in my head, it occurred to me that offering to buy Sam lunch would probably clinch the deal.

Juggle the order of your lists as seems sensible. Journalists were traditionally trained to write in *inverted pyramid style*—that is, to start with the most important story element and then successively work down to the least important facts or ideas. The reason: Editors prefer to trim articles to fit by cutting as much as necessary from the end, rather than reading every story through to piece together the most expendable bits. News articles are still generally written this way, and the method applies nicely to most business writing.

Consider your options in deciding which points to include and in what order. In the case of an e-mail, letter or online communication, this usually takes a simple sequencing of your brainstormed list. In the case of a lengthy document, it means stay clear on the major subtopics or sections identified in the planning stage, hold onto them through the whole document and sequence them logically.

FINALLY, END WELL

Note that in our Entrepreneur Group memo, the final sentences circle back to the lead and tell readers how to follow up:

> *If you want to be part of the best-ever Speaker's Program, drop me a return e-mail by this Friday telling me about yourself in a few lines. I'll assemble the team by the end of next week and set a convenient meeting time for kickoff.*

In the case of switching to a new vacation filing system:

> *I count on everyone to switch to the new system on March 3. Of course, let me know any questions about it ASAP.*

> *The report on the best software system would end with a conclusion:*

> *Based on our goals and the capabilities of the four systems tested, we recommend investing in System Green.*

Some more examples of closing statements:

> *Please let me know if you are available to meet on March 2.*

> *Contact Jane if this new process isn't clear.*

> *I look forward to receiving the application.*

The close is your call to action. In every medium, from letter to blog to website page, conclude with a call to action: what you want the reader to do upon reading the message, in context, of course, of your goal. But be sure it suits the task. Telling a prospective employer to "call as soon as you receive this résumé" isn't a good idea.

You may find that when you finish your draft, you end up saying something different than you intended. This is common with many short messages and it's one of the gifts of thoughtful writing: The process of putting the words down clarifies your thinking. When this takes you in a different direction than you began with, reassess what you want to communicate and either rewrite or rethink your message's goal.

If your focus has shifted, you may need a different lead. In the case of longer documents, when you surprise yourself with where a proposal or report ends up, accept that as a signal to revamp content. It's also a clue to plan more thoroughly next time. In the end, advance planning always saves you time and propels your success.

> *The act of writing is itself enough: it serves to clarify my thoughts and feelings. . . . ideas emerge, are shaped, in the act of writing.*
>
> —Oliver Sacks, psychologist and author

In the next two chapters we'll practice editing and refining the message to underwrite impact. But most important, determine to review content and tone by answering these questions:

How will the reader feel upon reading this?

Is what I want clear?

Is my message persuasive? Motivating?

Are the reasons the reader should give me what I ask for spelled out well?

Would *I* say yes to this message?

CHOOSE HOW TO ORGANIZE

Even if you've always felt that organizing a piece of writing was hard, you may find that thinking through the content before you write eliminates most of the problem. Writing is much more difficult when you just plunge in and start with what comes to mind first. That leads to a jumble of ideas that must be organized after the message is already written. Worse, your content is less effective because you deprive yourself of the chance to do a wide scan and delve into your reader's perspective. When you know your beginning, middle and end, and the points you want to make, organization becomes natural. You may find that creating a simple list, as described in the section "Brainstorming Your Content Points," goes all or most of the way toward good organization. But people are different. Here are more options to experiment with.

Use a Formal Outline

If the classic outline many of us practiced in school works for you, with major categories identified by numbers and subsections identified by letters, by all means use it. For an alternative that's specifically geared for business writing, try the approach described in "View From the Field: An Easy Organization Technique." Many people find this strategy helpful and it adapts to a wide range of purposes.

VIEW FROM THE FIELD: AN EASY ORGANIZATION TECHNIQUE

Most people plunge into writing without planning—which is fine for a two-sentence e-mail, but not for writing that is longer than a paragraph or two. They write one sentence at a time without being sure where they're going, and probably will cut and paste throughout their writing. This "plunging-in" approach will get the work done, but it's a long and painful experience.

It's better to do an outline. Come up with your main point, one that describes what your piece of writing is about. It should contain a key word that is generally a plural noun that relates to how the piece will be broken up. For example, if you're writing to communicate the reasons for something, the key word is *reasons*. Or, depending on your main point, the key word might be *benefits* or *steps* or *procedures* or *advantages*. Determining your main point and the key word within it helps you construct an outline, and the writing becomes easier.

Generally, your main point should appear as the last sentence of the first paragraph. Preceding your main point is a first sentence or two that explains why you're writing this e-mail or letter. Often it is in response to a person writing to you. At other times, you may be asked to do a piece of writing, or you may see a need to put something in writing.

Based on the above suggestions, here is an example of an introductory paragraph:

Two years ago, our firm instituted a certain procedure for cashing checks. Unfortunately, serious problems have arisen with that procedure, and we have been forced to change the process. Below are the three steps that you should now follow to cash checks.

Now you know what the next three sections, usually paragraphs, need to be. That is, each paragraph will deal with a new *step*, which is the key word.

The key word approach can help you create a good flow if you make sure to use transition words between sentences and paragraphs so people see how one statement relates to the next. Numbers can help: You can begin the second paragraph with *The primary advantage is. . . .* The third paragraph can begin with *Second . . .* and so on.

—Dr. Mel Haber, president of
Writing Development Associates

Tell It to Someone

Brain scientists find that writing involves complicated neurological processes that tap into memory, analysis, executive functioning and other mental capabilities scattered around different parts of the brain. In contrast, talking bypasses this complexity. Speech enables us to respond to immediate circumstances such as opportunity or danger. It preceded written communication by at least a few hundred thousand years, so little wonder that we're better at it. You can exploit this fact: To simplify a message and find its heart, tell it to someone.

This strategy works for a challenging memo, a blog or an important long-form document. When the task is important and/or involves numerous facts and ideas that are hard to sort out, explain it to someone else. If that person is not steeped in your subject, all the better. Often, expressing your goal gives you a good starting point. For example, "I want a new office because . . ." or "I want to recommend solving the problem this way . . . ," according to the situation. You'll find yourself speaking clearly and to the point. Your reasoning evolves organically to show you what's most important and how things fit together. If the person listening asks questions, figure out the answers and build them into your argument.

This is not, by the way, an unsophisticated technique. Feature writers use it all the time to figure out what's most interesting about a story they're developing. It connects them with their intuition and steers them toward the story's heart. Then they know how to create the story they most want to write and that is most likely to satisfy readers. You may at times find that the talking-through process dictates a substantial shift in focus. Don't resist this! It puts you on a better track.

To transfer your oral story to the written word, write down what you said as closely as you can. Then review it carefully. Good business writing seems conversational, but that is somewhat of an illusion. Writing is perceived differently than spoken language and must have a visibly logical flow and more "correctness" than spontaneous speech, which is here one moment, gone the next. Also, the writing-down process allows you to edit mistakes, cut extraneous information, and find flaws in an argument or gaps in your thinking.

A good technique, especially when you feel stuck, is to write out your outline and opening by hand. Neuroscientists are finding that the physicality of handwriting triggers the brain in a different way than using a keyboard. It also triggers recall differently. This is not illogical: Human beings have been "action" creatures eons longer than "thinking" ones. Many leading authors still handwrite their manuscripts, not necessarily because they're out of date or anti-technology, but because it helps them think better. See if it works for you.

Deploy Graphic Techniques

Whether your document is short (like an e-mail or letter) or lengthy (like a report or proposal), you'll find it helpful to stay organized by building in graphic options. This has a big payoff: It makes everything, regardless of length, more easily understood by readers. In fact, if you don't build in graphics while you're writing, you may have to add them later anyway.

Graphic tools are even more important to online writing because people tend to scan and their attention must be captured and managed. Website designers use graphics quite systematically to attract a reader's eye and move it from point to point, taking account of typical viewing habits, based on research. Online articles, blogs, profiles and other materials all benefit from the use of graphic devices as well as many forms of imagery.

To structure a document of any kind, many writers create a series of subheads before they begin to write. Then they juggle the sequence and—presto!—a ready-made outline materializes. They add the content for each subhead, and there's the blog or promotional piece or report.

GRAPHIC OPTIONS FOR ALL BUSINESS WRITING

Draw on your visual repertoire to organize your messages. Here are some options.

Use subheads to introduce a new thought or section. Choose the format you prefer:

A larger font

A different font

Boldface

Italic

Write them in sentence case, with just an initial cap, like this.
or
Write Your Subheads in Uppercase and Lowercase
You can combine some effects—bold with a different font, for example—but you must be consistent.

Use bold lead-ins for the beginning of a paragraph or section. Boldface, with or without italic, can also be used to **highlight a fact, figure, idea** or *point to remember in the body of your copy*. There are also times when underlining is a good way to highlight, but this looks outdated and falsely suggests that the phrase is a hyperlink. And of course color works, if the medium accommodates it. Take care when your material will be read cross-platform, because uncommon type and colors may not translate as you intend.

Use bullet points, but remember their limitations. They are good for

- listing ideas or facts telegraphically,
- summarizing,
- saving space,
- presenting at-a-glance information.

But do not depend on bullet points too much. While bulleting is a good way to present information for an audience with a short attention span—which, admittedly, is most of us—bullets need narrative context to deliver meaning. A collection of random-seeming stand-alone points is hard to absorb. Recall tends to be poor because they give the mind little to hold on to. More than four to seven at most is risky.

This applies to all media, including résumés. Listing responsibilities or accomplishments in bullet form doesn't work without narrative-style paragraphs to interpret the big picture. Remember, never expect readers to draw conclusions for you. They may draw the wrong ones.

Number your points. This can work well to pull a reader through your information or argument. Some reasons for this:

1. People like to know how much is ahead of them.

2. It's satisfying to feel a message has a beginning and an end.

3. A clear sequence can be easy to absorb and remember.

So, in print or speech, statements like "We can expect three basic results from this action" or "Here are the seven steps to filing the new form" are quite effective, followed, of course, by steps one, two, three and so on in logical order.

Incorporate graphic techniques. Use boxes, sidebars and pullout quotes—all demonstrated throughout the book you're reading right now. They enable you to incorporate relevant information without breaking the flow of a narrative.

Always, *extensive and strategic use of white space is critical to accessibility and eye appeal of EVERY message*. This is particularly true of long documents but deploy white space even with brief ones. Short paragraphs help break up space. And, of course, whenever you find ways to make your point visually, through a chart, graph, image or video, consider that. But keep the document consistent and keep visuals relevant.

Use the right font or typeface. Be sure you're using a very readable font and refrain from using capitals, italics or boldface for entire e-mails or large portions of text. As a general rule, don't mix more than two fonts, although you might use a distinctly different font for headlines and subheads. Traditional serif fonts, which have the little squiggles on the ends, are nearly always used for books, newspapers and long documents because they are considered more readable. However, sans serif fonts look more contemporary and are favored for websites, other online reading and résumés. (For specific advice on fonts and other graphic basics, see "View From the Field: A Graphic Designer's Advice on Presenting Well" in Chapter 6.)

Bottom line: Less is more. Don't jam in your copy, whatever the medium! Use formatting techniques in all media to support and clarify your message, make it reader friendly and invite the eye. Readability demands reasonable margins and thoughtfully used graphic devices.

SUCCESS TIP

We're all Screenwriters

Writers today must take account of how on-screen reading has transformed reader expectations for print as well as electronic media. In reading so much material on miniature screens, we have evolved into scanners. We check for what's relevant or interesting to us individually. We "dive" for information rather than systematically reading almost anything. We need choices. We bring this new attitude to all media and messaging.

Notice that few magazines or newspapers present us with dense, unbroken copy anymore. They use photographs, illustrations, pre-article summaries, charts, graphs, captions—all the access points they can devise to pull impatient people in and feed them at least a piece of the story.

A growing number of books (like this one) do the same. And note how sales letters and charitable solicitations are brimful of headlines, subheads, underlining, pullouts, "handwritten" notes and other devices.

Creating websites has been described as "packaging information," and this is a helpful way to think about most of what you write. Don't limit your attention to just the words. Consider the graphic presentation, your audience preferences and every technique you can draw on to deliver your message in a clear, attractive and compelling manner—while keeping it as concise and simple as possible. Wordiness and complex tricky graphics don't fare well viewed on smartphones. Notice how much simpler website design is becoming: an evocative image, a few carefully selected words and so on.

THE GOLDILOCKS PRINCIPLE: HOW MUCH IS JUST RIGHT?

Just like Goldilocks had to find the just-right bowl of porridge, and visual artists are challenged to recognize when a painting is finished, writers must decide how much to include in a message. How do you know when you're writing too little? Or so much that the ideas or facts or information may work against you?

A rule of thumb: Provide just enough to make your point well and resist adding anything that might undermine your goal. Consider this example of "too much." Jeb, a grad student who is a good writer, wrote to ask a nonprofit to partner with him on a project for his public policy thesis. He hoped to conduct an in-depth survey of the population served by the charity. His thorough three-page letter outlined the process he planned, the number of people he'd interview, his analysis techniques and so on. The executive director responded: "It doesn't sound like something we'd want to do."

By supplying information overkill, Jeb created a strong potential to strike a negative chord and give the reader a reason to turn him down. Probably, the extensive detail made the project sound like a lot of trouble. At his advisor's urging, Jeb wrote a one-page abbreviated message to another nonprofit, stating who he was, his proposed project, a few lines about carrying out the survey, and how the data would benefit the charity. He was invited in to talk.

In writing his original message, Jeb misperceived the goal. Rather than requesting project approval based on a very detailed description, he would have done better to articulate a more limited goal: an opportunity to present his idea—if not in person, in a fuller written version. Considering your goals, and the limitations of a platform, helps you judge the amount of information called for. In Jeb's case, he needed just enough to intrigue the recipient and spotlight the WIIFM. If, on the other hand, the message is a proposal for a research project, or funding, a detailed presentation is needed to move into round two.

"Audience" gives you a second clue. If you're asking your nontechnically minded supervisor to authorize a new computer, don't bury the ask under an avalanche of tech specs. If you want your company to pay for a course, dwell not on the benefit to you personally, but to your work and therefore the organization. Focusing on what's in it for them tells you what content is extraneous and which arguments and facts will further your cause.

As part of your editing process, check every message for the just-right amount test. There is too much if you

- overwhelm the point you want to make and it gets lost,

- bury or fail to state the benefit to the reader or listener,

- muddy the ask by presenting your request in terms that are too explicit or too expansive,

- give the reader a reason to say no,

- create a boring message that's tedious to get through.

Think "Goldilocks." It can save you a lot of time while enabling you to be more effective. A cover letter for a job, for example, isn't going to win you a job all by itself. That's unrealistic. Your aim is to introduce the accompanying résumé so it is read in a positive light and makes a good first impression. The best proposal is unlikely to bring you a check in the mail. You need to cover the information that earns a "yes" and the right to move one step ahead.

Anticipate that many of your wants require a multi-step process. It takes a string of letters or e-mails to build a relationship and establish trust. Often reaching "yes" is a back-and-forth process between written and oral communication. For example, you write for an appointment, interact at a face-to-face meeting, follow up with a thank-you note or written agreement, appear for another meeting and so on. And sometimes you build a sale by coordinating a combination of media: a social post to draw people to your website, which offers a giveaway in return for permission to send e-mails, newsletter issues or blogs, and eventually . . . you may score a sale. Ambitious achievements, such as asking people to risk money or time on you often requires big-time patience.

MANAGE YOUR TONE

As we've seen with some of the examples, a document can look well planned and written but still fail if the tone, or voice, hits the wrong note for readers. Just as with live interaction, the feeling you communicate in a written message strongly affects how your words are received.

In a person-to-person situation, tone clearly results from, well, tone of voice. The same words can mean many different things according to our voice inflection, pitch, rhythm, speed and so on—factors that reflect our actual state of mind and attitude. Moreover, in talking face to face, we also communicate via facial expression, body language, conversational pauses and a whole host of cues that signal interest, curiosity, surprise, impatience, resistance or a number of other feelings.

But when we read, our eyes and ears can't help us interpret meaning. Nonetheless, as readers we easily pick up emotional content, often subliminally, without being able to pinpoint a reason. For writers, controlling tone is critical. When you ask for something, clearly it's not a good idea to undermine your case by showing disrespect, ambivalence or any negative feeling about the subject or reader.

A counterproductive tone may result if you have negative feelings and don't take care to avoid revealing them. But you may also create this effect without intending to—and perhaps without even meaning it. For example, if your messages are influenced by texting and casual social media exchanges, you may write letters and e-mails in a staccato style that strikes some people as abrupt, discourteous and rude. Keep in mind that if someone perceives disrespect, you erect roadblocks, even if it just seems to you a matter of style. You can't know which people will react to texting style this way, so be aware of this pitfall.

Therefore be conscious of your tone, and work to align it with your goal and audience. Everything you write should reinforce and build positive relationships. The principle is the same for in-person situations. Take charge of your expression, body language and voice, because inevitably people pick up signs of disrespect, dislike or disinterest.

A 10-Point Tone Checklist

How can you sharpen your writing ear to achieve the tone you want?

1. **Recognize your feelings.** Just as with face-to-face interaction, your tone can easily convey your actual attitude. So if you're writing to someone you don't much like or respect, or communicating something you disagree with but should not express an opinion about, take particular care with what you say and how you say it.

2. **Think twice about writing in an emotional state.** You risk doing yourself long-term harm if you write when you're angry, frustrated, offended, envious, resentful or suffering from any other negative emotion. Writing that feels negative or seems to criticize the reader produces a greater and more lasting impact than an oral delivery. And a mean-tempered missive might be circulated. At best you will mark yourself as immature. If you must vent, try writing out your feelings and then burying the message. Never address such messages!

3. **Expect higher-ups to demand good manners in person and in writing.** Managers need respect to carry out their own function. VIPs, clients and customers need to feel respected too. And so do colleagues. Build in the full trappings of courtesy and often, in this age of careless communication, you stand out.

4. **Remember that subordinates also respond to courtesy.** A request or directive is better delivered with full respect. Tell people why something is necessary, give them the information they need to carry out tasks well, show appreciation. Your goals if you're the boss always include building the team, encouraging individuals and generating enthusiasm for the work. Those who report to you take their cues from you and treat others as they are treated.

5. **Remember that tone is contagious.** Projecting a negative attitude will provoke the same from your reader or listener. That never helps, so determine to communicate in a positive spirit. Don't earmark yourself as a complainer. If you want an enthusiastic response, show your own enthusiasm. Friendly, open and businesslike are good hallmarks to strive for in everyday communication.

6. **Stay appropriate to the subject and relationship.** If the topic is serious, don't be breezy. If you don't know the person, err on the side of formality. When you do know the person, call him up in your mind to automatically adopt the right tone. When it's someone you don't like, remind yourself not to worsen the relationship.

7. **Project a quiet confidence.** In informal channels like e-mail, aim to create the impression that you are reliable and resourceful, someone who has matters well in hand. For in-depth material like proposals and reports, avoid hedgy wording that sounds indecisive—"I believe that," "perhaps," "maybe," "might," "could," for example.

8. **Avoid ambiguity.** Double-check important messages and documents, preferably with a trusted buddy, to ensure that they cannot be misinterpreted in any way or lead to any conclusion against your interest. Imagine you were talking instead of writing: Would any statement require a particular tone of voice or facial expression or gesture to convey what you really mean? Irony and sarcasm are high risk!

9. **Adapt to the corporate culture.** Messages sent by Citibank staff may differ in tone quite a lot from messages written by employees at Facebook or a nonprofit, or they might not. An organization can be positioned along the formal to informal

scale based more on its own history and the nature of its leadership, rather than the industry it's part of. In a new work environment, invest time in analyzing the degree of formality, general style and appropriate subject matter of the written communication you see. Adjust your writing accordingly.

10. **Adapt to the medium.** Generally, a letter needs to be more formal than an e-mail. A report or proposal is typically more formal yet. Online writing, such as for websites or blogs, generally works best when it feels more casual, friendly and individual. Good websites look very accessible and spontaneous—though in fact, these qualities are always achieved through the most arduous planning, writing and rewriting.

avoid sarcasim or snark speak directly

Communicate in a positive, optimistic spirit and you will be amply rewarded. Avoid creating friction with coworkers or assaulting the boss with frequent complaints. If you encounter a problem and believe it's important, handle it proactively in a solution-oriented manner. Remember that people respond in line with their perceptions of you and how you treat them.

PRACTICE THE PLANNING STRUCTURE

Case 1: Drawing Important People to Campus

Let's see how the principles can be used to write speaker invitations.

The Entrepreneur Group is ready to write to the selected business leaders. What could entice these people to accept a speaking invitation?

Start with brainstorming what the group has in common. Most probably, they all

- face highly pressured schedules;

- like to be recognized as leaders;

- value community connection (or at least its appearance);

- want to support the region, especially schools that foster growth and make it a good place to live;

- might have an eye toward hiring future graduates, connecting with faculty and/or interacting with young people.

Here's one way to write a generic version of the letter.

Dear _____:

The Green University Martin School of Business is inviting the region's most prominent business leaders to address our students and faculty this coming year. Recognizing how important Premiere Industries is to both our area's economy and the community we share, and your own contributions as a leader, we hope you will accept our invitation to be part of this year's Executive Speaker Program.

We ask for just an evening of your time. In addition to an address of approximately one hour, including a Q&A, we hope you will be our guest for dinner and meet leading members of our business school community. We would be delighted to schedule your appearance for March and can offer you a choice of dates during the month.

The Executive Speaker Program gives our aspiring business managers the chance to become acquainted with the Quadruple Cities' most inspiring leaders. The Martin School of Business has worked hard to earn an impressive ranking internationally. We believe you'll find the discussion stimulating.

With your permission, we plan to publicize your appearance with the local media and videotape your presentation for our widely used archive. If it would be helpful, committee members will be happy to work closely with you to support your presentation.

I'll call you next week to ask if you accept our invitation and answer any questions. Or if more convenient, please call me at any time.

The letter takes account of the recipients' busy schedules and makes their commitment as convenient and pain free as possible, reminds them of the community and giveback context of a university, flatters (why not?) their importance and suggests some tangible benefit in the way of positive press and contact with faculty and select students.

It could work. But is it good enough?

Writing is more powerful when you personalize your message to the individual. When the stakes are high, take the trouble to find out what the person values.

How to do this if you've never met her? Start with questions you can answer with a little effort. In the case of our theoretical guest speaker, for example:

Is she

- a graduate of the school or parent of kids who have been or might be?

- a former business major? MBA?

- a donor to the university or school?

- connected with any particular community cause?

- proud of something in particular? Known for something in business circles?

- passionate about her work?

Does the company

- hire your university's graduates or those from your school?

- send employees to any university program for training?

- sponsor any campus programs?

Research the answers—online and by finding people to talk to who know the person or the company. Identify a professor, board member or school supporter who knows the individual personally or can connect you with someone who does.

This thinking applies to every occasion when you're requesting something important. Look for ways to successfully relate to your audience. Obviously, it helps if your potential speaker has direct ties to your school, a relationship with a professor or a strong community spirit. In each case, you'll use this information prominently, probably in the lead. One example:

> *I'm writing to you as a Green U. graduate because we'd very much like to include you as a Martin School of Business guest speaker.*

A basic letter can be adapted to each recipient's characteristics. Read the "Three Ways to Personalize Messages" box, and add the ideas to your tool kit. They work well for many documents, including job-hunting letters.

THREE WAYS TO PERSONALIZE MESSAGES

1. **Name-drop in an available and honest way.** In business, people respond to connections and references because it's far more comfortable to deal with someone who's vouched for than a total unknown. We trust people who are trusted by people we trust. If you have (or can find) a mutual connection, use it and use it early. For example:

   At John Black's suggestion, I am writing to ask . . .

   Professor Blue, whose class on corporate culture I am currently enjoying and with whom you also studied at White, believes I would be an excellent candidate for the internship your company is offering.

2. **Do your homework, and be sure it shows.** People like to know they're recognized or that you took the time to find out about them or their organization—especially when you can identify something they're proud of. For example:

   Our selection committee was particularly impressed with how you've established Brown Industries as one of the top in its field nationally in only 10 years.

   (Continued)

(Continued)

In addition to your business leadership, your support of the community through the scholarship program and hospital building fund makes you an exceptional model for future corporate leaders, so we will especially value your participation.

3. **Use compliments; they often work magic.** Like everyone else and perhaps more than most people, VIPs like to feel good about themselves and know that other people recognize how special they are. This is not to suggest twisting the truth but rather that you find something nice you can say *with sincerity.* (Try this technique sometime with a hostile boss or colleague and you'll be amazed at the turnaround.) For example:

Several classmates have told me that you are an exceptionally interesting and inspiring speaker, so I'm very pleased to extend this invitation.

I'd like to share that when we canvassed the committee members for their top speaker picks, your name came up repeatedly.

Knowing that your company has twice been cited as a "Best Place to Work" makes us particularly excited about your sharing your insights with us.

Case 2: Asking for Opportunities

Put yourself in the place of someone who's on the job for a few months and feels frustrated by the routine work. Interesting projects are under way in your department but you have no role in them and are not invited to the planning sessions. Deciding to speak up, your first impulse is to write to the boss (or tell him face to face) something like this:

Dear Chad:

I want you to know that I'm feeling very sidelined by my workload. I don't get to participate in the project planning meetings. I'm relegated to trivial assignments that don't require my qualifications and abilities. I can do so much more. Why don't you give me a chance? I know I can be a great asset.

The message is not likely to succeed. Why? The usual suspects:

Goal: *You're asking for responsibility and recognition, but undermine this desire by communicating only that you feel undervalued and bored. Concretely, what do you want the reader to do?*

Audience: *The message focuses on how you feel, unhappy and dissatisfied, which the boss may not much care about. It fails to consider reader perspective—WIIFM.*

Tone: *It's resentful and whiny, which doesn't speak well for the writer; nor does the touch of self-importance.*

Content: *The message makes empty claims about how good you are without providing evidence.*

This message makes a "me" statement and gives the supervisor no reason to accommodate a new, impatient employee by awarding more attractive work and privilege. Challenging him to make you happy could leave you in a worse situation than you're already in.

In contrast, if you use the strategic approach, it leads you to look at the situation through the boss's eyes and reason out why he should give you what you want. If you've built a profile of the boss, as recommended in Chapter 2, you have a good idea of what he cares about. But just considering how a manager thinks based on his position goes a long way toward helping you know what to say.

Assuming you've been doing a good job, the boss probably prefers that you stay and succeed. Replacing a hire is expensive and time-consuming. And all supervisors want their staff members to contribute more because it's how they in turn succeed. The question becomes: How can I connect what I want to what I assume Chad logically wants? If Chad said anything positive about your performance or an assignment, use that opening:

Dear Chad:

I was happy to hear that you're pleased with my work. I want to do a great job and look forward to contributing more to the team.

Is it possible for me to participate in some of the project development meetings? Understanding the big picture would help me see how my assignments fit in and help me do them better. The learning experience would help equip me to take on more responsibility and support the team more effectively.

I would value this opportunity and appreciate it.

Thanks.

This message gives you better odds because it's keyed to what Chad cares about, asks for something specific, and reflects a positive and appreciative tone. You want to contribute more. Now you're talking the manager's language!

Looking at a situation from another person's perspective and figuring out the WIIFM enables you to anticipate consequences. If he reads the first message, Chad will probably feel irritated and question whether you'd deport yourself well in team meetings. The second message gives him a concrete request to consider and suggests how granting it will benefit him, which disposes him to look at it favorably. The respectful tone communicates that you will honor the opportunity and handle it well.

Can the way you frame what you write make such a big difference? Absolutely.

True, Chad may say yes or no. But if he says no, you're still ahead. Chances are good he will provide a reason—perhaps that you don't merit that opportunity until you're on the job longer or that you haven't earned the right. If so you are now able to ask: *How can I show you that I am ready for this?* This may produce valuable guidance.

What if the boss says that the meetings will never be part of your role, and in effect that you should just stick to what you're given and not expect more? Then you gain important data for decision making.

Case 3: Resigning From a Job

Suppose you judge from Chad's response that your job will never grow into something better and you decide to leave the job and prospect elsewhere. How to go about resigning? You could just stop showing up—and in fact, a trend toward this tactic among younger people has been observed. This approach is not wise: You end up without a reference for the time you put in and may face a widely disseminated warning that loses you other opportunities.

If you do give notice, you might be tempted to write:

Chad—I'm out of here. I've had enough of being bored out of my gourd with work that hasn't much point. Send my last check to. . . .

Before delivering such a message, think about *goals* and *consequences.* Every industry is a small world, and every small world is connected by the global Internet. When you inconvenience and disrespect the boss, might he tell everyone in his network? And your immediate audience is bigger than the supervisor: It includes your coworkers. Unless you're moving to a desert island to live as a hunter-gatherer, your peers matter. In future they will be your major referral sources and perhaps your employers. A mean-spirited departure that leaves them holding the bag does not sow good seeds. So even if (and especially when) you're angry, take charge of yourself and write a professional message:

Dear Chad:

I've thought long and hard about our conversation and my prospects for advancement at WeGo Industries. I reluctantly conclude that this position just isn't a good fit. Please accept my resignation as of April 12. If someone else is appointed to fill the job while I'm still on it, I'll be happy to train them. I'll also work overtime to leave everything in good shape.

Personally, I want to say how much I appreciate having had this opportunity and everything I've learned from working for you. Thank you and best wishes, ——.

It is always professional to leave a job gracefully, no matter your grievances. While this resignation note may not thrill the boss, it leaves him feeling as positive as possible about his investment of time in you. A rude goodbye can diminish your options more than you'll know. Even a peer who shares your complaint might hesitate to recommend someone who left on a nasty note. So remind yourself that this too is a constant goal: to leave doors open and act in ways that accomplish that.

Case 4: Delivering a Bad News Message

Let's suppose it's your unhappy lot to develop a memo announcing that the company will cancel its tuition reimbursement benefit. Your boss gives you the draft she began:

To: All staff

Subject: Participants in Post-Ed Program

Please be advised that economic conditions dictate some employee benefit cutbacks. As of June 30, Rose Co. will no longer provide tuition reimbursement. It is regrettable if this causes inconvenience, but as you'll understand, the decision is in the company's best interest.

Talent Management Dept.

Here's why the message fails in both tone and content. The writer needed to consider two basic audiences—those who are directly affected and those who are not. A program beneficiary is bound to be upset when an entitlement is taken away arbitrarily. Worse, it sounds like more benefits may be on the chopping block—maybe even jobs. Even if you're not directly affected by this cut, you'd have the same uncertainties.

Further, because the bad news is delivered so impersonally—no one takes responsibility for the decision—you're likely to think bad thoughts about your employer. Not to mention that it sounds like the company is on the downslide. More than one member of the audience might come to the same conclusion: time to update the résumé.

Studies show that the manner in which bad news is delivered, even in worst-case scenarios like layoffs, strongly affects how employees perceive a company and feel about their jobs. This is no small matter because when times are tough and the staff is lean, management needs to build an everyone-must-pull-together spirit.

Good managers, therefore, put a lot of thought into anticipating reaction to bad news. They brainstorm about how best to frame it and whether anything can be done to offset the negative impact. And plenty of consultants find their bread and butter in telling executives how to handle these situations.

In the example we're using, then, the goals can be stated like this:

- Deliver the bad news in the most acceptable manner possible.

- Communicate honestly and realistically (anything else will backfire).

- Express empathy in a businesslike way.

- Reassure employees that there are no current plans for more cuts.

- Assure everyone that the company has a good future.

When you're not speaking for yourself, a situation you may often encounter, begin by gathering useful information such as this:

- Who made the decision?

- Exactly why was it made?

- Might the benefit be reinstated someday?

- Are other benefit cuts being effected or contemplated?

- Might layoffs follow?

- Is the firm's situation precarious? If so, to what degree?

- What has been the company's communication history and treatment of staff?

- What are the options for attributing the message's authorship?

Here's one way to reframe the message.

To: All Rose Company Staff

Subject: Suspension of tuition-reimbursement program

Dear Colleagues:

I'm sorry to tell you that as of June 30 the company will not offer tuition reimbursement.

As the management team has communicated over the past year, Rose Company has lost several important clients due to an industry-wide downturn. Additionally, a few clients have temporarily reduced their service level.

We're working hard to broaden our client base and diversify services, as you know, and see a promising business uptick. But right now we must effect some economies. We don't want to reduce staff beyond natural attrition. And we don't want to trim benefits like health insurance that are critical to our corporate family's well-being.

Accordingly, we have decided to reduce spending on tuition reimbursement as well as new equipment and conference travel. We realize that losing the program will disappoint many of you, and we continue to value our staff's commitment to continued learning. We'll be happy to reinstate this perk when it becomes practical to do so.

Meanwhile, I'm sure you'll agree with our priorities and our commitment to sharing the news with you openly and honestly. I know that, with your help, Rose Co. will weather the current industry downturn and provide a supportive employment climate for all of us.

I'll keep you closely informed of our progress.

Sincerely, Ed White, CEO

This memo tells readers why the cuts are being effected and puts them in context, establishes a team feeling, reassures readers about the company's future and makes them feel valued. It's hard to disagree with the expressed priorities. It sounds like management is handling the economic challenge well and that staying with the ship is a good bet. And employees can trust company leaders to communicate straightforwardly.

Note that there are various strategies for communicating bad news, such as "sandwiching" it between positive statements. For example, "Bob, it's been terrific to have you as a vendor all these years. But the company has grown and we're moving on. Let's remember the good times."

But this cushioning approach ill suits today's skeptical, impatient, even cynical audience. It's much more effective to impart the bad stuff immediately. Show caring, and give reasons when you can. Try to find something truly useful to offer rather than empty rhetoric. "I can suggest a contact who may have a job lead for you" or "We're bringing in some job search experts for you to consult with" is a lot better message than "With all your talents, I'm sure a great future awaits you."

These principles should help you avoid a bad news messenger's worst fate when you have that role. As you move up the ladder, remember that up-front honesty and compassion for others should guide your response to crisis. Introduce mitigating factors when possible. Where an apology is in order, offer it. Unfortunately, this lesson seems to be unlearnable in many corporate and political arenas.

The experimental memo from "Ed White" claimed a good communication history for the company only because I chose to assume that was true. Just as in personal life, good relationships must be built over time. This is true for external communication as well as internal. An institution needs to foster employee, public and media goodwill over the long run through good communication to successfully weather the inevitable crisis.

VIEW FROM THE FIELD: NEED TO APOLOGIZE? HERE'S HOW

Visiting hundreds of companies and writing about their crisis du jour, I noticed that organizations that apologize have better outcomes. And individuals who do it well rise higher and have better relationships. Clearly accountability—taking responsibility and rejecting defensiveness—is an important skill. So I started to put it together into a systematic approach, the 5Rs model:

- Recognition—acknowledge the specific offense
- Responsibility—accept personal responsibility, no excuses
- Remorse—there's no substitute for "I apologize" or "I am sorry"
- Restitution—here's what I'll do about it, concretely
- Repeating—I promise it won't happen again

You never know when the need to apologize will come upon you, but if you're not prepared, instinct kicks in—we want to defend ourselves, hide, deny responsibility. But the cover-up is always worse than the crime. Train yourself in small things and it will be easier to apply to big things.

Written apologies are more formal than spoken but work about the same.

These days, apologizing is a leadership skill. We see our decision makers dodging and weaving instead of accepting responsibility, and that disappoints us. We don't expect them to be perfect, just willing to learn. In the long run, apology leads to better outcomes and more durable relationships.

—John Kador, author of business books on leadership including *Effective Apology: Mending Fences, Building Bridges and Restoring Trust*

Chapter takeaway: Use this book's strategies not as manipulative techniques, but to communicate in ways that reflect your best self and connect with people authentically. Understanding another person enables you to frame your messages based on WIIFM—what's in it for her—and leads you to communicate from respect. It recognizes differences and acknowledges value in those differences. You own the ability to set the tone for your work relationships even when you're new or junior on the job. Speak and write with thought, caring, honesty and a positive voice. You will be a plus factor for the whole environment and will be appreciated.

In the next chapters, we'll start to look at concrete ways to improve the mechanics of what you write—the engineering. Good planning and substance are essential, but you also need to craft good sentences, choose the right words and produce cohesive documents.

PRACTICE OPPORTUNITIES

I. Write a Better Note for Amy

Ask her subordinate to deliver a report by a specific time in a way that will make her feel appreciated, part of a team and happy to work hard on Amy's behalf.

II. Group Work: Plan and Pitch an On-Site Visit

As a group, brainstorm to identify an interesting local company to visit. Come up with as many reasons as you can to justify the time required to plan, organize and make the visit.

1. Collaborate on a letter making your case to the professor.

2. Write a letter to the appropriate person at the company asking the firm to host the class.

III. Write a "Stop Order"

Write a convincing e-mail to the class telling everyone to stop texting, tweeting, Facebook viewing and so on during class time or business meetings.

IV. Draft a "Please Rescind"

Write an e-mail to a supervisor asking that the rule against texting, tweeting or Facebook monitoring during work hours be rescinded, explaining why.

V. Create a "How To"

Write a detailed document telling someone exactly how to do something practical, step by step. Make it as clear as you possibly can with thoughtful content, good writing and graphic techniques. Sample subjects: how to use the newest smartphone, fix a tire, make a paper airplane, choose a new computer, build an aquarium, catch a fish, train a dog to fetch or any subject related to your interests or knowledge base. Choose something you already know about or would like to research.

VI. Sum Up This Chapter's Content

Draft a 300- to 500-word summary describing the most important takeaways from this chapter. Create a complete message using the strategies explained and at least five of the graphic techniques. Exchange your draft with another student, and talk about the similarities and differences in content and how each of you handled this task.

VII. Find What's Wrong and Fix It!

Here are some real e-mails with counterproductive tone. For each, identify the problem and fix it.

1. To a supervisor:

Dana—I have a great idea for solving the problem we talked about last week. Let's meet on Thursday at 3:00 p.m. We can talk all about it.—Robin

2. To a professor:

Dear Prof—I looked online again for the syllabus you were supposed to post and couldn't find it. I need it by tomorrow—so last chance.—Mike White

3. To the employer's client:

Dear Mr. Black—I sent you the Kittredge draft last week but have heard nothing. Did I miss something? The deadline is close. Please advise ASAP.—Mark

4. From a travel agent to a client prospect:

Hello (no first name) Kennedy—Previously I had e-mailed you regarding your request for a quote for Waterworld Cruises Russia trip. There were a couple of questions that I needed answered in order to provide you with a more accurate quote. When is a good time to discuss your vacation plans?

I certainly can understand your being busy, or perhaps you did not get the e-mail. So if you can get in touch with me at your convenience, I would like to provide you with all the pricing, discounts, and details.—Jenny Jay

5. From a professional acquaintance asking for help:

Dear Ms. C:

Long time no see! You'll remember me as VP of marketing for Digital Extreme— you wrote a script for the company video under my direction about 10 years ago.

Now, alas, I've been downsized and am looking for new opportunities. Do you know of any job openings for people with senior experience like mine? Or can you give me some industry contacts to call?

Thanks—much appreciated! Mary Nova

SHARPEN AND IMPROVE YOUR WRITING

4 CREATE THE FIRST DRAFT

The discipline of writing something down is the first step toward making it happen.

—Lee Iacocca, automobile industry leader

LEARN HOW TO . . .

- Choose natural conversational words

- Build active verb-based sentences

- Assemble short, logical paragraphs

- Use good transitions

- Achieve a fluid cadence

The first three chapters focused on how to determine the content of messages and documents. Now let's turn to delivering the message well: expressing what you want to communicate in the simplest, clearest language possible.

As you'll see in many of the examples, there is not necessarily one "right" way to do this. Good writing is not accomplished with formulas. It's achieved through good thinking, according to each need. But you need not do all the thinking at once. That's the beauty of the three-step planning, drafting, editing process. First you brainstorm for the big picture: define what you want to accomplish, consider your audience, determine content. Then you create a first draft, as spontaneously and carelessly as you wish. And finally, you edit: review, correct, sharpen.

With a little practice, the three stages blend together. You refine your thinking as you write and, at the same time, automatically apply editing techniques to improve how you express yourself. But for now let's focus on creating the first draft. First come the words.

CHOOSE THE FAMILIAR WORDS OF CONVERSATION

In business writing, unlike parts of the academic world, you don't get rewarded for using long, "sophisticated" words. Instead, you lose readers. It seems obvious that using words that more people will understand, and whose meaning they agree on, is best. But too much business writing ignores this basic concept.

Today we're all speed readers. So even when your audience is highly educated, build your writing on the short words we use in everyday speech. How short? Generally, one and two syllables. This doesn't imply that you should never use longer words. It means to use short words as your basic building blocks and longer words where they are helpful for accuracy, impact or variety. Or when there's no available short word or you consciously want to spark things up or evoke an emotional reaction.

Does this sound like you need to simplify your thoughts? Absolutely not. It means that while you have a wealth of choices with which to express your precise meaning, you must work to be as clear as possible through words that really communicate this meaning to other people.

I love words but I don't like strange ones. You don't understand them and they don't understand you. Old words is like old friends, you know 'em the minute you see 'em.

—Will Rogers, performer and humorist

The English language evolved from short practical words (see the sidebar "Why English Has So Many Words and How That Affects Your Writing"), and to this day, we seem to trust those words most and find the "fancy" words suspicious.

WHY ENGLISH HAS SO MANY WORDS AND HOW THAT AFFECTS YOUR WRITING

The English vocabulary is rich, and there are often abundant word choices for expressing the same or similar thought. The alternatives for the most part reflect English history.

The short words mostly come from the language's Anglo-Saxon legacy, its original base. These include words like *mother, man, bad, good, work, dog, big, eat, love, in, out*. Some Scandinavian additions arrived with the Viking invasions (*leg, crawl, trust, take*).

But many of the language's longer words derive from Latin, or French, via the Roman and Norman invasions. Both occupied England as ruling aristocrats and introduced words relating to government,

the military, the arts, sophisticated living, philosophy and more. Many of these words represent abstractions—*justice, independence, materialism, intelligence, idealism*—and emotional states—*curiosity, excitement, annoyance*.

It's estimated that while Anglo-Saxon words compose only 1% of today's English, they remain the fundamental words, and half of what we typically write consists of those words. As Bill Bryson says in his interesting book *The Mother Tongue: English and How It Got That Way*, "To this day we have an almost instinctive preference for the older Anglo-Saxon phrases."

A big side benefit of using short words is that many of them are concrete. They represent tangible things we can see or touch or hear or feel and are automatically more persuasive. They keep us grounded in reality and help us write in ways that reach people more directly. Writing built on abstractions gives readers less to hold onto, and it also leads to needlessly complicated grammatical structures. This forces people to slow down and unravel your meaning. When you write for academic purposes, slowing readers down may help them absorb new ideas. But it's always a negative in business writing. Whether you're writing an e-mail or report or blog, you want to be understood immediately and unambiguously. You want to draw readers along smoothly and transparently so they absorb the content, rather than noticing (or battling with) the language.

Beyond this commonsense rationale for writing simply, clearly and concisely, today there's a physical reason. More and more reading is done on a smartphone or other mini-screen, so cutting to the core and tossing the extra words is imperative.

Here's a first-draft sentence I wrote for this book.

The amount of interaction in contemporary office contexts is continually diminishing because of technology. Therefore writing is today's preeminent skill.

Note all the long non-concrete words; the numerous prepositions (*in, of, to*), which instill clumsiness; and the structure of both sentences—they depend on the passive verb *is*. The result: a stilted rhythm and boring read that doesn't connect with readers.

When I put on my editor's hat, I came to my senses and rewrote this way:

Thanks to technology, today we talk less and write more. So writing is a more important skill than ever.

Does the rewrite have a somewhat different meaning than the original? Yes, but that's OK. Finding the best way to deliver a clear message helps you drill down to your core meaning and communicate it much better. Your first draft of any message, long or short, is unlikely to accomplish this. It may take several bouts of editing to find what you want to communicate. Moving from version 1 to version 2 in my example took several sets of changes.

However, the more you absorb the ideas that underpin good writing, the more you can build them into the first-draft stage. Editing becomes easier, and you can invest in strengthening the message rather than dithering about what it is. Relying on short, concrete words is a good principle to hold onto because, as you'll see in Chapter 5, checking word length and substituting short for long ones is often a good starting point toward clarity, readability and impact.

Help Yourself Use Better Words

Build your awareness of long words that have shorter alternatives. Here are some examples.

Instead of . . .	Try . . .
Approximately	About
Demonstrate	Show
Utilize	Use
Subsequently	Next
Construct	Build
Assistance	Help
Competencies	Skills
Initiate	Begin

In some context, the words in the first column might be more accurate or effective. But usually they're not. See the activity at the end of this chapter for more ten-dollar words to watch for. Jumpstart your writing skill by developing a personal repertoire of short words that can replace some of the long ones you often use. For example, *hard* generally works better than *difficult*. It's better to *fix* or *correct* a problem than *remediate* it. Instead of *investigate*, you may want to say *study* or *track* or *look into* or *follow up*. Scan examples of your existing writing to see what complicated words you tend to use, and start a list of alternatives.

Notice, too, that if you're like most people, your writing is full of phrases that can be reduced to a single word: *With reference to* is better expressed as *about*. Why say *in the event that* when you can say *if*? Here are some more examples to set you thinking. Scan your own writing for stock phrases that are wordier than they need to be, and pare them down.

We came to the conclusion	We concluded
At the present time	Now
We're in a position to	We can
The question as to whether	Whether
We wish to bring to your attention	Please note
Owing to the fact that	Because
For the purpose of	To
As a matter of fact	In fact

And to find better words as you write, use a thesaurus—nothing could be easier to do online. Choose a thesaurus you like or just search for the word plus "syn" (for example, "effectuate syn") and a choice of free resources pops up with surprising possibilities. Look up the verb *implement*, for example, and you'll find *apply, execute, carry out, put into action, enact, perform* and more. Observe that sometimes a set of short simple words may work better than a single long one—for example, *carry out* rather than *implement, in the end* rather than *ultimately*.

The thesaurus can also help you avoid using the same word over and over again, which dulls a reader's senses. Look up a frequently needed word like *develop*, for example, and you find a variety of one-, two- and three-syllable words: *grow, expand, spread, broaden, build, supplement, reinforce, begin, emerge* and much more.

The most valuable of all talents is that of never using two words when one will do.

—Thomas Jefferson

Do you still believe that sticking to simple words for your everyday messaging will make your writing vague and boring, or lead people to think you're simple-minded? It won't, but don't take my word for it. Take a close look at writing you like to read. I bet it's clear and easy to understand, no matter how complex the subject. And research has been done to assess how people react to both spoken and written language. Contrary to what you may expect, people who communicate in clear, simple language are perceived to be smarter and more educated than those who speak and write in a "sophisticated" way. It's true that some media, like marketing materials and scripts, achieve impact with colorful, graphic words. But most often this is accomplished by using simple words well, as covered in Chapter 6.

BUILD CLEAR, CONCISE SENTENCES

If a sentence, no matter how excellent, does not illuminate your subject in some new and useful way, scratch it out.

—Kurt Vonnegut, novelist

Now that you know that most of the words to write with are already in your head, what to do with them? Create sentences, of course. Good writing consists of good sentences. Improve your sentences and you improve your writing. Integrate them well and you're en route to becoming a powerful, flexible writer.

This book is about practical techniques for understanding good writing and how to accomplish it rather than principles of grammar. This doesn't imply a disrespect for grammar; the destination—clear and basically correct writing—is the same, but the route is different. If learning rules and a more formal foundation works for you, check out the resources listed at the end of Chapter 5. And when you identify specific shortcomings in your own writing that involve a grammatical point—like using apostrophes—it's a good idea to supplement this book's strategies with one of these resources and master the problem once and for all.

Let's look first at your choices for how to build a sentence.

In the beginning, there is the simple declarative sentence: Someone is doing something, or something is happening. Here are examples:

Jim wrote a proposal for a new client project.

He submitted it to his supervisor.

She read the proposal.

She didn't notice that Jim's calculations were wrong.

The client noticed the mistake.

Ellen blamed Jim.

Jim apologized.

The pitch failed.

Then there are sentences with more than one phrase, or clause (which is a phrase that includes a verb), often separated by commas, or words like *and* or *but*. Here are some two-part sentences:

Jack wrote a proposal to pitch a new client project and submitted it to his supervisor.

She reviewed the proposal carefully but didn't notice that Jim had made a mistake in his calculations.

More complex sentence can have three or more parts or sections:

The client, however, took the trouble to check the numbers and discovered that they were incorrect.

The supervisor blamed Jim, and although he apologized to everyone for the error, the bid for new business failed.

Which sentences are correct? All, of course. It depends on the information you're delivering, the tone of what you're writing and so on. But note that the longer sentences enable the writer to make connections between events more clearly without repeating words and ideas. And if you read the sentences aloud, their rhythms are quite different.

When simple declarative sentences dominate your writing, it sounds choppy and childish—much like a first-grade reader or some fourth-grade social studies textbooks. On the other hand, when writing consists entirely of long, complicated sentences, it becomes hard to follow and, pretty soon, boring. It picks up a cadence that, well, puts the reader to sleep.

For example:

Wanting to express subtle thoughts and ideas, Alice often used lengthy, complicated sentences in her business correspondence. When this problem was brought to her attention, she responded that she preferred not to insult her readers' intelligence. She was told that people found her messages confusing and might not read them to the end, and this bothered her. After thinking about the issue further, and consulting some writing resources, she decided to rethink her premise. When writing, she now varies her sentence length and is much more successful.

In fact, more of us share Alice's writing problem than the choppy "first-grade" approach: We tend to begin writing a message or document in a complicated, even convoluted way, disregarding how it "sounds," and need to work our way to simplicity and good rhythm. This is one of the central reasons you need to see every message as a first draft and edit it.

How could the paragraph about Alice read better? Here's one way:

Alice often used long, complicated sentences in her business writing. Told that this was a problem, she explained that she wanted to express subtle ideas and not insult her readers' intelligence. But her messages confused people. Often they didn't read them to the end. Facing these facts, Alice consulted some writing resources and decided to vary the length of her sentences. She finds this technique much more successful.

Do you agree that the second version is more engaging? The reason is simple but important: Version 1 repeats the same multiclause sentence structure, sentence after sentence—each is perfectly correct, but together they give the reader a tiresome experience. Version 2 breaks the pattern by combining sentences with different structures. Not incidentally, crafting the sentences one by one and dovetailing them neatly creates a shorter and more fluid paragraph.

You don't need to think specifically about structure. Just think about beginning each sentence differently. In the second version, for example, simple sentences like the first one for the most part alternate with more complicated ones that require commas.

Absorb this rhythm idea, and your writing may improve dramatically. It's easier to keep your reader's attention and sound interesting just by alternating the length and structure of your sentences. It pulls people along. *We live in an age of speed readers and scanners. The more naturally a piece of writing moves, the more people will stick with it. This elevates your success ratio.*

SUCCESS TIP

Listen to Your Writing!

Train your ear to help you review and edit your writing—this method will never fail you. *Simply read your draft aloud.* Notice rhythms: when they work and when they don't. Listen for the oral stumbling blocks that tell you that words and structures can and should be better. Another way to go about this is to use Google Translate (https://translate.google .com) or a similar app. Paste your copy into the box and click on the microphone or other icon for sound, and a fairly natural computer voice will read your copy to you. This can help you listen more objectively. Wherever you hear a sing-songy up-and-down inflection, see it as a clue to complicated sentences and lengthy words that need attention. We'll delve further into how to use this technique in Chapter 5.

Notice that "natural"-sounding writing doesn't really mean "conversational." You are unlikely to speak to someone about Alice's writing the way the written message does. You'd probably say something more like this:

Everything Alice wrote used to be really boring—a whole bunch of sentences, one after another after another. It just put you to sleep. Then she figured out that she could just alternate long and short ones, and it's amazing. The same stuff sounds so much more interesting.

How Long Should Sentences Be?

There is actually a semi-scientific answer to this question. It comes from readability research on what makes writing most understandable to the most people. As the sidebar feature "The Shrinking English Sentence" shows, the average number of words per sentence in written materials has radically fallen over the centuries. Today there is more or less agreement that sentences should average between 14 and 18 words to be most comprehensible.

And speech? Linguists have determined that the spoken sentence typically consists of 7 to 10 words.

How about online material? Somewhere between what works for print documents and what's typical for speech.

THE SHRINKING ENGLISH SENTENCE

People began studying readability and its relation to sentence length in the late 19th century. An English literature professor named Lucius Adelno Sherman analyzed sentence length historically and found (in his 1893 book *Analytics of Literature*) the following averages:

Pre-Elizabethan times	50 words per sentence
Elizabethan times	45 words per sentence
Victorian times	29 words per sentence
Late 19th century	23 words per sentence

Sherman observed that, over time, sentences had become simpler and more concrete as well as shorter. He noted that this was because spoken language was affecting written language—as it should: "The oral sentence is clearest because it is the product of millions of daily efforts to be clear and strong. It represents the work of the race for thousands of years in perfecting an effective instrument of communication."

Today, journalism experts believe sentences should be as short as 15 words on average for maximum readability. But not all written documents need to be understood by everyone.

Since the research agrees that sentence length is one of the two key ingredients of readability (word length is the other), it's important to consider these guidelines seriously. Here are a few takeaways for the business writer:

1. Academia remains partly immersed in pre-21st-century writing, especially for English majors. So the writing style encouraged by some professors reflects an earlier time and may be at odds with this book's guidelines, which focus on writing for today's high-speed business world.

2. The "rule" doesn't mean that every sentence should be at least 14 words and no more than 18 words long. It means the average length should fall within those limits. For example, the last few paragraphs here—from the "How Long Should Sentences Be?" head through the end of this sentence—average 17.9 words per sentence. But one sentence is 41 words long and some have fewer than 10 words. Using average length in this way promotes the alternating rhythm recommended earlier.

3. It's fine to vary the general rule according to the medium, your own writing style and the nature of your audience. Obviously, highly educated readers will understand difficult material more easily than less educated ones. If you're writing to an audience that ranges, say, from factory workers to managers, or you'd define the readers as average, keep in mind that the average American is estimated to read at a seventh-grade level. *And just because people with a lot of education can understand something difficult doesn't mean they want to read it—or will stick with it.* After all, we're not talking about writing required textbooks. Virtually nothing you'll write is mandated reading. There are no captive audiences in the business world: You have to earn your audience with just about every single document you create by writing it well.

4. To check how you're doing, you need not count the words of every sentence. Your Microsoft Word program, and others, gives you a marvelous tool that does this for you. It's the Readability Statistics Index, and you can ask your computer to bring it up every time you use spell check. The box materializes immediately after the spelling and grammar check and tells you the average sentence length of the document or highlighted piece, word length and more. We'll practice using this in Chapter 5, but it's a good tool to employ as you write as well as when you edit.

BUILD WITH ACTION VERBS

After improving what you write with shorter words and simpler but varying sentences, look to your verbs. Choosing action verbs is a transformative tool. You probably recall one of the main rules of most writing advice: Avoid the passive voice. This is totally relevant to good business writing. The passive is expressed by a form of *to be*—*were, was*—plus another verb, often ending in *–ed*: "The reason for the failure was identified." The problem with passive is that it doesn't say who did the deed. So beyond producing an awkward, dull sentence, people use it as an avoidance tactic, as in "A mistake was made."

The good news is that you need not understand the complexities of this rule. Just notice as you write: Does my verb suggest a feeling of action—something happening—or is it just a bland place holder? A "flabby" verb that just holds the sentences together and creates a need for wordiness? Look for these weak verbs in many situations other than the classically defined passive. Constructions with an *–ing* verb are often to blame. Here are a few examples:

Three writing tests are being administered by the ABC company.

Better:

The ABC company administers three writing tests.

He was seeing stars.

Better:

He saw stars.

As often as possible, center on the action and use the simplest form of a verb—the present tense or simple past tense. Then it's easy to cut unnecessary wordiness and build a forward-moving cadence that keeps readers with you. Notice how much more direct and compact the second sentence is in each case.

We were taking forward leaps.

versus

We leaped forward.

Many people are resistant to reading on screen.

versus

Many people resist on-screen reading.

To be your own editor is a skill we all need.

versus

We all need to edit our own work.

When you take a moment, more graphic verbs come to mind that don't need modifiers to make the idea clear:

The company's sales figures usually rise substantially in the first quarter.

versus

Company sales usually zoom in the first quarter.

Here's a more complicated example that typifies a lot of business writing:

This mistake has put us in the position of having to explain why business in the last quarter went down radically.

Notice the clues that tell you this sentence needs help. Read aloud, it dictates the sing-song cadence of poor writing. When you review it visually, you see that it contains four prepositions—*in, of, to, in*—and depends on words like *has* and *having*.

Spend a few seconds thinking about what the sentence means and you'll see other alternatives, such as this:

This mistake forces us to explain why business plummeted in the last quarter.

Simply substituting these stronger verbs for the roundabout versions cuts the word count from 21 to 13, produces a fast read with a natural cadence and gets the idea across more vividly.

Notice that many sentences with weak verbs and unnecessary wordiness can be fixed by using the present tense. *Resist* works better than *are resistant to*; *forces us to explain* is much better than *has put us in the position of having to explain*. Look at how these sentence pairs differ:

This rule can be applied to the problem we are confronting.

versus

This rules applies to the problem we face.

or

Apply this rule to the problem we face.

A subject line should really be focused on letting people know what the message is about.

versus

Focus subject lines on what the message is about.

To write a better e-mail, it's helpful to plan your message first.

versus

To write a better e-mail, plan your message first.

The reason you hate me is because I don't laugh at your jokes.

versus

You hate me because I don't laugh at your jokes.

The lesson here: Watch for the word *is*. You can't always eliminate it, of course, and certainly there are sentences that need it. But when you hunt for a substitute, you often find a much stronger statement lurking.

We also dilute meaning by using hedgy, lazy verbs like *make, can* and *get*. All are perfectly good words, but overusing them weakens your writing. A few examples:

He made a decision to leave the job.

versus

He decided to quit.

We can make this change in how we file expense accounts happen soon.

versus

Let's change how we file expense accounts soon.

You can get a start on the progress report tomorrow.

versus

Start working on the progress report tomorrow.

To make copy more colorful, use some long words.

versus

Use some long words to invigorate copy.

Words like *can* and *should* may also undermine impact. They feel evasive:

You can handle the challenge this way.

versus

Handle the challenge this way.

We should review this idea again next week.

versus

Let's review this idea again next week.

Notice how much more positive a sentence's tone feels when you use simple present, past or future tense. It's also good to resist temptations to use the passive to evade responsibility. This approach is sometimes called "the divine passive." A fact or event is presented as if it were an act of God. It doesn't work in the business world, no matter how often it's done. For example:

The wrong decision was made and an unproductive path was chosen.

Who made the decision? Beyond creating an impersonal tone, this evasion undermines credibility and does the cause no good. Here's an irritating quote reported by the *Wall Street Journal*, said by a News Corp. executive when his editor was convicted of hacking voice messages:

"We said long ago, and repeat today, that wrongdoing occurred and we apologized for it."

WORK WITH SHORT PARAGRAPHS

Simplicity is the ultimate sophistication.

—Leonardo da Vinci

Now that you know how to build effective sentences, it's time to move on to the larger unit.

You may remember being told in school to develop a thesis for an essay and a thesis or topic sentence for each paragraph. The paragraph should cover a single idea based on the topic and end with a conclusion. If that approach helps, use it. I found it paralyzing. Alternatively, start with the readability premise. Research tells us that for practical writing, the best length for a paragraph is three to five sentences. In many cases, even fewer sentences work best—for example, the lead of an article, online copy like websites and blogs, and promotional copy for marketing purposes.

Luckily, when you keep your paragraphs short, it's easier to stay on track and recognize when you stray off your intended path. It's also easier to know when to break your paragraphs, or "grafs." Basically, start a new graf when it feels logical to do so. Typically, this is when you're beginning a new thought or subthought, starting an item in a list or moving to a detail or clarification.

If you're the kind of writer who tends to spill it all out in a few long, breathless gasps, here's a solution: Consistently review your draft with an eye toward the white space. Have you produced a dense document with long paragraphs that break only a few times per page? Then splinter the material into shorter paragraphs of three to five sentences. Try scattering a few single-sentence paragraphs around as well, if they make a point worth emphasizing or act as a transition. Next, look at each paragraph to see if it makes sense or needs to be clarified.

Every document gains from short paragraphs in a number of ways:

- They more readily engage the eye and therefore readers' interest. A packed message skimpy on white space looks formidable and may even prevent people from reading the message at all.

- They increase the likelihood of keeping your reader with you, because the message seems to move so much faster.

- They produce a "spacey" document that is far easier to grasp than an unbroken dense one and is therefore more likely to succeed, whatever the goal.

In addition to checking that each graf works, check whether each leads logically to the next one and all relate neatly. *Short paragraphs are easy to move around, so you can experiment with making your message flow more logically.* You often find that the last sentence of one paragraph works better when you move it to begin the paragraph that follows.

And there's a magic tool for melding all those paragraphs into a fluent, convincing, logical message that makes what you write seem persuasive and even inevitable: the transition.

USE GOOD TRANSITIONS: WORDS, PHRASES AND DEVICES

Transitions play an important role in connecting your ideas, examples and overall argument. Take care with them, because successful writing requires that all connections are clear to your audience. You never want your readers to wonder, "Why is she telling me that?" or substituting their own reasoning for yours, even unconsciously. Ambiguous connections create misunderstanding or indifference.

Good transitions, on the other hand, instantly improve all your writing because they smooth it out and eliminate the choppy, disconnected effect that signals poor writing (and thinking). Think of transitions as the stitching that holds a patchwork quilt together.

Transitions are critical at the sentence, paragraph and full-document levels. For example, you could write:

John doesn't like sharing his reports. His supervisor wants him to do it.

The two thoughts don't connect. Instead they could read:

John doesn't like sharing his reports. However, his supervisor requires it.

On the sentence level, we typically use transition words instinctively. Simple words like *and, but, or* and *because* are handy—and may be used to begin sentences in all but the most formal documents. But connecting paragraphs well can take more deliberate thought.

It may be appropriate to end a paragraph with a transition, as an introduction to what comes next. Note the transitions between sentences as well as at the end of the paragraph:

The White Contract is scheduled for signing on the 30th. However, some problems have come up that we should discuss at Friday's meeting. In the meantime we can prepare for that conversation with the following procedure.

In many cases, transitions should be used to begin a paragraph so it links to what preceded it. Here are some of the useful words and phrases to draw on for both opening and closing a graf:

To sum up . . . in review . . . finally . . . in general . . . in other words . . . equally important

To the contrary . . . on the other hand . . . conversely . . . nevertheless . . . in spite of . . . otherwise . . . unfortunately . . . regrettably

Also . . . additionally . . . further . . . specifically . . . for example . . . accordingly . . . moreover . . . besides

Later . . . the next step is . . . recently . . . in the future . . . afterward . . . at that point . . . so far

To illustrate . . . for example . . . similarly . . . conversely . . . accordingly . . . in conclusion . . . finally

Some transitional words and phrases carry connotations that can help convey the tone you want:

Best of all . . . in fact . . . truthfully . . . of course . . . naturally . . . chiefly . . . inevitably . . . and yet . . . happily . . . it goes without saying . . . surprisingly. . . fortunately

In any message that matters (and as you know, I think they all do), check how each paragraph connects to the one that precedes and the one that follows. If you can't make these relationships clear, you may need to rethink your content and your own understanding of the subject.

In long documents like reports and proposals, use transitions to ensure that the sections connect logically. Go out of your way to clarify the links with phrases that act as transitional devices:

Here's why . . .The result . . . Our conclusions . . . There's more . . . What did we learn? . . . How will this help you? . . . The solution we came up with . . .

You can also use whole sentences to introduce a section and tie it into the document's logical pattern. Apply some creativity to these transitions, and they'll really support your cause:

We base our conclusions on the following trials.

We focused on similar projects for five years and learned a number of lessons.

The sales projections are especially interesting.

Here are the questions most frequently asked—and the answers.

A brief review of the problem's background.

It sounds great. But . . .

That's what we used to think, too.

Setting up a sequence via a numbered list is another good tool for promoting clarity and holding a document, or section, together:

Four factors weigh most heavily in making the decision.

The process can be completed in seven stages.

Here's the plan for the next eight months.

One more great benefit to transitions: Consciously used to better communicate a message, they help you organize your material more easily. And for your reader, a message that feels clear, logical and cohesive is much more convincing than one that holds together less tightly.

SIDESTEP TONE TRAPS

The tone of any piece of writing rises, sometimes mysteriously, from the integration of words and sentence structure, what's included, what's left out. Tone must suit the subject matter and your relationship to your reader. Control tone if you want your messages to succeed. Here are some pitfalls to avoid.

The Meant-to-Be-Funny

Humor is a tremendous asset for a speech, a presentation or a conversation. Unfortunately, unless you're a talented and confident humor writer, it's risky to depend on it in writing.

A piece of writing lacks the advantages of personal interaction. There is no facial expression to underscore or counter the words; no subtle body language to suggest your true meaning; and, above all, no tone of voice to communicate the real message. What would be funny in person can easily come across as insulting or cruel. Especially because e-mail (like social media) is infinitely forwardable and accessible, a moment's entertainment can have unwelcome consequences.

This is a particular drawback with using irony and sarcasm. One solution is to use emojis to suggest that you're "just joking" and soften a message. But they may be misinterpreted, especially by people unfamiliar with them. And they are still seen as inappropriate in many business environments.

So here is the rule: In business writing, avoid the temptation to make fun of someone or something others might care about. Don't joke at someone else's expense. Be wary of injecting any humor that might be misunderstood.

Prejudicial Wording

Don't undercut your message by building in a negative slant, consciously or not. Suppose, for example, you receive an e-mail that begins with one of these phrases:

As I already told you . . .

This is to reinforce our conversation . . .

You did not provide . . .

You are apparently unaware that . . .

I am at a loss to understand . . .

Don't fail to let me know . . .

As you should have foreseen . . .

I thought you realized the importance of . . . .

Obviously, you're on full defensive even before reading the rest of the message. The takeaway: Avoid this tone and wording. It's not a productive way to address people, no matter what their relationship to you or how you feel they failed you. Amazingly, however, companies will often write to customers in a similar off-putting manner:

This is to inform you that we are unable to ship your product at this time . . .

Our policy clearly states that purchases are only refundable if . . .

For your information, we no longer provide support services for . . .

Please understand that we cannot make exceptions . . .

SUCCESS TIP

Keep a Lid on Your Emotions

In business, the line between expressing passion and emotion can be a fine one. Your colleagues, superiors and subordinates certainly want to feel your conviction, enthusiasm and confidence. But these qualities must appear to be based on an objective reality—not inappropriate personal investment in a subject or unchecked feelings.

Obviously, it's bad to lose your temper at a meeting, act defensively, sulk or cast blame. In the business world, like the political, such behavior marks you as the loser. Results can be even worse if you send a hostile message. It may circulate or rankle forever. Therefore:

- Never let what you write show anger.
- Never criticize anyone in writing (unless it's part of a structured evaluation process).

- Work hard to maintain a balanced, reasonable tone.
- Avoid words that can be negatively interpreted. Don't sound judgmental.
- Monitor your messages so they don't betray any attitude, emotion or feeling that will undermine you.
- Always pause before sending a harsh message and ask if it might damage a relationship.

However: It can be very helpful to *write* a message that tells someone how you feel; just don't *send* it. Compose and polish a complete e-mail, letter or post and then burn it; that is, file or discard it. Mentally processing an emotional situation this way enables you to put it in perspective and move on more easily. It's a good idea not to address it, to prevent a Freudian click.

The substance of a message may in fact be negative, as in the customer service examples. When this is the case, take special care to present the information in as positive a way as possible. The first statement, for example, might be put this way:

We're delighted that you've ordered our Product #65 but sorry that because it's proved so popular, we are unable to fill orders as quickly as we'd like. Each #65 is individually crafted . . .

Here's how one smart retailer responded, in part, to a return:

We'd love another opportunity to please you. Please accept this offer of free shipping on your next purchase in our catalog or online at . . .

Note that when a company produces a flow of impersonal these-are-the-rules-and-we-don't-care-if-you-like-them-or-not messages to customers, its policies merit review. The marketplace is too competitive to treat customers this way. Writing well can only go so far to cover up bad thinking.

The Pompous and Pretentious

> *If you can't explain something simply, you don't understand it well enough.*
>
> —Albert Einstein

We often see overblown, pretentious language that combines long words with awkward construction. These messages fail to communicate when used in place of real substance. Here's an empty sentence built on abstractions and adjectives:

The nostrum of "regulation" drags with it a raft of unexamined impediments concerning the nature of markets and governmentality, and a muddle over intentionality, voluntarism and spontaneity that promulgates the neoliberal creed at the subconscious level.

Spot a sentence like this and rewrite if you can. When writing is so bad that it communicates no meaning at all, it's impossible to fix it.

The Cold and Impersonal

People today value messages that feel authentic and personal. Whether you're writing a memo explaining a company benefit, a promotional piece selling a product or a letter responding to a complaint, make it personal. Often this means taking the "you" viewpoint: For example, rather than

The new policy on filing for overtime claims is . . .

try

To file an overtime claim, you need to know . . .

For pitching a product, rather than

The newly designed Inca 247 offers a number of features to help the graphic designer.

try

Inca 247 saves you 20% of your graphic design project time and . . .

This tactic ties right in with your need to instantly engage readers and pull them through your document. Remember, when people decide whether a message is worth reading, self-interest rules. Figure out how to phrase the sentence, and the whole message, building on the word *you.*

PRACTICE OPPORTUNITIES

I. Practice Sentence Rhythm

A. Correct Choppy Cadence

Rewrite this paragraph. First read it aloud to identify the problems. When you've written a new version, read that aloud as well and see if you're satisfied.

> Carol is working on an MBA. She finds the pressures very demanding. She has almost no time to spend with friends. She doesn't even have time for phone calls. She doesn't have much time for e-mail or keeping up with Facebook either. The only time she sees other people is in class or team projects or study groups. She recently decided to change this pattern. She'll begin by brainstorming ideas for how to set aside some personal time each week. She also needs to think about whom she can spend that time with. Everyone she knows is constantly working.

B. Fix Monotonous Cadence

Rewrite this letter asking for a recommendation. Again, read the before and after versions aloud.

> Dear X,
>
> Not only are you an exceptional business adviser whose unique vision adds significant value to the company, but your constructive management style helps the entire team to develop new skills each day. Because you are a leader in your field, I was wondering if you'd write a letter of recommendation supporting my application to the Green University International MBA program.

While this job affords me constant learning and I continue to enjoy my experience here, I hope that gaining an MBA will enhance my management skills at the international level. It should also prepare me for a future in management, since I hope to become a great manager, like you, one day.

I realize that my acceptance would mean my departure from the firm, but there should be ample time to train a replacement. If permitted, I would love to help secure a replacement and provide thorough training as well as feedback to ensure that the new role maximizes efficiencies and focuses on future growth. And after I've completed my schooling, I hope I have the opportunity to work with you in the future.

If you do decide to grant me this request, I have prepared a folder that includes a letter outlining specifics and a prepaid envelope for mailing. If for any reason you don't feel comfortable writing a letter on my behalf, I completely understand.

II. Review and Rewrite a Recent Message

Identify an e-mail, letter, networking message, report, online post or other piece of your own recent writing. Carefully review:

Word choice

Sentence length and structure

Paragraph length

Unnecessary wordiness

Use of transitions

Cadence when read aloud

In what ways do you find your writing at odds with the principles presented in this chapter? How would you write the message or material differently now? Try a rewrite, thinking within a business context.

III. Translate Your Academic Writing for a Practical Real-World Purpose

For this activity, choose a recent paper you wrote, on any subject, for an academic class. Now invent a business-like reason for the message the paper contains. For example, if you analyzed a piece of literature, review it as if you'd been asked whether to recommend it as required reading for your coworkers; if it's a research paper, think of an appropriate person to whom you might need to report your findings, such as the chief of IT, HR director, or head of accounting. Rewrite the gist of the paper as a recommendation in simple, concise, active language in line with this chapter's guidelines. Draw also on the concepts of goal and audience covered in the previous chapters to produce your best message.

IV. Review Your Verbs

Assemble five pieces of your own writing in any media. Go through each methodically, and bold or color the verbs. Then create a document listing all the verbs. Scan the list: Do many reflect a passive voice or feeling? Are they dull placeholder verbs? How many can you replace with more active, interesting verbs? Where can you substitute the simple present tense?

Choose one of the documents and change the weak verbs to strong ones. Notice the changes that the new verbs suggest. Does the message become shorter? Less wordy? More effective? Do you like it better?

V. Write Notes to Yourself

Create pages, real or virtual, with these headings:

Word Choice

Verbs

Sentence Structure

Paragraphs

Transitions

Cadence

On each page, note the changes you'd like to effect in your writing based on the ideas in this chapter. Take account of the analysis you did in the preceding exercises, and review more of your writing against the guidelines.

Print these pages out and keep them as reference. You now have a checklist that will help you improve your writing immediately and a strong start on creating your personal writing improvement plan!

VI. Build a List of Short-Word Substitutes

Think of short-word alternatives for the following list of words. Expand the list with additional frequently used long words you find in your own writing and your everyday reading.

Substantial

Subsequent

Indication

Aggregate

Culmination

Disseminate

Eliminate

Construct

Convoluted

Imminently

Prevalent

Verbose

Fundamental

Additionally

Fraudulent

Initiate

Optimum

Curriculum

Assistance

Substantiate

Component

VII. Group Activity: Assemble a Master List of Shorter Words

In small groups, share and discuss your substitute word lists and brainstorm for more. Each group then contributes its full list to a central committee or individual (perhaps accorded extra credit) who integrates the lists to produce a helpful handout for everyone.

5 EDIT YOUR WRITING

Fix it . . . NOW! Periods and commas are everything! Attention to detail, grammar and ease of use are the most critical things on the site.

—Mark Zuckerberg's "laws," described by Noah Kagan, Facebook employee #30 and founder of AppSumo

LEARN HOW TO . . .

- Approach editing systematically
- Identify language and structure problems
- Improve messages with commonsense strategies
- Sidestep common tone and grammar problems
- Use helpful resources, tools and professional tips

Many people are wary of editing, as if it requires a mystical skill or rare native talent. But just as with writing, a strategic approach guides you through.

Knowing you will improve your document and fix problems later is liberating. It frees you to write more spontaneously and even experiment in the first draft. This is true whether you're a get-it-all-down-at-once type of writer or one who crafts each sentence thoughtfully.

Contrary to some popular assumptions, editing and proofreading are not the same. Editing is your review of big-picture content, language and impact; proofing is your check on the mechanics and final polish. I recommend doing both even with everyday e-mails, but of course, important materials demand closer attention. Here are some guidelines for these instances.

TEN PRINCIPLES OF POWER EDITING

Half my life is an act of revision.

—John Irving, novelist

1. Give It the Time

On a typical project, many professionals allocate a third of the available time for planning, a third for drafting, and at least a third for editing and rewriting. If your project is big, build in a good amount of time for editing and proofing as the last stage.

2. Give It Some Space

Try to put an important document aside for a week or a few days, or an hour. Objectivity grows with distance. When you read the draft after even a brief lapse, errors of tone and substance pop out, as do technical mistakes. Stash even a significant e-mail for a few hours so your eyes are fresh and your emotional antennae are up.

3. Consciously Switch Roles

When you edit your own work, approach the piece as if you've never seen it before. Don't be influenced by how hard a particular section was to produce. In fact, many fiction writers follow the advice "Kill your darlings," meaning that passages they especially love are suspect—they probably distract from the piece's intent—and should be cut.

4. Use Track Changes to Edit On Screen

If you're not familiar with this valuable Microsoft Word tool, see the Success Tip box. Track Changes helps you follow your own improvement process and is a must for collaborating. You can also use a program like Google Docs for this.

5. Print It Out and Use Your Red Pen

Copy reads differently in print form than on screen. Mistakes and typos are easier to spot. Therefore, consider printing out résumés, letters, reports, blog posts, website copy and other materials that matter. To make it more efficient and fun, try using proofreaders' symbols, a shorthand that writers and editors employ to communicate with printers and each other. Just Google "proofreading marks" and you'll find a number of demonstrations.

6. Edit in Successive Stages

When you make changes, you often introduce new mistakes or expose awkward wording. So always review your new version. This consistently reveals more opportunities to improve the language and make the content more persuasive.

7. Use the Read-Aloud Test

Read a short message aloud or, in the case of a lengthy document, read at least selected portions. Or have your computer read them to you. Both methods are described in Chapter 4 and immediately key you in to language and structure glitches.

8. Use Grammar and Wording Tools

A handy and reliable feature of Microsoft Word is the Readability Index, which shows you how easily understood the material is. It is detailed later in this chapter. Online resources such as Hemingway.com and Grammarly.com also can help you achieve simplicity. Check the clues that tell you to liven up your verbs and language, explained in the rest of this chapter.

9. Find a Co-Reader

Backup is invaluable. Scout your environment for a colleague or friend to read your important documents, play "audience" and provide honest feedback. Pay attention to how your buddy perceives and understands your important messages, and revise accordingly. Perform this service in turn for your partner, and learn a lot about editing your own work!

10. Proofread. Finally.

After you're satisfied with your content and language and flow, proof for correctness: spelling, grammar, transitions and, again, sentence rhythm.

SUCCESS TIP: TRACKING YOUR CHANGES

Microsoft Word offers a way to record your edits as you make them and retain as many versions as you want so you don't lose the variations. It also allows a number of people to review and make edits, which show up in different colors so you know who is doing what. To find this tool, choose Review on the Word toolbar. Then click Track Changes to turn tracking on. In the box at top right, choose All Markup if you want to view every change; Simple Markup lets you write without being distracted by the changes. You can also look back at the Original. The Markup Options box gives you choices for how you want changes to show up. Under Reviewing, the toolbar also presents Accept and Reject boxes. You can go through your own or someone else's document and incorporate each change, one at a time, or reject it. You can also accept all the changes in part or all of the document by highlighting. Using Track Changes takes a bit of experimentation, but once absorbed, it saves you considerable time. Once you've finalized a document, be sure to save it with all changes accepted to avoid sending out a version demonstrating your revision process.

Now let's look at practical editing strategies, including some professional tricks of the trade. Note that a garden-variety e-mail might need just a quick run-through, while a major document like a proposal, résumé or how-to manual demands careful step-by-step attention. But do commit to rereading everything you write at least once, with an eye toward improving content, fixing mistakes and protecting yourself from misinterpretation.

PRACTICAL EDITING STAGE 1: CONTENT REVIEW

Start by focusing first on the big picture—*what to say*. Conveniently enough, you can recap the same checklist that led you through the planning and writing processes detailed in Chapter 4:

Review Goal:

1. Is the message clear on what result you want to achieve? Does it communicate that goal—the reason you're writing?

2. Do your points support the goal?

3. Is anything missing? Ideas, data, evidence, detail, and so on?

4. Are you delivering too much information? Any irrelevant points? Does anything distract from the result you want?

5. Is the sequence of the material logical? Convincing?

Review Audience:

1. Will the reader recognize that the message is directed to him and care about the subject?

2. Is the content right for the specific reader or group you have in mind?

3. Did you take account of the reader's probable knowledge base and attitude toward your subject?

4. Did you leave out anything that matters to your reader?

5. Did you consider possible audience sensitivities?

Review Tone:

1. Is it appropriate to your goal and audience?

2. Is it right for the particular relationship and relationship building?

3. Can anything be misinterpreted?

4. Is the message courteous and positive in spirit?

5. If you were the reader, how would the message make you feel?

Review Message Structure:

1. Is the document well organized?

2. Does it have a clear, engaging lead?

3. Do you see good transitions so the thoughts flow naturally and connect?

4. Did you build a strong close, with a call to action as needed?

5. Is the response you're asking for perfectly clear?

Bottom line: If you were the reader, would you give you what you want?

And always consider the overall impact on your company, and on you, of broadcasting the information. Everything you send digitally might reach unimaginable numbers of people. Careless e-mails create confusion and mistakes. Thoughtless reports lead to poor decisions. Personal posts on social media can cost you a job or the future presidency when employers or voters check you out.

The possibility of embarrassing yourself online grows daily, as everything becomes more findable and difficult to erase. All too many people are scouting for shareable material to entertain their "friends." On a bigger scale, as companies post more and more content on their websites to demonstrate transparency, misjudgment looms.

The content review tells you what cuts to make in your document and/or additions to develop. The process is a lot less time-consuming than it looks spelled out. Once you absorb it, an everyday e-mail will just need a fast minute, but a report or proposal or marketing piece merits more. There's little point in working on language if your message content doesn't work well. But once you believe it does, move on to sharpening *how* you say it.

PRACTICAL EDITING STAGE 2: REVIEW LANGUAGE AND STRUCTURE

Much advice on good writing is really advice on revising. Because very few people are smart enough to be able to lay down some semblance of an argument and to express it in clear prose at the same time. Most writers require two passes to accomplish that. And after they've got the ideas down, now it's time to refine and polish.

—Steven Pinker, psychologist and linguist, author of *The Sense of Style: The Thinking Person's Guide to Writing in the 21st Century*

If you're editing a printout and haven't done so yet, take out your red pen. Or make changes on screen. Better yet, try both and see if there's a difference!

As promised, here's more depth on two basic strategies for improving the quality of your writing technically: how you use and structure language. We'll explore the Readability Index and the read-aloud method for editing. Keep in mind that they blend together. Experiment with both in assembling your personal editing toolkit. They are easy to use and will help build your writing common sense.

Use the Readability Index

The Readability Index, mentioned in Chapter 4, is as close to a magic bullet for better writing as we have. I'm always surprised to find that many professional writers don't know about it. The Index is simple to use, it's free, and it's right in Microsoft Word.

To find it, go to File, Options, Proofing. In the spelling and grammar section, check the last box: "show readability statistics." Thereafter, every time you finish a document, after the grammar and spell check (which you can use but cautiously) a box comes up to tell you:

Counts: number of words, characters, paragraphs, sentences

Averages: sentences per paragraph, words per sentence, characters per word

Readability: Flesch Reading Ease, Flesch-Kincaid grade level, percentage of passive sentences

You can also select any part of a document to check as you write or after the draft is done.

The Flesch system is named for its creator, but there are similar systems you can access and use online, such as the more graphically named Fog Index.

The Flesch index shows you instantly whether you're writing within the guidelines recommended earlier: short words, sentences in the 14- to 18-word range on average, short paragraphs. Moreover, it tells you the document's percentage of passive sentences.

These factors are automatically calculated to show the percentage of people who are expected to understand the writing and what grade level they would need to have achieved.

Knowing the problem goes a good part of the way toward solution. If Flesch says your sentences are overly long when averaged, break some up. Same with paragraphs. If your words are lengthy, substitute shorter ones for some. If your passive percentage is high, review your sentences to spot the passive constructions Chapter 4 discusses. How much passive is too much? I take a serious look at my writing when it measures more than 10%. I'm happier when it's below 5%. I celebrate when it hits 0%.

How about reader grade level and readability? What percentage to aim for?

That depends partly on your audience—another reason why understanding your readers is critical. If you aim for 100% of people to understand you, a choppy first-grade cadence might result. But note that Ernest Hemingway, perhaps the most emulated of modern writers, created novels that communicate profound ideas with a fourth-grade reading level. And that the *Wall Street Journal* scores at eighth grade, as do most popular fiction writers. Only academic papers and many government communications score above 11th grade.

True, a scientist writing a research report doesn't need the average person to understand it. She's communicating with peers. But if the scientist is writing for a general interest magazine, or crowdsourcing an experiment, readability and grade level rule.

As a general guideline, aim for your everyday business messages and materials to calculate at a Readability Index of at least 60% with a reading level below ninth grade. If you're addressing a diverse audience—for example, managers, stockholders and factory workers—you might choose to write on a relatively low grade level with perhaps 75% comprehension. Better yet, write different messages for each group—segment the audience, as marketers say. For example, announcing a new "company mission" suggests different content and writing style for different groups because their concerns, need to know and educational levels probably differ.

However, always remember that everyone welcomes simplicity and clarity. You will never be criticized for achieving this, as long as you follow other guidelines such as using energetic verbs and good sentence rhythm so it doesn't look like you are dumbing down your material. On the other hand, nearly everyone resists the overly complex, passive and boring.

The comparison of the Readability Index for Version 1 and Version 2 on the facing page illustrates an example of how I used the Flesch Index to improve a piece of writing.

Use the Read-Aloud Method

This simple strategy supports you in the drafting process, as covered in Chapter 4, and is invaluable at the editing stage. Don't think it unsophisticated; it's a favorite of many professional writers. Of course, you can do it silently when you're not alone, but practicing it aloud when you have the chance tells you more. To distance yourself, you might record the read-aloud version and then listen. Or have the computer read it back to you via Google Translate.

What are you listening for? The cadence: Does it sound natural? Or is your voice forced into an up-down-up-down sing-songy cadence, like a nursery rhyme or tattle tale?

Readability Index for Version 1

Readability Statistics

Counts
Words	137
Characters	660
Paragraphs	1
Sentences	5

Averages
Sentences per Paragraph	5.0
Words per Sentence	27.4
Characters per Word	4.8

Readability
Passive Sentences	60%
Flesch Reading Ease	44.4
Flesch-Kincaid Grade Level	12.0

OK

Readability Index for Version 2

Readability Statistics

Counts
Words	80
Characters	409
Paragraphs	2
Sentences	6

Averages
Sentences per Paragraph	3.0
Words per Sentence	13.3
Characters per Word	5.0

Readability
Passive Sentences	0%
Flesch Reading Ease	54.7
Flesch-Kincaid Grade Level	8.9

OK

Text Version 1—Original

There have been a diminishing number of young people in the region, according to a variety of studies that have been issued on the subject by organizations ranging from smart growth groups to the offices of the county executives. Universally, it is agreed that a brain drain is untenable. The impact of losing our best and brightest would be that the region could become less vital and would offer fewer opportunities, which can only increase the problem. If this happens, Green Island is going to become a place that is dominated by an aging population, a situation that would have dire economic and social consequences. To solve this challenge, we need to be able to understand the perspectives of a variety of stakeholders and determine what program we can put into place in order to move forward.

Text Version 2—Rewrite

Young people are moving away from the region, a number of studies confirm. We all agree that preventing a brain drain is essential. If we lose our best and brightest, Green Island loses its vitality.

As young adults find fewer opportunities, more and more will look elsewhere, leaving us with an aging population. This outlook threatens our economy and social well-being. To address the challenge, we must understand the different stakeholders' perspectives and decide on a program so we can move forward.

Use the Readability Index to monitor your own success in the process of writing as well as at the editing stage. And see the Practice Opportunities at the end of this chapter. Employ this resource often to measure your "general" writing. This helps you create your own plan for becoming a better writer.

Do you hear stumbles? If the words are hard to say, consider replacing them with simpler ones. Do you hear awkward pauses? Or keep running out of breath? Examine your sentences to see how you can simplify them. They are probably wordier and longer than necessary. Does it sound active—like something is happening? If not, review your verbs and try to liven them up.

These writing shortfalls tend to come together—one careless element brings on the rest. Use the fact that mistakes hang together to advantage.

For example:

The new managers are embarking on a fundamental shift in accounting methodology, in the hope of circumventing financial embarrassment in future situations.

Read that aloud and note the up-down-up cadence it forces your voice to take. Then read this version:

The new managers plan to introduce a new accounting method to prevent the risk of embarrassing the firm in future.

Better:

To prevent future embarrassment, the new managers will introduce a different accounting method.

Often you can improve a sentence in one editing step. But often three steps is the charm. An intermediate version helps you clarify your meaning and enables you to go the last mile with a version 3 that says it best. I'll give you more of these three-stage examples as we move along. For each example, try to improve the sentence yourself before reading the revised versions. If you come up with a different rewrite, compare it to the one presented. Remember, there's always more than one way to rewrite. And don't worry about "losing" your individual voice and style. You can't; it creeps in anyway through all your choices. Like writing, editing is not a science. Certainly it's a craft—and, many would say, an art.

COMMONSENSE FIX-IT TECHNIQUES

Perfection is achieved, not when there is nothing more to add, but when there is nothing left to take away.

—Antoine de Saint Exupery, author of *The Little Prince*

When you identify by sound that your sentences need help, how can you fix them?

Look closely at what produces the up-and-down rhythm. This section lays out the usual suspects, the signals that beg for your real or virtual red pen. Some of these alerts will sound familiar because they support the first-draft process. Here's how the ideas apply in the editing stage to ensure that your messages succeed.

Strip Redundancy

Repeating words and sounds detracts from the message. This is because repetition deadens impact. Repetition is boring. Therefore try not to repeat. Avoid repeating anything if possible.

Did the last few sentences annoy you? They should. Review everything you write to check for repetitive ideas as well as sounds, words and phrases. The above sentence might better be stated:

Avoid repeating words and sounds. These echoes bore readers and deaden your message's impact.

Substitute Short Words for Long Ones

For example:

We can postulate with a high degree of confidence that we expect the outcome to be positive.

Why not just say:

We can confidently predict a good outcome.

Better:

We expect a good outcome.

Of course there are exceptions: A short word substitute may not exist or may not work as well for the purpose; or a long word may be necessary to make a particular point. In the example, the idea of confidence might be important, so it would be a mistake to omit it, as in the third version. Pay attention to context.

Also, for some types of writing, simplicity is not the only measure of success. You may need colorful words to market a product or idea, graphic images to move people emotionally, language that paints a picture to communicate a vision and bring the abstract to life. Some of these techniques are covered in other chapters, and you may want to draw on them in your more everyday writing as well. See Chapter 6, on techniques of persuasion; Chapter 9, which focuses on major business documents; and Chapter 11 on spoken media.

Minimize Words That Create Abstract Sentences

Most commonly these are words that end in *–ing, –ed, –ious* and *–ion*. As mentioned in Chapter 4, many derive from the French and Latin overlays to English and are less concrete than the plain, short, everyday words. Others are verb forms that create diffuse and unnecessarily complex sentences.

These word forms force you to write abstractly—or reflect abstract thinking, whichever way you want to look at it. Either way, here's a quick and easy editing method: Routinely count the number of such words in each sentence. It's easy to overlook the pile-up they produce when you write. This scan helps you pin down your problem. Better yet, a quick fix usually follows. Finding a workaround is easy once you pinpoint the need.

Therefore, develop your awareness of the following:

Words Ending in –*ing*

They are often useful, but contemporary writing relies on them too much. For example:

Giving the audience the responsibility of interpreting your writing is a bad idea.

A rewrite:

Don't make the audience responsible for interpreting what you write.

We're implementing a system for tracking how well we're measuring performance.

A rewrite:

The new system will track how well we measure performance.

The fix: Review your sentences and, as often as possible, limit yourself to one –*ing* per sentence. If you check to see whether this book follows its own rules, you'll see that writing about writing makes it tough to resist adding more words that end in –*ing*. So yes, I know this rule can be hard to follow. But if you doubt its importance, consider this line I was surprised to see in a newspaper article:

The company said the water table was making work on fixing the second line challenging.

Words Ending in –ion

For example:

The function of the communications department is the production of newsletters.

A rewrite:

The communications department's job is to produce newsletters.

Our intention in providing the presentation is to provoke a reconsideration of the salary guidelines by management.

A rewrite:

We're giving the presentation because we want management to reconsider the salary guidelines.

Words Ending in –ious

For example:

We're suspicious of the division's anomalous performance report and believe the Board should be made conscious of this situation.

A rewrite:

We suspect something isn't right about the division's performance report and think we should tell the Board.

Words Ending in –ed

For example:

The aforementioned executives were astounded to have experienced the result the report achieved, which was unintended.

A rewrite:

The executives were astounded by the report's impact. It was unintended.

You're always trying to trim everything down to absolute rock, solid rock. I will sit there for 15 minutes to make it one syllable shorter.

> —Jerry Seinfeld, quoted by John Jurgensen in the *Wall Street Journal*

Limit Use of Prepositions: Of, To, For, By, In, On

A sentence is suspect when it has more than one of a particular preposition or too many prepositions altogether. Writing that's cluttered with these little words becomes verbose and hard to understand. It might read like this:

The plan for the department by the partners is to restructure in order to implement the best principles of management.

You might say instead:

The partners plan to restructure and implement the best management principles.

Here's a three-stage example:

1. *Mark is of the opinion that the leadership team will reconsider the facts of the matter.*

2. *Mark's opinion is that the leadership team will reconsider the facts of the matter.*

3. *Mark believes the leadership team will review the facts.*

Notice that often the magic fix for too many *ofs* is the *'s*. *The CEO's decision* is better than *the decision of the CEO*. Here's another three-step example. Notice how much better the simple present tense works.

1. *The impact of the new regulation on profits is negative.*

2. *The new regulation's impact on profits is negative.*

3. *The new regulation brings down our profits.*

Here, the repeating *in* hurts the sentence:

In case the contract doesn't reach you in time, please look into the reason and keep me in the loop.

Better:

If you don't receive the contract in time, find out why and let me know.

Limit Adjectives and Adverbs

Both are descriptive word sets, and while they are perfectly nice in themselves, using too many of them undermines your messages. Many adjectives are basic to English and describe qualities or attributes of nouns. A person, for example, can be happy, dark, small, young, nice, silly, pretty, good and so on. The much-admired 19th-century writer Mark Twain wrote this famous advice to a 14-year old boy who sent him a letter. It relates nicely to 21st-century business writing.

I notice that you use plain, simple language, short words and brief sentences. That is the way to write English—it is the modern way and the best way. Stick to it; don't let fluff and flowers and verbosity creep in. When you catch an adjective, kill it. No, I don't mean utterly, but kill most of them—then the rest will be valuable. They weaken when they are close together. They give strength when they are wide apart. An adjective habit, or a wordy, diffuse, flowery habit, once fastened upon a person, is as hard to get rid of as any other vice.

Then there are adverbs. Often they're created by adding *–ly* to an adjective: for example, *sadly, colorfully, ultimately, perfectly*. Again, piling them up kills your flow:

Fortunately, he knew perfectly well that it was highly impossible to maximally exercise in a dangerously extreme manner.

Try reading this example aloud:

The report by the committee was happily generally positive and gave us a blueprint to revamp policy by rethinking the guidelines.

A rewrite:

Overall, the committee's report is positive. It gives us a blueprint to rethink our policy guidelines.

Take a close look at your descriptive words in editing and you may be surprised at how few of them you need. Often, they only contribute extra verbiage. Overuse can make you look childish. Businesspeople often fall into this trap when they write absurd hyperbole that fails to disguise a lack of substance. Here are excerpts from a goodbye message that Marissa Mayer, ex-Google VP and then CEO of Yahoo, delivered to the staff after she'd sold Yahoo (at considerable personal profit):

Dear Yahooers . . .

We set out to transform this company—and we've made incredible progress. . . .

Imagine the distribution challenges we will solve, the scale we will achieve, the products we will build, and the advertisers we will reach now with Mavens—it's incredibly compelling. . . . The teams here have not only built incredible products and technologies, but have built Yahoo into one of the most iconic, and universally well-liked companies in the world. One that continues to impact the lives of more than a billion people. I'm incredibly proud of everything that we've achieved, and I'm incredibly proud of our team.

This message was widely disseminated and not admired.

Count Your Conjunctions: And, Or, But, For, Nor, Yet, So

These little words are usually the culprits in wordy sentences—long meandering statements that lead readers to lose track of meaning. Break up long sentences when they combine thoughts in a way that's hard to follow. For example:

All these ideas are excellent, and you can find an approach that works for you to supplement the practical strategy we've been pursuing, but try not to upset the budget.

Better:

These ideas are all excellent. Use them to supplement the strategy we planned, but don't upset the budget.

Here's a three-stage example:

1. *We're ready to communicate to all stakeholders and interested parties and want to ensure that best information and current thinking are available to the media and the public.*

2. *We're ready to communicate to stakeholders and interested parties. We'll deliver the most current information and current thinking to the media, as well as update the public.*

3. *We're ready to communicate with the media and the public. We want to give all stakeholders our best thinking and most current information.*

Creating two or even three sentences from a runny one is an easy fix. It may cost you a little space or, as in the foregoing example, save some. Is it OK to begin sentences with a conjunction? Opinions differ, because the old grammar "rule" forbade it. But you may notice that all are frequently used as starters in this book, except perhaps *nor*. The technique works for creating a conversational feel—for websites, blogs, and sales messages, among other platforms. Not so much for cover letters and other relatively formal materials.

Find Those Action Verbs

Replacing dull place-holding verbs with active, high-energy ones transforms your writing. Sentences based on the *to be* verb are tempting to write but boring to read. So is writing that depends on verbs like *have, get, can* and *make*. Eliminating such verbs isn't possible or desirable, but the less you rely on them, the more effective your writing becomes.

Be especially cautious of sentences that begin with *There is* or *There are*. They deprive you of power right at the start. Note the difference in the following pairs:

There is a section describing the new technology inside the report.

versus

The report includes a section describing the new technology.

There are strong indications that this is not the time to ask for a raise.

versus

Clearly, this is a bad time to ask for a raise.

Yes, the last sentence still depends on *is*, because finding a different verb is hard in this case and the structure works OK.

Notice that *is, are* and *will be* sentences often demand words ending in *–ed*. This is another signal to substitute a livelier verb.

Different parts of the brain are involved in writing as opposed to speaking.

versus

We use different parts of the brain to write and to speak.

Have-based sentences also tempt us when we're lazy. Here's a silly example to make the point:

To have edited your work after having written it is always advised. Upon review, you'll find that mistakes have been made. But editing is not a subject many of us were ever taught in our lives.

versus

Always review your writing. You'll find mistakes. Unfortunately, few of us ever learned to edit.

Some examples of *get* and *make*:

I suggest we make a decision to have a meeting to discuss the issues that may make problems for our company's image.

versus

Let's talk about the risks to company image.

Sometimes taking a few more seconds will bring to mind an active verb that produces a more honest, to-the-point statement.

We need to get ready for the bad publicity.

versus

We must brace for the bad publicity.

When I see a paragraph shrinking under my eyes like a strip of bacon in a skillet, I know I'm on the right track.

— Peter DeVries, comic novelist

SIDESTEP BUSINESS-SPEAK

Jargon, buzzwords and empty rhetoric variously confuse, bore or conceal meaning. Sometimes a word or phrase accomplishes all three! To counter this effect, cultivate mindfulness in your use of such language.

The Trouble With Jargon

Whatever industry we belong to, we typically absorb a specialized repertoire of words and terminology. This is useful and necessary. It enables us to exchange information built on common understanding. A lawyer's "inside" language naturally differs from a biologist's, a financial manager's, a graphic designer's and so on.

But industry shorthand can create problems.

Jargon Problem 1

We forget that a client, funding agency, journalist, investor or member of the public does not share our insider knowledge. Here's an example from education, a passage (admittedly out of context) from an alumni magazine issued by a major university's Department of English. The article is about how writing instruction must adapt to changing technology.

> *Apply this domestic generational paradigm to the English Department and we begin to see how the ethos of space might affect students and teachers, perhaps even an entire discipline.*

It's easy to laugh at how people in other industries use jargon but harder to notice when we do it ourselves. A business example:

> *This change will allow us to better leverage our talent base in an area where developmental roles are under way and strategically focuses us toward the upcoming Business System transition where Systems literacy and accuracy will be essential to maintain and to further improve service levels to our customer base going forward.*

SUCCESS TIP

Don't use writing to evade responsibility; it doesn't work

Here's how Ford Motor Co. responded when reporters questioned a rumor that the company would lay off 10% of its global workforce:

> "Reducing costs and becoming as lean and efficient as possible also remain part

of that work. We have not announced any new people efficiency actions, nor do we comment on speculation," the company said.

Countless companies, government agencies and other organizations use such business-speak as if it distracts people from reality. It isn't creative to make up new phrases like "people efficiency"; it's insulting. It's one reason so many institutions face a credibility problem. To establish or reestablish credibility demands that organizations be honest, transparent and clear.

Writing (or speaking) jargon-laden drivel makes you part of the problem. Writing well makes you part of the solution—whatever work you do and whatever role you now play.

Jargon Problem 2

Using code words with ambiguous meanings that can be interpreted in different ways destroys clarity. *Protocol,* for example, has different meanings to a diplomat, medical researcher and computer specialist.

Consider the word *overload.* To physical trainers, it means building fitness through progressive weight bearing. To computer scientists, it's using a single definition for different classes of objects. To some college professors, it means teaching extra courses. Not to mention that overload is also a chess tactic and a Pakistani band. Of course, context usually tells us which meaning is intended, but if we're talking to someone from a different field of expertise, or the public, this assumption can be costly.

Jargon Problem 3

We use jargon to veil our meaning or avoid expressing one—such as when we say nothing at all in a supposedly impressive way. For example:

> *With risk-weighted profitability metrics implemented in a consistent manner across the organization, both financial and staff resources can now be optimally allocated based on maximized overall business performance.*

There's no way to make this statement meaningful because it appears to have no substance at all. Here's an example from another annual report:

> *The company is maniacally focused on ensuring that all of this software meets stringent benchmarks and product criteria for best-in-class ease of use, simple installation and overall ease of ownership to ensure that mission-critical networks are safeguarded and protected not only by redundancy, but also by the most innovative technology available today.*

The Trouble With Buzzwords

I don't know the rules of grammar. . . . If you're trying to persuade people to do something, or buy something, it seems to me you should use their language, the language they use every day, the language in which they think. We try to write in the vernacular. Our business is infested with idiots who try to impress by using pretentious jargon.

—David Ogilvy, quoted by Kenneth Roman in *The King of Madison Avenue: David Ogilvy and the Making of Modern Advertising*

A first step toward resisting buzzwords is to recognize them in your own environment. Here are a few business expressions to avoid when possible, along with better alternatives.

Instead of *core competency*, try *skill*.

Instead of *thought leader*, try *expert* or *authority*.

Instead of *proactive*, try *take the lead*.

Instead of *doubling down*, try *work harder*.

Instead of *curriculum*, try *content*.

Instead of *optimum*, try *ideal* or *best*.

For more examples, see the Practice Opportunities at the end of the chapter. Don't be surprised at how hard it is to find less clichéd substitutes for some of the words. It may require more words, rather than less, to express the idea.

The Trouble With Empty Rhetoric

When you make meaningless claims without substance or backup, you typically end up with a pile of jargon and buzzwords that fail to communicate: statements like "synergistic out-of-the-box best practice." You can have some fun and play with online buzzword generators. But many businesspeople generate the meaningless combinations without humorous intent.

Individuals are prone to this mistake as well. If you don't think so, check out some résumés in your industry. How to recognize empty rhetoric in your own profile and other writing? One signal is when your statement could apply equally to any number of businesses or individuals. Here are some tactics to counter verbal emptiness:

- Know what you really mean and say it clearly. When you draft generalizations that lack true substance, face it and think, "How exactly would I explain this to a friend, using simple language that requires no translation?"

- Be concrete. What is truly original or different about you or your product? What does it do? What do *you* do? What value do you really offer?

- Find the positive facts and use them. "97% of our customers told us they'd buy our product again" is a lot better than "We've got a phenomenal satisfaction rate." "I showed my employer how to save 10 minutes managing each order" is way better than "I'm responsible for processing order forms."

- Go for evidence. "We've been recognized for innovative products three times in the past five years by the Consumer Advice Board" is more convincing than "We are the most innovative." "We have partners in 23 countries on five continents" works better than "We're very international."

Chapter 12 gives you specific ways to improve your job application materials by substituting concrete statements for vague generalizations. Communicating something real that is relevant and valuable always serves you better than rhetorical claims.

The Trouble With Idioms

Idioms—phrases that we use all the time that mean more than the sum of their words—are so built into the English language that we hardly notice them. Many of them are more graphic than "straight" wording, and even though they're overworked, they tend to add color to our interactions and speed them up. However, because they are generally untranslatable, many nonnative English speakers have no idea what they mean and may totally misinterpret them.

Since so much of what we write will be read by an international audience, it's important to take care with idioms and jargon. Moreover, today most organizations' internal audiences include many nonnative speakers. So when you communicate knowingly with a nonnative speaker or language-diverse audience, look for simpler ways to say what you mean.

Here are some sample idioms that can confuse readers whose first language is not English.

Against the clock

Draw the line

By word of mouth

Face value

Lose track of

Make a stand

Zero in on

Set the record straight

On the shelf

In a nutshell

Get to the bottom of

Let it ride

Across the board

Change of heart

Be especially wary of analogies that derive from sports that may not be popular outside your own country. American English is rife with expressions that are opaque elsewhere: *end run, hit it out of the park, thrown for a loss, step up to the plate, out of left field* and *Monday morning quarterback.* British idioms drawn from cricket—such as *gola, sticky wicket* and *hit someone for six*—are foreign to Americans as well as people in other countries where cricket isn't played.

Even this smattering suggests how entrenched many idiomatic expressions are in our language. Eliminating all of them, even from a short document, is hard. But when your audience is diverse or the document will be translated, try to use them sparingly. Again, the antidote is to delve behind the meaning of what you want to say and find the clearest, least ambiguous way to put it.

Will your writing lose color and interest without idioms? For native English speakers who read well, yes. For all others, the loss of color matters much less than clarity.

> *Easy reading is damn hard writing.*
>
> —Attributed to Nathaniel Hawthorne or
> Thomas Hood, both 19th-century writers

FIXING SOME GRAMMAR GLITCHES

> *I tell subordinates, don't give me your mediocre material to try out. We need you to produce your best work before you give it to us so we know we can trust you. Otherwise we can't let you deal with the client directly.*
>
> —Arik Ben-Zvi, managing director of the
> Glover Park Group, a strategic communications firm

This isn't a grammar book. There are excellent print and online resources for this, some of which are listed at the end of this chapter. But I know that even many good writers share some common problems that undermine their success and professional image. Naturally, if you must take a writing test to qualify for a job, these are the mistakes the tests focus on. So here is some practical advice to help you identify your weaknesses, quick fixes that you can supplement with other resources.

Using Commas

The read-it-aloud method will reliably show you where to put commas—always, or close enough. Say your sentences s-l-o-w-l-y with attention to what they mean, talking in a natural way. The commas usually go where you want sustained pauses. No long pause, no comma. If you're in doubt, try removing the comma and see if clarity is lost. If so, put the comma back.

Read the following sentences aloud to develop your ear:

Commas tell readers where to pause, making it easier to understand a sentence immediately.

Use commas carefully, because when they're in the wrong place, they mislead the reader.

Jack, who studied grammar books for years, failed the writing test because he became so confused he couldn't decide where to put the commas.

Full disclosure: Throughout this book I use the "pause" method of placing commas, and a grammarian may find many inconsistencies. My imperatives are clarity and fast reading. Commas slow reading down and this may be an advantage for some communication, but not for business writing. My view: Commas should signal cadence and therefore meaning. However, some style manuals dictate other practices—most notably, using commas before the next-to-last item on a list (the serial comma). If your company follows a specific style guide, find out.

Periods

Despite a trendy idea that you should omit periods from the end of sentences because it feels "less sincere," as I was amazed to read recently, you need them. Avoid omissions that may be read as mistakes. Also, don't be caught misplacing punctuation marks, a favorite writing test "gotcha." In American English, periods and commas are always placed inside quotation marks, not outside. Also, when you have a quote within a quote, use single quote marks inside the double quote marks.

"The deadline has been moved up to the 28th," Jack said, "and you must be ready with the data."

"How can this all be true?" Jean said. "You'd think that no one knows the expression 'a stich in time.'"

Exclamation Points

Exclamation points represent a whole separate issue. Five years ago, universal advice was to avoid using them lest the message look childish. But the challenge of personalizing virtual messages has led to an exclamation point renaissance. They're used often to show enthusiasm or excitement or agreement. OK, but do that sparingly, and visualize your reader to be sure they're appropriate. Exclamation points may still look immature to many of your important readers.

Dots and Dashes

Dots and dashes are another stylistic choice. You may have noticed that both are often used in this book to connect thoughts quickly or, in the cases of three dots (known as ellipses), to suggest a leap, or that something is missing. However, in the editing stage, I typically trim them back—too many become annoying . . . do you agree? Often breaking the sentence works better, or a small rephrasing. Colons are handy for expressing an emphasis or to signal a list.

Agreement

Pay close attention to nouns and people's names. Take care that words such as *it, they, he* and *their* used later in the sentence match the singular or plural situation. A student kindly provided me with this example of multiple non-agreement:

The blog's main goal is to get their readers to stop lying on social media in order to make their lives appear better than it may be.

Wandering Sentences

To identify too-long sentences, read them aloud and you'll hear them wander. Or just look at them, especially if your Readability Index check shows your average sentences are long. Break these sentences into two or more, or find a more concise way of delivering the message.

Danglers and Misplaced Modifiers

These are sentences that confuse the basic "who did what" structure:

Paddling the canoe up the river, the alligators scared me out of my wits.

The mosquitoes will descend on you while sleeping, so use a net.

Walking along the shore, a pig suddenly jumped out of the water.

Obviously, the alligators didn't paddle, the mosquitoes didn't attack in their sleep and the pig didn't walk on land and jump out of water at the same time.

Parallel Construction

Try to be consistent in how you use verbs and combine phrases. Here's a terrible sentence from an e-mail. It demonstrates a number of awkward constructions:

One of my colleagues is trying to build a WordPress-based site for a client and a major feature they need integrated is the ability for a client to design a shirt and then the order to be placed—similar to CafePress.

A hint on fixing this: Break it up, and focus each new sentence on who is doing what.

That Versus Who Versus Which

When you don't know whether to use *that* or *which,* try *that.* Only use *which* when the sentence sounds really strange with *that.* But please don't use *that* when you're referring to a person—use *who.* The following are incorrect:

ABC members are looking for business professionals that would like to expand their business relationships.

I have a colleague that is also a good friend.

Who Versus Whom

For everyday business language, it's best to ignore the finer points of this distinction and write in a way that sounds natural. "With whom are you going to the conference?" feels pedantic. Few people would say it. If "Who are you going to the conference with?" bothers you, work around it—for example, "Who is going to the conference with you?" "About whom were you talking" is annoying. Keep it "Who were you talking about?"

Ending With Prepositions and Conjunctions

Similarly, the classic "rule" against ending sentences or clauses with these small words can lead you into unnatural paths. A famous way of demonstrating this was supposedly given by Winston Churchill—the attribution has been debunked but the example holds:

> *This is the sort of English up with which I will not put.*

Sentences like the following are fine:

> *There's nothing to be afraid of.*

> *Where did that idea come from?*

> *Who did you vote for?*

Double Negatives

Avoid using more than one negative word in a sentence because it confuses readers. Here is a triple-negative sentence attributed to the comedian Groucho Marx:

> *I cannot say that I do not disagree with you.*

And here is a three-*not* sentence written by a student, responding to a complaint he received in his work life:

> *Although the report concluded that there is not enough evidence yet to say whether the dust and smoke cloud produced by the terrorist attack caused cancer, it does not mean the Registry or other surveillance programs may not find such evidence in the future as a result of the ongoing investigations.*

THE FIXER TAKEAWAY

Yes, it's often a challenge to clarify, simplify and tighten your writing. But the payoff is real. People find you more interesting, credible and professional. As a result, they do what you want more often.

You need not memorize rules or even attack a piece of writing using every one of these guidelines. Your goal is to identify which techniques and tools work for you and absorb them into daily practice. Experiment with the various clues and find those that help you strengthen your own writing.

The really good news is that, like all roads to Rome, most of the clues lead to consistent problems. And they come in sets. Abstract words associate with complex, indirect sentences.

Piling up words ending in *–ing* or *–ious* produces clouded, wordy statements. It's like pulling one strand of a cobweb: Identify one problem in a sentence, fix it and the rest begins to fall into place more easily than you may expect. So start with reviewing the words, repeat sounds, sentence structure or the *is* and *are* sentences. Or just look for wordiness and figure out ways to cut it back. Or use your online or software tools like the Readability Index.

Every writer has a personal set of repeat problems. Start recognizing your own and consciously make the fixes. You'll soon accumulate your own set of solutions—a personal editing program.

EDITING DOWN LONG COPY

Sometimes you'll work through a document and find you've occupied more space than allocated for it, or more than your subject is worth. Trimming it can be hard.

First, apply the guidelines: Cut everything inessential to your goal—ideas and information, words, perhaps whole sentences and paragraphs. If you've shortened your message as much as you can and it's still too long, think about whether you can pull out some material and supply it as an appendix. This works well with a report or proposal, for example. If you're writing an e-mail, the subject might be divided into two or more messages.

One helpful approach is to think about exactly what you need to get across and then, without looking at what you wrote, draft a new version. It will probably be much stronger as well as closer to the length you want.

But resist the temptation to just condense everything you write into a shorter space. This approach often saps all the interest. Journalists prefer to sacrifice whole sections of a piece rather than lose an interesting quote or sidelight that brings their story alive.

Don't try to deliver everything you know about a subject in a document—or speech. It's much more effective to deliver less, more powerfully.

HOW CORRECT MUST BUSINESS WRITING BE?

It depends. That may sound weaselly, but your audience, purpose and platform determine the answer. Think of it as a sliding scale.

Text messages. Abbreviations and shortcuts are inevitable, but make sure the specific audience understands the ones you use and don't take chances when it matters, spelling included. A text to your boss saying "cant cum in today sory" can produce dire results. Spell it out when clarity counts. This applies to informal in-house exchanges as well. Resist asking emojis to carry a business message or soften a remark that might be taken amiss.

E-mail. Keep writing concise, clear, to the point and basically correct: the right spelling, grammar that looks correct. Informal styles are fine, such as beginning sentences with *and* or *but*, or a single-word sentence like *Maybe*. Contractions carry the informal feeling—*won't* instead of *will not*. But avoid giving the impression that you're careless and disrespect the reader. Texting shortcuts are out of place here. And skip grammar overkill: no need to write something in a way that would sound silly or pompous if you said it.

Letters. If you're writing a cover letter for a job application or proposal, a thank-you note, a request for an appointment or anything else where you want a stranger to think well of you, strive for scrupulous correctness. Spelling and grammar are critical because you are what you write in these cases. Sloppiness gets you trashed. But as with e-mails, avoid unnatural language. Then go the extra mile and find a workaround to avoid ending with a conjunction. For example, instead of "Who will I meet with," you might write, "Who will be at the meeting?"

Major documents. Reports, proposals, business plans and marketing materials must be completely error-free. You need to demonstrate trustworthiness, authority and judgment. These documents should be well organized and easily understood, read fluidly and concisely, and feel objective and concrete.

Guidelines for oral and online communication are covered in the relevant chapters of this book.

FINALLY: PROOFREAD

When your final document is in place, proof carefully. Scan for spelling and grammar problems. Note whether your transitions work. See if you have enough white space and if not, consider shortening paragraphs. Try a final Flesch Readability test. And do a final "tone" test: Any unwise feelings lurking under the words? Are they carried by prejudicial words, or a staccato rhythm that sounds angry?

Extra eyes are helpful so enlist your buddy when the message or document is important. A useful strategy some professionals like, when they've read material so many times they can hardly see it, is reading it backward, starting at the end. You pick up typos and repeats that you wouldn't otherwise notice. This works well for proofing numbers and statistics. Or, read figures aloud to someone else who reads them as you speak, reversing roles periodically.

If you make even a small change or correction at this point, always proof again—the whole message if it's short, or the part that might be affected. Often new mistakes materialize and when you substitute a different word, or trim a sentence, additional changes are needed.

How much should you rely on your auto-correction system on the computer, smartphone and other devices?

Not very much. At best, your devices don't know when you mean "soul" or "sole." Nor do they know when you've chosen specific structure or wording to achieve an effect. The more aggressive typing programs become in guessing your intent and fixing your mistakes, the bigger the potential for embarrassment or disaster. In a recent last-moment check of a simple e-mail I discovered that Word had changed "mediation" to "meditations." Worse, it interpreted "toolkit" as "toilet."

As President Ronald Reagan is known for saying in a different context, "trust but verify."

REMEMBER: MANY WAYS CAN WORK

Keep in mind that there is nearly always more than one way to solve a problem, in writing as in life. Here's a sentence that I asked a group of professional writers to rewrite:

> *A performance system will allow the development of innovative training techniques and methodologies and allow companies flexibility in tailoring their training to the specific job duties of their employees.*

Here are three different results. All are workable.

1. *A performance system will allow companies to develop innovative and job-specific training techniques for employees.*

2. *A performance system gives companies access to new and innovative training techniques and enables them to tailor learning to specific responsibilities.*

3. *A performance system allows companies to develop new training techniques. Companies also have more room to create customized training for each job.*

Notice that each interprets the original sentence somewhat differently. Editing other people's work carries an additional set of challenges. When it's poorly written, the meaning can be hard to pin down, and a rewrite might slant it the wrong way. Revising your own work is a relative snap—you usually know what you meant.

PRACTICE OPPORTUNITIES

I. Explore the Readability Index

Grade levels for various publications and authors have been calculated as follows:

Ernest Hemingway novels: 4th grade

Wall Street Journal: 8th grade

Most popular nonfiction: under 9th grade

Most popular fiction: under 8th grade

Academic papers and government acts: above 11th grade

Affordable Care Act: 13th grade

A.   Discuss: Do any of these ratings surprise you? Why does reading level matter? What level do you want to aim for?

B.   Use Microsoft Word's Readability Index to determine what grade level your favorite magazine is written for. Then check out the *Wall Street Journal*. Is it

really written for eighth graders? Does readability vary according to the writer—
what range do you find? Also check out your city's daily newspaper and online
publications and blogs that you like.

C. Discuss results in class: What surprises you? Were the publications
consistent in their grade-level appeal, or did different parts of them vary?
Did the online media produce grade-level calculations different than the
print media?

II. Compare Readability Tools

Check out the Gunning-Fog and SMOG indexes, and compare them to each other and the
Flesch. Are the formulas different? Which is most useful and why? Are there any others you
prefer? Write a report suitable for a blog.

III. Rewrite Your Past Writing

Select one page from a recent piece of your own writing; classwork is fine. Put on
your editor's hat. Improve the piece according to your best judgment based on
the principles covered in these chapters. Aim for better sentences, word choice and use
of verbs.

Then use the Readability Index to check out the stats on your original piece and the
newer version. Is there a difference in the word length, words per sentence, total number of
words, percentage of passive verbs and the readability indicators?

If the index doesn't show an average of 18 or fewer words per sentence, and/or the percentage of passive verbs is more than 10%, rewrite the selection again and see if you can hit
these targets.

IV. Edit Someone Else

A. Exchange your final version from the rewrite exercise with a partner. Edit each other's
piece as if you were preparing it for distribution or publication. Try doing this both
on paper and on screen with Track Changes. Compare the results of both methods.
Which worked better for you?

B. Discuss your editing with your partner and vice versa. Explain why you made the
changes you did, and listen openly to the other person's reasoning on the edits he
or she made on your work. What did you learn about your own writing? About the
editing process?

V. Write a Memo to Yourself

We all have our own individual writing problems and tend to repeat the same mistakes.
Review this chapter's strategies against your own writing patterns, and think about which
specific ideas can help you improve. Then write a memo to yourself describing how you plan
to make your writing work better in terms of sentence structure, rhythm, word choice, use
of verbs, unnecessary use of –*ing* words and so on.

VI. Class Discussion: Poor Writing at Work

You arrive at your new job determined to write well: clearly, simply, persuasively. But you find the organization is entrenched in a wordy, overly formal style that wastes time and creates confusion. You assume you're expected to write that way too. What's your course of action? Discuss this dilemma in small groups, and then compare the recommendations each group comes up with.

VII. Sentence Fixer-Uppers

Try your hand at improving these sentences. Focus on improving the verbs, cut unnecessary words, use shorter words where possible and simplify each sentence.

Watch for the clues, including intrusive use of *–ing, –ed, –ion;* constructions involving *has, is* and other inactive verb forms; and an abundance of prepositions and conjunctions.

1. There isn't an exact number yet of how many people we will need to hire, but we are going to try to keep the number as minimal as possible.

2. It has become a rather difficult time for our industry.

3. We're very appreciative of your interest in the products our company produces.

4. Want to put your expertise in the spotlight?

5. Please note that the central speech you will present should focus on the new style of leadership.

6. We gave them warning that it would be necessary to develop additional funding sources to establish the new service.

7. You might have hobbies that lead you to an in-depth understanding of a subject.

8. When writing to a prospective employer, ask yourself, do they have a need that they may not have perceived yet that I could fill?

9. In addition to their financial contributions to the candidate, the support group had the intention of increasing her public profile.

10. His presentation on the skills of negotiation has been scheduled to be delivered in March.

11. We need to be able to understand the perspective of a variety of stakeholders and what needs to happen in order to move forward.

12. New development is making our suburban sprawl become even worse.

13. Few things affect the quality of our life as much as the removal of intrusive sound in our environment.

14. People who do not have the support of a partner accord more value to their friends.

15. The work of the lab is to develop nano-engineered particles that can be much more powerful in catalyzing combustion.

16. Our greatest awareness of the complexity of movement is a by-product of watching babies' development.

17. Jones needed to do something to revitalize the association.

18. We review your publications and websites and advise you on how to improve them.

19. The supervisor did an investigation of the accident and came to the conclusion that the agency had been in violation of safety regulations.

20. A decision was made by the nominating committee that due to the fact that applications were tardy, an extension of the application period would be made.

VIII. Real-Life Fixer-Uppers

Individually or in small groups, review the following statements or paragraphs. Diagnose each one and rewrite. Then check the Readability Index to compare the old and new versions, and be sure you're satisfied with your new ones. Try the read-aloud test as well. Finally, proofread. For an added learning experience, compare your version with those of classmates.

A. From a Respected Online Newspaper in a Weak Moment

The core values of an effective community leadership program help create among stakeholders and participants a shared sense of destiny in devising strategies for implementing a common set of community goals based on holding the community in trust for future generations.

B. From an Interoffice E-mail

Dear X Department Staff:

On June 18, at 2:00 p.m., a meeting has been scheduled to follow up on our previous conversation of May 10, and I would ask you to make arrangements to be in attendance. It is anticipated that approximately two hours will be necessary to cover the agenda thoroughly and review the various recommendations that were previously made. Please advise me of your availability.

C. From a Wall Street Journal Op-Ed

At the most basic level, however, capitalism has become the world's economic ideology of choice primarily because it demonstrably unlocks a higher fraction of the human potential with ubiquitous organizational incentives that reward hard work, ingenuity, and innovation.

D. From an Advertorial

With risk-weighted profitability metrics implemented in a consistent manner across the organization, both financial and staff resources can now be optimally allocated based on maximized overall business performance.

E. From a Website

Design happens at the intersection of the user, the interface, and their context. It's essential for interface designers to understand the gamut of contexts that can occur, thereby ensuring they create designs that are usable no matter what's happening around the user.

F. From an E-Mail Promotion of an Event Called "The Harsh New Media Reality"

Insights on the need for more precise media training that emphasizes a contextual sentence that stimulates a reporters lead and to provide compelling quotes, which together manipulate the reporter's script, giving you the ability to control the edit.

RESOURCES FOR PART II

You may want to review the basics, address specific problems in your writing or just know where the resources are when you need help. Excellent books are available as are online advice and reference materials. Here are some choices. Check out the ones that sound promising to find those that resonate for you.

Books

Robert Allen, editor, *Pocket Fowler's Modern English Usage.* A classic, updated with new entries on the language of e-mails and the Internet.

The Economist Style Guide (https://shop.economist.com/products/style-guide). Excellent set of brief basics followed by exhaustive alphabetical list of writing problems and advice.

Karen Elizabeth Gordon, *The Deluxe Transitive Vampire: The Ultimate Handbook of Grammar for the Innocent, the Eager, and the Doomed.* This book does a better job than you might imagine of making grammar fun.

Constance Hale, *Sin and Syntax: How to Craft Wickedly Effective Prose.* A guide to English prose drawing on pop culture for a really up-to-date take on language.

Joseph Kimble, *Writing for Dollars, Writing to Please: The Case for Plain Language in Business, Government and Law.* Excellent advice on clarifying materials for consumers, a must-read for government agency work.

Richard Lanham, *The Longman Guide to Revising Prose: A Quick and Easy Method for Turning Good Writing Into Great Writing.* A specific system for revision you may or may not like.

Patricia T. O'Conner, *Woe Is I: The Grammarphobe's Guide to Plain English in Better English,* An easy-to-read rundown on most problem areas presented with a humorous tone.

William Strunk and E. B. White, *The Elements of Style*. The classic case for simple writing revered by writers.

William Zinsser, *On Writing Well*. A fine manifesto on clarity, and you get the message in just the first few chapters.

In Print and Online

The Associated Press Stylebook: www.apstylebook.com

Merriam-Webster's Collegiate Dictionary: www.merriam-webster.com/dictionary

Roget's Thesaurus: http://thesaurus.com

Online Resources

11 Rules of Writing, Grammar, and Punctuation, http://junketstudies.com/joomla/11-rules-of-writing/the-rules: Surprisingly concise problem solver.

The A–Z of Alternative Words, http://www.plainenglish.co.uk/the-a-z-of-alternative-words.html: A free and helpful resource, an alphabetized list showing good substitutes for long words and phrases, plus other useful writing guides.

Grammarly, www.grammarly.com: Grammar errors and tool to check for plagiarism.

Guide to Grammar and Style, Jack Lynch: http://andromeda.rutgers.edu/~jlynch/Writing: An alphabetized list of problem areas.

The Guide to Grammar and Writing: Interactive Quizzes, http://grammar.ccc.commnet.edu/grammar/quiz_list.htm: Teaches by quizzing you.

Hemingway Editor, www.hemingwayapp.com: Shows you how to translate your writing to be more like the author famous for his simplicity.

The Online Grammar Guide, www.world-english.org/grammar.htm: Another alphabetized list of problem areas.

Plain Language: Before and After, https://plainlanguage.gov/examples/before-and-after: A payload of terrible but true "before" examples with the illuminating rewrites—a must-see especially if you're looking toward government work. See also https://plainlanguage.gov/resources/humor for examples that make the point by being funny. There are also plain language initiatives in Canada, the United Kingdom, Australia, and New Zealand—check the websites for great "before and after" writing examples and advice.

College and University Writing Help Websites

Capital Community College: The Editing and Rewriting Process, http://grammar.ccc.commnet.edu/grammar/composition/editing.htm

Purdue University: Online Writing Lab, http://owl.english.purdue.edu/owl

University of Calgary: The Basic Elements of English, https://english.ucalgary.ca/grammar/menu.htm

University of Illinois at Urbana–Champaign: The Center for Writing Studies, Writers Workshop, http://www.cws.illinois.edu/workshop/writers

6 USE THE TECHNIQUES OF PERSUASION

Simplicity is all. Simple logic, simple arguments, simple visual images. If you can't reduce your argument to a few crisp words and phrases, there's something wrong with your argument.

—Maurice Saatchi, co-founder of Saatchi and Saatchi Advertising

LEARN HOW TO . . .

- Deploy the tools of persuasion and advocacy

- Build trust and credibility

- Support your message with writing techniques

- Find and develop your own story

A basic premise of this book is that everything you write asks for something. Obviously we need the techniques of persuasion when we're selling a product or service, pitching an idea or marketing ourselves. But they are equally valuable on an everyday basis. When you write an e-mail to request an appointment or ask for flex time off or a role on a coveted team project, you must be persuasive. When you develop major documents like a report that recommends a plan of action, a proposal suggesting a new initiative or a résumé for a job application, persuasive writing is essential.

Visual media like video and social platforms also benefit from the tools of persuasion. So do presentations. Even an important conversation, to negotiate the terms of a job, for example, demands the ability to make our case convincingly. You need the tools every time you want to advocate for something and every time you're called on to present or defend a belief or value. In general, you need your persuasion toolkit whenever you need people to care about your idea, grant your request or judge your capabilities favorably.

The world around us abounds—indeed, overflows—with blogs, ads, commercials, offers, solicitations, opinions, arguments. Supplement the ideas in this chapter by exercising your powers of observation. Cast an analytic eye and ear toward all these asks. Notice which ones engage your interest and how they accomplish this. Read opinion pieces critically, especially those you disagree with, for more illumination. Think about how to adapt the strategies to your own writing.

This chapter focuses on ways to write and present persuasively. There are many viewpoints on what works, so insights from different specialists are included.

LINE YOUR TOOLKIT WITH ESSENTIALS

Nobody cares how much you know until they know how much you care.

—President Theodore Roosevelt

Persuasion involves elements of psychology, negotiation and intuition as well as strategic use of platforms. The evergreen principles explained in earlier chapters provide your starting point. Let's recap these basics from the perspective of persuasion.

Know What You Want

Be clear on the result you want to achieve, and set realistic goals. You're unlikely to change 100 years of tradition with one proposal, no matter how good. Typically the world's best résumé can only win you an interview. The world's best PowerPoint will not enable you to change 100 people's opinion on the spot. Persuasion is usually a building process, so view each piece as a contribution to what you aim to achieve. Take care that what you want or recommend is 100% clear to your audience—the action you endorse, or the amount of money you need, or your own bottom line.

Clarifying your goal makes content decisions easier for every platform. If you want funding, bottom-line numbers and proof of your own capabilities belong in your proposal. If you want publicity, come up with some angle that interests an editor's readers—or create a new element that will. If you want a job that requires particular qualifications, center a résumé on evidence that you possess them. Know exactly what you want your reader or listener to do.

Define and Understand Your Audience

If you want people to care about your message, see things through their eyes and frame your content based on what matters to them rather than to you.

An approach built on "give me this because I want it" seldom works. Messages that pile on assurances of how important something is to you seldom reap good results, unless, perhaps, the audience is your mother. For the individual as well as a business enterprise, good communication focuses on audience needs, problems and hopes. Why should this person or group give you what you want? It's up to you to connect these dots.

When you're out to persuade, identify your primary readers' self-interest, what they know about your subject, what assumptions and beliefs they hold. What will these people resist, which arguments and evidence will they find compelling, what will make you credible? Statistics? Anecdotes? Expert opinion? Historical context? Immediate bottom-line impact or long-range advantage? It depends on the individual or group you're addressing.

Multiple audiences are often the target. If you want to persuade people to conserve water, the message to those living in an arid place will be different from one directed at people living in a rainy region. If you're changing a company benefit, you communicate different information to different groups and use different language.

Here are some additional general principles to guide the substance of your persuasive messages across media.

Believe It!

If you want people to believe in something, first believe in it yourself. Ask a master salesperson, a public relations executive or an entrepreneur to name the one essential of persuasion, and they're likely to say it's personal conviction. To sell something you must believe in it. Many media call for an objective tone, but this can be combined with passion. Proposals, for example, should feel fair-minded and reasonable, rather than showing a personal emotional investment in what you recommend. But here, too, a rock-solid conviction should shine through. And when you want to pull people into your orbit, or ask them to risk investing in you, it's always in style to project a passion for what you do.

You may wonder, then, how a lawyer is able to present a winning argument for a client she believes to be guilty. Or how a public relations practitioner can represent a company that does not reflect his personal values. Lawyers explain that the cause they fight for is more truly viewed as *justice*, which embodies a higher value than a single individual. A PR specialist might say that truth is complicated and, in understanding an issue fully, it is always possible to find an element worth promoting. Or almost always. An attorney might decline to defend someone who commits a crime especially reprehensible to her. Some public relations agencies draw the line at representing an industry they deem to function against the public interest.

But especially when you're new to the career place, here's a helpful takeaway: Avoid jumping to conclusions when you disagree with a policy or decision. You may have to support an initiative you don't personally sympathize with—perhaps even argue for it. In such cases take the trouble to understand the reasoning that motivated the decision or policy. Like the PR person, you are likely to find a positive to believe in and will have expanded your perspective.

> *Believe in the argument you're advancing. If you don't, you're as good as dead. The other person will sense that something isn't there, and no chain of reasoning, no matter how logical or elegant or brilliant, will win your case for you.*
>
> —President Lyndon Johnson

Know Your Story

Drill to the core so you don't get lost in detail. With a long-form document or multidimensional medium like video, unless you focus on your central message and base content decisions on it, you miss the mark. Challenge yourself to think like a scriptwriter pitching a producer—you've probably seen it done on film and television, and it often works that way: In a single sentence, the pitch must distill the heart of the project—what it's about, who the main players are, why people will care. Here's author J. K. Rowling's description of how she came up with the idea for the first *Harry Potter* book. Riding on a train staring out the window, she thought:

Boy doesn't know he's a wizard, goes off to wizard school.

This simple idea was all Rowling needed to guide a legendary series of books.

Keep in mind that even a 50-page document is ultimately a "message." If it's an in-depth message meant to influence decision making, it may require a lot of backup detail and support material. But still it must present the story in a cohesive, simple-to-follow, convincing way.

Focus on Benefits, Not Features

This mantra drives marketing and advertising. A feature is a fact or attribute, such as a car's high horsepower engine, a skirt's A-line shape, a customized training system. The benefit is what the feature will do for you—the hot car will make you feel young and powerful, the skirt will help you look slim so you feel confident going to the party, the training program will teach your employees to use the new software and save time.

Effective marketing sells benefits, not features. Figuring out benefits takes some work. Look at a product from your customers' perspective, for example, and ask: What will this feature do for me? Why would I want it? Why would I want to change the services I buy? Human beings generally resist change, so aim to give them good reason to do so, in terms that matter to them.

This pattern relates to marketing yourself as well. See "benefits" as your credentials: college degree, job experience, certifications and so on. "Features" are how you can apply your experience to help the employer, solve her problems and make a difference. Can you troubleshoot software snafus? Train a team of interns? Manage a social media marketing campaign?

Communicate to Inform and Educate

Never patronize your audience or allow that sense to permeate your messages. Think about why you hold a certain conviction and how you can share that reasoning with others. Provide information. Bringing readers along the sequence you followed yourself in coming to a conclusion can open their minds to your ideas. It's especially powerful to give people facts and ideas that lead them to draw their own conclusions. Stories have this potential, which is one reason that so many orators rely on them.

Keep in mind that it's hard to ask people to make huge leaps in a new direction all at once. Good teachers are satisfied to move students along in increments. Start where your audiences are.

But give people a vision. We all want to believe in a better future, a solution, a dream. If what you offer contributes in any way to a better, easier, healthier, happier, more convenient, more productive, more interesting life, let people know. Give them the biggest picture that legitimately applies. When you read or hear something that feels inspirational, it's usually because you've been given a vision.

VIEW FROM THE FIELD: DON'T BURY THE VISION

To me a writer is negotiating. It's about painting pictures with words to create vision—being conscious of the purpose of this paragraph, this sentence. A writer invests effort into bringing about agreement to what he's saying or delivering.

We often destroy vision by overloading the knowledge.

—Jim Camp, founder of Camp Negotiation Institute, author of *Start With No and No: The Only System of Negotiation You Need for Work and Home*

Try, Try, Try Not to Bore

If you've done a project and are reporting on the results, or recommending an operational change, or asking for money to fund your start-up, the message isn't boring to you—and it must not bore your audience. Remember, when it comes to communication, we live in an opt-in world. To succeed, craft messages in that light.

Draw on all these techniques to determine the right substance. Then apply the techniques of good writing and good graphics to carry the message.

ADOPT PERSUASION'S TRIPLE PLAY: ETHOS, LOGOS, PATHOS

The Greeks, who gloried in public debate and argument, set the stage for a productive way to think about influencing people. Aristotle defined rhetoric as "the faculty of observing in any given case the available means of persuasion." He pinpointed three basic audience appeals, loosely interpreted for our purposes as follows:

Ethos: establishing credentials, using appropriate language, expressing yourself well, creating common ground

Logos: providing facts, statistics, historical context, analogies, logical arguments

Pathos: arousing emotion and sympathy through language, examples, stories, tone

Ultimately, messages that convince other people—to give us an opportunity, consider our viewpoint or buy something—employ all three factors, in varying proportion. The ideas that follow fall into these three basic categories. When you assemble an important document or argument, Aristotle's three principles give you a good checklist against which to review what you wrote.

VIEW FROM THE FIELD: A PSYCHOLOGIST'S ADVICE ON ADVOCACY

To communicate your viewpoint or effect change, first listen and look for common ground. Make a genuine effort to understand the other person's point of view and identify things that you can appreciate. When people feel listened to and understood, they are more open to another's perspective. Then when you engage in a discussion about alternative possibilities, the person is more likely to be receptive to your perspective.

You must be genuinely respectful and authentic—people are very intuitive and will sense any effort to manipulate them. Be sensitive to their frames of reference and speak in a language they will understand. Talking to a technologically oriented person when you're a businessperson, for example, can be like speaking English to someone whose language is French. When you're advocating, it's up to you to adapt your language. You have to translate, put your proposal in a language that takes into account the other person's way of looking at the world.

Don't stop listening. Pay attention and don't make assumptions. If you get caught up in your own ideas and forget the other person, you lose your connection. Always show respect for the other person and don't focus so much on trying to sell your point of view that you forget to do this. Remember, people are more responsive to what you offer when they feel respected.

Concrete examples help, such as how well something worked for other people. But the examples must draw on something real and feel like something the person can see himself doing. Acknowledge your reader's concerns, and even when you seem far apart, thoughtful language can help bridge the gap: "I wonder if you've ruled out . . ." or "I understand that . . . but let's look at what might work."

—Susan H. Dowell, psychotherapist, co-author of *Workplace Genie: An Unorthodox Toolkit to Help Transform Your Work Relationships and Get the Most From Your Career*

WRITE TO BUILD TRUST

The salesperson's imperative: Get in the door. Then use the opportunity to connect in person and show yourself to be credible, knowledgeable, likeable and on the same wavelength as your prospect. This *ethos* principle gives you a chance to establish common ground by listening and posing questions. Reading the other person's responses equips you to gauge the person's problems, and the needs of the entity she represents, and present a solution. The process builds trust.

Of course, you can't depend on face-to-face interaction to create trust with written messages—but you can listen in a different way. Mine your audiences' RFP, website, white papers, Twitter feed and anything else that helps you understand their viewpoint, concerns and values. Establish credibility in every message as if you're starting from scratch. A proposal, for example, must communicate who you are and why you are worthy of belief, not just how you'll handle a particular project. And why should a reader grant you the appointment, read your blog, learn more about your product or even accept a free sample or e-book? You are asking people to risk, at the least, their time.

A bio appropriate to the medium is usually essential. Note that business pros believe many proposals fail because they don't prove that the team is right for the job.

And—always—people respond, consciously or not, to the quality of your writing. Whatever you argue for, strong, concise, accurate writing demonstrates your worth and suggests your sincerity. How well a report or proposal or tweet or e-mail is written is its best proof of value. Most people don't think about this, so don't ask them to confirm this observation. But notice your own positive responses to messages from unfamiliar sources. Good content and delivery doesn't necessarily get you to yes. But it does give you your best shot at being heard.

As in all endeavors, trust is built over time. Be honest, reliable and consistent. Deliver everything you promise. In today's world, the path to trust is often via a succession of coordinated media. Marketers refer to this as the "sales funnel." We like someone's newsletter or blog or podcast or video, for example, and subscribe via e-mail. We follow him on a social channel and find value. After a while he offers a free chapter of his new book and we take him up on it. We like it, and a few more e-mail pitches later, we decide to sign up for a workshop, pay to join a network or buy the book. Perhaps we become fans.

VIEW FROM THE FIELD: BUILDING RAPPORT IN PERSON

Connecting with others and forming positive harmonious relationships will help you advance your career, build your business and ultimately yield trust and respect. Take every opportunity to build rapport at work and other venues. When you're in sync with a single person or a group, you are in a better position to exchange ideas, influence and open up new opportunities.

How can you begin to establish rapport, especially with someone you don't know? While some people have a flair for bonding with others quickly, most of us need to develop the skills. A good way is to show an interest in the other person by asking open-ended questions and listening actively. Find something you share in common: Perhaps you both love Italy or skiing, or you went to the same college, live in the same neighborhood, etc.

Listen! Stay focused on your conversational partner's face. Good networkers always encourage "new" people to speak first to find the connection points that guide their responses.

Remember that you need more than words to build rapport. Body language is important. Notice that salesmen match their posture, gestures, and facial expressions to the other person to create alignment. Your body language and tone will reflect the interaction in a natural way if you listen well and focus on the other person rather than yourself.

Don't forget to smile—it shows warmth and puts people at ease. Use good eye contact, and lean in a little toward the person so you look like you want to connect. If you're presenting to a large group, telling stories is effective. Engage the audience with true personal anecdotes that relate to their own feelings. For instance, if you're presenting on how to overcome a fear of public speaking, you might relate that you once had the same problem and can now share the techniques that work for you.

—Marla Seiden, Seiden Communications, Inc., presentation skills specialist

ACKNOWLEDGE OTHER VIEWPOINTS

Rather than disparaging or omitting the opposition's ideas, it's more effective to show respect and cover at least one of their important points. It's a "but" argument: Look for ways to absorb the other side's arguments into your own. For example:

As recently as last year, Strategy X was the standard way of doing things. But today, new technology empowers us to choose a more efficient, less expensive model.

Certainly, investing in Opportunity A offers some immediate advantages. Opportunity B, however, gives us a long-range potential in a new market and will ultimately pay bigger dividends.

Three other products are available to clean clay floors. However, Miracle Wax J is the first and only one to restore their original color.

This technique can be adapted for personal situations too:

My background in chemistry is different from candidates who studied journalism or public relations. But I'll know how to really question a researcher when I write about research, in business as well as science.

I know the team members are all older than I am. I'm sure I'll learn a lot from them, but I think I can help them understand how people my age look at things.

Also, in both writing and communicating orally, always anticipate objections and speak to them. You'll disarm at least some resistors and deprive them of their counterarguments. (See Talking Points in Chapter 11.)

VIEW FROM THE FIELD: ESTABLISHING CREDIBILITY

The first step is always to start with your goal and work backward from there. Too often people in business skip that step and jump right into tactical or narrow-focus questions.

A lot of times companies will throw in a lot of spin—a cardinal mistake—and will try to cover five points. Whether you're writing an op-ed or speech, if you're trying to persuade an audience, make a single argument—know your core argument and then support it with evidence.

The most effective technique for business, politics, nonprofits is credibility. Build trust with your readers by acknowledging valued points of the other side. This has disappeared from politics, which is why people are cynical and frustrated. It's much more successful to take account of an opponent's points or rebut them: "Yes, you have a good point per se, but here's why ultimately it's not convincing."

—Dan Gerstein, president of Gotham Ghostwriters, political strategist and commentator

BUILD PERSUASION INTO ALL YOUR WRITING

No matter what people tell you, words and ideas can change the world.

—Robin Williams

Set the stage for your own frame of mind. Whether you're writing an opinion piece, a speech or proposal, whenever possible *write with a particular person in mind*. This helps focus both your everyday messages and more substantial forms of communication.

Pick someone you know who typifies the audience you're addressing. Visualize that person as you write, and you'll have a good sense of her level of knowledge, concerns and probable questions. It's easier to gauge what might be relevant to one individual than a sea of unknowns.

Keep writing super-simple. As with all media, short, concrete words, short sentences and short paragraphs resonate best. Stay with basic sentence structures, alternating between simple declaratives (I recommend we purchase the Model XYZ) and longer, more complex ones (However, should IT project a volume of more than 3 million, HJK will serve us better). There are additional reasons why total clarity promotes agreement: Simplicity conveys authenticity and transparency. And the converse is true as well. If you employ $2 words and write in long, tangled sentences and dense paragraphs, even if you're read, you're less credible. People will feel that you're hiding facts—and that you don't know your own story very well. No matter how complicated your message is, think it through thoroughly so you are able to crystallize it into simple, clear writing.

Also, aim for material that reads as fast as possible. A forward-motion momentum keeps people with you. Apply the "say-ability" test: Read what you write out loud, and where you hear that sing-songy sound, or stumble, rewrite and then retest. Check that the ideas connect with transitions that clarify how things fit together.

SHOW DON'T SELL!

This is the business world's version of the fiction writer's mantra, "show don't tell." Aristotle called it *logos*. Instead of telling people how great you or your products are, give them proof. Think creatively about evidence to bring a particular message alive and make your case. Here are some routes:

Illustrate with stories, anecdotes and examples. They're hard to come up with on the spot, so experienced speakers and writers collect them over time. Most magnetic are stories that center on people to illustrate a point; a success; a problem and, ideally, a solution. Examples give you effective mini-stories—how you solved a challenge, how a similar investment paid off, how someone succeeded wildly with this approach. Notice how good journalism presents big problems and trends through personal stories. Editors call this technique "storifying." (See the section on personal storytelling later in this chapter.)

Kill hyperbole and generalizations. Avoid abstractions and empty, inflated claims for your product, company, or yourself. When a company says, "We are exceptionally sophisticated strategic innovators" or "We take pride in our unique craftsmanship," they bore busy skeptical readers. Demonstrate innovation by citing some actual examples of how the team defined a new direction. Show craftsmanship with images of the product and perhaps video of the creation process. Use this tactic for personal websites and résumés, and to help you prep for interviews. Dig for concrete realities. Rather than saying, "I possess excellent teaming skills," recount how you coordinated a successful team, whether at work or on the soccer field.

Find your proof. Data is your best friend when you're in persuasive mode. To support the case you want to make, consider using your track record, testimonials, case studies, examples and any other indicators of your merit. Incorporate other authorities. One way is to use prominent quotes from experts, as this book does. They make reading livelier and provide more perspectives that offer different angles, in different language.

Visuals are often your best evidence. Turn statistics into charts, graphs or infographics. Use photographs, video, illustrations. Some studies say that using images boosts the credibility of written material by 75%.

More sources of evidence: third-party testimonials, case histories, statistics, trend charts and much more according to your imagination.

USE LANGUAGE MAGIC

A point made poorly doesn't take you far, no matter how good you believe it to be. Here are some language-specific techniques to help you write and present more persuasively.

Painting mental pictures is essential to fiction writers and makes business writing far more effective. Abstract ideas—and words—generally appeal only to the intellect and are seldom persuasive outside of academic realms. Simple, concrete, graphic words that are familiar to readers (and listeners) work better. Using them to draw forth the visual sense is especially powerful. Which do you prefer:

I found that this book was interesting and provoked me to generate new ideas.

or

This book lit up my mind—it felt like a world of windows opening around me all at once.

Use familiar frames of reference to make the abstract more real. A simile is a figure of speech that make comparisons using the words *like* or *as*:

Eliminating System A without replacing it would be like removing the pillars that hold up a bridge.

A metaphor is a more subtle comparison that doesn't use *like* or *as*:

The region is a crazy quilt of farmland, suburbs and urban patches loosely knit together. Today the quilt is fraying around the edges.

An analogy is a comparison that can make an idea more vivid and explain something technically difficult. To express a key theme of this book, I could say:

It's critical to write well, because although few people seem to notice when you fail to, they may nevertheless respond negatively.

or

Bad writing is like bad breath. People won't mention it, but they may keep their distance.

Creating visual analogies is especially powerful. A website that advocates against buying bottled water states:

Bottled water produces up to 1.5 million tons of plastic waste per year.

A television commercial for a water filtration system, on the other hand, says:

Americans drink enough bottled water every year that, laid end to end, the bottles could stretch around the world more than 100 times.

Writers work hard to come up with original metaphors and images. It's not easy, but the impact can be worth the effort when you're pitching something important.

VIEW FROM THE FIELD: A FICTION WRITER'S TAKE ON GRAPHIC LANGUAGE

Mention the word *graphic*, and you may think of graphic novels, those long-form works that convey a story with comic images. In works of fiction, graphic refers to the language used to convey a writer's ideas in a way that grabs the readers and drags them into the colors, smells and details of a scene.

Graphic language makes fiction more relatable, transporting readers into the story. When creating a scene, writers consider how each of the five senses applies. Use of words that describe sights, smells, sounds, textures (touch) and tastes will draw the reader in. For example, let's look at this sentence:

The boy licked the ice cream cone.

Now, consider the same idea presented through graphic language:

The boy's frozen tongue lapped at the sticky melt of gelatinous goo running down the ridges of the waffle cone, his nose tickled by its syrupy scent.

Vivid language can also be used to provoke the reader's emotional response to a character. When you add descriptive language that "shows" rather than "tells," readers get to make their own decision about a character's persona. Rather than write, *He was mean*, an author finds ways to display the character's meanness. For example: *He loomed in the doorway, his face contorted and fists raised while glaring at Pat's crumpled body.* Words such as "loomed," "contorted," and "crumpled" give readers the clues they need to decide that the man is mean.

—V. L. Brunskill, novelist and memoirist

Consider colorful language. When you read V. L. Brunskill's "View From the Field" explaining how a fiction writer uses language, you probably question whether such colorful writing has a place in business writing. The answer is: sometimes. Sharp, descriptive language can be a tool to help you stand out and get noticed in a crowded field. However, you must know your industry, your organization and the people you report to. A law firm would probably not welcome highly graphic language. Many technology companies probably would not—but some of the newer breakthrough companies might. And probably everyday e-mails should employ, well, everyday language. Colorful wording that calls attention to itself might work counter to your purpose.

But before you dismiss its value, think about those platforms where you want to stand out as an individual—as your online persona, for example. Note that Brunskill's attribution in her View From the Field is cited simply, in the nonpromotional style of all the book's bylines: V. L. Brunskill, novelist and memoirist. But here is how her self-description originally read:

V. L. Brunskill ditched journalism class after landing her very first interview with the late, great, punk icon Joey Ramone. A retired music journalist, she is the author of the Savannah novel *Waving Backwards*. V. L. lives in Savannah, Georgia, with her bass-player husband, above-average daughter, and delightfully bad dog. She blogs at vlbrunskill.com.

Does that give you the feeling that you know V. L. a bit? That she's an interesting person? That you'd like to check out her blog? And does it give you ideas about how you might present yourself more individualistically for a Twitter or LinkedIn profile, blog, byline or social channel?

Use your judgment to decide when an individual style with graphic wording is right for the medium and your goal.

Use vigorous verbs to carry a feeling of action. Use the present tense as much as possible. "This tool performs a variety of functions" is better than "This tool will be able to perform a variety of functions." Cut back on all those extra words and phrases: "This system can be adapted to . . ." works much better as "This system adapts to. . . ."

Avoid trite wording, jargon and descriptives. Find substitutes for generalities to express what you really mean. Edit out the adverbs and adjectives—*very* is a prime example.

Formal business documents offer good reason to explore a thesaurus for word choice. Find one you like in print or online—or simply Google the word and a ton of options will appear. (For example, to find alternatives for *simplicity*, just type "simplicity syn" in the search box, and a choice of instant resources comes up.)

Perhaps the most common problem . . . is that a well-intentioned and informed writer simply fails to get the message across to an intelligent, interested reader. In that case, stilted jargon and complex constructions are usually the villains.

—Warren E. Buffett, financier

But never choose color at the expense of clarity. Pinterest and other online platforms are rife with advice on writing, and some of it is helpful. But I see dozens of pins along the lines of "100 substitutes for 'says.'" Journalists almost never use any of them, in part because they're often prejudicial—*he barked, she blustered*. He *said* or *she says* are the least intrusive words for a narrative. Colorful words can be excellent to engage the senses, but only when they support the idea. If they call attention to themselves, they may undermine the message.

Manage your tone. No matter how formal an industry or enterprise may seem, almost always, most business materials benefit from a feeling of warmth. Simplicity, directness and genuine concern for what your readers or listeners care about contributes to this. So does crafting energetic language, communicating vision, using relevant anecdotes and stories, acknowledging counterarguments and perhaps your own errors. Try identifying how Warren Buffett uses such elements masterfully in the activity at chapter's end.

And finally, here's a favorite technical tip for writing persuasively:

Use transitions brilliantly. With careful attention, these small words and phrases connect every fact and thought to what precedes and follows. Good transitions are the cement that holds your structured content together and reinforces the logic of your argument. Check the discussion in Chapter 4 for how to use transitions between sentences and paragraphs. Try building them into every sentence—you can always cut some later when you edit. Connect paragraphs the same way so that one leads directly to the next. And whole sections of a complex document should relate and be justified by strong transitions. The strategy will force you to make sure your thoughts do in fact proceed logically. The payoff is that your presentation will appear cohesive and seamless, your arguments logical and your conclusions inevitable.

WHEN THE STORY IS YOURS: FINDING, SHAPING, TELLING

> *Marketing is "the art of telling a story that resonates with your audience and then spreads."*
>
> —Seth Godin, online marketing expert

Professional communicators have recently rediscovered storytelling for every conceivable purpose: marketing, branding, speech-giving, PR, advertising, employee engagement. We all love stories. Why not? They're so much more fun than being confronted with mounds of data or long logic-based arguments about why we should do or buy something or change our minds about anything. They entertain us. They give us perspective. They're memorable. They connect people with people and humanize organizations. And they reach right past our defensive reasoning to inspire, influence and motivate us.

Neuroscientists who watch the brain in process of reacting, thanks to new technology like fMRI (functional magnetic resonance imaging), report that when we hear or read about someone undergoing an emotionally charged experience, our brains respond as if we were living that experience ourselves. This effect persists, too. And it's true of stories we hear and also see, as in TV and film, and stories we read.

Storytelling is a prime way to enliven all business communications. And it's a terrific tool for your persuasion toolkit, whether you want to build a career, start a business, support something you believe in or all of the above. Use anecdotes—which are short stories—to enliven every type of presentation, your answers in a job interview, blogs and much more. They're hard to find on short notice, so do what professional speechwriters do: collect and squirrel them away for when you need them.

A more serious enterprise is finding a story (or stories) that represent who you are. Here are a few ways to identify and develop your story. Experiment freely and combine elements of the different approaches to discover what works for you. I challenge you not to find the process interesting and illuminating!

How to Dig for Your Own Story

Do you think you don't have a story? I promise that you do—you may have many, in fact. It's worth recognizing your overall life story because it gives you perspective and clarifies your goals. Psychotherapists, life coaches and career advisors find the storymaking experience so illuminating that they make it a staple of their repertoire. Personal storytelling leads you to look more closely at your own experience, motivation and expectations. You become aware of opportunities you may be overlooking and limitations you place on yourself. You can develop a clearer vision of what you want, which helps you know how to get there. Better yet: Therapists help people invent new endings. A thoughtful process enables you to do this too.

A personal story is useful for speeches, "about us" pages, a personal video and more. They are invaluable for job and promotion interviews. But a story's deepest value is in how you internalize it. Even if you don't envision ever standing in front of an audience to tell it, owning your story expands your sense of yourself and informs how you communicate in spoken and written media alike. It gives you a special power.

Here are some ways to think about your story. First of all, *develop it in writing.* You might even try handwriting it, because many people find that fashioning their thoughts through their hands ties right into the brain's creative centers where connections are made. *But edit stories orally.* Storytelling is an oral tradition; even in written form, stories must "sound" and reach other people like spoken language and read naturally. For expert speech-makers, comedians and other performers, creating new material is an endless loop of write/say/edit/rewrite/say and start again.

DRAW ON THE TRANSFORMATION STORY MODEL

The classic formula for "story" goes back at least to the Bible and Greek playwrights: It's about the hero's journey and transformation. One way of summarizing it:

Hero/heroine . . .

sets out on a quest

meets increasingly difficult obstacles

discovers his/her own weaknesses and, ultimately, higher capacities

experiences personal triumph

articulates his/her accomplishments and what he/she learned

is now ready to . . . be king? Win the princess? Or in more contemporary terms, help customers and clients achieve their own goals? Win the coveted assignment or job or promotion?

A more targeted-to-the-moment formula derived from Dale Carnegie (author of the famous *How to Win Friends and Influence People*):

Share a personal incident relevant to the goal or audience.

Describe the action that solved the problem.

State the benefits of the action.

Thinking within a structure like one of these, or others described below, gives you a much easier way to find and develop the story about yourself than blue-sky thinking. And working it out helps you with many tough challenges. Consider, for example, the standard questions job interviewers ask: How have you overcome a challenge? What did you learn? What mistakes have you made? What are you proud of achieving? How do you handle setbacks? What's your worst fault or mistake? What experience opened up your thinking? Imagine how satisfying it would be to have a sincere personal story that communicates who you are as a human being, rather than another set of application papers.

Consider the process suggested by Ginny Pulos, a business story coach, in her View From the Field.

VIEW FROM THE FIELD: A STRUCTURE FOR FINDING YOUR STORY

Storytelling is the most underutilized persuasion skill in business. A great business story is about you, your company or someone you work with intimately. It must be brief, true and engage emotions with twists and turns—and end on a high note.

To help people mine their stories, I use this process: First, write a list of the major events in your life—birth, death, graduation, marriage, divorce, winning a race, your triumphs and pitfalls. Next, write a few words about each situation and what happened; then, your age at the time; and

(Continued)

(Continued)

finally, what you learned from it—how that event changed your life.

You need never share this list but must choose one story idea to write out fully: What did it sound like? Taste like? What were you wearing? How did you feel? What did you see? Use all the senses. Paint pictures for people. And this is key: Write in present tense, like, "Picture this. I'm walking down Main Street and it's 2001. The sky is crisp and clear. I hear. . . ." When you've got it right, introduce your story directly: "This is a story about overcoming failure." At the end, say something like, "That's how I learned to turn failure into. . . ."

Edit to no more than 850 to 900 words; aim for five minutes or less orally. You'll save time and words if you act the story out a bit. For example, tilt one shoulder forward if you're talking for one person, the other shoulder for the second person, so you don't have to keep saying, "I said," "she said."

Now you have a great story for many occasions, by heightening one aspect for one audience and muting it for another. And you can make it much shorter (what I call a vignette), to the 30, 60, or 90 seconds you need to for networking events. Or you can expand the story over lunch or a long flight. Once you've done the entire process, you'll have unlocked a powerful skill set.

Remember: Stories work best when you risk revealing who you truly are because it's a key way others come to trust you, your ideas, your character. You'll not only gain the confidence that gets you the job, you'll be able to bring that power to your business and the relationships you build there, make self-introductions at meetings and persuade clients and colleagues which path or pitch will add to their success.

—Ginny Pulos, Ginny Pulos
Communications, presentation
skills, media training, storytelling

Identifying your own transition points can give you ideas to explore. Here are some more situations to start you thinking.

- losing a job—through a mistake you made, personal interaction or company layoff

- witnessing an injustice or experiencing one

- losing something you worked hard for

- getting your first good grade (or bad grade)

- scoring the winning goal—or failing to and being booed

- having someone express confidence in you or question your value

- learning something eye-opening from a specific person

- feeling friendless and having someone reach out to you or vice versa

- receiving a gift or piece of advice that took you in a new direction

- handling an unusual amount of responsibility at an early age

- losing someone important to you

- recovering from a major setback of any kind

- leaving home, family and friends to forge a new path

- deliberately choosing a harder road

A good story idea is one that makes a reader or listener want to know what happened, what you did about it and how you changed. Perhaps you were led to see past the obvious, dedicate yourself to standing up for others, reassess your life goals, practice patience, redress injustice in the world or commit to being your best self. Think about how the experience relates to your immediate goal.

Do some of these ideas echo your memory of writing a college entrance essay? Not a surprise, because it's true that there are just so many themes in the world. That doesn't make your story less unique if it's *specific and individual.*

If you are established in your career, working for an organization or running your own business, draw on additional possibilities, such as how you

- decided on your career path or got your idea,

- found your inspiration or sense of mission,

- dealt with losing an opportunity you worked for,

- handled a difficult project that came without a blueprint,

- took an unorthodox route to a goal,

- persevered through a series of setbacks,

- managed a team enterprise with problem members,

- created success for other people.

Here's a tactic to move you ahead: *Ask yourself* **why** *you want to succeed in your chosen field, win the opportunity, pursue a goal, take a new direction. Probe for* **why** *you care so much about what you're doing or what you want, the ultimate reason*: Do you want to build bridges because you grew up next to one? Do you want to design robots because someone gave you a kit for your seventh birthday? Or you see it as the solution to a major problem you care about? Do you want to help people because someone helped you or a loved one, or you were touched by a specific experience? Do you love empowering people to reach *their* goals?

> *People don't buy what you do, they buy why you do it.*
>
> —Simon Sinek, motivational speaker, marketing consultant,
> author of *Start With Why: How Great Leaders Inspire Everyone to Take Action*

Dig into your memory. The answer to a question on the list may surprise you and provide the seed of a unique story. Notice especially a memory that keeps coming back without apparent reason. It may be a small happening on the surface, but could represent something important to you and relate directly to your current situation. Tap into your instincts for a seed worth growing.

TIPS FOR WRITING THE STORY

Writing well means never having to say, "I guess you had to be there."

—Jeff Mallett, developer of Yahoo and other Internet startups

1. *Find a strong lead.* You can start in the middle, at the point of crisis, then go back to cover how-I-got-there and what you did to emerge successfully. Or tell it sequentially from the beginning. Opening with the bottom line can spark interest: "This is a story about how I lost my dream job and what happened after that." Don't wait so long to introduce a challenge that you bore your audience.

2. *Be specific and concrete.* A story may lead to an abstract kind of conclusion—like "I learned to always give people a second chance"—but how you got there must be spelled out and feel real. Fiction writers take trouble to use colorful language and uncommon words. Graphic language is evocative—see V. L. Brunskill's View From the Field—but simple, unassuming language can work wonders: short everyday words, simple sentences, a natural flow.

3. *"Show don't tell."* The mantra for novelists, playwrights, choreographers and artists is a good one for storytelling. The more you can bring people into an experience, the more you engage both their emotional and rational sides. Work with the language to recreate the experience for the senses so they see, hear and touch what it was like to be there. Comparisons help. To explore using metaphors, think about what the experience felt like—and what else that experience reminds you of or can be compared to. Use your imagination to connect two things that are ordinarily thought of separately. (Remember Forrest Gump's "Life is like a box of chocolates"?)

4. *Use the simple present tense or past tense, and try to tell what happened.* Aim to give your audience the facts that created a strong feeling. Rather than simply saying, "I was devastated," for example, say something more like, "I felt the floor start to crack. I felt my left foot slip in. . . ." Many storytellers like to use the straight present tense for a feeling of immediacy. "I hear a creak. I look down. The floor opens up. My left foot slips in. . . ."

EXPLORE THE EMOTIONAL DIMENSION

Storytelling is a major tool for reaching people on the emotional level—Aristotle's pathos. In addition to stories, there are many ways to generate emotion. Here's why you want to know about such tools: Most human decision making has a strong emotional component. Good salespeople seem to be born knowing this, and the advertising world has relied on the concept for generations. That's why we see so many ads that show cute babies to sell investment opportunities and car commercials with insanely happy families having fun. And equally, sad-eyed children in ruined playgrounds when the goal is to raise relief money.

Recent research supports the premise of emotion's primacy. Neuroscientists use technology to track how the brain functions during decision making, and behavioral economists study the process by live experiments with people. Both groups find that human beings make most decisions based on emotions, or intuition, often instantaneously. Then they use facts, logic and reasoning to justify that decision.

This suggests that whatever you're marketing (including yourself), *consider people's emotional disposition and anticipate their feelings*. For many professionals this means identifying the problem that keeps prospective customers up at night and what frightens them, or at the other end of the emotional scale, linking to things that ring positive bells and trigger good associations.

Another working truth is that people buy more readily—and find arguments more persuasive—when they like the person delivering the message and feel they are on the same wavelength. The best salespeople encourage other people to talk, listen carefully and respond appropriately.

Managers, communicators and marketers commonly assume that decisions are emotionally driven. They therefore want their audiences to like them and to believe that they share the same values. So they sponsor nonprofit initiatives, hire popular spokespeople and mount campaigns accordingly.

If the target audience is young, for example, organizations may mount strategic campaigns on social media to show the brand is fun, creative and right on the audience's wavelength. They work to create emotional appeal for their brands rather than relying on pricing, old loyalties and convenience. Many newer enterprises build community values into their DNA.

Integrate Ethos, Logos and Pathos

The importance of connecting emotionally does not imply that in the interest of persuasion, you should throw logic overboard. Most of us validate our emotionally driven decisions based on the data relevant to us individually. We may love a $1,000 pair of boots at first sight. But few of us make the buy without ascertaining whether the quality is excellent, comfortable and/or will incur fashion envy. We probably read what people like us share online about the product. We may calculate what to give up in order to balance the purchase. So the shoe company gives us the emotional glitz *and* the specs as well as the user testimony to prove the product credibility. When what you want is important, do this too.

The nonprofit community has led the way in this thinking for some time, as Allen Mogol explains in his View From the Field.

VIEW FROM THE FIELD: ENGAGE BOTH HEAD AND HEART

Writers have a lot to learn from not-for-profit organizations, which create messages encouraging donations, volunteering and other forms of engagement. Ideally, these messages connect with audiences on two levels: emotionally and intellectually, sometimes thought of as "right brain" and "left brain," respectively. Sometimes, we give of our money and time for purely emotional reasons. Sometimes, we do so for intellectual reasons. Most likely, it's a combination, with both motives resulting in a stronger call to action than either would create individually.

Here's an example of how an organization with a strong story—the Metropolitan Museum of Art—misses an opportunity to tug at the heartstrings on its Donate page:

Your support enables us to preserve our collection, mount once-in-a-lifetime exhibitions curated by leading scholars, present education programs and resources to visitors of all ages, and more.

Help us continue the story of 5,000 years of art and sustain an exciting, accessible, and relevant Museum for future generations by making a gift to The Met today.

Please note that your contribution may be tax deductible within the limits prescribed by law.

The Met misses the chance to more fully engage by evoking the transformative power of art. Instead, it just states it.

In contrast, recent copy on the American Heart Association's (AHA) Donate page includes the lines:

For the littlest baby and the oldest grandparent, you can change and even save their life. With your donation today, you are why families will stay together after heart disease threatens to tear them apart.

Emotional.

The visitor to the AHA's About page reads a compatible credibility-driven message:

Founded by six cardiologists in 1924, our organization now includes more than 22.5 million volunteers and supporters. We fund innovative research, fight for stronger public health policies, and provide critical tools and information to save and improve lives. Our nationwide organization includes 156 local offices and more than 3,000 employees.

Most effective: Tug on the heartstrings *and* give credible reasons to act.

—Allen Mogol, writer, editor,
adjunct professor of writing

You may have noticed that the grammar in the Heart Association appeal is imperfect. Clearly, the charity reaps benefit from the message as is. Observe how the whole construction is based on "you."

Use the Power of Specific Language

"Specificness" appeals to both our heart and mind. Images do this powerfully. A good chart that demonstrates a trend reaches our logical side. A photograph of an abused puppy who needs a home, or a homeless man with the same need, grabs our heart and may inspire us to reach for our wallet. Nonprofits long ago learned that symbolizing a need through a single individual does this far more effectively than citing statistics about homelessness, hunger or any other cause. Over time, particular images have come to trigger a collective or even universal emotion—a screaming child fleeing from napalm, a small body on the beach after a boatful of immigrants capsized. They haunt our imagination and sometimes frame how we see a whole war or other crisis.

However, good writing also plays a role in persuading people to a cause. Here, too, specificness—focusing on a single example—is key. Words can paint pictures to bring an individual child's plight alive for us. Comparisons can resonate to influence our perspective even in material that might otherwise be dry.

Attending to the guidelines for creating simple, direct statements presented throughout this book help you make copy persuasive. Sometimes a small shift in language creates a world of difference in how a statement affects us. Notice what happens to this sentence with a simple change:

The mission is to help homeless people.

Ho-hum—a passive statement without much emotional appeal. Not much motivation there. Is this better?

We help homeless people rekindle their lives.

A well-established group called Elder Hostel recently changed its name to Road Scholar. Research highlighted the fact that today's seniors don't like being labeled or thought of as old. What do you think happened to this nonprofit's popularity after the shift?

Relabeling doesn't work as a superficial tactic, however. It must reflect or serve as a touchpoint for a true change of heart and be used to inspire new ways of filling the mission—or as the basis of a new mission.

REMEMBER THE GRAPHIC DIMENSION

Even when the medium is not a visual one like a website, appearance always counts. From e-mails to proposals to blogs, people unthinkingly decide whether to read a message based on how it looks. Moreover, they assess your credibility and authority based on appearance. Is this unfair? Perhaps, but realistically this is how we all react. It's the equivalent of judging people by how they present themselves physically—hair, clothing, posture and all the rest. Does the written message look accessible and inviting? Or confused and crowded and complicated?

It's especially tough to pull people through long-form documents. You need your full tool kit if you want to create documents that are enticing and readable. When you compete for a substantial project as a freelancer, assume your competitors will take the trouble to make their materials look good, and so must you.

In some industries, extraordinary skill goes into the visual appearance of proposals. Whole creative teams are devoted to this effort. But even on an everyday basis your messages will more often succeed when you invest a little extra time into checking for white space and clarity. Fortunately, improving the graphic element coincides with the process of sharpening language and wording. A lack of white space, for example, signals that your paragraphs are too long and perhaps your sentences are, too.

Whatever your goal, represent yourself with a document that makes a good impression. Design a title sheet—simple is fine. Build in headlines for sections and subheads as well as lots of white space to rest the eye. Short paragraphs are especially helpful. Use a very readable typeface even if it's less slick and "modern" than one that's trendy.

VIEW FROM THE FIELD: A GRAPHIC DESIGNER'S ADVICE ON PRESENTING WELL

The general rule for just about all documents, in print and online, is keep it simple and keep it clean. Here are some guidelines.

About Typeface

The point is readability and accessibility.

- Consistency counts. Don't mix two different serif faces—those are the ones with the squiggles at the ends. Stick with one font. But you can mix a serif face with a sans serif (squiggle free) face. For example, Times New Roman or Garamond for body copy works well with Arial for heads and subheads.

- Sans serif can also be used for body copy if you don't have a lot of it or if a pretty face counts, like in an advertisement.

- Size matters: In general, keep to the 10- to 12-point range.

- But size is subtle: Fonts have different "x heights"—meaning that the bottom part of a lowercase letter in one face will be higher than that of another. The higher one is more readable. For example, Helvetica has a higher x height than Berkeley. So if you're using a small type size—like 8 or 9 points—Helvetica is a better choice. You can check this effect visually.

- Caps and italics are hard to read, so use them only for emphasis or headlines. This is true for bold as well.

- Don't justify: Run copy for most purposes flush left and rag right—justifying forces text into unappealing letter spacing and makes readers feel uptight. Rag right is calming.

Break It Up

Use all the tools available for creating air and space.

- Let your lines breathe: Don't cram copy in so the lines run too close to each other. If your column is wide, try adding space between lines (if you have control over this, use at least 2 points between lines such as 9 on 11, or 10 on 12). On your computer, see how it looks for your purpose if you add 1.5 spaces between lines on documents rather than 1.

- Keep substantial margins on left, right, top and bottom—generally no less than an inch and, yes, even on résumés.

- Use bullets and indenting deliberately as a way to break up space.

- When using subheads, leave more space *above* the subhead to separate it from the body copy than the space left *after* the subhead; it offers a better visual break.

- Headlines: Be consistent in using caps or upper/lowercase and making them flush left or centered—don't alternate.

For Proposals and Other Big Documents

- Take the trouble to make proposals inviting. This will increase the likelihood of winning the bid.

- Be sure proposals reflect your brand identity. Use the colors associated with it.

- Choose fonts and arrange your pages for instant readability.

- Build in LOTS of white space and page breaks—wide margins, subheads, pullouts, indents, bullets, colored boxes, a rule element, images. Designers love white space because of what it says to the audience. People associate white space with higher value and quality, luxury, simplicity, sophistication, calmness, design savvy, concern with aesthetics and thoughtful attention to their preferences.

- Use relevant graphics and keep to a single style: Don't mix and match cartoons and photographs, for example, and keep visuals in line with your graphic image.

- Clip art: Stay away from it! If you can't find an appropriate image resource, get your message across with color boxes and other variables.

- Spark up graphs and charts with color. Think about a more intriguing way to present them rather than plain and static. Try to build in a feeling of motion and action.

—*Tina Panos, president of Panos Graphic Services*

LEARN FROM A MODEL BUSINESS WRITER: WARREN BUFFETT

Financier Warren Buffett is widely admired as a master communicator looked to as a model by Wall Street and beyond for his writing as well as moneymaking ability. In this excerpt from his July 26, 2010, report to shareholders, notice the tone, language and approach to delivering good and bad news:

> *Charlie and I hope that the per-share earnings of our non-insurance businesses continue to increase at a decent rate. But the job gets tougher as the numbers get larger. We will need both good performance from our current businesses and more major acquisitions. We're prepared. Our elephant gun has been reloaded, and my trigger finger is itchy.*

Buffett's communication style makes it easy for the reader to engage and keep reading. Beyond being clear, the document is more enjoyable than you'd expect of an annual report letter. Moreover, it conveys sincerity.

Buffett also sets a wide stage. Later, in the same letter, he presents a vision of the big picture that comforts and inspires:

> *No matter how serene today may be, tomorrow is always uncertain.*

> *Throughout my lifetime, politicians and pundits have constantly moaned about terrifying problems facing America. Yet our citizens now live an astonishing six times better than when I was born. The prophets of doom have overlooked the all-important factor that is certain: Human potential is far from exhausted, and the American system for unleashing that potential—a system that has worked wonders for over two centuries despite frequent interruptions for recessions and even a Civil War—remains alive and effective.*

We are not natively smarter than we were when our country was founded nor do we work harder. But look around you and see a world beyond the dreams of any colonial citizen. Now, as in 1776, 1861, 1932 and 1941, America's best days lie ahead.

The more concise, easy to read and lively you make your document, the better it will work. The more you bring information alive by communicating vision, telling stories and crafting vivid language, the more convincing it becomes. Like Warren Buffett—who I'm willing to bet plans and edits his writing obsessively—practice good writing strategies to communicate persuasively.

PRACTICE OPPORTUNITIES

I. Analyze the Advertising Around You

Review three print ads, three television commercials and three online ads. Answer the following questions, and write about your observations:

1. Who is the target audience (or audiences)?

2. What persuasive techniques can you identify?

3. How effective is each pitch?

4. Choose one: Can you think of any ways to make it more effective?

5. What differences can you observe in the tactics used in the three media?

II. Discuss: How Decisions Are Made

Do you agree that people make decisions, from life choices to minor purchases, on an emotional rather than a rational basis?

Pick three of your own recent decisions, such as choosing a school, selecting a smartphone, making a donation to a charitable cause, pursuing volunteer work or making a major purchase like a car or computer. Carefully analyze the process you followed and assess what motivated your decisions.

Does reviewing the decision lend support to the emotion-first concept? Does it affect your outlook on using persuasive techniques?

Research emotional decision making for a more in-depth view, and think about whether the concept makes sense to you and to what degree. The pivotal (and interesting) book is *Thinking Fast and Slow* by Daniel Kahneman.

III. Write and Present an Anecdote

Can you identify an occasion when you changed your mind about something such as an idea, a person, a decision? Think analytically about *why* you changed your mind and the experience of doing so. Write a short anecdote (e.g., two minutes) to present to the class or a subgroup. After all the anecdotes are shared, discuss as a group whether changing an opinion is difficult, and why. What factors lead us to hold onto our beliefs? Should we be more open-minded? Also discuss what worked well in the various anecdotes.

IV. Write Your Story

Use one of the approaches outlined in this chapter to select a moment in time that represents something important to you. Remember that you may not exactly know why an event matters to you before developing it into a story. Build it in writing, in the length you feel it merits. Say it aloud, review it, edit it into a two- to five-minute version to tell the class. Listeners should offer positive comments only.

V. Discuss: What Works in Storytelling?

After everyone has presented, discuss as listeners what techniques were most effective in both story content and delivery. Focus on the techniques rather than the storytellers. If desired, create a set of written guidelines for personal storytelling.

VI. Research and Report on a Corporate Story

Check out some of your favorite companies and identify one that tells its story in an effective way, whether on its website, on social media or in print. Write a report that capsulizes the story, explains why it's successful and describes how the company uses it. Is the story used differently in the various media?

VII. Write a Persuasive Letter or E-mail

Select something you feel strongly about from your school, business or personal life. It can be an idea, such as why companies need to enforce strong ethical guidelines or give new hires more access to leaders. Or why the person you're writing to should buy a different computer, take a particular course, read a book, build an aquarium—whatever. Choose something that you know is a hard sell. Write a persuasive memo to the relevant person using as many of the techniques covered in this chapter as you can, including the graphic guidelines. Then list the techniques you incorporated and identify the corresponding examples.

VIII. Write a Rebuttal Letter

A friend tells you she pays a service to write her papers because "it's the smart way to get through college with less stress and more time." Create a written argument against this practice, drawing on the various techniques of persuasion and the Talking Points process presented in Chapter 11.

IX. Read and Analyze Warren Buffett

Find and read at least three pieces of Buffett's writing, easily available online. Identify all the persuasion techniques you can identify, and try to add more not covered in this chapter. Consider, too, when his general style is appropriate. And to what media. Share your findings with a small group of classmates and assemble one master list with examples. Then review other groups' results and develop a comprehensive list of persuasion techniques.

X. Word Choice Practice: Dump the Clutter

When we write An Important Document, the process seems to trigger our most traditional and even old-fashioned instincts toward the formal and pretentious. Here are some phrases that are wordy, interfering with the reader's ability to absorb the big picture or even get through the document. How would you replace the following? And what phrases can you add? Notice where your own wordiness comes from and consciously replace those phrases with more straightforward language every time you write.

At this point in time

In consideration of

In a position to

Reach a conclusion

In view of the fact that

It is important to note that

Notwithstanding the fact that

The manner in which

Following the conclusion of

In the event that

Contrary to the assumption that

In mitigation of

The purpose of this document

In a very real sense

As a matter of fact

At an early date

In the use of

SELECTED RESOURCES FOR CHAPTER 6

A number of interesting websites and blogs connect psychology research to marketing and other persuasion needs. Here are a few I like. Notice that most of the sites have taglines. Which do you think work best?

Changing Minds: "How we change how others think, feel, behave and do." Large resource of ideas about tactics of persuasion (http://changingminds.org/techniques/general/overall/overall.htm).

PsyBlog: "Understand your mind." Psychologist Jeremy Dean's website covers scientific research that relates to everyday life (www.spring.org.uk).

Psycho Tactics: "Why customers buy (and why they don't)." Sean D'Souza on psychotactical strategies for small business (www.psychotactics.com).

Neuromarketing: "Where brain science and marketing meet." Roger Dooley blogs on this subject and recommends other current material. He is also the author of the book *Brainfluence: 100 Ways to Persuade and Convince Consumers With Neuromarketing* (www.neurosciencemarketing.com/blog).

Social Triggers: Derek's Halpern's take on applying psychology science to business (http://socialtriggers.com).

You Are Not So Smart: "A celebration of self-delusion." David McRaney's observations on the flawed perception and reasoning behind what happens in the world (http://youarenotsosmart.com).

The Web Psychologist: "The science of online persuasion." Nathalie Nahai applies persuasion techniques to online writing. Her book is *Webs of Influence: The Psychology of Online Persuasion* (www.thewebpsychologist.com).

Influence at Work: "Proven science for business success." The website of Robert B. Cialdini, PhD, a leading researcher in the field and author of widely respected books including *Influence: The Psychology of Persuasion* and *Pre-Suasion: A Revolutionary Way to Influence and Persuade* (www.influenceatwork.com).

Neville Medhora's Kopywriting Kourse Blog: "Learn how to write like you speak and sell like hell." A lively, sometimes irreverent take on writing good marketing copy geared to online media (https://kopywritingkourse.com).

A Few More Books

Thinking Fast and Slow, by Daniel Kahneman. Published in 2011 and already a classic, this Nobel Prize winner explains our two thinking systems and how they interact to determine the decisions we make, large and small.

The New Rules of Marketing and PR: How to Use Social Media, Online Video, Mobile Applications, Blogs, News Releases and Viral Marketing to Reach Buyers Directly, 6th edition, by David Meerman Scott. An up-to-date approach to dealing with the media and using PR tactics.

The Micro-Script Rules—It's not what people hear. It's what they repeat, by Bill Schley. How to create the perfect pitch to communicate an organization's core value in eight words or fewer. Fun and useful for website copywriting, marketing materials and many other purposes.

Tell to Win: Connect, Persuade, and Triumph With the Hidden Power of Story, by Peter Guber. Entertaining view of "the story" and how to use it in business by a Hollywood/sports/business power broker.

THE BASICS OF BUSINESS COMMUNICATION

7 BUILDING RELATIONSHIPS WITH EVERYDAY MESSAGES

Simple English is no one's mother tongue. It has to be worked for.

—Jacques Barzun, historian and educator

H ow you communicate with your supervisors and coworkers probably determines how successful you are at your job, whatever your responsibilities and industry. The platforms an organization depends on vary according to its culture. When you start a new position, pay close attention to its communication systems, preferences and styles. How people communicate as a group is central to how things get done and close observation yields big dividends. Notice: Who sends messages to whom? Do you see a strong hierarchy or more open cross-messaging? Is information readily shared or parceled out? Are people practicing brevity and writing clearly? What channels are favored?

Obviously there's no point in sending messages on social media if everyone else uses e-mail or Slack. And if your inbox is full of e-mails that lean toward the formal, think twice about writing breezy careless ones yourself. But even if you perceive that the general standard of writing is poor, take the trouble to write every message as well as you can. You'll stand out.

E-mail is the medium of choice today for most companies, nonprofits and government agencies. It represents an important learning curve for many people new to their chosen careers, so it's the major focus of this chapter. If your organization uses its own communication network, the principles are the same. But you may need to adapt the format and style.

USE E-MAIL STRATEGICALLY

If you think e-mail is an antique way to communicate and that you can bypass its use, think again. The most thorough research on global platform trends is done by the Radicati Group, which recently reported that "email use continues to grow even as other methods of

> **LEARN HOW TO . . .**
>
> - Use internal communication to shine
> - Strategize e-mail with structured thinking
> - Represent your interests well
> - Create messages that solve problems
> - Handle challenging conversations

interpersonal communication, such as instant messaging, social networking and chat are seeing strong adoption." Here are a few statistics the last report projected for 2017:

- 269 billion e-mails per day sent and received

- More than 3.7 billion e-mail users—about half the worldwide population

- Continuing growth of 4.4% per year

E-mail is serious business in today's workplace. It may be supplemented by other platforms where you work, and you may rely on social media to connect in your personal life. But e-mail connects the business world in all directions: with colleagues, supervisors, subordinates, collaborators and services. When we deal with people outside the organization—from customers and clients to suppliers, partners, media and industry contacts anywhere in the world—e-mail is usually the vehicle. One study estimates that the typical office worker spends 27% of his time on e-mail. Another found the typical office worker checks e-mail 74 times per day.

In fact, for work purposes we typically turn to other communication channels only when we must: if in-person contact is essential, for example, or when the occasion demands more formality or even faster speed.

What could happen in a given company if everyone wrote good, clear, appropriate e-mails day in, day out? Without question, efficiency and productivity would rise. The number of mistakes and misunderstandings would sink. Customers would buy more and behave more loyally. Many relationships would become more congenial.

But more to the point, what will happen if *you* write effective e-mails each and every time? Your work life and career prospects will improve—perhaps dramatically. Supervisors, colleagues and customers will find you capable, logical, credible, persuasive and professional, probably without knowing why.

Think of it this way: The caliber of your everyday messages builds a total impression of who you are, adding up to a subliminal résumé in the minds of those you work with and for. Not to mention, well-written e-mails will get the responses you want much more often, whether you're asking people to meet with you or supply resources or refer you to an employer or client.

And don't think humble e-mail is an unsophisticated communication tool. In the last few years marketers have turned full circle to see e-mail campaigns as the most effective way to sell products and services. E-mail is a key way for online marketers and "influencers" to build their reputations and contacts, deliver their blogs and channel people to websites and online points-of-purchase. It's their door to closing the sale, whatever the pitch.

One more carrot: Learning to write first-rate e-mails equips you to write "big" materials like proposals, reports, résumés and blogs. The same process applies to presentations and less formal but no less important in-person interactions, like conversations with the boss. It's the perfect way to practice the universal plan-draft-edit process introduced in the previous chapters. So here's how to write e-mails that work for you and also manage "live" interactions in ways that represent your interests.

Commit to Crafting Your E-mails Well

Dance like no one is watching; e-mail like it may someday be read aloud in a deposition.

—Posted on LinkedIn

E-mail may be easy to send—but that doesn't mean it's easier to write than other media. Each message merits full attention because you can't know which ones are important. E-mail was the first medium with that most special and frightening feature: limitless forwardability. You may address a progress report to your immediate supervisor, but she might send it right on up the food chain. You may dash off a casual message to a buddy who ends up forwarding it to half his address list or includes it as part of a long message thread to people unknown and inappropriate.

So never write anything you'd be embarrassed to find on the CEO's desk, a billboard, or the front page of a newspaper. Don't write anything you won't want dug up years from now, either, when you're up for CEO or running for office. E-mail has another special feature: It's indelible. It may sleep, but it seldom dies. Invest the time to draft and revise every message so it represents your best writing, and thinking, in every respect. And remember that what you *don't* write can matter as much as what you *do* write.

That said, there are occasions when timing counts more than quality. If your boss calls from China to say she's signing a contract and needs the research results e-mailed *now,* don't labor over your wording. But here's the good news: The practice you give yourself when less pressured makes handling emergencies a snap.

VIEW FROM THE FIELD: USE E-MAIL TO YOUR ADVANTAGE

E-mail is one of the principal ways you can distinguish yourself because you do it constantly. If you get a reputation for being able to write concise, to-the-point e-mail that says only what needs to be said, people will always open your message and read it. Showing that you have the ability to summarize and wrap up is a fantastic way to show what a capable person you are. It should be a top skill for a person entering the business world to master.

—Leila Zogby, president of
Leila Zogby Business Writer, Inc.

Write E-mails Based on Their Purpose

Keep in mind that e-mail is essentially a delivery system, despite the fact that it supplements or even replaces earlier systems like "snail mail" and faxing. It began the trend toward diminished in-person contact and even telephone conversation. Certainly it's replaced all those typewriter memos painfully produced by armies of secretaries and delivered by mailroom clerks a day or so later. *But e-mails should not all be created equal; the goal of every message determines your best choices for format, style and tone.*

Realistically you won't spend as much time crafting an e-mail that says "let's get together at 10" as you would if you're asking the boss for a work-from-home day. But all too many people send sloppy cover notes when presenting a résumé or proposal. This often disqualifies them instantly. It's a mistake to view a cover note as a casual throwaway. It may be delivered via e-mail, but it is nonetheless a *cover letter* and will be evaluated as part of your application. A proposal may be delivered by e-mail, but you're asking the reader to invest in you, so it demands careful thinking, supportive content and relatively formal writing. These kinds of messages are specifically covered in Chapter 8.

In contrast, the everyday e-mails that connect you with coworkers and supervisors are today's version of face-to-face and telephone conversation. So they serve you best when they are more informal and communicate a personal feel that takes account of the reader as an individual.

While abstractly e-mail is not an ideal relationship-building tool, we rely on it to introduce ourselves and it's often the only practical way to build and maintain connections. *So consciously use e-mail to build relationships—one little increment at a time.* Judge in each case whether you're contributing to this goal with your choice of content and tone. Style must suit the occasion; for example, a client communication may fall somewhere in the middle between "friendly casual" and "business formal," depending on the person and how well you know him.

Know When E-mail Is *Not* the Right Channel

"Traditional" advice says to use e-mail for short messages and stick to one idea, but in fact this rule is often ignored. However, never forget that most people don't like reading long documents on screen and resist scrolling. They tend to skim subject lines and leads and decide whether to invest time in reading the rest. Moreover, most people today read e-mails on their smartphones or other mini devices. So long complicated messages full of ideas or instructions don't work. Of course, you can attach a complex document—provided you're pretty sure the recipient will open it. Or you can link to online materials to provide backup detail. Or break your complex subjects into graspable pieces and write a series of messages.

Look for a communication channel other than e-mail when

- the occasion calls for more formal documentation, with a potential legal aspect or a need to go on record. Contracts are routinely signed online these days, but sometimes it's wise to protect yourself with a print document. A physical document may also be useful for a "live" interaction: when you're negotiating an agreement or delivering a performance review, for example.

- you're asking for something personal, especially a favor: a donation to a good cause or a reference, for example. Depending on your audience, e-mail may be fine, but fundraisers and salespeople invariably look for an in-person audience, for good reason.

- the person you're addressing is e-mail averse. Consider, for example, that many wealthy investors and donors to charitable causes are over 65 and, especially if they no longer work in office situations, may use e-mail minimally at best. Important audiences need to be addressed in their own terms. At the other end of the scale, many young people would prefer texting or a social channel.

- the message should be delivered privately. Generally speaking, don't criticize anyone by e-mail, fire someone, resign, or break off a relationship of any kind. It's not only cruel and cowardly but apt to backfire on you in unenjoyable ways.

- confidentiality matters. A printed letter or other document can be sent with an assumption of privacy: Only the intended recipient will read it. But with e-mail, once you click "send," you totally lose control of where your missive goes. That's why lawyers and accountants still depend on the post office.

In general, don't make e-mail a substitute for in-person contact. It's not a great relationship or team-building tool compared to face-to-face interaction or even telephone calls and online meetings. Like all written communication, it doesn't come with cues like facial expression, tone of voice and body language. *So avoid negotiating by e-mail or using it in any give-and-take situations.* The medium's impersonality leads some companies to mandate weekly e-mail-free days, or daily e-mail blackouts, forcing employees to pick up the phone or walk down the hall.

However, e-mail is an excellent way to introduce a subject when you'd like the other person to think before conversing. For example, if you want to approach your supervisor for a nonstandard raise, asking for the conversation in writing may give you a better chance. When asked in person seemingly out of the blue, the boss may produce a reflexive "no." If you have a good case you can prompt more serious consideration by citing your reasoning in the e-mail. For example, you can request a meeting and say, "I'd like to talk about bringing my salary in line with the extra responsibilities I've been carrying the past six months."

Model Messages on Your Own Response Patterns

Are you impatient with meandering e-mails of dim purpose or those that require time to decipher? So is everyone. This tells you that relevance, conciseness and clarity count.

And all the human interaction factors do, too: sincerity, honesty and courtesy. We're the same people in the work setting as we are outside of it. Most of us want to feel included, respected and appreciated––liked and maybe even cared about.

You've probably noticed that even the briefest written message, even in context of work, can convey subtle emotions when you're on the receiving end. Every message you send includes such a subtext, intended or not. Practice awareness of what you communicate in the emotional dimension. *Ask, "How will this message make my reader feel?"* Think "platinum rule" and monitor for a positive tone (see the Success Tip later in this chapter). You'll accomplish your goals and build good relationships far more easily.

Build the Subject Line and Lead Paragraph

A strong opener is essential for e-mail. Each message is a fight to keep the reader's finger from clicking "delete" and her eye from moving back to its inbox scan. Many people receive 200–300 e-mails at work daily. Naturally they look for any reason to ignore most contenders. Therefore fashion concise, to-the-point subject lines that clearly say what the message is about. Puzzle out a way to put the important words on the left where the eye tracks first and to keep them from being cut off in an inbox window. Collect good subject lines and adapt them. Here are a few "cold call" lines that enticed me to open the messages in my e-mail inbox today:

Open Sky: You have $100 in credits . . .

The Repositioning Expert: When Price is Your Only Dif . . .

Today Everyday Sol . . . The 1 tip to help you leave work s . . .

And here are a few I deleted without opening:

AWFD: Last Chance to Register for . . .

SUV Choices: Discovered amazing deals on SUV's

Merriweather: Shocking News!

Notice that the sender's identity is part of the subject line. Like me, you no doubt open messages from friends, colleagues, bosses and other known sources. If the message is from a "stranger," you open it only if it hits an alignment—I'm not in the market for an SUV, so why bother with that one? But material on pricing a service might be of interest, so I'll check it out. After I read the first paragraph of the message, I may continue, or not.

The lessons apply to everyday work e-mails as well as every kind of sales pitch. Go right to the bottom line. Focus the subject line, and then the opening sentence or paragraph, on why you're writing and immediately address the scanner's implicit question: Why should I care enough to open and read this? It's the WIIFM principle in living color (see Chapter 2).

VIEW FROM THE FIELD: HIT THE E-MAIL MARK

It annoys me when an e-mail goes on and on, especially when it's a solicitation—getting a long complicated e-mail from someone I don't know and am not engaged with is a fast way to make me hit the delete button. So keep it simple. If you need to elaborate, send an attachment or have a conversation. Once in a while I get an e-mail that's fast, right to the point, doesn't include a lot of rhetoric or misspell my name, or approaches me in some way the person knows will be relevant to me. That shows they did their homework and figured out what's in it for the audience.

—Laurie Bloom, director of marketing and communications at the law firm Rivkin Radler LLP

The need to closely identify your subject applies even when you're writing to a work connection or friend on a known subject. If you write "Re the Blue Project," response time is probably quite different from a subject line that reads, "New deadline for Blue Project!" A clearly identified subject supports personal messaging, too. One friend writes simply "Hi" for the subject line of every e-mail. This creates small resentments because it's hard to recognize a new message in the inbox, and if I need to find a specific one, the search is needlessly time-consuming.

APPLY THE PLANNING STRUCTURE

To write successful e-mails, approach the task systematically. This process will become second nature with surprisingly little practice. The structure is explained in detail in Chapters 2 and 3. Here's a recap for e-mail:

1. Define your *goal*—what you want to accomplish—as closely as you can, and consider your *audience* and its *characteristics*.

2. Figure out what *substance* will accomplish that goal with that particular audience, and put the elements in a logical order beginning with the most important WIIFM (what's in it for the reader).

3. Decide what *tone* is appropriate to the reader, taking account of the person's status, personality, your relationship with him and the nature of your goal.

4. Based on the first three steps, figure out a direct, clear *lead*. For e-mail, that's the subject line, salutation and first one or two sentences.

5. Write the *middle*, which typically contains technical information, backup for your request and the reasoning when you aim to persuade.

6. *End* strongly, with a call to action that states what follow-up you want.

7. *Review, edit and tighten.* Business e-mails (and I would say all your e-mails) must be concise and error-free with correct spelling, punctuation and basic grammar. Sloppy writing interferes with comprehension and makes you look incompetent and uncaring.

Now let's apply this framework to a workaday e-mail.

You notice that you're not included in a flow of reports relating to a major department project, one you're not directly involved in but would like to be. Here's how to plan your message, preferably writing down the answer to each question as in this example.

Goal? Immediate: to be added to the distribution list. Long range: to better position yourself for interesting and more important work.

Audience? Primary: your supervisor. Secondary: possible higher-echelon executives who may make the decision.

Audience characteristics? What do you know about these people? You're writing for a range of personalities, but since they are all managers, you can safely assume they have a few things in common: self-interest in "getting the job done" and, one hopes, grooming new talent.

Tone? Must be very respectful. Even if your manager is a pal, you're asking for something, and her bosses may not even know you. But avoid sounding artificially formal.

Substance? The questions to always ask: What can I say that will make my case with this audience? Why should my target readers care?

Look at the situation through the other persons' eyes to find your best clues. *If you were the supervisors, why should you grant the request?* Don't write an e-mail asking for something until you have an answer, because knowing that tells you what to include and what to leave out.

Understanding the company culture also tells you whether your request is a hard sell or not. Is information flow generally good, or is there a knowledge-is-power mentality? Are there rigid guidelines on pecking order entitlements or flexible ones?

If you assume your request is an easy sell, you could simply write:

Dear Jack,

I'll appreciate having my name added to the Carter Project distribution list. I'm interested in seeing how it goes.

Thanks, Jane

But this would be a mistake. You can't predict whether the recipients will see the change as insignificant or as a departure from protocol. So you need to make a case. Think about possible advantages to the other parties. For example:

- The information will help you do your current work better.

- You possess some special background or experience and could make a contribution.

- When you're involved in similar projects down the line you'll be better prepared.

Draft 1

Subject: Request to be added to Carter Project distribution list

Jack:

I'd like to ask if I can be added to the information distribution list for the Carter Project.

Since I'm currently working on several smaller-scale but similar projects, seeing how the challenges are handled will be helpful and could save me a lot of time. Also, the chance to review the materials will prepare me to handle future large-scale initiatives in the future.

As you know, I have a background in the medical imaging industry, so I believe I'd have some useful thoughts to offer on Carter.

Thanks so much.

Jane

This brings us to Step 7, editing and revising. Here's how I'd rewrite my own draft after reviewing and thinking about it.

Draft 2

Subject: Request for information, Carter Project

Dear Jack:

I'd appreciate it very much if I can be added to the Carter Project distribution list.

I'm working on several similar smaller-scale projects right now, and seeing how the challenges are handled will be a big help. Also, reviewing the materials will help prepare me for future large-scale projects when those opportunities arise.

Thanks so much for considering this request.

Jane

Is this version better? Why did I make these changes? Here's the reasoning, along with guidelines that apply to all e-mails.

Subject line. Focus it tightly or your recipient may trash your message without reading it. The subject line in Draft 1 is long and wordy—probably only part of it will show up on the reader's screen. It needs to be tighter and more direct. Also, a good subject line enables you or the recipient to easily retrieve an e-mail in the future.

Salutation. Pay attention to tone in salutations. In Draft 1, using the name alone is abrupt, often not appropriate in a request to a superior.

The lead. The first sentence in large part determines whether your message will succeed. Take time with it. Draft 1 begins OK in that it gets right to the point. But it's a little obsequious, asking for permission to make a request. So I took out "I'd like to ask" and substituted words that set an appreciative tone. *When you're asking anyone to go out of his way, do something for you out of the ordinary or take a risk on your behalf, showing appreciation is your magic wand.* In cases like this example, you're expressing advance appreciation, since the request is not yet granted. But it works because you're saying thank you for *considering* the ask, whether the answer is yes or no.

Message substance. *Always aim for just the right amount of content to make your point—not too much and not too little.* Draft 1's substance works reasonably for the purpose, but on more careful consideration—which is easy once you have the draft in front of you—paragraph 3, offering to help on the project, seems a bit arrogant. So I cut it, though it's a good point to hold in reserve for a conversation.

The close. *End strongly by underlining your request, or whatever other purpose motivates your message, as specifically as possible.* In Draft 1, the very general ending doesn't really close the natural circle of your message. In this case, you're asking for a response to a request; at other times, your close might say, "Let me know when you're available to meet with me" or "I look forward to hearing the project is a go-ahead."

Writing style. *Simple, direct, conversational language that moves naturally to pull the reader through is always best.* Draft 1 overall sounds rather stilted and clumsy. To instantly discover where the language needs attention, read the message aloud. If it's hard to read any part of it smoothly and rapidly, and you hear an awkward rhythm, look for ways to reword.

You can also find wording that interferes with speed by searching out repetitions—for example, there are two phrases using the preposition *to* in the first sentence. Paragraph 2 also fails to meet the reading-aloud test and sounds "hedgy." You may notice the word *help* appears twice, but that's OK, because that's your subject—asking for help.

Do you write telegraphic e-mails, leaving out words and relying heavily on abbreviations? Break the habit! You'll get better results with cohesive messages that don't require readers to fill in what's missing or figure out what you mean.

Tightening the message. *A major goal of editing is to make complicated sentences simple.* So always look for alternative ways to say the same thing more directly and plainly, eliminate unnecessary words, and rephrase the thoughts. I did this with Draft 1, sentence by sentence, and ended up cutting about 25% in the process. Notice that once you cut words back, it becomes obvious that they aren't needed. You can always check your editing this way: If eliminating words or thoughts makes a message read less well or seem less convincing, don't do the cut, or look for another way to say what you mean.

Review Chapter 4 for clear writing principles and Chapter 5 for a full rundown on almost-grammar-free editing techniques and tools that enable you to improve your own writing.

Review the total message for the big picture—What's coming across? In the case of our example, how will the different versions make the primary reader feel? Is Draft 2 respectful and courteous? Have any negative feelings crept in? Does the content appear to make the case with clarity and logic? Are the transitions good? Can anything be interpreted against the writer's interests?

Also, does the message read quickly and easily? The faster your writing reads, the better it works and the more convincing it becomes. Contemporary means short: words, paragraphs, sentences and documents.

Compare Drafts 1 and 2 to see how much faster the second one flows, how much more convincing it seems and how it projects a professional image for the writer while being very respectful.

Are you reluctant to take time for this kind of planning and editing? Know that if you can achieve what you want with your first draft you're unique. Professional writers don't expect to and nor should you. There's an old adage that writers like: "A writer isn't someone who writes but someone who rewrites."

And know that if you don't invest the energy, you're gambling against your own success.

The good news is that just a little practice will put you way out in front of the field—and once you've built the habit of writing it right, you'll find it doesn't take much time at all. No need for mental meandering about what to say, how to start, how to judge your chances. You earn confidence. Of course you won't always get the answer you want, but when you make your best argument it often pays off in the long run by contributing to how you are perceived and treated.

BUILD IN THE RIGHT TONE

In line with the discussion earlier in this chapter about each e-mail's function, adapt tone to your audience and purpose. A "let's plan a meeting" note to your peers suggests a different tone than "I'd like 15 minutes of your time" to a VIP. It's all too easy to ruffle feathers with e-mail because we typically dash it out with our own needs in mind and overlook the other person's realities and the nature of the relationship. Here are some universals in content and style that affect tone. Whether you're addressing a subordinate, equal or superior, avoid the following:

- abrupt language that sounds angry: short stilted sentences without variation

- disregard for your reader's priorities such as a crunch period or recent absence

- content that absorbs time but contributes nothing new or is irrelevant to the recipient

- meandering messages that force the reader to dig for your point

- careless writing and mistakes in grammar and spelling that imply you don't consider the reader important

- cultural inappropriateness: unless you work for a startup or organization dominated by people younger than 30 years old, use a casual breezy style only if it's the norm

You may want to ask: Why should I adapt to a writing style that I find stuffy and old-fashioned rather than writing quick efficient messages that get the job done?

First, if you're the newbie, it's your role to adapt to the culture you're entering. Second, you may not be gauging your audience well; even a young boss may prefer respectful careful messages. Third, you aren't defining "the job" productively. Part of your goal, always, is to build relationships. Your own tone creates the spirit and other people react to it.

Here's an example that may strike some echoes with your team project experience.

As project coordinator, it's your job to pull together a team report. The group consists of your peers and a few subordinates, and each has been working on a different section. The deadline is approaching, and you need the pieces to come in on schedule.

Here are two possible ways of writing the e-mail.

Version 1

Subject: Assignments due!

Everyone on Martin Proposal Team:

As you know, I expect you to deliver your assigned part of the Martin proposal on Wednesday, April 3, by 2:00 p.m. via e-mail. Unless I hear otherwise from you, I'll expect you all to meet the deadline. This is important. Thanks. John

Version 2

Subject: Due April 3: Martin Proposal Sections

Hi team—

I look forward to having all sections of the Martin Proposal on my desk by Wednesday at 2.

An e-mail attachment will be fine. If you're having any last-minute problems pulling your part together, give me a call ASAP.

The plan calls for me to review everything by the end of the week, so please be available to answer questions. Marian needs all the pieces in hand by Monday so she can edit the full proposal and make it cohesive in time to meet the client's April 12 deadline.

I know we'll have a great proposal and a good chance of landing this contract. Thank you, Mark, Jane, Eric and Marie, for all your hard work on this.

Sincerely, John

Which version would you rather get? I assume it's the second one, so let's analyze why. Technically Version 1 is okay—correct spelling and grammar, clear and to the point. The big difference from Version 2 is in the tone and its probable effect on the recipients.

The subject line in Version 1 is vague and at the same time threatening. It makes the writer sound like a teacher calling for essays and expecting the worst. The negative voice sustains throughout.

Version 2, on the other hand, projects a positive attitude and a team spirit. It gives context to the proposal process, so the deadline doesn't seem arbitrary. It offers help with problems—better to find out any hitches now rather than later, no? It conveys enthusiasm for the result, reminds everyone that something important is at stake and extends appreciation to each team member as an individual, treating everyone equally.

If you think the difference is trivial, consider: Which writer would you rather work for, and would work harder for, on this and future projects? Which person would you want to team with again?

Yes, structure your messages well and craft your language. But achieving the right tone is equally critical. *Remember, the complaint that employers most often make about how younger staff members write is a failure of tone.* So let's further explore where tone comes from and how to control it.

Thanks to text messaging and the modern business tempo, with a boost from Twitter, many people have learned to get to the point quickly with the least possible number of words. But what can get lost in this minimizing is tone. Most noticeably, both respect and warmth are often absent.

Generating an effective tone starts with how you think through your content in terms of your goal and your reader.

In our e-mail example, Version 2's writer considers what he wants at a level below the obvious: He needs everyone's report, but beyond that, he wants them to do a first-rate job—not just supply him with information. If I were in their shoes, he asked, what might I want to know, and what would inspire me to do my best work? I'd like to know why I'm doing this task, what I should do if I have a problem, whether this extra effort will be appreciated.

As every good manager knows, there's everything to gain by making people feel included and important. Taking the time to write the thoughtful message is therefore a smart investment.

Many managers have trouble projecting warmth. But if you begin by looking at the situation from the other person's viewpoint, it usually happens naturally. Consideration shows. But you may also have to consciously think about how to frame the message from the other person's point of view. For example, writing, "If you don't send your work in by Friday, you'll mess up the whole team project and it will be late" is very different from "Please send your work in by Sept. 5 so we can fit it into the final project and meet the deadline."

If you're just entering the workplace or your career is in the early stages, you may be more "managed" than "managing." Let's see how the same process can help when the situation is reversed. Consider Marie, who worked all weekend on her part of the project, delivered on time and heard the proposal was sent out. But the boss has offered not a single word of acknowledgment. Marie simmers for a few days and then writes:

John: I gave up my whole weekend working on the Martin proposal so you could have it Monday morning. You said it was really important. But now you haven't said a word. Can you at least let me know you got my contribution?—Marie

Poof! Marie displays her resentment and the value of her hard work goes up in smoke. Her accusatory tone sounds childish and John will feel attacked. What would work better? Perhaps:

Hi John—I was wondering how the Martin proposal was coming and whether the backgrounder I gave you Monday was what you needed. Anything else I can do to help?—Marie

This note may reap a belated thank-you or a no-thanks. Either way, the impact is positive. If John takes Marie up on the offer to contribute more, she's advanced her cause. This doesn't suggest that John is right not to acknowledge and encourage his staff—but often, we don't have the luxury of working for perfect bosses. It's up to us to help them give us what we need. With thoughtful communication you have more power to accomplish this than you suspect.

SUCCESS TIP

E-mail Knows No Boundaries

Because e-mail (and all electronic media) leaps oceans and crosses national borders so readily, we forget that we're communicating cross-culturally. This can cause problems for writers of American-style English, whose e-mails tend to be highly informal and may sound brusque or even rude to people in other countries. Counter this by being scrupulously courteous and considerate. Be aware of other countries' individual cultural norms—for example, whether requests are best made directly or indirectly and whether it's in order to express personal interest in your recipient.

To internationalize what you write

- use short common words and short declarative sentences
- cut the jargon and idioms
- use lists when appropriate
- phrase everything as straightforwardly as you can
- avoid passive structures and those with get and have
- don't pile up long strings of nouns

In general, write more formally though not in ways that sound unnatural in ordinary English (however, messages may sometimes feel rather stark).

Remember that most businesses today must also consider internal audiences whose native language is not English, so the guidelines often apply. More ways to internationalize your writing are covered in Chapter 8.

DON'T BURY THE LEAD!

I write as straight as I can, just as I walk as straight as I can, because that is the best way to get there.

—H. G. Wells, novelist and historian

Journalists warn themselves of this danger constantly, but spell it differently—for historic reasons, the phrase is "don't bury the lede." It happens in stories when the writer either fails to recognize the important point himself or doesn't use the fact or idea where it belongs—right up front where it signals the reader that this piece is worth her time.

Let's go back to the meeting-invite situation to see how this occurs in e-mails. Marcy wants to call a team meeting to solve a serious problem that arose with a client. She writes a subject line:

Subject: Dyer Project, Meeting March 7

Then she writes five paragraphs recounting the project history, background of the client relationship and remaining steps to completion. Paragraph 6 reads:

Clearly, this client and this project are important to our company future. So it is most unfortunate that an accounting glitch has occurred that led us to underbid by $2,437,458. Please come to the meeting with your best ideas on streamlining production and approaching Dyer so they are willing to meet us halfway.

Getting to the point so late in the game kills the message's urgency and probably loses most of the audience. The antidote: *Restate your message's goal to yourself before you write and when you review it.* Remember that every point you make must support your central message and not get lost in ancillary stuff. It's obvious how this can happen with long-form documents, like reports, but it happens shockingly often in high-stakes e-mails. Thus we see a message about a company's achievements that takes until paragraph 11 to announce that a workforce division is being discontinued and 500 people are "excessed." The first 10 paragraphs laud the company's recent achievements, and the closing section explains how much better off the company will be without the division.

At the other end of the spectrum, avoid overwhelming the lead with so much detail that the action point gets lost.

SUCCESS TIP

An E-mail universal: Smile when you write that!

Your business e-mails should almost never convey negative emotions or anything the reader could possibly interpret as disrespect, dislike or disapproval. Never send a message when you're angry or frustrated or impatient. The impact of expressing such sentiments in writing can be disproportionate and indelible. People may not forget or forgive.

If you're writing to someone you dislike, ask a friend to check your message. Attitude creeps through. Remember that e-mail lacks social feedback—the reader doesn't see your face and gestures or hear your voice inflection—so skip the sarcasm, irony and most humor, alas. Avoid a complaining tone—as a general principle, don't complain about anything in writing. Problems are best communicated in an objective, neutral-sounding manner, preferably with a solution, or at least a request to discuss the matter or follow up in some way.

A positive tone says you're in control and capable. Show enthusiasm—it's contagious. Convey that you care about the subject in an appropriate

(Continued)

(Continued)

way—that's persuasive. While you don't want to end every sentence with an exclamation point, err on the side of cheeriness. It's the same as with in-person contact: Would you rather relate to a gloomy, complaining person who seems unhappy with his work or a positive, engaged person who wants to help solve problems and creates good feelings?

Here's a thought to help you maintain good spirit in writing. Psychologists observe that the human mind—ever alert for threats—tends to put a negative cast on what we hear and especially what we read. We often interpret a neutral or ambiguous statement as negative even though the writer or speaker did not intend this. For example, suppose you send a résumé to a leader in the field you're interested in to request an informational interview. She writes back:

Sorry. . . . so busy right now, maybe some other time.

Your immediate reaction might be "she won't help me, what a mean person" or "she sees me as a loser" and maybe even "no use asking any industry VIP to help me." Spelled out, this is clearly counterproductive. Salespeople who take rejection this way don't last long.

Negative bias is natural but needs to be countered. Here are some tactics:

1. Take some messages literally: The VIP might well have meant "try me another time."

2. Remind yourself that things are seldom about you. Everyone has their own problems, pressures and quirks.

3. Think of other explanations that are not undermining or self-blaming; they have at least equal chances of being true.

When you write, accentuate the positive. Smiling helps you do that. It's physical, try it: A smile controls your tone of voice. It's impossible to sound angry when you're smiling. Customer service employees are trained to smile when they pick up a call. Experiment with smiling when faced with a difficult message or face-to-face situation.

Choose language that reinforces your positive tone: Use polite salutations and closing words. And:

- Say "please" and "thank you."

- Prefer contractions ("I'm happy" versus "I am happy").

- Use the word *you* a lot—cut back on *I*.

- Use affirming energetic words.

- Use the reader's name in the message body.

- Convey enthusiasm and confidence.

- Avoid prejudicial words and phrases: *Obviously . . . as I made perfectly clear . . . as you should recall.*

COMMUNICATING ABOUT WORK PROBLEMS

It may surprise you to know that many supervisors prefer that you tell them you're unhappy with an aspect of your job rather than remaining silent. They may be willing enough to accommodate a need when they know what it is. Remember that people's assumptions differ. Those who have been part of the workforce for many years didn't expect to be taken seriously until they proved themselves and ascended the ladder gradually over time. Today people come on the scene with higher expectations and, in their supervisors' eyes, little patience. For their part, higher-ups are caught short when a recent hire says nothing, puts in the hours and then stops showing up. Bridge this divide with communication.

Of course, it's counterproductive to complain about everything that doesn't satisfy you. "Choose your battles" is a perennial workplace mantra. But when something matters to you, consider speaking up rather than abandoning the field. This needs to be done with care, but everyone benefits. Here are some examples of reasoning through such situations. Notice that these problems naturally suggest a combination of written message and face-to-face conversation. Whether you need to ask for an appointment in writing or can walk in the manager's door to talk, preparation is the key to success. And some interactions suggest written follow-up.

Asking for Help

You come in on time, work hard, sometimes skip lunch. But you feel overwhelmed: Your desk and inbox are jammed with so many tasks you don't know what to do first and what merits the most effort. You feel resentful, overworked and underappreciated. A conversation is your best tack here, but even when that's achievable, you may need a good e-mail to justify the boss's time.

Think it through this way:

What precisely is my *goal?* Basic answer: to know what's important to focus on so I don't go crazy. But I don't want to appear unable to do to my job. My personal agenda is to be perceived as a capable, efficient, resourceful self-starter.

Who is the *audience?* My boss—but who *is* she? Consider both her role and individual traits: what's important to her, how does she likes people to communicate with her, what problems is she facing and so on, as relevant. Assume that as the boss she cares about getting the work done and maximizing your contribution.

What's my *tone?* Respectful, confident, positive, not whiny.

What to *say?* One possible message:

Subject: Request for input

Dear Cindy:

A number of assignments are on my desk right now and it would be very helpful to know which ones to take care of first. When convenient for you, can we take 10 minutes to prioritize?

Then I can plan the work flow to be sure you have what you need on time. And once I understand the deadlines and how to evaluate each assignment's importance, I'll be better able to work this out myself in the future.

Thank you! Garrett

This is an "ask" hard for a supervisor to refuse. It clearly communicates the what's-in-it-for-me: Garrett will perform better and be more useful. He's taking the initiative in a positive way and both immediate and future benefits are likely. Based on his thoughtful communication, Cindy can expect Garrett to learn quickly and not waste her time. What's not to like? By asking for help thoughtfully, and framing it in the supervisor's perspective, Garrett improves his perceived value. What if Garrett wrote based on his emotions instead of strategizing? Something like this:

> *Cindy, I just can't keep up with the assignments you keep piling on! I'm frustrated and tired of working late and feel that I can't make you happy. I'm about to give up!*

Here, Garrett communicates in a way that leaves Cindy no room to respond, other than "what can I do to make you happy?"—which is unlikely.

The bottom line: Speak up when you need help, feel unfairly treated or ignored, and do it strategically. Check your assumptions about other people's priorities and attitudes rather than acting on your own needs without thought. One of life's hardest lessons is that usually *it's not all about you!* Managers, coworkers and other people in your life generally fixate on their own issues and it doesn't occur to them to understand your viewpoint if you don't explain it. Often, starting a conversation with a simple, neutrally toned ask leads to meshing different perspectives and, magically, a solution. But the ask must be concrete and specific. It must offer the other person a benefit or fit her framework.

Of course, we can't always know why people behave as they do or control their responses. Suppose Cindy responds to the better message by saying she just can't make the time. Garrett might do his best to prioritize on his own, create a list and present it to the boss:

> *Cindy, here is my best judgment on how to prioritize my assignments, based on my current understanding.*
>
> *I'll appreciate your taking a look when you have a chance. Please set me straight if I'm off the mark so I can be sure to give you what you need on time.*

Preparing for Face-to-Face Conversation

Let's look at a more sustained situation. Put yourself in Matt's position: He's worked for his employer almost a year and feels frustrated that he's not learning anything new. He decides to see if he can gain momentum by bringing it up to his supervisor. Since this type of complaint calls for negotiation, it is best handled face to face. But it demands the same strategic thinking as you're practicing for written messages. Moreover, you can use writing to prepare for the important conversations.

If Matt goes to his boss intent on sharing how he feels and plays it by ear, he's likely to begin, "Al, I'm very unhappy here. I don't like my assignments, you're not trusting me with more interesting work, I'm not learning anything, I feel like I'm going nowhere."

Now consider Al's probable reaction based on his own role as supervisor. What if he's unhappy with aspects of Matt's performance? If so, Matt gives him a ready-made opportunity to send him out the door. If Al is reasonably satisfied with Matt's work, his approach still doesn't work well. Matt's tone is accusatory. It puts the burden of making him happy on the boss. But the boss isn't a parent or friend—Matt's happiness is not Al's priority.

Matt can create a conversation that is both more cordial and more likely to achieve his own goals. First he must decide:

1. **What are my goals?** "To be happy and learn more" is too vague a target. It asks the person in charge to figure out what would make you feel better. Achievable goals are specific and tangible. And they are more easily accomplished when you identify what would move you closer to them, rather than asking for the ultimate prize to be thrust upon you for the asking. Matt should also consider:

2. **Who's my audience?** What matters most to Al? By virtue of his role, his focus is on a bigger picture than any individual employee. He cares about office productivity, cooperative teaming, efficiency, progress with the mission. Al values Matt according to how well he contributes to these goals. So Matt must consider as objectively as possible what he is contributing, in Al's perspective. Matt knows Al as a person, too, so his observation and intuition will further help him frame his requests in terms of WIIFM—what's in it for Al. To the good: Whatever the boss's opinion of his work, Matt is already on the team, so Al is to some degree invested in him and would like to escalate his value. Based on this reasoning Matt can identify:

3. **Match points for building content**. What can he ask for that will move him forward and also benefit Al? This can be thought through using the Talking Points approach described in Chapter 11. A brainstormed list might look like this:

   - permission to sit in silently on some meetings to better understand team projects

   - some regular one-on-one time to ask questions and get feedback

   - Al's advice on how Matt can demonstrate that he is ready for more responsibility

   - Al's input on something Matt might learn to increase his value to the team

   - some extra work to take on that showcases Matt's capabilities

With specific ideas in mind that Al will probably react to well, Matt can plan to . . .

4. **Strike the right tone**. Clearly, it must be respectful and courteous, solution rather than complaint oriented. Since he has asked for the conversation, Matt owns the chance to . . .

5. **Lead well.** What he says will set the conversation's tenor and parameters. Once he moves away from the "I'm unhappy, fix it for me" way of thinking, Matt can imagine a useful opening. Here's a universally failsafe tactic when you sit down with the boss: *"How am I doing?" "How can I do better?" "How can I contribute more?"* If Matt introduces his concerns this way, he can

- find out what his boss thinks of his performance (he should expect some surprises);

- feel reinforced in his positive contributions (which may be different than he assumes);

- discover ways he can become more valuable *in the boss's eyes* (provided he maintains an open, listening attitude and resists reacting defensively);

- understand the work better, as well as his supervisor's priorities and team needs;

- adjust his specific requests to what he hears so he can frame asks in terms of mutual benefit.

Most important, Matt's established a friendly atmosphere of genuine communication. He and Al will probably emerge knowing each other better as individuals. Probably Al will be impressed with Matt for taking the initiative in a positive spirit—most bosses take an active interest in staff members who want to do more and prove themselves. Matt may leave the talk with at least a partial roadmap to help him get where he wants to go.

It's also wise to prepare to field your own potential emotions in advance. When you invite input, you may well hear some criticism that is hard to swallow. Avoid letting disappointment or anger shut you down by practicing a line like this:

"That's a lot to think about. I'll spend some time doing that."

To get ready to handle a live conversation with high stakes, do your homework. Create Talking Points for all the possible ways the conversation might go. Marshall all the evidence that speaks for you—for example, *I've been taking on extra work at crunch times . . . I've become the office go-to person for software glitches . . . I came up with the idea of doing X to save time by. . . .*

Also list all the questions or responses the other party might come up with, especially the tough ones. As needed, research the facts, perhaps consult friends, ask people you trust for advice. Like Matt, translate your long-term goal into doable specific requests. Then ask yourself why the supervisor should give you a yes. If you're asking for a plum assignment, for example, take time to thoroughly understand its components, provide evidence of an applicable strength, show how you can handle this "extra" without hampering the usual workflow and so on. Look at your answers from the other person's perspective.

Good preparation earns you ownership of your message. It enables you to listen well, participate effectively, speak from strength and keep your cool.

Of course, good communication doesn't guarantee you'll get what you want every time, from the boss or anyone else. But when you represent yourself well, even if the response isn't satisfactory, you're still ahead. You have more solid ground for deciding whether to temper your expectations, work differently or invest yourself elsewhere.

Writing Confirmation and CYA Memos

Many times, it's a good idea to write an e-mail to confirm an understanding. You may need to follow up a conversation, clarify an agreement or decision, or—let's face it—ensure that you're not left holding a bag you don't want. Consider too that in all good faith, a group of people can attend the same meeting and emerge with wholly different interpretations of what happened and what actions were agreed to. Even a one-on-one conversation is open to interpretation and faulty memory. Write confirming memos in a low-key, matter-of-fact way:

> *To confirm what we talked about yesterday, I'll put the White report on top of my to-do list.*

> *I'm glad we reached agreement yesterday. We'll move full speed on the Kwik project this September.*

> *Thanks for spending the time with me on Monday to discuss Blue Devil. Here's what I'll do next. . . .*

> *FYI: As discussed, I'll call Marjorie Marks tomorrow and tell her she can have a 12% discount on orders over $5,000 the rest of the season.*

Notice that writing about what happened and follow-up-action puts the writer in a position of strength. Other people usually accept the version they see in writing as "true." So rather than duck opportunities to be the note taker and reporter, welcome them.

If you're running your own enterprise, summing-up e-mails are critical. Voice-only agreement is high-risk, no matter how much you think you trust the other party.

Responding to Angry or Mean-Spirited People

A good technique when your own temper is roused and you're in the grip of an emotion is to write what you feel, but don't put a recipient's name in the "to" space. Then never send it. Vent without doing yourself harm.

Determine to look at emotionally laden situations dispassionately and aim to defuse them. If your boss or another important person sends a stinging reprimand, for example, take some time to think through the facts and your response. Are you at fault in relation to the charge? Did you make a mistake? If not, can you see any justification for the attack? Any mitigating factors, like the boss just lost a promotion? *Find ways to abstract yourself from your own strong emotion so you can handle the problem to your advantage as much as possible.*

Try beginning a memo with words like these:

> *Jerry, thanks for taking the time to explain where I misunderstood the assignment.*

> *Ella, thanks for the in-depth review that shows me how to improve my job performance and become more valuable to the team.*

Then see if you can develop a reasonable response from there. You may find it easier than you expect. I promise: You will find great satisfaction in handling such challenges strategically.

A valuable defusing technique that customer service representatives use is mirroring, or echoing. They simply repeat back what the angry customer said. You may have experienced something like this yourself:

> *I understand that you're very upset because the product arrived broken, and when you tried to call, five people told you it wasn't their problem and passed you on to someone else. Is that right?*

Straightforward acknowledgment often calms an angry person down most of the way, and then the problem can often be easily resolved. This works in writing as well as face-to-face confrontations. For example:

> *Jed, I understand that I misinterpreted the instructions and that this created problems. I will work hard with the team to address the issue as quickly as possible and ensure that this doesn't happen again.*

The key here is to resist a defensive posture, acknowledge a mistake, make amends and suggest a solution as possible. Maintain an even, objective, dispassionate tone. It is bound to improve rather than worsen the story.

SOME E-MAIL Q&A

Q: Is the "hey there" tone of casual communication appropriate for e-mail today?

A: With highly informal "private" channels like Slack or texting, spontaneous and unedited may work fine. But many people don't expect this style in e-mail and usually the subjects you're writing about need more thought. Certainly think twice about using it when writing to anyone outside your workplace or personal circles. It's appropriate in limited contexts. For example, people pitching services online to a relatively young target market often begin e-mail messages with a greeting like "Hey, Mark." But it may undermine your purpose to start and continue in that vein without knowing how your target audience will receive this style.

Q: Abbreviations: Y or N?

A: Many people are unaccustomed to the abbreviations that are second nature to frequent texters and instant messaging. They may fail to fully understand your message, misinterpret it, disregard it or read it resentfully. None of these outcomes is good.

An additional large number of people understand the abbreviations fine but do not like to see them in another medium—even e-mail.

Collectively, both groups probably include a lot of people important to you, such as clients, future employers and supervisors. Therefore, it's sensible to avoid most abbreviating.

Q: Attachments: When?

A: Concern for computer viruses is one reason many people make it a rule not to open attachments. But when you have a lot to say, it's challenging to write a short e-mail. In the case of a report or other lengthy document, it's impossible.

The best solution is to know your audience. Ask if necessary whether your recipient will open an attachment and prefers it. If the answer is no, then incorporate the material in the body of the e-mail, but use formatting to distinguish it from the e-mail message—for example, draw a line between the message and report, and give the report a clear headline. And make the rest of the document as readable as possible with subheads, some white space and so on.

Alternatively, use a safe cloud meeting point like Google Docs or Dropbox.

Q: How to communicate with people on the go?

A: Aren't we all? A huge proportion of your e-mails will be read on a tiny screen while the person is online at a checkout, taking a walk or eating lunch. Your best strategy is nevertheless to write in complete sentences, not fragments, and avoid abbreviating. But use those little screens to remind yourself that e-mails must be easily read and understood; simplify content and language, use tight sentences and short words, employ white space and just enough information to deliver your message.

Q: What about emojis?

A: Essentially, emojis help fill the gap between wanting to express our feelings and the impersonality of written communication. You may use them effectively and creatively in your personal messaging to friends. But be cautious about bringing them to work. Recent research carried out in 29 countries found that rather than increasing their perception of warmth, readers think the writer who uses an emoji is less competent than someone who sends the message without it. Further, when "smileys" are used, writers tend to share less informational content, which shortcuts workplace communication. The research conclusion accords with common sense: Don't use smileys or other emojis in business communication unless you know the other person well, and preferably, wait until she has done so first.

CHECKLIST: PRACTICE YOUR E-MAIL KNOW-HOW

Do

- Answer in a timely way—24 hours or less. People expect this with a medium geared for speed.

- Send only necessary messages. You need not have the last word, especially if it's just "got the message"; people appreciate hearing less rather than more.

- Include only what's needed, and write short messages. Speed readers may miss the point when you bury it.

- Use accurate subject lines to identify your message, change it when the discussion shifts and make it audience directed and findable. Use must-read elements when justified—for example, "DATE CHANGE, Miller meeting."

- Create a strong lead—bottom line on top.

- Build in a clear close, asking the reader for what you want—and make it easy for him to do.

- Use graphic devices to support clarity and stay organized: numbers, bullets, subheads and so on.

- Use an easy-to-read typeface in a substantial size—12 point minimum.

- Use the signature to your advantage. Cite your most important contact points, such as your website, blog and social media addresses— limit the length.

Do Not

- Betray negative emotion. You will irritate people and be seen as unprofessional.

- Communicate overly emotional investment in your subject; this arouses skepticism.

- Say anything ambiguous that could be interpreted against your interests.

- Employ sarcasm, irony and humor in general, which is always open to misinterpretation.

- Include anything you'd cringe to see on Facebook, your boss's desk or your competitor's e-mail inbox.

- Say anything you'd be embarrassed to have forwarded to anyone.

- Use jargon and abbreviations beyond the minimal.

- Include philosophical ponderings. This is not the place.

And Never

- Write whole messages in italic, bold or capitals.

- Use smiley faces or other emojis when the relationship is formal or the audience unknown.

- Forget to edit and proofread.

- Forget to take a big picture view of how your message *might* strike a reader and *might* make her feel.

See also Chapter 12, which focuses on how to use e-mail to network, apply for jobs and accomplish entrepreneurial goals.

PRACTICE OPPORTUNITIES

I. Assess Your Manners Quotient

How well are you exercising your social skills in the work context, past or present? Does any of the advice in this chapter lead you to rethink how you've handled relationships and whether you might have resolved a problem differently? Write a personal list of 10 things to remember and perhaps improve on in handling yourself successfully to create collegial relationships with colleagues and supervisors and solve problems.

II. Group Work: Plan and Write a Communications Policy

1. Together, brainstorm how workplace supervisors should communicate in writing with younger employees: E-mail? Texting? Social media? Intranet? Other?

2. Draft an e-mail presenting your recommendations and reasoning to an older supervisor one of you works for now or worked for in the past. Begin by profiling the supervisor through asking questions of the group member who knows the person.

III. Make a Difficult Request in Writing

As a class, come up with a set of requests that would be a hard sell on the job. For example, going to an expensive conference, buying a glitzy new computer, obtaining a better office. Write all the ideas on paper and put them into a "hat." Pair up and pick one idea from the hat. Student 1 acts as supervisor and Student 2 as a staff member with the request. Student 2: Write an e-mail to the supervisor asking for what you want. The supervisor articulates his reaction to the e-mail—what worked and what didn't work. Together, rewrite the e-mail.

Be prepared to present your thinking and ultimate written results to the class.

IV. Plan a Challenging Conversation

Imagine that your supervisor has agreed to speak with you about something you want that will improve your personal life: a work-at-home day or two, permission to leave early once a week to take a class, a recommendation for a different job in the organization. Plan out in writing what you will say—the central message to communicate—and how you will answer all the responses you can anticipate.

Then partner with another student and take turns role-playing the supervisor and the person asking for a "yes." Debrief each other: How well prepared did you prove to be for the interaction? What surprised you? How is handling a request in person different from writing for what you want?

V. Write an E-mail to a Friend Who Writes Poor E-mails

Explain to your friend why she should take more care with e-mail, and share the most important points you learned from this chapter about how to write them well.

VI. Write a Complaint E-mail to a Person or Organization That Disappointed You

Choose a business rather than personal situation. Write it strategically, using everything you've learned. Then wait a few days and reread it. Have you changed your perspective? Does the problem look different now? What effect did writing it out have on you?

VII. Evaluate an Important E-mail From Your Past

What resulted? Did it gain you what you wanted? Did it meet the guidelines established in this chapter? Would you write it differently now? Try it!

VIII. Group Project: Create Guidelines for Writing E-mails

Your committee is asked to draft a set of guidelines to help the company's new employees communicate efficiently and effectively by e-mail. Together, brainstorm the points to make and present them in a user-friendly format. Aim for a document of about 500 words.

IX. Questions for Discussion

1. How do you think written communications like e-mails should take account of generational differences? Who has had a problem that relates to this? What did you learn?

2. What words do you typically use to communicate with a friend by e-mail that would be inappropriate when writing to your professor? A supervisor? A client?

3. How can you project a feeling of respect in an e-mail when the situation calls for it? Warmth?

4. In what e-mail situations is it suitable to "be yourself"—with little thought to content, wording, grammar and punctuation?

5. Do grammar and punctuation matter anymore? Why or why not?

6. Should emojis or emoticons have a place in business communication? Debate: Half the group should argue for; the other half should speak against their use.

8 WRITING MORE FORMAL MESSAGES

Chapter 7 showed you how to make a good impression on the job or in any situation where you work with and for people. Let's look now at how the structured thinking process—using goals and audience to guide content—applies to communicating when more formal messages are called for.

Yesterday, meaning maybe 15 years ago, sharp distinctions existed between business communication formats. Internal memos followed set guidelines and were circulated solely in house. It could take a day or more for a typed memo to reach the recipient, hand-delivered by a mailroom clerk! Letters were of course snail-mailed (often taking three days). Pitching the media demanded rigid format and style. But today, with some exceptions such as legal documents, delivery systems have blended together under the flag of digitization. In other words, almost everything is e-mailed or shared online. Messages arrive instantly and most can be forwarded just as quickly around the globe to journalists, critics and competitors, as CEOs often find when they write especially shortsighted e-mails.

However, media distinctions still matter and need to be considered. Today they have less to do with how a message is delivered and more to do with its importance to you. If you're thanking a prospective employer for interviewing you, treat that note as a letter, even though you're delivering it by e-mail. If you're hiring someone or firing someone, consider it a letter. The same is true of any note to a customer, a pitch to speak at a conference or contribute to a blog, or a cover note for a proposal. Thinking "letter" helps you avoid the carelessness that electronic speed induces. "Letter" reminds you to think content through carefully, craft your best writing and edit for correctness. You also find it natural to take a somewhat more formal and courteous tone—which often serves you better.

> ### LEARN HOW TO...
>
> - Decide on the right degree of formality
>
> - Plan, write, and format letters
>
> - Write messages that build relationships and networks
>
> - Strategize messages to solve business problems
>
> - Create messages for global audiences

WHEN TO WRITE LETTERS—AND HOW

I consider it a good rule for letter writing to leave unmentioned what the recipient already knows, and instead tell him something new.

—Sigmund Freud, founder of psychoanalysis

While you may not routinely write letters to friends and relatives, and might be surprised at how common the practice was before digital communication, the art is still essential to many business venues. You may need to write letters, by digital or other means, to clients, customers, government agencies, suppliers and many other people and organizations.

One virtue of pen-and-paper letter writing is that in an age when so much of what we communicate is virtually public, a physical letter remains private. Only the intended recipient can read it. Of course, he can choose to share and even copy it to send out wholesale, but this happens a lot less often than with a careless e-mail or social post. Most people accept the for-your-eyes-only premise of an actual letter. So when the matter is personal—or legal—a letter is a good way to go. Given privacy concerns, we may even see a letter-writing revival!

Although you may be able to use some standard prefabricated pieces in some letters, for the most part, every letter you write must be individual and specific to your purpose.

Characteristics of Successful Letters

Unlike e-mails and very unlike text messages, *letters are natural relationship-building tools.* They carry more weight than casual, spontaneous-seeming e-mail. Treat them as a way to make a good impression or risk accomplishing the reverse.

It is particularly important to write clear, concise letters that come to the point quickly and move fast. Even if your message is delivered by hand or in an envelope, don't visualize your reader as putting her feet up on the desk and perusing it in a relaxed, contemplative manner. Few people have those moments at work anymore. Visualize an overburdened, stressed executive who needs to solve problems and find answers. Write to that person.

Make what's in it for the reader loud and clear. Apply all the principles of economy—short, immediately understood words (mostly one and two syllables), short sentences (14 to 18 words on average) and short paragraphs (three or four sentences on average). Express one idea per paragraph.

Write in a conversational tone, but more carefully and formally than e-mail. Pay more attention to grammar. This may move your writing toward a more stilted pattern. Counter this by simplifying the language and thinking of concise ways to phrase your message. Pay special attention to good sentence rhythm, alternating long and short sentences.

Consider relationship-building. Adopt a "you" orientation. Build in respect and courtesy. This isn't always easy. Figuring out how to frame some messages courteously can take effort. When a client, for example, has repeatedly ignored your request for a conversation, focus on your most important goal: You want the information, sure, but you want to keep the client. So don't allow annoyance to creep into your tone.

VIEW FROM THE FIELD: TONE IS CRITICAL WITH CLIENTS

Many people I supervise use the wrong tone when they write to clients. If a client owes you a response, that's never an excuse for an e-mail that sounds like you are barking orders. Start off requests with the magic word, *please*; end any request with *thank you*; and always indicate that you are prepared to help facilitate whatever response you need. If an e-mail to a client on any topic sounds like something a parent would say to a child, a drill sergeant would say to a new recruit or your boss would say to you—rewrite it.

—Arik Ben-Zvi, managing director of the Glover Park Group, communication strategists

Create letters that look well thought out and constructed. This means logical organization, painstaking editing and attention to the visual—neat, clean documents with enough white space, a readable font in at least 10 point, graphic balance. Letters must feel personal. Even if you're sending out a mass-audience letter to 100 employers, for example, address each one individually.

Always write to a person. Always know who you're writing to. It's off-putting to a human resources director to be addressed by his job title, for example, or his predecessor's name. If you write a letter that begins "Dear CEO" or "Dear Psychology Department," you're less likely to receive an answer. Almost always, a little research will give you the name—you can call the organization and ask.

Engage the reader quickly, tell her why she should care, and maintain focus. It's up to you to do the matchmaking between the other person's perspective and what you want. Throughout, use words that tell readers what to especially notice—for example, "the main idea," "more important to consider," "my most significant qualification" and so on.

End with an appropriate call to action. Do you want an appointment? A reference? A connection? Say so clearly but considerately. "I look forward to hearing whether I may make an appointment soon" rather than "I'll be in your vicinity Thursday at 2 p.m.—please confirm."

The guidelines we followed in earlier chapters for determining your goal, audience, tone, structure and content will see you through every letter, no matter how challenging. They apply to "cold call" letters and even direct mail, but I'll demonstrate with your most probable needs.

VIEW FROM THE FIELD: LETTER-WRITING TIPS FROM AN EXPERT

1. Always start by putting the reader in the picture. So much material begins with *I*, and that's not nearly as effective as finding a way to start with *you*. For example, rather than saying, "I appreciated your taking the time to speak with me," say, "Your taking the time to speak with me is appreciated" or "Thank you for taking the time to speak with me." "You will see my schedule attached" is better than "I'm attaching . . . " and "Your presentation was excellent" is better than "I enjoyed your presentation very much." This approach may mean using the passive voice, which you're told generally to avoid, but it gives you a better opening. You can use *I* and avoid the passive in the rest of the letter.

2. Don't use all the jargon that makes so much writing meaningless. "Feel free to call me" says nothing—of course the person feels free to call you. "As per your instructions" is so stilted; "as we discussed" is better. Don't say "Call me at your earliest convenience." It's never convenient. Be specific: "Please let me know by December 15."

3. Take care not to sound condescending. When we reviewed letters written at an urban housing agency, we often saw language like "We will not tolerate people sneaking into the facility." There's never a reason to write like that. It's better to sandwich a negative between two positive statements. For example, "We're pleased to count you as a tenant. Please note that the recreation facility is not open after 10:00 p.m. Thank you for keeping this in mind."

—Carol C. Weeks, corporate training specialist

Format: Keep It Simple but Classic

Sometimes it's a good idea to make a letter look like a letter, e-mailed or not. A formal-style cover letter for a job application or proposal, for example, represents your interest better and signals your seriousness. In such cases imitate the classic letter format as seems reasonable for the occasion.

If you're writing a "real" letter that will be delivered physically, or one that can appropriately be sent as an attachment, use letterhead or build a serviceable one for yourself. Include your name, address and contact information. It doesn't have to be fancy and should not employ an obscure typeface that other people's systems may not recognize. Note that hiring managers prefer receiving application materials in Word rather than a PDF, because Word documents are more easily scanned. For the sake of personal branding, if you're applying for a job, the letterhead and résumé heading should match.

If you choose not to use letterhead, then type in your name and address at the top, flush left.

If the e-mail itself is the cover letter, rather than serving as a cover note for an attached cover letter, it's more natural to put the appropriate contact information under your signature. An exception is any message where reaching you is critical—as in a media release. Then put your contact information first.

Start the rest of the document with the date, flush left. Skip a few lines, and put in the full name, company and address of the person to whom you're writing. Skip a few more lines and write your salutation, generally "Dear Ms. X" or "Dear Jane," ending with a colon or comma.

Skip a few lines, and start your message in block paragraphs, flush left. Single space the body copy, but skip a line between paragraphs rather than indenting.

When your message is complete, sign off—with, for example, "Sincerely." Under the signature space, put your name and contact information (if the letterhead didn't take care of that) and/or social media information and direct phone line. If you're writing on behalf of an organization, under the signature space type your name, your title, the company name and suitable contact information.

That's about it. When you're done, if you are printing the letter out, take a minute to center it on the page vertically so it looks balanced. Even if you're sending it electronically, it's good to know your message will print out well should the reader do so. If it's a long message, begin page 2 of a print version with a line that says something like "Mr. Bob White/ August 3, 2012/page 2." Use boldface to set it off. The heading ensures the continuation won't get separated and lost.

If additional material is enclosed or attached, say so at the bottom of the page: "Enclosed: Résumé, three work samples."

The major exception to the style described here is when creative license is called for. Note the solicitation letters that many savvy charitable causes send out these days. They use color, pull quotes, "handwritten" messages in the margins, subheads, images and whatever else they can come up with to engage attention and entice us to read at least part of the message.

You can take a similar tack in a low-key way to ensure that those who skim business letters before investing real time in them—which is just about everybody today—are pulled along and absorb the most important points. Your tools include subheads, bold lead-ins, numbered and bulleted lists of key points, summaries, pull quotes.

Use your judgment about deploying graphic techniques. A job application letter should be conservative (unless you're trying to demonstrate creativity); a sales letter, on the other hand, needs to capitalize on techniques that attract and direct attention. If your message is lengthy and essentially a report or proposal, at least work in headings so readers can identify what's important.

In general, keep letters to one page. When you suspect a letter may be viewed as an integral part of an application, consider sending it as an attachment and write the e-mail itself as a brief cover note:

Dear Ms. Smith,

I am pleased to present my materials in application for the Lab Assistant position advertised in Jobs Inc.

Thank you for reviewing my qualifications.

Sincerely, Tom Brown

We can't cover every type of letter you may need to write, so let's practice the thinking-through process with some useful examples.

Some Frenchman—possibly Montaigne—says: I never think except when
I sit down to write.

—Edgar Allan Poe

CRAFT LETTERS FOR SPECIFIC SITUATIONS

Thank-You-Very-Much Notes

We haven't lost romance in the digital age, but we may be neglecting it. In doing so,
antiquated art forms are taking on new importance. The power of a handwritten
letter is greater than ever. It's personal and deliberate and means more than an e-mail
or text ever will.

—Ashton Kutcher, actor

Good thank-you letters are hard to write. Just ask a communications specialist who works for a nonprofit. Coming up with credible ways to say "thanks for giving" is a constant challenge, especially since important donors give periodically and gratitude must be expressed differently each time. But every organization knows that future contributions depend on effective thank-you letters.

Thank-you messages are equally important to you. They're in order when someone interviews you for a job, introduces you virtually, suggests a good contact, recommends you—and in a host of other situations where an in-person or telephone thank-you is insufficient or impractical.

To work out the characteristics of a good written thank-you, consider what you'd like to receive from a charitable cause to which you contributed. No doubt, you'd prefer it to be

- sincere: conveying a genuine sense of appreciation;

- personal: appearing to be addressed to you, not a mass audience;

- specific: describing how your contribution will help the cause;

- timely: reinforcing your good deed quickly.

Suppose you've asked friends and relatives to contribute to a cause close to your heart, a library in a Nicaraguan village. What could you write to thank those who made a donation? Here's one approach, which I'll also use to demonstrate the basic format previously outlined.

Does the letter come across as sincere, personal and specific? Would you write it differently? Always consider the other person's perspective and think about how you'd feel receiving the message.

Jacob Slater
135 Rodeway Place
Washington, D.C. 01234
202-123-5678

November 14, 2015

Mr. Joe Constant
246 River Road
Washington, D.C. 10235

Dear Joe:

Thank you so very much for your contribution to Library Build. Your support for a cause I believe in so deeply means a lot to me.

As you know, when I visited Nicaragua as part of a student group last year, I was struck by how happy the children were—and adults, too—with the few Spanish books we had thought to bring. We wished we'd brought more.

Now your contribution is helping us do that. We're collecting books right now, and a group of us will travel to the village of Perdita in the spring to set up a small library.

So, Joe, from all the people of Perdita, and from me, thank you for your generosity. I look forward to sharing pictures of the new library with you soon.

Sincerely, Jake

Jacob Slater
Volunteer Director
Books for Perdita

Don't overlook the advantage of creating handwritten thank-you notes for many situations. They come across as much more personal and appreciative. Notice how often people post them in their offices, which gives them extraordinary staying power and reach, too. Here's a real example of a handwritten note acknowledging a donor on a similar occasion. It is much more informal but no less sincere in spirit, pleasing the recipient so much he reproduced it on his popular blog:

Navid—

You are AWESOME! We are so grateful for your classroom donation. We are blown away by your generosity. Thank you for helping us change many lives in Kenya. We cannot wait to show you the classroom.

Thank you,

World Teacher Aid

Which tone is "better"? It depends. Are you writing to your boss at work? A friend? An anonymous donor or someone you've never met and know little about? The first letter is probably more in line when you don't know the person or are unsure how she will react. If you're writing to a classmate or colleague with whom you're comfortable, the second style might feel natural. Use the visualizing technique described in Chapter 2 to mentally put yourself in the person's presence, and you will intuitively know what kind of message will be best received.

If you're writing an interview thank-you, the more formal tone is called for by nature of the relationship and the organization. But thanking someone at an online startup who wore jeans when interviewing you suggests a much less formal style. Is a handwritten note a good idea if you're looking for a law firm or Wall Street job? Carefully done, it might be. Someone I know beat out the competition for a top-level job by delivering handwritten thank-you notes to every member of the company's board who had been present at her interview.

As a rule of thumb, think of it the same way you decide how to dress for an interview, presentation or other spotlight situation: Aim for one degree of formality above what you expect your listeners or interviewers to wear. If you're pretty sure an interviewer will wear blue jeans, you would probably opt for neat pants but not a suit. Write thank-you and other business messages in ways that personalize the interaction but with a conservative tilt. Even the blue-jeans startup people may want to know you can handle yourself with their relatively conservative clients.

VIEW FROM THE FIELD: WHY SAYING "THANK YOU" MATTERS

A number of studies show that thanking people makes us feel good and improves relationships. But recently a pair of psychologists (Adam M. Grant and Francesca Gino) studied the effects on individuals who are being thanked. Interestingly for us, the example they chose was to ask people to help a fictitious student named Eric with a job application cover letter. Half the people got an e-mailed thank-you back.

When Eric then asked for more help, 66% of the thanked people agreed to give it, while just 32% of those who had not been thanked were willing. The investigators followed up by sending an e-mail from a second invented student, Steven, asking for similar help. Among the group whom Eric had failed to thank, 25% offered to help Steven; by contrast, 55% of the group that had been thanked were willing.

The lesson: Expressing appreciation not only rewards you with more help should you need it, but contributes to how people respond to others asking for help in the future.

—From "A Little Thanks Goes a
Long Way: Explaining Why Gratitude
Expressions Motivate Prosocial Behavior,"
Journal of Personality and Social Psychology

The same principle of expressing appreciation applies to many office and networking situations. If someone you work with does you a favor or helps you look good, if a subordinate goes to extra lengths so you can meet that deadline, or if a supervisor gives you a special opportunity or a client refers you to a prospect, it's smart to say thank you. And a written message tends to resonate even more than a spoken one.

Be sure to make your response timely. In fact, if someone connects you with a person you want to meet, it's best to thank the go-between before the meeting happens. You owe appreciation whether the event goes well or not. It's a good idea to write again to report on the meeting itself—or telephone. Better yet, take your matchmaker to lunch.

What if the meeting doesn't actually go well? This raises some interesting questions about what to put in writing. Here's an example. Sam virtually introduced Angela to a former employer with a job opening in Angela's field. After the meeting, Angela wrote:

Dear Sam—Thanks so much for making it possible for me to meet with Mark White. I saw him yesterday. He was very nice to me, and the job sounds great. Unfortunately, I totally blew the interview. By the time we met at 4:00 p.m., I'd had a really bad day, and on top of that, I was unprepared for questions about the gap in my résumé from a few years back. I apologize for letting you down but no one could feel worse about it than me.

I promise to do better next time. —Angela

What do you think Angela's chances are of seeing a "next time"?

Of course, it's always awful to flub an opportunity, especially when someone else has put himself on the line by recommending you. But it happens. When it does, write yourself out of the worst scenario by focusing on your goal and desired outcome: Here you want to inform Sam that the interview wasn't perfect, sure, but you need to maintain his confidence in you. This means there's no point in telling your benefactor that you disgraced yourself and took him with you. Here's one solution:

Dear Sam—Thanks so much for making it possible for me to meet with Mark White. I saw him yesterday.

He was very nice to me and obviously thinks very highly of you. Mark generously spent more than an hour with me and gave me a very good understanding of the open position. At this point, I don't know if he considers me a good match for it, but I'll be very happy if he does.

In any case, I learned a lot about the industry from our conversation and I got some new ideas about how to position myself more effectively for the right opportunities.

So again, thanks so very much for introducing me to Mark and enabling me to have this valuable experience. —Angela

Do you think it's dishonest to send such a message?

Consider that (a) Angela can't know that Mark was as critical of her as she is of herself and (b) she's not made any false statements. The letter puts things in a way that encourages Sam to feel good about himself, which is only fair. It's clear that Angela values the experience whatever the specific outcome. While she might worry that Mark will tell Sam that she messed up, this is not likely. At worst, he's more apt to say something like "Thanks, but it wasn't a good match," so as not to insult Sam's judgment.

> *Never send a letter or a memo on the day you write it.*
> *Read it aloud the next morning—and then edit it.*
>
> —David Ogilvy, the "father of advertising"

Writing Effective Requests

Many of the ideas for writing thank-yous apply to request letters. Suppose you're Jacob Slater, who wrote the sample thank-you letter in the preceding section, and you're writing to friends and acquaintances to ask for a contribution to your personal charity. Here, too, you want to come across as sincere, personal and specific.

A good way to start is to tell readers why you're writing and why it matters—to you. Here's an example:

Dear Jean,

I'm writing to ask you to support a special cause that means a lot to me.

When I visited Nicaragua last year with my school's student aid group, I was struck by . . .

The key to a request letter is figuring out *why* the person or group should give you what you want. When you're asking, in effect, for a personal favor from people who know you, they will be motivated by their feelings for you. So tell them why your request matters to you. Of course, unlike my example, don't write the same letter to thank them if they do give.

What if you're writing to strangers? They are much less likely to respond to the same strategy. In such cases, you need to find a reason for them to care about the cause or relate to it, rather than to you. This is easier if you already believe the audience is interested in your project. For example, if they're members of a literacy or library support group, you might begin:

Dear Mr. Black,

There's a village in Nicaragua where the children have never seen a book.

When my school group visited Perdita last year, the children were awestruck to even touch the few books we brought. . . .

A $25 contribution will enable us to bring 10 books . . .

Solicitation letters from established charities are among the most sophisticated communications created today and are usually written by PR or direct mail specialists. Pay attention to the techniques they use to engage your interest and make you care. Always effective: telling a story about a single individual, preferably with a photo.

Nine-year-old Manuela is an alert and curious girl eager to learn. But she had never seen a book. When we unwrapped the four children's books we had added to our luggage at the last minute, Manuela was afraid to touch them . . .

Many letters asking for donations tap into the "giving back" sensibility that motivates many successful people. Will granting the request make them feel good about themselves or look good to other people? Will they have reason to feel satisfaction in giving to this cause? Can you offer anything they will value—like formal recognition? Of course, as covered in Chapter 6, you must also give people rational justification for contributing to a cause. People who don't know you will especially look for proof that their money will be used well by a responsible organization.

If you're writing letters for personal career purposes—like securing an appointment or a reference—the process is similar. Figure out why the reader should agree to your request using the basic what's-in-it-for-me (WIIFM) thinking process explained in Chapter 2. Go light on communicating how supremely important the favor is to you. Rather than telling readers how much you will gain from an informational interview, for example, find a reason for them to connect with you and feel positive about investing time in a worthy individual.

Writing thoughtfully and carefully is the way to do this. Edit thoroughly. In such situations, you are exactly what you write—no more, no less. People are willing to extend a helping hand to an amazing degree provided you demonstrate respect for their time, are appreciative and appear likely to reflect credit on them.

For more ideas on writing "asks," see the e-mail examples in Chapter 7. And remember that many requests are best done in person—as a negotiation. Both in interviews and on the job, aim to represent your own interests and speak up for what you need. Don't assume other people will automatically give it to you—or, on the other hand, will say no. Often they don't know what you want. It's up to you to explain why buying you that new computer, for example, will make you more efficient or that you will use an early leave time once a week for a class that teaches you a useful skill. Take the lead. Understand other people's viewpoints and find WIIFM—the benefit for them. Use writing to articulate your viewpoint and prepare for a productive conversation. Here are some specific tips from an expert, Laura Fredricks.

VIEW FROM THE FIELD: HOW TO ASK FOR WHAT YOU WANT—AND GET IT

Asking can be extremely difficult for all of us. Why? Because we want what we want and we want it now. Or, we should have what we want without asking. Or, we second-guess that we won't get it anyway, so why should we ask?

I developed a five-step process that anyone can use, especially bright, enthusiastic students who are ready to ask for something they need to enhance their careers. Recently, as I explained this process—its organization, structure and focus—to

(Continued)

(Continued)

a group of students, one young woman said, *"You mean you have to do all this work just to ask for something?"* I answered, *"Do you want to get exactly what you ask for, or do you want to leave this to chance, luck or, even worse, poor timing?"*

These five steps will get you exactly what you want IF you put time and effort into the process and do each step in this order. As an example, let's say you landed a great job and now it's time to negotiate the terms. Here are the steps to follow in the exact order:

1. Know exactly what you want, with numbers and dates.

   For example: *"I want X salary, a start of September 5th and three weeks' vacation."*
   This works a lot better than *"I want to be paid what I'm worth, start in the fall and have the maximum time you offer for vacation."*

2. Prepare the conversation.

   Write down 15 responses you think you might get and then prepare your answers to those responses. For example, someone might say to you after your ask, *"We can't do that,"* *"We've never done that before"* or *"That's what we offer for entry-level positions."* Then you can say, *"Can you explain a bit more WHY you can't do that? I'm sure we can work this out,"* *"I can appreciate that this is the first time, but let me share with you how it will really benefit you and this*

company," or *"While this may be an entry-level position, I bring to it advanced skills both personally and professionally."*

3. Deliver with confidence.

   It's time to shine, so make sure your dress is professional, your body language is convincing, your tone of voice sounds confident and your direct eye contact is strong.

4. Reiterate and clarify what you THINK you heard.

   For example, you hear, *"We have to think about giving you that salary level."* But does that tell you what the company needs to decide? No. So say, *"Thank you for sharing that with me. It would be helpful for me to know what you and the company are thinking about. I'm sure we can work this out together."* Get on the same page by clarifying what you think you heard. This way you both will be in sync and you can close your ask to your advantage.

5. Plan your next move on the spot.

   Ask for a specific time when you will follow up: *"This has been a terrific meeting. May I call you next Tuesday at 10 a.m. to continue this conversation?"*

—Laura Fredricks, CEO/founder of
The Ask and author of *The Ask for
Business, for Philanthropy, for Everyday Living*

USE MESSAGES TO NETWORK

In today's world, we connect more and more through the written word. To meet with people in person, we often ask for that opportunity in writing. Once you've begun a relationship, it's sensible to maintain and nurture it through writing. And in many cases, even ongoing work relationships may remain entirely virtual. We may never meet a collaborator or supervisor at all, other than through writing and perhaps online meetings or social media. So from a career perspective, the messages you send demand your best thinking and execution. Communicating for job opportunities and connecting with career help is serious business!

How to Ask for Informational Interviews

Suppose you want to tap your school's alumni network for advice on your career path and perhaps even some direct job leads. How to think this through?

Start with why. Your goals are clear, so think first about audience and how to answer the why question: Why might a graduate of your school take time to talk to you? Here are a few possible reasons that may help shape your content:

- Graduating from the same school gives you common ground and experiences.

- "Giving back" is a popular sentiment for many successful people.

- Asking for advice flatters and reinforces people's view of their own accomplishments, especially if they're relatively recent graduates.

- Building goodwill and networks is a lifelong endeavor for many people, so a bright, ambitious young person might prove a good contact now or in the future.

- Attracting new talent to the industry and their own organization is a priority for many business and professional leaders.

Next consideration—tone: Respectful and appreciative. You are, after all, asking for a personal favor you're unlikely to return in the foreseeable future. Communicating a positive and energetic manner helps. And, of course, so does enthusiasm.

Content: Remind the recipient of your common bond. Connect with his probable motivation to help you. Provide evidence that you are worth helping because you'll probably be successful and a person who'd be good to know.

Here are two examples that someone I know received from fellow alumni requesting informational interviews, reproduced essentially as received. Which works better?

Sample 1

Subject: White University career network

Dear Ms. Lewis:

I'm a senior at White, majoring in science and anthropology. I was hoping you could tell me a little about your job—what does an average day entail and how did you get to where you are today? Im interested in what working for a non profit is like.

Thank you and I hope to hear from you soon.—Sally

Sample 2

Subject: Requesting an informational interview

Dear Ms. Lewis,

My name is Jessica, and I too graduated from White. I obtained your name and contact information from the university's Career Network.

I am writing to request an informational interview. I am very interested in pursuing a career in high-level research and analysis—I hope on an international level. As a result, I would very much like to learn more about the work you do for FLU and your prior professional experiences.

Just to let you know a little bit about myself: While working on my degree, I was president of the International Club and active with the Speaker Committee. I spent a full year as an undergraduate in Dubai and interned at the National Association for Freedom.

I am eager to utilize my international background, and as I am brand-new to this career path, any advice will be greatly appreciated.

I will be in your area on Thursday and Friday, July 27 and 28. If you are available either of these days and willing to meet with me for 15 minutes, I will be most grateful.

Thank you for your time, and I hope to speak with you soon.

Sincerely, Jessica

Which e-mail would you probably respond to? If you agree that Jessica's e-mail is better than Sally's, think about why.

To begin with, Sally didn't trouble to carefully draft or proofread what she wrote. It comes across as off the top of her head and a bit illiterate, suggesting she is (a) not so smart, (b) not respectful, (c) not really appreciative or (d) all of the above. Further, her note is very unspecific, so it's hard to understand what she wants to know. Her message shows that she didn't trouble to make a good match between herself and her hoped-for information source.

Jessica, on the other hand, thought the connection through and clearly related Ms. Lewis's experience to her own goals. Her advance gratitude is expressly stated, and a few significant details about her background are referenced. Her request is brief but specific in regard to what she asks for and why she merits the time.

The result: Jessica sounds like a winner—someone who'd be interesting to talk to for 15 minutes, by phone if not in person—and worth the investment. You would assume she'd present well to any contact you refer her to.

All this achieved by a solid, planned-out message that says the person did her homework and knows how to interact? Absolutely.

Use Strategies That Build Your Connections

Should you always write a thank-you to the person who talked to you about your future for 20 minutes, or referred you to a colleague? Well, only if you're seriously interested in your career. Earlier in this chapter we analyzed how to express appreciation. Let's look now at how applying this thought process helps you stand out in an impersonal world.

VIEW FROM THE FIELD: TO BUILD YOUR CAREER, NETWORK!

Networking is one of the most important skills to develop, and it builds both your business and social skills. Many people struggle with networking, so now is the time to work on it. Remember, only 12%–14% of hires come from job boards and most openings are not advertised. Even if you don't see the necessity now, there may come a time when you need help, and having a network already in place will be a lifesaver. Building a network takes time and patience.

1. Work at growing your contacts. Attend industry events or volunteer at industry associations. Don't just rely on social media connections. Get out, invest the time and meet new people.

2. Don't stop connecting. Maybe you started to network at job fairs and events, and that's smart, but don't stop just because you find a job. Keep your contacts current and growing. Make sure you are active in your Alumni Association and let everyone know what you're up to. You don't have to interact every week, but do so at least twice a year.

3. Be brave. Don't be afraid of people. Networking with only people in your age/skill group is not necessarily helpful. You want to meet people of different ages with different skills and backgrounds. You never know who will help you.

4. Be yourself. If you are natural and comfortable around people, they will be that way with you. You can't force any type of friendship—just let it happen.

5. Follow up. It's great to have business cards, but they are only a start. To turn an acquaintance into part of your network, engage them. Talk with them, ask questions and then follow up by note, phone or e-mail.

—Marie Raperto, owner of Cantor Integrated Marketing Staffing Inc.

If someone helps you or invests time in you, make it a practice to let her know you are grateful, in writing. Do so even if you didn't like the advice or it proved irrelevant.

Use the same strategies to connect with people you meet in many situations—the woman you sit next to on an airplane, the man who mentions a colleague you should meet, someone you meet at a conference or workshop. Savvy networkers routinely follow up by figuring out how to provide a small bit of value to another person they'd like to know better. For example:

> *Hi Jed—I really enjoyed talking with you at the TGF meeting on Tuesday. You mentioned that you'll be traveling to New Zealand soon, so I'm attaching a great article I just ran across. It suggests a bunch of things to see there that are below the general radar.*
>
> *Happy travels—I'd love to hear how the trip turns out!*
>
> *Best, Nate*

You might, as appropriate, send someone a lead to a job, a virtual introduction to a colleague or friend if both parties may benefit, the name of a special restaurant for an upcoming celebration she mentioned—such strategies take just a little time, memory and imagination. FYI, professional fundraisers, salespeople and other serious networkers take systematic notes after meeting every valuable person. Many make it a practice to talk with everyone in every situation. One top sales coach I know rarely leaves a checkout line or airport queue without a new lead to follow up.

If the idea of telling strangers what you do (or want to do) is daunting, practice your elevator speech, explained in Chapter 11. This prepares you to take advantage of opportunities more comfortably. But don't feel compelled to talk to strangers—unless you're at a conference, meeting or other venue related to your industry of choice. In such cases, regard everyone as a potential friend and contact.

People who practice the connection habit often maintain contacts years later by writing thoughtful, planned e-mails that trigger positive memories and responses.

Social media offers amazing ways to initiate, maintain and revive business contacts. As noted in Chapter 10, the access to VIPs and influencers is a remarkable gift of online communication. And maintaining contact with former coworkers and supervisors via your medium of choice is plain smart. But your messages must be just as carefully crafted based on good thinking and writing practice. Be sure you choose channels appropriate to each person. Adapt the techniques presented here to social media style and platforms.

Practice Job Application Courtesies

Should you always write notes to follow up a job interview? Yes. Unless you're explicitly told "no thank-you notes"—seldom the case—give yourself the edge that courtesy and a well-written letter can produce. Accept that every job you deeply want is intensely competitive. The employer is deluged with excellent résumés, good cover letters, confident interviewees with good answers and high motivation. The decision maker's challenge: who to gamble on. If she chooses someone whose performance disappoints, or proves a poor personality fit, the work suffers. Unpleasant interactions follow, and the time-killing hire process starts all over again. So what tips the balance? More often than you might suspect, the follow-up letter.

Suppose you've just been interviewed by the assistant manager of a large multinational for a spot in the marketing department. This thank-you letter is more complicated to create than those we've been talking about and should be based on the structure we've practiced with e-mails. Here's how it might work.

Your goal: To advance your candidacy for a competitive job.

Your audience: An individual you spent time with and observed—so you know something about personality, communication style, company status and so on. That's all relevant, *but*—because this is a structured interaction between a prospective employer's representative and you, a candidate—plan further this way:

Your writing tone: Formal and businesslike. And just as for a charity's thank-you, the letter must feel sincere.

Content: What will work? Express appreciation for the interview, show enthusiasm for the job, indicate that you understand the skills needed *and* support your candidacy with additional information or evidence of your qualifications.

A simple structure works:

- a paragraph expressing appreciation, enthusiasm and confidence in your ability to perform

- new information about you

- a good close confirming your availability for further interviews or to start the job

To fill this out, draw on your personal impressions: Replay the conversation, visualize the person and figure out ways to distinguish yourself that the interviewer, and/or the company, will value. It's also the time to think through any points in your favor that you forgot to make in person or that occur to you in post-analysis, now that you know the job better. Did you have a smack-your-head moment after the interview because you failed to make a point in your favor? Did you miss any opportunity to provide an important piece of information? Can you figure out a relevant "side skill" you didn't think to mention? Did a qualification occur to you as especially important to doing the job well? This is your chance to say it.

Here's a simple example.

Dear Ms. Royal:

Thank you so much for speaking with me Thursday about the Marketing Associate position at Brandon. I enjoyed our conversation and appreciate your taking the time to tell me about the company and the job.

Your description of the role convinced me more than ever that it is the right opportunity for me and that my background is an excellent fit with your needs. Thanks to my three years of experience with Malibu Inc., I'll bring a solid grounding in retail marketing practice backed by my course work in White University's MBA Program.

I'd also like to share that over the past five years, I've found additional opportunities to build the communications skills that are so important to this job. I serve as managing editor of White's Management Department newsletter, which has helped me advance my writing skills, and I've been active in Toastmasters International for two years. Recently, I helped the debating club team I belong to win a regional competition.

Again, thank you for encouraging my application, and I look forward to the next step.

Sincerely,

You've no doubt written letters like this already and won't be surprised that even a straightforward one takes plenty of time and thought. I won't lie to you: It doesn't get easier. The more advanced your credentials or experience, the more difficult these letters are to write—and the more important. If you're applying for a creative job, you must really work to show off your originality. But stockpile pieces that feel well articulated to draw on for future occasions.

Writing a Rejection Message

If you haven't yet been in the position of having to write a rejection letter, you may not believe it, but these are famously tough to write, too. To illustrate how to apply the principles you're learning to unfamiliar challenges, let's try it out on a rejection message.

Suppose you're in charge of the internship program at your organization and must tell several candidates that the decision has gone against them. Your goal is a letter that considers their feelings but unequivocally delivers the bad news. This is important: Beyond the fact that any rejection process deserves care—we've all been on that receiving end and the experience stays with us—maintaining the candidate's goodwill toward the company is important.

Delivering the bad news immediately is almost always the best tack, so finding a lead is not hard:

Dear _____:

Your interest in working as an intern for the Ivy Company this summer is greatly appreciated. Unfortunately, we will not be able to offer you a place.

The hard part comes next: What reason can you give? Brainstorm the possibilities. Here are a few:

We had a large number of outstanding candidates this year and had to make a tough decision.

More than 100 people applied and we have room for only three.

We needed to coordinate different skill sets to build a balanced team.

We recognize that you are highly qualified, but other candidates had specific experience that applies to the role.

If any of these rationales strikes echoes, it's because colleges as well as businesses use similar terminology—and not lightly: How to word rejection letters can keep admissions officers up at night, and the results don't always succeed in spreading goodwill.

When you're writing to a particular person in a business context, rather than to thousands of people, brainstorm for ways to soften the blow or even to be directly helpful. Such an element enables you to maintain good feelings and, in practical terms, gives you a good closing. Here are a few examples:

We invite you to apply again next summer.

We'd be happy to talk with you when you graduate should a full-time position be open.

I suggest you talk to Mr. X at Y Company, which has a larger summer associate program than ours.

If it's not appropriate or honest to say any of these things, and you can't come up with an alternative, then you might close with simply a "good luck" statement.

WRITING TO FIX BUSINESS PROBLEMS

In today's business environment, well-written messages are critical to maintaining good relationships with clients, customers, vendors, collaborators, investors and more. In the past this goal was often accomplished person to person: We established trust face to face, learned how to use a product from the salesperson, negotiated a pricing disagreement over lunch, explained a need in conversation. But now the impersonality of many transactions produces more questions, dissatisfactions and complaints. In many situations we depend on writing to solve the problems.

Because these messages are typically delivered electronically, digital media's "spontaneity" often misleads writers to overlook their ultimate goals: securing both immediate and long-range results. Often they undermine their own objectives by writing thoughtless messages that yield unintended consequences. When you're the writer, constantly remind yourself that the *relationship* comes first. Framing the message more formally as a letter helps, even though you may choose a spontaneous-sounding style.

Fielding a Supplier Challenge

Failure to consider tone is often the culprit in business messages that go wrong. For example, suppose you head a department and learn that a supplier has been overcharging for fabrications. It's your job to rectify this, and the problem needs to be resolved in writing.

Your audience: Bob Brown, your contact at the supplier. What you know: Bob has been pleasant to deal with for seven years. The relationship is cordial but not personal. Until now, Bob's firm has been reliable, provided good-quality products at reasonable prices and accommodated you in difficult scheduling situations.

Your goal: You want the error acknowledged and restitution made. The options you see:

1. Fire the supplier immediately—maybe even sue for the overcharge and perhaps damages.

2. Let Bob know you're angry and demand an apology as well as restitution.

But does either route serve your interest and keep the supply chain going economically, reliably and efficiently? If you follow Option 1, you instantly embark on the search for an equivalent supplier and must build a new relationship. An untested supplier carries risk, and the effort will be time-consuming.

Option 2 is tempting: It's always nice to vent—but rarely productive. And it's possibly unfair. You don't know whether the error was deliberate or a billing mistake. Is there an Option 3? Of course. Once you move past the sense of personal betrayal, you can consider another option:

3. Ensure that the error is acknowledged and rectified, and you are never overcharged in the future. And allow room to reestablish trust and maintain the productive working relationship.

The takeaway: Resist taking a short-term perspective on your goal. In this case, getting the job done, once the error is rectified, matters more than instant personal satisfaction. Look at business situations dispassionately to determine what's important. Often, you'll find it better to give people the benefit of the doubt, or a break. Chances that you're confronting a genuine mistake are at least equal to assuming Bob deliberately cheated you.

Your tone: The occasion calls for fairly formal business style with a no-nonsense, nonjudgmental, very matter-of-fact tone.

Structuring the message: The principles we've established tell us to lead with strength and immediately engage the reader with the subject, organize our points in the simplest way and end with a confirmation or call to action. Here's one way to handle the message:

Dear Bob:

I've learned that your invoice #5742A of July 7 is in error.

The price of #12 fabrications is calculated at $34 per thousand. However, the correct price according to our most recent contract is $31. Thus, on our order for 3,000 boxes, it appears we've been billed $9,000 too much.

Of course, we'd like this corrected immediately. Please confirm that you'll send a corrected invoice.

Acme and Ideal have been working together a long time, Bob, and I hope this matter can be quickly resolved so we can continue to do so collegially.

Sincerely, Joan

Responding to Complaints

The great majority of messages that companies receive from the public are complaints about a product or service. Prior to the last decade or two, many complaints were ignored, but the digital age is putting an end to such carelessness. More and more goods and services are now purchased online, and this escalate customer correspondence—questions and complaints. Today's consumer is instantly able to reach the offending organization and/or voice her dissatisfaction via online channels potentially reaching millions. Accordingly, many well-run organizations employ staff to monitor negative reviews and comments and respond effectively.

If you're in business for yourself or are charged with this work by an employer, always see such messages as letters. Use the full planning structure to articulate the goal, consider the audience, build content and adopt the appropriate tone. Craft your writing and edit carefully—this demonstrates respect. Take a critical look at the messages you receive yourself when follow-up service from an online vendor is necessary. How does a supplier respond when you complain about receiving the wrong order, are disappointed in the product, need help negotiating the return process, object to a policy or report a problem with telephone assistance? Sometimes such challenges are handled well, but all too often they are not. The cost: offended customers who don't come back and, worse, may leverage the digital world to vent their frustration.

So important to remember: How will this message make my reader—also known as my customer—*feel?* The emotional response your message generates may have an impact well beyond the actual problem and create far more serious problems.

Collecting Money Due

Another situation, often encountered by independent workers, is trouble collecting money owed. Even happy clients cause such grief. Sometimes it's through carelessness, or a policy of "aging" bills, and sometimes it's because gratitude for a job well done fades quickly when the bill comes. Assume you've finished a freelance assignment and it was accepted, but the check isn't in the mail and hasn't been for two months. Start by assuming the reason is benign. You want to maintain the client. So you might write short and sweet:

Hi Penny—

A friendly reminder about the invoice I sent you on June 20th. Can I expect a check ASAP? It will be appreciated.

Thanks—Julie

It's seldom helpful to say how badly you need the money or how disappointed you are at the lateness. An impersonal tone is best. But another month goes by and you are more seriously inconvenienced and annoyed. Maintain your cool with a more formal, distancing approach:

Dear Penny,

My accountant called to my attention the outstanding invoice in the amount of $2,750 owed to my service by your company. Can you jog the machinery so this is taken care of immediately? The work was completed April 28th and I supplied the invoice on May 2nd. Please let me know right away.

Thank you, Julie

What if you are still not paid? At this point you care a lot less about continuing a relationship that looks counterproductive. Time to get really formal. A good technique is the "history" approach:

Dear Ms. Blank:

On January 17th, you engaged my company, Navel Training Inc., to design and present three customer service training programs for your staff in Baltimore and Boston. The signed contract is attached.

We consulted with you in person on three occasions, designed the programs and revised them to meet your new specifications, and created print and online materials to accompany the training.

On March 1st you officially approved the plan and materials. Your signed letter is attached.

On March 15, 17 and 20 we trained a total of 90 employees in four locations. The reviews were excellent (attached). You stated on site that you were "delighted with results" and sent a letter of appreciation, attached.

. . .

The total amount due immediately is _____. Please remit so we need not charge interest, per the contract (attached).

A letter like this may work because of its formality and legal overtones. It sounds like you might have consulted a lawyer—or, at least, that you are ready to take the next step and have a good case.

Writing contracts is beyond this book's scope, but experienced independent contractors protect themselves with written signed agreements that spell out each party's responsibilities—including prompt payment at specified intervals. Asking for an advance deposit is always smart, and so is specifying interest charges for late payment. Even buddies have been known to renege on agreements, so act in a businesslike way in the "safe not sorry" mode.

THE INTERNATONAL DIMENSION OF BUSINESS WRITING

English is today's language of business across the world. It's also the language used by scientists and other professionals everywhere to collaborate and communicate, and the language used for teaching at a growing number of universities. However, this does not mean that people in other countries think like native English speakers or interpret written messages the same way.

Digital communication is the most common medium internationally, and its ease of use further obscures our awareness of cultural differences. This can be a problem in communicating across borders. Even in its more formal moments, American English style feels brusque and discourteous to many people whose primary language is not English. In some countries more than others, many businesspeople have become accustomed to this style and overlook it, even adopting it to some degree as their own.

But it's good to be cautious: When writing to someone whose native language is not English, adopt a more formal style that is scrupulously polite and considerate. Be aware of other countries' individual cultural norms—for example, whether requests are best made directly or indirectly and whether it's preferable to open with small talk (e.g., Japan, but not on a personal level) or avoid it totally (e.g., Russia). *People are offended by different things according to their culture.*

Online help like Google Translate (https://translate.google.com/) is getting better. But when you draft an important e-mail message to someone overseas—as part of a job application or to introduce a business arrangement, for example—try to consult with a native speaker of the language in the specific country. Spanish has many varieties, for example, depending on location.

Here are some tips to start your thinking:

- Know which salutations and sign-offs are expected. They are often not intuitive and may result from ancient traditions (e.g., in France).

- Know how to address people. In many countries, formal titles are required, and some (e.g., Germany) demand full respect for all their formal education and other qualifications.

- Use short, common words that do not have more than one meaning.

- Build with short, declarative sentences; avoid long, complex multiclause statements.

- Spell things out rather than use contractions—"I will visit" rather than "I'll visit."

- Eliminate jargon—especially sports-based—and clichés that may puzzle people from different cultures.

- Use lists when appropriate.

- Phrase everything as straightforwardly as you can.

- Avoid passive structures. Write as much as possible in present and simple past tense.

- Minimize use of wordy structures that depend on words like *get* and *have*.

- Avoid piling up long strings of nouns.

- Skip the humor, sarcasm and irony that can confuse nonnative speakers.

- Pay attention to graphic effect. Write with short paragraphs, and build in white space.

Overall, write simply and more formally, though *not in ways that sound unnatural in ordinary English.* This will prevent you from insulting fluent English speakers by appearing to talk down to them. Will messages feel more stark and perhaps less colorful when you strip them of so much color and personality? Will they be less interesting? Probably. But what you gain in comprehension and response is worth the price.

It's hard work to read a business message in a language when your fluency is limited. But it's a hundred times harder to answer in a relatively unfamiliar language. Some experienced businesspeople write in English but invite recipients to respond in their own preferred language. Then someone who speaks that language can easily translate. This facilitates the exchange and ensures better mutual understanding. Again, you can use online translation in both directions, but when the matter is important, a knowledgeable eye is better.

Internationalizing business English is a huge if surprisingly unacknowledged need in today's workplace and that of tomorrow. The emerging workforce in the United States and everywhere else is increasingly global. It's an unusual enterprise of any size that does not prominently include people whose native language is different from our own. Write with this awareness.

PRACTICE OPPORTUNITIES

I. Request an Informational Interview: Write and Review

1. Write an e-mail requesting telephone or in-person time with a friend's relative (or someone else) who works in your chosen career, to ask for advice and possible job leads.

2. Exchange your draft with a classmate for review and editing. Discuss results with each other, and revise if you agree with the suggestions.

3. Expect to be evaluated on both the quality of your own e-mail and the quality of written input you provide to your classmate.

II. Ask for a Special Favor

Write to a specific person to ask for a reference, connect you with someone she knows or request a special assignment on the job. Then assume your request is granted, and write her a thank-you note.

III. Respond to Rejection

You've applied for an associate job you wanted, at a company where you hoped to find a foothold, and just received a rejection letter. You're very disappointed but know it would be smart to send a response, because you're planning to try for a full-time job there after completing your degree. Write a complete letter.

IV. Write a Rejection Letter

You're called on to write a rejection letter to internship candidates. What can you add to the list presented earlier in this chapter of possible reasons for rejecting those not chosen? Do you see more ways to soften the blow? Draft a complete letter rejecting an internship candidate. Produce a cohesive, thoughtful message with an effective closing statement. Try for a letter that would make you feel as good as possible if you were on the receiving end.

V. Group Discussion: What Makes a Good Rejection?

What's the best rejection letter you ever got? What made it good? And what was the worst one? Where did it go wrong, and how did it make you feel?

VI. Manage a Client

You're an accountant. A client has provided a carton of information, and after sorting through it for hours, you find it doesn't contain some of the major items you asked for: tax returns for the past three years, documentation about technology expenses, correspondence with the IRS about tax shortfalls. Write a letter to the client requesting these materials within three days.

VII. Draft a Letter About Writing Letters

Your department head has noticed that some embarrassing letters are going out to clients and prospects and wants to assemble a short how-to guide for everyone's reference. She's asked for staff input on guidelines to include. Consider what you've learned in this chapter and the preceding ones, and draft a letter presenting your best advice. Use graphic techniques to make your message clear and readable.

VIII. Write a Letter of Complaint

Were you disappointed recently in a product or service you bought? Or did someone you know have that experience? Write a letter to the company using this chapter's techniques to resolve the problem to your highest satisfaction. Then take the company's probable perspective and write a letter in response to the complaint.

IX. Write a Meaningful Letter of Appreciation

Think of someone who has had a real impact on your life in any way, at any point: a teacher, parent or other relative, friend, employer, stranger. Write a true, sincere, detailed letter to that person expressing your appreciation and how he or she has influenced you. If practical, consider sending the letter. We all too seldom say thank you on this level, in person or in writing. Note that every teacher who receives even a short note treasures it forever. And even well-loved teachers receive few of them.

X. Write a Message to an International Audience

Select a letter e-mail or other message you've written—or received—and review it from the viewpoint of someone with limited English proficiency. What idioms, abbreviations, contractions or wording might such a reader have trouble understanding? How would you rewrite the message? If you can't identify a message that suits this exercise, create one for a student coming from another country to attend your program. Describe the academic program, how to find social opportunities or other aspects of the experience you can share.

9 | CREATING STRONG BUSINESS DOCUMENTS

Nothing is particularly hard if you divide it into small parts.

—Henry Ford

Your everyday writing enables you to demonstrate your professionalism and open doors. Of course, you also need to know how to handle opportunities once they're in hand. Among your likely challenges are creating contemporary versions of traditional long-form documents such as reports, proposals, presentations and business plans.

Whether you work most immediately for yourself, or a company, nonprofit, professional enterprise or government agency, you'll probably need to handle at least some of these formats well. The techniques are useful even when you occupy an entry-level job and are not yet responsible for exercising these skills formally. They are relevant when you want to demonstrate readiness for an assignment, value to a team and willingness to go above and beyond.

As you move up, information-sharing materials like reports and proposals may become make-or-break opportunities, whatever the industry. They can earn you in-house support for your projects and win outside contracts or funding when that's part of your role. And, because a growing number of organizations function on a project basis, you may be called on to constantly compete for assignments with proposals.

If you become an entrepreneur full or part time, good proposals are key to your success.

Knowing how to create effective business documents is an asset to carry along wherever your career migrates. Happily, the basic guidelines for everyday media like e-mail and letters work equally well for more substantial business staples, with some adaptation. Each writing challenge is different, and only a few can be explored here, but absorb the approaches and they will see you through every challenge and help you stand out.

First, I'll recap the writing style that suits long-form business documents.

LEARN HOW TO...

- Apply writing principles to business materials

- Create an Executive Summary

- Prepare project and personal reports

- Write formal and conversational proposals

- Develop grant applications

WRITING TIPS FOR BUSINESS DOCUMENTS

As different as various business formats are, as well as their subject matter, the writing style is similar for all. These guidelines, detailed in earlier chapters, are important to in-depth materials that incorporate different types of information and a lot of detail.

- Write crisp, simply constructed sentences that read fast.

- Use an objective third person tone and relatively formal language that is also accessible and clear.

- Choose short, vivid, concrete words, and avoid jargon and clichés.

- Choose action verbs rather than dull, boring ones.

- Maintain an upbeat, positive, "in charge" tone that communicates good judgment and conviction.

- Avoid hedgy words and statements (e.g., *about, we hope that, we could, probably, we'll aim to, it's possible that*).

- Write a strong lead plus informational headlines and subheads to attract and retain your target readers.

- Employ good transitions between sentences, paragraphs and sections to ensure your argument flows logically and the relevance of each part is clear.

- Check that the copy is sayable—read portions aloud or listen to your computer read them.

- Use a clear call to action as appropriate: What should the reader do in response?

When the material is complicated or technical, some writers like to read portions to a teenager, or another "outside" person, to check that the document is easily understood and see what questions come up. *Remember that the higher most readers' level and knowledgeability, the less time and patience they have for deciphering a message.* So writing in a pretentious academic manner hurts your cause.

Expect to edit through a series of revision cycles. If your first draft (or two) is too long, as it probably will be, look for redundancies in thought and word. Cut empty phrases as well as unsubstantiated hyperbole to tighten the writing. Suspiciously eye any vagueness and boilerplate-style material that is not completely customized to the occasion—readers spot the one-size-fits-all approach and feel insulted. Sharpen language. Polish, polish, polish. But don't edit the life out of the material; aim to energize and enliven it.

And don't let the technical challenge of creating a major business document overshadow your message. You must know your core message—be able to state it in a sentence or two—and stick to it throughout. Everything included must support, prove or demonstrate the truth and relevance of your message.

For best results, steep yourself in your own conviction and the excitement (or need) that drove you to prepare the document. Write from inside your own commitment. But at the same time, remember that *it's not about you*. Especially for proposals, or any pitch, immerse yourself in the audience perspective. Invest in understanding your target readers and the problems they want to solve, whether you're preparing the document for your boss or a client or the public.

You cannot manipulate language to cover a lack of basic understanding, knowledge or perspective.

Logically examined, each project will suggest what to include. For a report, as an example, you might plan a long message similarly to a short one—shape a beginning (reason for the project, why the reader should care, definitions, orientation to the subject), middle (technical material, evidence, research, details) and end (a strong conclusion that brings the content and bottom-line recommendations home to the intended reader). A long document also requires a table of contents, Executive Summary, and perhaps an appendix, where you can stash the backup without distracting readers from your story line.

SUCCESS TIP

Use a folder system to jump-start big projects

When a major writing project looms, ease your path by collecting ideas, thoughts and resources in file folders, either real or virtual—or both. If you use paper folders, colorful ones are better than plain manila. You can color-code by subject. If you're working on a business proposal and your outline has 10 sections, make up 10 folders. Then, as random useful thoughts or information come to you, make notes and place them in the applicable folders.

If you allow reasonable time for the project, you end up with a batch of ideas and information for every topic. The writing feels less formidable, and good material is right at hand. The system also keeps you organized. Best of all, this simple collect-as-you-go method builds your thinking much more powerfully than if you sit down and try to create the document from scratch, all at once.

You can also use online systems to organize, such as Evernote, Scrivener or Google Docs, which facilitates sharing on collaborative projects.

CREATE REPORTS THAT WIN SUPPORT

People often underestimate the value of required reports.

If you hold a job that obliges you to submit regular accounts of your own activities or your unit's to a supervisor or client, see them as opportunities rather than rote chores. Supervisors value staff reports not only as a way to hold people accountable, but as information sources: They are often the executive's means to stay in touch with events at ground level and to communicate degree of progress (or its lack), problems at an early stage and signals that intervention is needed. Reporting well on your own work showcases your writing–thinking skills and rewards you: with recognition, help when you need it, more responsibility, more interesting assignments and, ultimately, promotion to the next level.

Many reports are platforms for decision making. If you're reporting on an initiative, whether it's a social media experiment or research into what software to buy, or you want to justify further support for a project, anticipate that what you share and how you share it will have a tangible impact on your reader's decision.

If you are part of a service business or perform research or analysis for your company's clients, your nonprofit's donors or your own enterprise, reports are how you tell your most important audiences what you've accomplished.

The following sections cover personal reports and project reports. When the reason for writing a report falls somewhere in between these two basic types, draw on the strategies that suit the case. The techniques are also helpful when you need to make a convincing case in a range of situations. For example, if you write to the boss asking for help, a good report-style statement may gain your point persuasively, even if it's only a single paragraph.

DEVELOP BIG-PICTURE PROJECT REPORTS

In creating reports, even professionals with sophisticated technical skills often fall into traps that undermine the value of their hard work. Some pitfalls:

1. Getting lost in the bog. People today don't necessarily welcome more information and data—we all feel overburdened. It's the writer's job to digest the information and develop a clear perspective based on what that audience needs to know.

2. Oversupplying process and undersupplying results, recommendations and interpretations. In most cases readers care little about what you did to obtain your data, information and results: They want to know what it means.

3. Delivering the message in a dull, non-engaging manner. You may not see a report as a source of entertainment, but readers must choose to spend time on it. Just because busy decision makers want information doesn't mean they happily slog through tons of lifeless material to find what they need and interpret it.

If you do the work well and understand the subject, rarely is a report's substance boring to you. So why bore or confuse the reader? Here are some techniques to make your reports at once more interesting, clear, readable, useful—and valued.

Find Your Story

Journalists typically start by gathering as much information as possible, then ask themselves, "What's the story?" It can be far from obvious when a lot of research is involved, and the original concept may have evolved into something quite different than the start point. The reporter's mantra applies here: *Don't bury the lead.* Identify what's important, interesting and valuable about your message to the reader; lead with it; and organize the rest of your story (or document) to support it.

To uncover the message, try telling your story to someone else. This taps into your oral instincts, bypassing the more complicated way your brain works for writing. It also gives you more direct, simple language. Or ask yourself these questions: What is this really about? What did I find? What do I believe should result from the audience reading this report?

Another route to core meaning is to frame the question your audience expects you to answer, such as: What does the evidence or analysis indicate to be the best decision? What are the alternative courses of action, and what are the risks and benefits of each?

Once you know your narrative, organize its elements into relevant sections. Highlight it in the Executive Summary, covered later in this chapter. Use it to offer a complete perspective on what's in the report, what's important, and your recommendations or conclusions. Usually, the bottom line is your most captivating lead.

View the rest of the report as evidence and backup. You can cross-reference the sections within the Executive Summary so people easily find the detail they want. But don't weigh those sections down with all your research and analysis. A report works best when relatively nontechnical readers can move through it quickly without becoming embroiled in too much data they may not understand or care about.

The bottom-line-on-top strategy works for all of a report's sections. For each part, first figure out the main import and put it in perspective. Don't slow down or interrupt the narrative flow with too many calculations. Use accessible charts, graphs, or other "evidence" to explain your points visually without challenging the reader to decipher them. Most readers care about conclusions, not process. Put any backup that slows down understanding . . . in back.

Here's a quick formula for a technical report:

Executive Summary/overview

Narrative describing goal and actions

Major findings

Interpretation of results

Recommendations/conclusions

Appendix with relevant data and detail

Note that decision makers often read just the summary and depend on accountants or tech specialists to vet the rest for problems.

Use Action Heads and Subheads

Pull readers along with action headlines and subheads that say something, rather than labels.

Instead of writing, for example,

Pension Fund Forecast

Try

Pension Funding Inches Up

Or use the label and add a headline that says something specific:

Pension Fund Forecast: 14% Rise Seen for First Quarter

This technique automatically makes the material more interesting and snags reader attention. Being more specific helps people identify the must-read pieces, too—which is good. Today's reader, trained by the Internet, is active rather than passive and decides what to read based on the clues you provide.

Use content-based headlines everywhere, including the Executive Summary. You can still use the label approach when necessary to align with company style, but amplify it meaningfully. For example:

Executive Summary: Three Routes to Funding Pensions That Meet New Legal Guidelines

VIEW FROM THE FIELD: WHY GOOD REPORTS MATTER IN INTERNATIONAL WORK

In international work, you need to communicate with people in different time zones, so writing is really the only way to do it. And a documented paper trail may be necessary. Government agencies, for example, as well as many other kinds of organizations, must include for the record why something was done.

Often reports must enable people to make good decisions, and to do it without your being present. In my work we communicate a lot verbally, but not everyone is at the meetings. Even if they were, given the amount of information flow, they won't remember everything that's said. So a coherent, clearly written document that gives people everything they need to know is essential.

Getting people to come together around a document to agree on major conclusions can, if it's concise and clear, generate the underlying decisions needed. For an internal audience, if I'm presenting research, I need the takeaway and justification for what I believe to be the case.

So writing is very important to me when I hire people. When I interview, I ask, "How would you explain this to the person who will make a decision about it? And how would you explain it to a group of curious students?" I walk them through different groups, and it's quite telling to see how people would write for different audiences.

—Alicia Phillips Mandaville, vice president for global development policy and learning at InterAction (alliance of international development and relief organizations)

WRITE SOLID PERSONAL REPORTS

Reports are universally needed because accountability matters, on every level. And as more firms scatter themselves geographically and personal contact diminishes, reports become more important. A project may come with its own communication channels, and its own protocols for sharing. When that's the case, of course follow the guidelines. But look for opportunities to incorporate some of this chapter's ideas to enliven your delivery and highlight your accomplishments.

As with a research or project report, open when possible with the big picture that gives context to the period's activities or communicates what's most important. Starting with a tight Executive Summary may work well. If the format disallows this, try drafting one anyway to find your perspective; just don't include it. Or incorporate it in your overview statement.

When you report on your activities, see it as a "what I accomplished" opportunity rather than "how I spent my time." Ask yourself all the questions about why the reader cares about the information, what it means, why it matters, what you need. Go for a proactive, upbeat tone and deliver the bottom line immediately. If you're writing about the month of January, for example, rather than beginning in a hum-drum just-doing-my-job fashion such as

This month, I continued to work on the software issues for the project I'm assigned to. Twenty hours were spent on research. I analyzed 47 possibilities. I also made some telephone calls . . .

Try something more like this—more like Warren Buffett:

I'm happy to report that I will complete my analysis of software for the Zilch Project by January 17th. Good news: We can accomplish all our goals and come in under budget. Here are some of the purchases I plan to recommend, which coordinate for efficiency . . .

If you want help on the project, add something like this at the end of the summary:

I can deliver the report a week sooner if I can get some help with . . .

Reports give you a major opportunity to demonstrate that you are a responsible, resourceful and capable individual who understands the organization and contributes to its bottom line in the best way your current job allows. Show that you're a problem solver and that you're committed to your role. This applies even to an entry-level job where your tasks don't seem very lofty. If you spent a bunch of time filing, for example, it might legitimately be reported as "organized the quarterly financial reports using adapted online software, saving two hours." Of course, what you say must be true. In fact, if you visualize how you will report on a mundane activity at month's end, you might be prompted to find a more effective way to accomplish it.

THE EXECUTIVE SUMMARY: TECHNIQUES AND OPTIONS

The Executive Summary is a critical element for many kinds of materials: business plans, proposals, white papers, reports, grant applications and more. The busier everyone gets, the more vital a role the summary plays. In many cases, it is the only part of the document your key audiences read. If they like it, they may read the rest—or take action based on the summary alone.

How to Identify Content for Reports

When you have trouble establishing perspective on what you or your department accomplished during a given time period, or aren't sure what's worth sharing, ask yourself some of these questions.

- What's important about the period's events in terms of company or department goals, immediately? Long-range?

- What has changed or progressed?

- What initiatives did I take? How did they turn out?

- What challenges or problems did I encounter? How did I solve them?

- Did I see new opportunities and act on them?

- What surprised me?

- Did anything occur that bears watching or should be taken into account in planning?

- Can I share anything thought-provoking?

- What (if appropriate) do I recommend based on recent events?

So leave plenty of time to develop this piece. Don't pull out excerpts from the full document and tack them together. Use the summary to tell a complete, self-contained story. In some cases, its role is to fully present your idea and recommend a course of action, supported by evidence. In other cases, it must convince readers that they need the information and that it's relevant to their interests.

Touch on every element of the whole document to put the pieces in context, but give center stage to what matters most to the reader. If you're writing a business plan for a new venture, focus the summary on communicating your idea vividly as well as why it matters and why it's viable. A research report summary should concisely relate what you did, why, how, basic results and perhaps next steps. A proposal summary typically identifies the problem and your solution.

Use the Executive Summary to put the whole document, and therefore your subject, in perspective. Think of it as an elevator speech for your document: It tells readers what the rest of the material means and why they should care. And aim to accomplish it all in one to two pages—rarely is a longer summary called for or welcome. The rule of thumb is to limit a summary to 5% to 10% of the full document.

VIEW FROM THE FIELD: THE EXECUTIVE SUMMARY AS INTERNAL ADVOCACY

My goal in writing an Executive Summary is generally some form of advocacy: to get my point across, to influence, to make a compelling argument that can be fully trusted. Very often your audience has limited time, so the Executive Summary needs brevity—but it should also show a solid organization and logic

in respect to a business issue. The most successful Executive Summaries are self-contained. You may get approval based on just the summary.

It's good to show your audience that you know what came before and use it for context. Don't discredit it. And it's sometimes appropriate to make one recommendation but show other possibilities. This lends credibility, and people like to have a choice.

Move with gentle guidance into key findings or data points to support the recommendation, putting the most compelling ones on top. Know your audience: If you're appealing to the CFO, you may want to arrange your data points to address return on investment, cost saving and other financial aspects. Think of your audience's core responsibilities to help you plan your arguments and prioritize what you say.

Avoid flowery language and too many superlatives. I like to use language that shows an attempt at objectivity, focusing on the facts of the situation. The Executive Summary is not the time to put your heart on your sleeve. Err on the side of formality. Decision makers expect a level of seriousness when you ask for buy-in—chummy doesn't work. And accuracy is really important: It's a first impression thing. People will focus on a typo rather than your argument.

—Lisa Cuevas Shaw, senior vice president and managing director, U.S., for Corwin, a SAGE company

Marshal your writing tool kit to make this intro as interesting as you can. This is the place to recreate your own excitement as an entrepreneur or advisor making a recommendation. But use an objective tone based on facts rather than emotion.

SAMPLE EXECUTIVE SUMMARY FOR A REPORT

Summaries are best written after the full version of the document is drafted, but you may find it helpful to draft a preliminary version first to guide you through the development process. Just expect to rewrite it later, when your own understanding is more complete.

At that point, you may feel like you're buried in a morass of material and have lost your story line. Ideally, step away from it for at least a day or two, and then think about what settles out as significant and important. Or try the tell-it-to-someone-else method. Find a way to lead with the idea or viewpoint or need that rises to the top. In most cases, whether you're writing a project report, proposal or business plan, your goal is to solve a problem. So start with that and the rest will fall into place. For example, here are three leads.

1. To find out the best social media platform to promote our new Dance It fitness program to teenagers, we ran three-week campaigns on five platforms.

2. In the past six months auditing errors have cost Vantage Point Inc. $137,495 in federal government fines. This report identifies the cause of these mistakes and recommends adoption of four new safeguards to prevent recurrence.

3. It's well known that 75% of new businesses fail. But why? Are entrepreneurs overly confident? Do they make poor decisions about location, pricing or staffing? Do they fail to compete for adequate funding? Dover Analytics researched 1,320 businesses launched in 2018 to pinpoint the reasons for failure. This report provides the first analysis in this region and suggests some ways entrepreneurs can overcome the human biases that most often undermine success.

Notice that in each case the lead suggests a natural organization for what follows.

Organize the Executive Summary to parallel the rest of the document, although you may want to present the solution early in the Executive Summary but at the end of the full report.

Outline-Style Versus Narrative Executive Summary

You can use an outline style for your Executive Summary rather than a narrative. Here is an abbreviated version of the summary for a white paper on an environmental situation targeted to the media, government officials and civic groups.

Craven County's Brownfields

Analysis, Recommendations and an Action Plan

The problem: Craven County is home to 5,450 brownfields. These contaminated parcels of land

- pose health and environmental hazards,
- put our undeveloped land at risk,
- prevent logical economic development,
- cost the county millions in lost taxes, and
- create suffering in disadvantaged communities.

How we got here—a complex set of interrelated problems must be faced:

- bewildering state and federal laws and confusing local regulations
- lack of leadership: who takes the helm?
- lack of centralized information
- uncertainty that makes developers reluctant to invest
- community resistance to change

Craven County Citizens for Cleanup will take a leadership role in a comprehensive campaign to

- develop community understanding,
- build a database of sites and data,
- advocate for more effective laws and incentives,
- serve as a clearinghouse for information and ideas, and
- provide guidance and road maps for stakeholders.

Resource needs:

- corporate partners

- government grants

- bond issue potential

- citizen contribution campaign

A narrative version for this paper might, in contrast, begin like this:

Craven County is home to 5,450 brownfields—contaminated parcels of land—twice the number of any other county in the state. Every one stands undeveloped or abandoned. Ranging from former dry cleaner shops and gas stations to industrial sites, they exist as eyesores in many communities but compel our attention for more serious reasons.

The rest of the summary follows in the same sequence as the bullet version but in narrative style with action subheads.

Which approach is more effective? It depends on the nature of the project and audience. Technical subjects may present well with the outline format. But narrative style offers more potential to create emotional impact and tilt the reader in your direction.

WRITING PROPOSALS THAT WIN

Writing leads to wealth.

—Jeffrey Gitomer, sales trainer, in
Little Green Book of Getting Your Way

Whether you're pitching a project, contract or grant, proposals must be first rate. There just aren't many piles of money sitting around without a horde of applicants buzzing around, vying for a share or the chance to do the job. Lean times and industry shifts tempt less qualified applicants to try for every opportunity, so in many fields, competition rises.

With adaptation, most of the proposal ideas that follow apply to the corporate, nonprofit and government arenas. The same set of tools works for consultants and independent contractors. If you're starting your own business, the same thinking applies there as well, whether you aim for supplemental or total income.

Business proposals aimed at securing work of any kind can be formal, informal or somewhere along the line between the two. Judge the circumstances and context to decide. A large company or government agency may present a formidable set of instructions and, in many cases, a highly specific form to fill out. But even when a strict format dictates your presentation, follow good messaging guidelines to succeed. This often takes some imagination. Here are some universals.

Know your audience. Can you tell who will read the document? That may determine the content and level of technical detail to include and what angle to take—a CEO and COO and CFO have different interests, not to mention an engineering chief or HR director. In most instances, assume a variety of people will review it. This is not a problem if you write with the relentless clarity and simplicity that everyone welcomes.

Know your goal. As with a résumé, you want the proposal to qualify you for the next step—usually an in-person presentation or conversation. Rarely is a group hired based solely on "paper." A proposal succeeds when it gets your foot in that door.

Know the problem the organization wants to solve—and why it's important. Read the RFP 20 times if the problem isn't stated outright, and look for clues. Is a tight deadline mentioned over and over again? Are there an unusual number of checkpoints that may suggest a prior bad experience? What skills and capabilities are stressed? Read between the lines, do research and investigate industry trends and challenges.

Know your story—the big-picture message. Try writing a brief crystallization of what you'll say in person at the next stage should your proposal reach the "call" pile. Why are you the best choice? Answer this basic question as a guideline for the full proposal. It may evolve into a good Executive Summary.

Give them proof. Marshal the evidence of how well you'll handle the work, and deploy it as appropriate. Proof may include previous jobs, results, client roster, client testimonials, team credentials, special expertise, graphics, photos and more. If there's an issue with deadlines, or coming in on budget, include factual proof of your consistent performance.

Don't bury yourself or your reader in detail. Provide what is asked for, but never lose sight of the message you want your audience to hear.

Remember that people hire people. Take opportunities to get across who you are and what you care about, how the team coordinates skills and works together, any special advantages you bring and why you're nice to work with (perhaps via testimonials). Trust me, likability counts a lot. The more enthusiastic you sound about the prospect of the work, the more appealing you are. The better you present your qualifications and your team's on every level, the better the impression you create. Experts say that painting the picture of credentials—why *this* candidate or company is best for the job—is too lightly handled in many proposals and a reason they lose.

Write in clear, jargon-free language. Use short words, sentences and paragraphs. You may have heard proposal advisers claim that a pitch for big money from a big source should be written in big language: a weighty, formal, impressive, fancy-word style commensurate (their word, not mine!) with the value of the prize. That's usually absurd. Your substance must be

VIEW FROM THE FIELD: PROPOSALS FOR PRIVATE VERSUS GOVERNMENT SECTORS

It rings true in both the private and public sectors: Always know your audience! For corporate proposals seeking new business, focus not on you so much as on the clients. You need to really know them, what they're thinking, and what their true objective is (besides revenue). Here's what I found works with engineering proposals, for example.

First, look at all the hot buttons mentioned in the RFP. Repeat them throughout, and incorporate them into the cover letter. If the RFP says, "Here are our goals and what we hope to achieve from this project," great. If not—dig a little, interview key stakeholders and research the project's history.

Establish a theme for the entire proposal. For example, if it's a redevelopment project and the main goal is to create jobs, our theme would be economic development and we would carry it through the captions, images and photographs in addition to the cover letter and technical scope section.

The proposal must read well and easily flow between focus areas. Use an active voice, keep sentence length to 15 words or less, be positive and remove unnecessary words. Write it so that someone outside of the field can review it and understand it. Proposals are often reviewed by committees that include members of the broader community and must be understood by the layman. Appealing graphics are an extremely important component of the proposal. Use them to engage the reader. Remember, the goal is to pass the first stage and get an interview!

For government grants, such as the National Science Foundation proposals I currently create, it is the quality and promise of the proposed research that is the focal point and probably accounts for 80% of the scoring. With federal grants, the agency will detail what it wants to see in each section. The project summary is most important and should be written in the third person (in the case of NSF). It includes character limitations and requires details about the broad impact of the research—its intellectual merit and how it will affect the community and world at large. The emphasis is still on the story, which appears in the form of a project description. A technical committee will review the proposal, but it must be understood by nontechnical people, since the entire process is in the public domain.

A Cover Letter Example

For a private sector proposal, an individual, well-thought-out cover letter is important. If it doesn't appeal to the clients, they won't go further. A guideline to follow: Restate the client's goals in the first paragraph so that from the beginning, it's not about "us," and you show your understanding. The second paragraph should introduce the team members, not just who they are, but why the client should care: Have they worked with the company before? Do they have relevant experience? Then, take a look at the RFP and the evaluation criteria, and show how you meet the criteria and how your team benefits the client. It's matching "our" story to "theirs."

Next refer to what is unique about your proposal: Shortened timeline? Coming in under budget? Ideally, something that makes you special. And don't forget to include contractual matters, such as "This contract is good for 180 days."

The cover letter should be clear, concise and one page when possible—two at the most. Here is the closing section of one applying for a major construction project when I worked for an engineering firm:

We have a passion for bicycle projects. For us, they are not a side business; they are a stand-alone practice area. Furthermore, our team includes avid cyclists and bike advocates. Our enthusiasm translates into focused attention to quality and service, and we take special pride in and ownership of these assignments.

On behalf of the project team, thank you for this opportunity to present our qualifications for this interesting assignment. We hope to have the opportunity to discuss our experience and approach further. Please feel free to contact me at xxx-xxx-xxxx should you require any additional information.

—Christine M. Cesaria, director of grants/ communications, Department of Computer Science, Stony Brook University, and former marketing director for engineering firms solid, but aim to be a breath of fresh air in how you present. I don't promise you'll win all the time—just more often.

How to Work With Rigid Formats

In private industry as well as the government sector, you often don't have the freedom to choose the shape you prefer for your presentation. An RFP may dictate a standard set of categories and set strict word limitations on each section. Follow the guidelines scrupulously. Watch for the "do nots" as well as "dos." If the RFP specifies, "do not write more than one paragraph" for a section, don't sneak in a super-long paragraph. You will be disqualified. The thinking: If you can't follow instructions at this stage, why expect a good performance?

Still, apply ingenuity and find ways to incorporate the idea of an Executive Summary. Usually RFPs have a project overview section that lends itself to this use. Predetermined formats can make it hard to maintain your narrative, but you are more likely to be rewarded when you do.

How to Write Informal, Conversation-Based Proposals

Especially for service providers who operate on their own or in small groups, writing a proposal is a formidable task. As a result, many people produce generic boilerplate pitches that go on at length about their wonderfulness and devote perhaps a few paragraphs to the work at hand. A better alternative is a conversation-based proposal that zeros in on the job without spending a ton of time writing.

Typically, a client has a problem to solve and hopes you will solve it. With a little encouragement, she will gladly tell you about that problem, why it matters, and what has already been tried. If you have the chance to present your idea in person, resist the temptation to tout your qualifications! It may sound counterintuitive, but once you're in front of prospects, most take your credentials for granted. They want to know you understand their problem and will solve it.

Use the in-person opportunity to find out as much as you can about that problem as well as the person and the organization. To prime the conversation, try open-ended questions such as these:

What do you want to gain? Why is that important?

What would you like to see different about _____?

How would that make your life better? Improve the organization?

What are you losing because of this (money, efficiency, opportunities, image, competitive edge, etc.)?

How have you tried to solve this problem so far? How did it work out?

Listen for below-the-surface clues. Often people with problems are conscious of symptoms rather than underlying causes. Someone tells you his website doesn't draw because it's not optimized well, for example; this may be true, but dull content may be a bigger factor.

From this point, you might develop a solution right on the spot, working collaboratively with the prospect. It's often better to end the conversation, make a second appointment if possible, then draft your analysis and recommendation on your own time. Two pages are enough for a simple synopsis that spells out the problem and its importance, followed by your solution.

For example, if I'm selling e-mail-writing workshops to a company and have spoken in reasonable depth with the person in charge, by telephone or in person, I could write in a simple letter format like this:

Dear Anne:

It was a pleasure to meet you and learn about the interesting work ABC does.

I'm sure the Can-Write team can help you meet the challenge we discussed. Here is how I understand your need.

- *ABC's junior managers are alienating the firm's wealthy, elderly investors by sending abrupt e-mails perceived as rude.*

- *These staff members also produce internal messages that are confusing and inefficient, which creates dissension and wastes time.*

- *An estimated 14% of staff productivity is lost through poor e-mail skills, costing the company an estimated $xxx annually.*

And so on. Three to seven points are usually enough. Then:

We propose a set of customized workshops led by writing experts who are seasoned presenters and work frequently with busy professionals. A series of five three-hour interactive, lively learning experiences will train your staff members to build good relationships with customers and coworkers in all e-mails. Specifically, they will learn and practice how to do the following:

- *Understand the needs and expectations of ABC's audiences.*

- *Create messages that demonstrate respect and consideration.*

- *Plan and strategize all e-mails to accomplish specific goals.*

- *Write with clarity, brevity and impact.*

An effective proposal can be built this way, along with a few more sections according to the occasion (see the example below). Notice the emphasis on what will be accomplished.

Typically the *how*—the process used to perform the work—is secondary. Good proposals, whatever their length, give the reader a vision of how much better life (and/or profits) will be when the project is accomplished.

A proposal in this letter format can easily be converted to an agreement—just amend it based on your prospect's input, add any provisions needed and dedicate space at the end for signatures and dates. If a more formal proposal is called for, it's easy to adapt the written pitch along these lines:

Proposed by Can-Write for ABC Inc.

A training program to improve e-mail communication company-wide and build customer relationships

The Problem—*in narrative style with bullets*

The Solution—*narrative with bullets*

What We'll Do—*some detail on what you'll provide (e.g., content of the workshops)*

How We'll Collaborate—*some detail on the process (e.g., interactive client process to sharpen goals and deliverables)*

Who We Are—*a tight profile of you/your team showing why you're the best for the job and your excitement about the project*

What We'll Accomplish—*a tempting vision of the problem solved and the wonderful future that beckons*

Mutual Responsibilities *(and perhaps deadlines, relevant logistics, etc.)*

Fees *(which should have been discussed earlier, but not before defining the problem's scope and importance)*

The conversational approach automatically produces a you- rather than me-based way of selling your service and writing proposals. And except perhaps for celebrities who tire of reading about themselves, if there are any, this approach never bores the audience. Also, clients are often more receptive to your solution when you lead them to clarify the problem and give it a value, typically higher than they originally would have assigned.

Here are four more tips for a competitive advantage in all proposals:

Practice the art of omission. Adopt the attitude of the popular fiction writer Elmore Leonard, who said, "I try to leave out the parts that people skip." Do the same. A concise proposal is more apt to be read all the way through and hold reader interest. Leave out the boilerplate statements full of empty hyperbole that anyone, in any industry, could use and everything that does not support your story.

Skip the tech-speak. Pile it in back as a separate section or appendix if you feel it's needed, but don't break the narrative flow with details your prospect will not understand or care about. A businessperson, for example, doesn't want to know what programs a web designer will use to build a site. What that new website will accomplish, however, holds infinite charm.

Go for speed. In today's hyperactive world, the faster your writing reads, the better your chances of reaching other people and persuading them to your viewpoint. This in large part translates as "write short"—words, sentences, paragraphs, sections.

Inject energy and enthusiasm. Above all, evidence your passion for what you do. You want the work or the project or the grant—don't be afraid to make that 100% clear. Enthusiasm coupled with thorough understanding of client needs is hard to resist, sometimes even when the price is higher than the competition's.

SUCCESS TIP

Collaborative writing projects

In both classwork and the business world, you're often called on to participate in collaborative writing projects. This is a challenge: People have different levels of capability, especially when it comes to writing. In many instances, strong writers feel like they are expected to hold a very big bag.

The best solution is to plan the project carefully: Break out the tasks and distribute them as fairly as possible. The work may encompass planning, research, obtaining information through interview, collecting and analyzing statistics or other data, creating visuals, graphic design and production, perhaps preparing an oral presentation—and writing, editing and proofing. Agree on a project leader or coordinator, who should be given extra recognition.

Each person can take responsibility for one or more of the functions, according to the team's size, so that everyone agrees the workload is fairly distributed. Set a timeline that specifies when each phase must be completed, allowing for the time needed to accomplish all subsequent phases. Also set parameters for completing each aspect of the project: in what form the research, data, interview, and technical information must be delivered; what the finished project should look like; checkpoints for the coordinator to manage so he can field problems.

Consistent, structured communication is essential. Determine what tools for sharing are most appropriate, and set guidelines for their use. Ideally, launch the project with an in-person meeting, but if that's not possible, set up online meetings in which people can see each other. The full group should maintain regular contact and review each member's progress on a preset schedule.

Put the plan in writing and mark deadlines clearly. Keep a checklist.

Be sure to allow enough time for the individual or team responsible for final writing to produce a smooth and integrated document that doesn't sound like it was written by a committee. And at least one other person, preferably three, should thoroughly proofread.

SUCCEEDING WITH GRANT APPLICATIONS

An application for funding or project support from a government agency, foundation or corporation shares the essentials of proposal writing, with some additional requirements.

Foremost: Take the grant-giving organization's mission seriously. Invariably, those that invest money in a good cause or project of any kind feel passionately about their mission. *Be sure you understand the nature of that mission, and dovetail your application so it directly relates to it.* This mission orientation is one reason foundations and companies prefer to fund projects rather than support "operational expenses."

Another guideline: Don't be boring. *Besides getting to the point quickly and succinctly, tell your story.* This might cover why and how your organization was created; what it has accomplished, preferably told through people you've helped or goals achieved; and a vision of how much better the world will be if your application is funded.

Avoid repeating material more than necessary. In the case of grants, most reviewers will read the full document and you need not keep regrounding them in the same ideas. If necessary to repeat, find another way to say it.

Stick to your central message: what you'll accomplish with the funding. Organize the document to correspond to the RFP and specific format requirements, but have a clear idea of the message you want to deliver and build a cohesive narrative as best you can. Each answer should stand on its own, contribute new information and add up to a compelling story.

VIEW FROM THE FIELD: A GRANT REVIEWER ON WHAT LOSES, WHAT WINS

What annoys me most is that people just do not answer the questions. They talk around the issues and don't get to the heart of things, the core interest of a donor or funder: Why should we give money to you and not another organization that's doing similar work?

Many grant applications are particularly light on the organization's impact. One, for example, asked for more money to do more work in the same area. They talked about how horrible the problem is that they deal with but not the agency's impact. I asked about it: "You've been using the money for 15 years—what difference have you made?" They talked themselves out of the funding.

Don't just cite numbers to show success—saying "we trained 500 people" isn't going to make me invest in your organization. I want to know what happened to those people a year later. It can be hard to track results with figures, but you can show them anecdotally.

I notice bad writing, I don't notice mediocre writing and I do notice good writing—when you see something written well, it has stars around it, sparkles. Good writing stands out.

Given that the application shows capacity and evidence that the organization can do the work, good writing gets the grant.

—Ann Marie Thigpen, director
of the Center for Nonprofit
Leadership at Adelphi University

Grant Application Strategies

Get in touch. Talk to the grant administrators. Ask questions about the level of detail they'd like to see, data to include and even whether a particular project is a good candidate. This enables you to perfect your pitch.

It is a rare funder that will mind hearing from you, as long as you speak with intelligence. Making awards is a grueling business for funders as well as for the applicants. They're happy to help you meet their needs. Moreover, the interaction works toward building a relationship. We all prefer to work with and invest in people we trust. If you must pose your questions in writing, do it well and carefully.

Define the problem and focus on outcomes. Show clearly that you understand the problems to be solved and what will be accomplished should the money be awarded to you. Funders often complain that many grant applicants fail to provide enough information on outcomes, which must be meaningful: "We will train 50 farmers to use the new agricultural method" is a so-what statement. But this is not: "We will train 50 farmers and show them how to train their peers. Each will train an additional 25 per year, and they in turn will share their training. Within two years, the program will reach half the co-op's farmers and yield a collective crop increase of 15% to 20%."

Connect to the action. Link outcomes to the activities and methods you believe will bring them about. For example, if a program's objective is to help failing students improve their math grades by 20%, and the application says only that this will be accomplished by presenting 15 workshops, you haven't said what the students will learn, who will teach them and what innovative strategies will be adopted. Show a track record for the methods if you can.

Demonstrate accomplishments and set the stage for future applications. Understandably, many nonprofit organizations cannot afford expensive follow-up studies to prove a program worked. When you're responsible for managing the grant, look for tracking options at the very beginning and build them into the work. For example, field workers can be asked to make note of clients' input on how they were helped. In-person testimonials shot with a simple system, such as a smartphone, offer an excellent option for showing results in the human terms everyone responds to.

If you do win an award, don't forget to say thank you! In fact, it's smart to write an appreciative note even if you don't win.

And always, report project results to the funder in writing, whether that's a formal requirement or not. Many requestors fail to do so and wonder why their new applications fail. Evidence of success is always welcome: photographs, statistics, notes from people you served thanks to the funding and so on as appropriate and possible. Find a way to demonstrate how you fulfilled your promise and helped the funding agency advance its own mission.

A WORD ON BUSINESS PLANS

Business plans are highly individualized documents that can take months or even years to evolve, because developing a new enterprise is tough. Writing the plan pulls entrepreneurs through the tough work of thinking through how to implement the idea and meet the many challenges that lie ahead.

Develop the written document much like a proposal. You'll need sections explaining the mission—why the idea has value and why it's needed, who it will interest, how it will operate, what it will produce. A business plan also needs a full marketing strategy, a convincing

VIEW FROM THE FIELD: PROPOSAL ADVICE FROM AN NGO PROGRAM DIRECTOR

We start with knowing the audience and the language it speaks. We aim with all our writing to be very clear and direct. Saying it in simple terms is important. People often want to overexplain things in a proposal, but then the less clear it becomes. Focus on only the essential details that provide context and demonstrate expertise. Thread in too much detail and you lose directness and intensity. Put in too much mechanics and people start to get lost in the machinery.

There's an art to finding the most direct way to say something about a sophisticated idea in a short amount of space. Usually we have 10 pages to explain what we'll do with millions of dollars.

The underlying structure we use:

- rationale
- political context
- why it's important
- why we're the best to do the work
- what the work will actually be
- timing
- results we expect

I recommend outlining what you're trying to do, so you go into a document with a road map of how it all fits together. This tells you where questions will arise and what research you have to do so you have a game plan to avoid unnecessary preparation work and prevent repetition within the document. The document may not end up much longer than the outline. This process helps people distill the ideas and concepts down to bullet points—then they have the luxury of adding detail and can figure out the sequence people will understand. An outline also lets us brainstorm with other people, who many times are overseas, so it's easy for them to contribute, and you build buy-in and consensus in advance.

Always put the bottom line up front. If you're asking for something, whether in a letter or proposal, come out with it right away. Be unambiguous. It gives the reader a unifying idea of what the document is about.

This is important also because of another element: how you want readers to think of you. They learn about the team, and the project, by how the document is written. You want to be seen as straightforward, direct, easy to understand and an expert. You need them to trust you and feel they can get a very direct answer in a quick amount of time.

—Erin Mathews, international development consultant

portrayal of a capable leader and team, and a detailed financial plan. All the techniques of persuasive writing apply to the presentation, including a strong Executive Summary that shows off both your passion and practicality.

Asking for money is a serious business. There is help out there: the Small Business Administration, Small Business Development Centers, local business advisory groups. Many regions have SCORE offices, which offer entrepreneurs free mentoring and workshops by industry professionals. Also check out college programs and online sources of advice and business plan formats.

Today, crowdsourcing is a tempting way for many people to finance a bright idea. If you have a compelling story for a business or project, you must articulate it well, use professional-style graphic presentation and create a video to demonstrate your idea and/or talk about it effectively. Most successful crowdsourcing appeals also have a stepped incentive program of rewards for different levels of support. If you want to try this route, start by studying pitches on the platform that interests you and observe how people with similar appeals go about it. Notice which techniques work for you personally and would apply to your own pitch.

See also the techniques and tools of persuasion discussed in Chapter 6.

PRACTICE OPPORTUNITIES

I. Group Project: Invent and Propose a New Course

Collaborate in small groups on ideas for a new course that would add to your capabilities and qualifications. Pick one and brainstorm its benefits. Divide up the responsibilities, and collaboratively write an Executive Summary for a formal proposal to your school's director. It should explain what you recommend and why, using techniques of persuasion.

II. Group Project: Develop a Nonprofit Project Proposal

1. **Propose a cause.** Brainstorm in small groups. Each group decides on an idea for a new local charitable cause or a major project you agree would be of value to the community and is practical (e.g., cleaning up a park, collecting used clothing for a children's shelter, volunteering for an after-school tutoring service, helping housebound senior citizens with shopping or household tasks).

2. **Plan a proposal** to raise funds for the idea from local businesses or a civic group. Identify what needs to be done, set a timeline for each stage and determine how to collaborate, each team member assuming an appropriate part of the work. Decide together on the central focus of your story, and include why the project is needed, who will benefit and how (including the sponsoring organization), the extent of demand, the precise support you're asking for, activities and anticipated outcomes. Include ideas for reaching the audiences you'll need.

3. **Create the proposal in line with your plan.** Include an Executive Summary. Draw on the writing and persuasion techniques presented in this chapter and Chapter 6. Include appropriate graphics (or describe what they would consist of).

4. **Present the proposal.** The full class reviews all the proposals and votes on which to support, taking the role of a civic group or committee on corporate giving. If desired, the class can also conduct Q&A sessions with each group (which will uncover any missing information).

5. **Discuss results.** What characterized the most successful proposals? What persuasion strategies did you observe, and how well did they work? Were opportunities missed? And how did the collaborative process turn out? Can a best practice set of directions be assembled for collaborative writing?

III. Create a Business Proposal

Have you had an idea for a business or service you'd like to develop that could be begun on a small scale? Working on your own, brainstorm this idea in practical terms or invent an idea on the spot. Write a concise but complete proposal to the television show *Shark Tank* asking for a chance to pitch the show's investors on air. Based on this chapter's guidelines and this book's writing advice, figure out what kind of information to include and list the sections. Then plan and write an Executive Summary introducing the idea and making all the most important points.

IV. Write a Report

Create a written report on what you accomplished in this course during the past month. What did you learn, why does it matter, and how will you use it? What problems do you need to work on? How do you chart your progress? What recommendations can you give yourself for further improvement? Where do you need help, and how might you get it? For this, you (along with the professor) are your own audience.

V. Class Discussion: When You Don't Agree With Your Employer

In the business world, you may well be called on to write memos, letters, social media posts and other materials that speak to a viewpoint you disagree with or for which you have no natural empathy. This happens often in professional communications work. When should you voice your opinion? Where do you draw the line? Must personal values reconcile with job demands—and if so, how? Consider a concept public relations specialists espouse: There are many truths. Do you agree with that? Does it lead you to broaden your perspective or feel more receptive to other viewpoints?

WRITING FOR ONLINE AND SPOKEN MEDIA

10 CRAFT YOUR WRITING FOR THE INTERACTIVE WORLD

Have something to say, and say it as clearly as you can. That is the only secret.

—Matthew Arnold, 19th-century philosopher

If you're reading this book you may be preparing for your career, even if you're not yet sure of your path. It's equally probable that the Internet is an integral part of your life and a central source of entertainment. It's how you obtain information, communicate with friends and peers, connect with new people and perhaps exercise your creativity. Here's the question to consider: Should you start using online media thoughtfully? Choose media and create content that supports your long-range aspirations? Consciously build an online presence to help position and qualify you for your future career and networking?

This chapter shows you how you to apply strategic thinking and good writing to your online life. Many benefits attach to adopting a business-like framework for your digital communication. For virtually every organization—whether corporate, nonprofit, governmental or professional—digital media are tools to share information, create communities and achieve marketing goals. You can adopt the mindset and techniques to achieve your own goals or set the stage for doing so. These approaches will serve you well in job hunting, demonstrating value to employers and running your own business or side gigs if that is on your agenda.

In a word, it is smart to think of your online life strategically. At the least, to paraphrase what medical students learn, do yourself no future harm.

STRATEGIZING YOUR DIGITAL PRESENCE

The best way to increase your social media engagement is to share content your audience is truly interested in.

—Nathan Ellering, Convince & Convert blog

The basic principle for using the Internet strategically is the same one this book recommends for succeeding with all communication: First, know what you want to accomplish, and know your audience.

231

For professional marketers, the ultimate goal is usually to sell a product or service or charitable cause and build a loyal following. Much of the challenge is in defining *audience*. Marketers ask: Who do I want to reach? What does a typical member of this group need? What interests and concerns motivate this person? And, as appropriate: What is my typical prospect's age, gender, education level, income level? Consider his buying habits, problems and much more, according to the product or service. Professional communicators and businesspeople input all the relevant factors to create a "persona" to represent the typical individual they target.

They create content—meaning the collective material they post online—based on this envisioned audience (or audiences). In earlier times marketers depended on mass-audience vehicles like advertising in print and television. But the digital revolution transformed these tactics. Rather than hoping to reach the "right" fraction of the audience through a mass communication TV commercial or magazine ad, organizations can now narrow their gaze and reach the specific people they want. It's at heart the same tactic Warren Buffett describes, writing with his sisters in mind, described in Chapter 2.

See the Digital Revolution in Perspective

We're still adapting to the seismic shift in how we communicate. Today, traditional sources of information like books, newspapers and television remain with us but are challenged to adapt to the digital marketplace. The same is true of "brick and mortar" purchasing, which steadily moves online. The digital revolution also reduces the need for "colocation." Instead of working in a shared physical setting, more and more of us work in dispersed environments with coworkers, bosses and collaborators who may be virtually anywhere in the world, in any time zone.

The Internet also opens the playing field for small low-budget enterprises and startups, empowering them to compete with established enterprises. If they use the opportunity well, they can connect with their target audiences and, like big organizations, reach across geographic and cultural borders to sell, collaborate, partner. And by providing the infrastructure of the gig economy, the Internet opens up a world of possibilities for you if you want a side job or aim to become your own boss.

The digital tools that we use to connect with others and that influence us—social media, websites, blogs—add up to the new word of mouth. Given infinite choices we look to friends and trusted strangers for advice on what to buy, use, experience.

Here's the bottom line lurking in this quick overview: Online channels give us additional ways to communicate with our audiences, but work differently from traditional channels. Organizations and successful online personalities have learned: *Instead of broadcasting what they want their target audience to notice and respond to, they must bring that audience to the message.* This requires delivering the message in media the audience members like and frequent, and giving them material they will seek out and value. Today, readers and viewers must be earned.

To use an analogy, if you want to see hummingbirds, scattering breadcrumbs to feed many kinds of birds doesn't make sense. Hummingbirds don't eat breadcrumbs.

Marketers today decide which birds they want to attract and endlessly analyze which food—or content—will pull them in and keep them coming back.

Online Media and You

It's important to remember that while social media are incredibly effective for distribution and engagement, it's just another tool in your marketing and communications tool bag. I get excited about new technologies because the possibilities for engaging supporters increase exponentially. But what always matters most is having a powerful story that you can share in an authentic way.

—James Wu, brand and business strategist

Unless you want to use online media to see yourself talk or share your life with a few friends, the key for you, too, is to understand the audiences you want to reach—and others that may matter to you down the line. Consider your personal goals. At this point in time, do you want to stay in touch with friends? Find new ones? Share experience or knowledge? Have fun? Experiment with your creativity and show it off? Learn about something that interests you and connect with people who share that interest?

All fine. But are you ready to find career leads or foresee a time when you will? Do you want to build networks and relationships that will support your future aspirations? It's never too early to take these goals seriously, because the building process is slow. And it's cumulative. Everything you post becomes who you are, and online media have long and mostly indelible memories. With any activity at all, you are already building a reputation and online personality.

Take an honest look at whether you are building an online self that is positive and embodies how you want to be seen in the long run. The online world is your open-to-everyone electronic résumé, and it's wise to assume everyone who wants to know what you're about—prospective employers, clients, friends, dating partners—will find it all.

Another general principle that can work for you: The Internet is incessantly hungry. It devours information at a breakneck pace. Organizations of every kind devote more and more resources to feeding it with blogs, press releases, websites and social media posts. You may have noticed that as new social platforms emerge, they become "professionalized": Experienced marketers mount well-financed campaigns, sometimes successfully, other times not.

On the other hand, the abundance of material makes it increasingly difficult for both companies and individuals to gain attention. Material must be of high quality and real value to readers. If you don't build it really well and deliver what your readers want, they will not come, or keep coming. This is where we arrive back at writing.

Why Online Writing Matters

If you think of digital media as offering principally visual experiences, think again. Study after study demonstrates that the words are pivotal. Yes, people naturally relate to and love visuals: photographs, video, gifs, other graphic forms and good design. But in many communication channels, the role of visuals is to engage attention and pull people into the written material. Even in video, words are essential to delivering the message or at least providing meaning and context. The words may ultimately be few—but they must be just the right ones, which is a challenge.

Communicating visually via your favorite social platforms may be part of your daily life. But recognize the limits of what you can communicate purely with visuals. You can deliver the elements of your daily experience with friends through creatively used images, but not ideas, or much information. Without writing, it's hard to plan beyond the moment. You can't collaborate. You can't share or transfer ideas beyond the most basic. Remember, writing enabled human beings to record what they learned so that others could build on the collective knowledge over generations. That's how we developed civilizations and every field of knowledge. All of which still depend on writing.

People in your work life need you to communicate in words—written and spoken. Use writing to communicate with yourself, too. Create a written plan for your career and you'll give yourself a head start on developing your ideas so you can move naturally toward your goals. A written plan serves especially well for strategizing your online life. What do you want to accomplish? Who do you want to reach? What is the best way of doing so? This may lead you in better directions you haven't considered—for example, investing energy in platforms like LinkedIn, where employers, hiring managers and prospective customers scout for talent.

A plan will also reinforce your personal commitment to good writing. When you view the various channels strategically, you are more apt to choose those that matter to your future. Then it becomes more obvious that *you are what you write. Online, credibility depends on writing quality.* Consider how you judge unfamiliar material yourself. Do you not unconsciously judge it by the writing? The digital world empowers anyone to be a seller, author, critic or expert. So the intrinsic question is: Why should I trust you? What signals tell me that you are authoritative and honest? That I should take you seriously?

Good writing demonstrates that you relate to reader interests, communicate clearly, and have something to say. Without good writing, good ideas don't matter—they don't really exist if they aren't well expressed. And when people look for insights into what kind of person you are, it's the content and quality of your writing that generates a positive impression, or not so much.

One more reason to write well in everything you post: Today's online world is alarmingly competitive. To access its remarkable opportunities, whether to promote your career long range or find an immediate job, client or customer, you must contribute outstandingly and thoughtfully. So much good stuff is online, free for the taking, that even giving it away is a hard sell.

ADAPTING TO INTERACTIVE MEDIA

There's more "content" than ever. But it's also harder than ever to find signal amongst the noise and facts amongst the fiction—let alone inspiring ideas and high-level discourse, which is what the internet was meant to be.

—Ev Williams, CEO of Medium and cofounder of Twitter

Do you need to master a whole new skillset to write well in digital formats? No. The basic principles are the same as you've practiced for everyday writing, with some adaptation. A primary rule for e-media: Aim for a lightning speed read. People scan and dive to find out if a website, blog or post interests them. Therefore, almost always, get to the point immediately. Never force readers to dig for what they came for. Tell them immediately they're in the right place, and keep them going with good information and strong writing.

Guidelines for the Mechanics

Stay Short and Simple

- Use familiar one- and two-syllable words.

- Write straightforward, clear sentences without a lot of clauses, averaging 6 to 14 words long. Work in an occasional one-word sentence for punch.

- Keep paragraphs between one to three sentences long, and use some one-sentence paragraphs.

- Keep pages short enough to read with minimal scrolling.

Stay Active and Lively

- Build with strong action verbs, preferably present tense. Don't water things down with tentative language like *will be, can be, should be* and passive constructions.

- Choose concrete nouns rather than abstractions—even when writing about an idea.

- Don't bog sentences down with unnecessary words and repetitions.

- Minimize descriptive adjectives and adverbs (*most* experienced, *amazingly* efficient, *revolutionary* idea, *groundbreaking* innovation, etc.).

> *The road to hell is paved with adverbs.*
>
> —Stephen King, novelist

Stay Positive and Upbeat

- Keep the tone light and bright unless common sense dictates otherwise (on a funeral home website, for example).

- Use a conversational tone. Warm and friendly works; a spontaneous feeling is great, but not easy to achieve.

- Show confidence and avoid hedgy words like *sometimes, possibly, perhaps.*

Helpful Online Techniques

Use inverted pyramid style. Anticipate that your readers may stop one-third of the way through a blog post or your home page. So know your core message, and communicate it early.

Imitate journalists: Put the most important information at the beginning of each page and each copy block. And put the most important words of each headline and sentence on the left.

Find ways to say you. Rather than "Customers will save hours of time with G2," say "G2 saves you hours of accounting time." And rather than using the abstract third person (he, she, they) frame your ideas in first person (I, we) to more easily achieve the personal, warm tone you want and lead you to use wording that's more friendly and direct.

Opt for we *rather than* I. If you're representing an entity rather than yourself, say *we*. It's more credible. You're usually entitled to do that even if it's a solo operation. If you're a designer and a job requires a writer, you'll bring one in, right? If you're out of town and can't handle a call for computer repair, won't you ask a friend? Therefore you're engaged in a team endeavor.

Create information chunks. Small chunks are easily absorbed and remembered. Cognitive psychology research claims that the brain can remember only seven or eight pieces of information at a time, whether words, numbers, sentences or bullet points. Unless you're deliberately writing for people you've profiled as liking a lot of long, dense information, break material down into short pieces.

Position yourself specifically. If your company focuses on telecommunications or recruitment, say so, rather than referring to "management services." If your filtration systems are designed for water in hot climates, say so. If you serve customers only in Delaware, say so. Concrete information works best online. Many websites make it hard to figure out what the organization does. Don't be like that. Tell people what you do, who you do it for and where, if relevant.

Take liberties to keep writing sayable. A conversational style works best for online writing, so test it with the read-aloud method. Be ready to take liberties with conventional English. You don't need formal "literate" statements. Fragments are fine if meaning is clear. You needn't (and shouldn't) say:

> *If you're interested in finding out how we at GBH can customize our consulting services to increase your company's telecommunications efficiency, please call us at xxx-xxx-xxxx.*

Better:

> *Need more efficient phone service? Let's talk. Right now. xxx-xxx-xxxx.*

But take pains to look correct! Don't write in any way that the reader might interpret as a mistake. You can write informally and build in dramatic effects, but your language and grammar must stay basically correct and your spelling must be perfect. If it's not, poof! Say goodbye to your credibility.

Attend to your search terms. It's well worth some research and testing time to figure out your best keywords and search terms—the words people will use to find you. Include them in copy and headlines. But don't try to game the system. Google finds more and more ways to penalize those who try to manipulate their ranking process. Above all, substance counts.

Build in graphic techniques. In addition to using photos, illustrations or graphs as appropriate, engage the eye and help readability with strong headlines, subheads, bulleted lists, bold lead-ins, numbered lists and plenty of white space. But generally speaking, aim for simplicity and a consistent style. Don't mix a lot of fonts and colors or juxtapose cartoons and photos. Avoid graphic busyness that confuses the eye.

Guidelines for Building Your Positive Image

While certainly you can use your favorite platforms in a spontaneous way, it's smart to create a personal big picture. As part of your Internet planning, decide how you want to be seen. This guides you to make good decisions, safeguard your reputation and build for the long run. Not every message needs to accomplish long-range goals—but then, it's hard to know what might have impact or staying power.

The line between personal and professional is harder to draw every day. You may run the purely social side of your online life separately from the strategic side, but never imperil yourself by posting a careless remark, offensive language, hostile post or *anything* that might undermine you. You probably know people who've lost something they value with a single ill-conceived remark, not to mention the high-profile cases of entire careers obliterated by a tweet. Perhaps worse: losing opportunities you're not even aware of.

So here's your "never" list for online posts:

- Don't disparage or insult anyone.

- Don't use irony, sarcasm or any humor open to negative interpretation.

- Don't lose your temper.

- Don't use "bad language."

- Don't contribute to questionable sites.

- Don't post photos—or anything—you don't want your grandmother or employer to see, now or ever.

- Don't post anything with incorrect spelling, bad grammar or bad thinking.

TEN TIPS FOR USING ONLINE MEDIA

1. ***Grab your readers with a good accurate headline and a visual.***

Alert scanners that the material is relevant to their lives. Use a visual whenever possible, *if* it's appropriate to the message.

2. *Maintain interest with substance.*

Online readers simply will not stick around for unhelpful material unrelated to their concerns. Whether your subject is a product or a new idea or an opinion, and whatever the platform, provide your best thinking and information. Show a generous spirit: Share without worrying whether people will steal your ideas or perform whatever it is themselves.

3. *Distill and crystallize your messages.*

Reading on screen makes us grumpy. Even the best desktop screens flicker undetectably, tiring the eye. Moreover, the tiny screens of smartphones and watches just don't have the space for anything beyond a core message. So avoid posting wordy, meandering, repetitive material. Refine your messages.

4. *Dispense with all empty claims and inflated rhetoric.*

Statements along the lines of "I am the greatest expert in my field" or "This is the most innovative product ever conceived" are dead ends. You must demonstrate or prove your claims. Figure out what evidence could make your case: images, testimonials, results and so on.

5. *Don't waste a reader's time.*

Never ask your audience to decipher what you're saying or block their path to navigating the platform easily. Websites must provide clear connections to what's next. Don't force visitors to figure out how to turn off music or visuals (or ads if possible) they prefer not to experience. Always deliver on what your headline or promotional blurb promises.

6. *Keep a lid on your emotions.*

Enthusiasm is fine, passion for a subject is great, but don't get carried away. Overall, an objective-sounding but positive tone is most persuasive. Showing negative emotions like anger, frustration and impatience can harm you and your cause.

7. *Exercise good people skills.*

The digital world is social, so use your best manners. Respond to comments and criticism—courteously. Share generously. Give your best. Other people are doing so, and so must you.

8. *Soft-sell the commercial.*

If you're selling or promoting something, don't do so overtly if the channel suggests it's out of place. Try to make it part of the value you offer. Many businesspeople elect to self-promote in only one out of five tweets, for example. A blog can showcase your special knowledge or viewpoint, yet not be *I* centered.

9. *Build in the interaction.*

Aim not to give lectures and pronouncements. Expect, feed and encourage audience participation. Work at presenting ideas or information in ways that entice a response.

Ask thoughtful questions, request opinions and input, share an idea that's a bit edgy or controversial. And follow up with responses to keep the conversation alive.

10. Foster relationships creatively.

Just like in the face-to-face world, building online relationships takes time. Don't expect to post a comment or blog and become an overnight sensation. The online world is already heavily populated. Emulate the way children make friends or join a social circle: They watch a group from the sidelines for a while and feel things out by observing the interaction and rules of the game. Then they'll "kibbitz" a little—make comments about the action. Eventually they feel comfortable asking to join the play. Similarly, research the blogs, groups and content communities that relate to your interests and goals. See what people talk about and what concerns them. Contribute thoughtful comments. Ask questions, start conversations, follow what others say and continue to contribute. Absorb the culture and you'll start to see what it values, where the gaps are, what of value you might contribute.

WEBSITE WRITING: WHAT'S DIFFERENT

Websites over the past few years have evolved from "one more marketing tool" for organizations to front and center in the marketing/communications/PR/branding mix. For many buyers and information seekers, websites are the main port of call for finding what they want. Many organizations use social media, e-mail campaigns and even paid advertising as conduits to a website, where in-depth substance lives and the sale is closed (or not).

Whether you need your own website depends on where you now are in terms of your career and what you want to accomplish. If an online résumé will best showcase what you offer, a website is a core need. If you are marketing something other than yourself, or plan to, a website is also essential. Thanks to online do-it-yourself platforms like WordPress and Wix, building a website has melded into blogging. So you can create a website or a blog or something in between. Whatever works for you, the strategies that have evolved for website creation and online writing are useful to know.

Highlighting the differences between print and digital writing is helpful. Foremost, online writing involves more dimensions. It's not about "just" writing. Websites, and most other online media, are visual and dynamic experiences. Planning must cover design, site architecture, navigation, images, perhaps video. Who should oversee this complicated venture? Many sites are planned by design and production specialists—but this process often produces ineffective sites. When graphics are created, and then someone is called on to fill in the copy blocks, little thought is given to the site's set of goals and how it fits in with the organization's overall marketing.

At companies and nonprofits with resources, the best sites are produced collaboratively by a team led by marketing and communication specialists. The team's designers work to translate these decision makers' ideas into visuals that support the message, and the technical people make it happen.

If you are a one-person band, feel secure that your knowledge of your subject—whether a product, service or yourself—combined with your strategic writing and thinking skills gives you the best base to build with. You can use online platforms to supply design and adapt it according to your capabilities. Or you can hire art and production help. But it's up to you to decide what you want your site to accomplish, who you want to reach and how to communicate your core message. Good websites are not technology-driven—they are message driven.

Here are a few more differences between print and website writing.

1. **Interactive thinking.** Traditional print media have a one-way direction: "here's the word from the author" or the firm or the government. In general, online media aim to foster comments, dialogue, opinions, sharing, contributions, content. (Notice that newspapers and magazines have picked up on this approach and also try to foster dialogue and input.)

2. **Nonlinear nature.** Print documents were traditionally conceived as linear information flows with a beginning, middle and end. Few website visitors start at A and finish at Z. They search for specific information and may never see your home page. So each page should be self-explanatory and may need to repeat content from other parts of the site, including contact information and a call to action.

3. **"Information packaging" outlook.** Because the digital world offers so much material, to draw people in and keep them engaged, information must be "chunked" into short, digestible lumps; use alternate ways to pull visitors along; and develop interpretive visuals.

4. **Scanability.** Online writing must take account of scanners and divers and robots. We dive for what we need—for example, a product to fix a leaking pipe, a plumber, advice from people who solved a similar problem, tips for dealing with plumbers. To be found by robots, pages must incorporate well-planned search terms. Copy must get to the point without fluff or empty verbiage.

5. **Clear channeling to "what's next."** Most effective websites include a strong call to action on every page—"Buy today!" "Call us now at . . ." "To find out more . . ." "For a peek behind the scenes . . ." "Subscribe to our free newsletter!" Since visitors don't read your pages sequentially, each page should lead them where you want them to go, or to what you want them to do. For example, "Check out more products you may like," "Read what our clients say about us," take this quiz, read my blog, order now. Many websites fail to smooth the buyer's path toward the ultimate goal.

6. **Build to evolve.** Websites can be used as "online brochures" that remain basically static, but ideally, they should incorporate ways to update and morph in response to user response and analysis. Traditional documents took a long time and heavy investment to prepare, print and deliver. And then they were immutable. But once created, digital media delivers instantly and is highly changeable. Because constant

updating is possible, people expect it. Figure out how to keep your site alive: new blog posts, comments, guest appearances, news of any kind relevant to your audience. And notice content and graphic trends. For example, many effective sites today feature fewer words and a dominant visual. But the words must be exactly right.

SUCCESS TIP

The Evolving Digital Language

Leading websites have steadily evolved to speak more through images (photos, illustrations, video, infographics) and less through words. Language gets tighter and tighter. When the first edition of this book was written five or so years ago, General Electric—whose website is widely admired—positioned itself on its home page in formal language:

> GE IS IMAGINATION AT WORK. From jet engines to power generation, financial services to water processing, and medical imaging to media content, GE people worldwide are dedicated to turning imaginative ideas into leading products and services that help solve some of the world's toughest problems.

Two years ago, a similar statement appeared on the "consumer" home page this way:

> GE works on things that matter. The best people and the best technologies taking on the toughest challenges. Finding solutions in energy, health and home, transportation and finance. Building, powering, moving and curing the world. Not just imagining. Doing. GE works.

Most recently, GE's various home pages include no explanatory text at all.

Dominant focus is on the site's interior content: stories, or information sections relating to each site's target audience, promoted with an image and teaser blurb to lead readers to click and read. Sites that aggregate information (e.g., travel sites, celebrity news, book sites) use similar approaches. The content inside must justify the click.

HOW TO STRATEGIZE A WEBSITE

Even if you're a one-person band doing your own graphics, HTML and copy, start with a written plan. The approach for online media is close to the one you're practicing for an e-mail, speech or report.

Define Your Goals

Decide what you want the site to accomplish. For context, here are various ways that enterprises of any size frame their goals (which were formerly accomplished via other media and channels, and still are; websites are additional though important delivery systems).

- sell a product or service

- communicate with the public, investors, board members, government agencies and so on

- provide customer support

- build brand awareness and loyalty

- attract quality new employees

- announce news and build media relationships

- establish credibility

Websites also enable organizations to more easily accomplish goals that were once formidable. For example:

- personalize service by interacting with and learning from customers

- create an organizational personality

- present a unified face to a complex multidivision, multilocation firm

- unite geographically scattered staff and consultants

- rally staff to the mission and to contribute to marketing

- demonstrate social commitment

- market individuals as experts, speakers, personalities

- educate relevant audiences

- create a fan base among identified groups

Nonprofit organizations, which also function as businesses, typically share these goals and add a few of their own—for example, to attract and recognize donors and volunteers, support grant applications and humanize the organization. Government entities leverage opportunities to put a human face on their work and make their services more accessible and appreciated.

Put your own goals in writing. Assuming you want a website (or blog) that supports your immediate and long-range job prospects leads you to . . .

Think About Audience

Who might help advance your career ambitions: Employers in your field? Human Resource professionals? Career employment agencies? Your peers? Use some of the people-analysis tools in Chapter 2 to characterize the people in such groups and what they will want to see or look for. Build personas, like marketers. With your goals and target audiences in mind, it becomes easy to . . .

Decide on Message and Content

Very much like you're practicing with e-mails, reports and other media, think about the message you want to communicate to your chosen audiences. (For some ideas to help with this, see the sections on preparing elevator speeches and stories in Chapter 11.) Once you define this message content, decisions become easier. For example, if you want a site that demonstrates excellence in your field, should you show examples of your work? A good "About Me" self-introduction page and/or a video? Testimonials from former employers, professors or others?

The thinking process also clarifies what not to include. For example, photographs that make you look unprofessional, comments that are controversial or overly personal, a passion for something that's at odds with the idea that you will be a dedicated employee, material that contradicts how you want to be perceived. In fact, determine to put up only what shows you as your best professional self.

Choose Your Tone

If you want to impress people who are highly conservative, you need not produce ponderous old-fashioned copy, but you may not want to go to creative extremes that may offend them so they consider you unfit for their environment. Be cautious about creating a funny or witty site; try it out on members of your intended audience and collect honest opinions.

Most of us love sites that are spontaneous-sounding, humorous and edgy. But that's not easy to achieve. It typically takes the organization's A-team a ton of time to create that charming quirky touch. Fortunately, a solid, effective site can be built with a straightforward tone. In fact, some sites formerly renowned for their cleverness now strive for simplicity—in language, visuals, navigation. The effort is to crystallize the message and achieve a friendly, accessible, lively feeling. Clarity always trumps cleverness.

Site-Building Practicalities

Once you've set your guidelines, decide on the pages you need and their sequence—how each will connect to the others. Some planners think of this structure as a plant: The home page is the leafy "pretty face," and below ground, pages branch out as a network of roots.

Think about how you envision the site now and also down the line in a month, six months, a year or more. That helps you build a framework that easily accommodates growth and development.

Even for a blog, you may want a stable section of the site that remains basically unchanged. Consider the essentials that have become classic for organizations:

Home Page: Represents the site content and leads to it. The main elements are headline, tagline, positioning statement, links to inside content

About Us: Your story. Who are you? Why do you do what you do? Why are you good at it?

Services or Products: What needs you fill and how what you offer is unique, will make your visitor's life better

Newsroom: About your company and the industry, media releases, appearances

Examples: Your product or service in action

FAQs: Ask and answer probable visitor questions

Testimonials: Often—surprise!—the most-read part of a site

Contact Us: E-mail, telephone, social media as appropriate

Links and Resources

Do you need all this? No, of course not. It depends on your goal–audience analysis. Your blog can be your home page, you can add a bio page, use testimonials there or on a separate page, use a page for work samples. But keep in mind that people are accustomed to finding and exploring websites in a common progression. They dislike searching for a profile, for example, that is hidden under the title "Of past and present." They dislike cute icons with unclear meaning. For example, the three little lines often used to represent "menu" remain a puzzle to a large percentage of viewers. Aim to be totally clear and honest in the buttons and titles and clicks of your infrastructure, your message and the customer's path to purchase or other end point.

Translate Print to Online Language

Online reading demands that language be more concise and to the point. Too many websites read as if an old print brochure had been recycled into uncomfortable digital life. Let's use an example to demonstrate the difference and suggest some effective techniques for online writing generally.

Suppose that Jack has come up with a niche service and wants to develop his business. He might write a **print handout** that reads:

> ### Introducing Kung Foe: Martial Arts Lessons Designed for Women
>
> *We're happy to announce the opening of the Kung Foe Studio, a martial arts training center that focuses on women.*
>
> *Created by Jake Lane, a black belt practitioner of the martial arts since 2010, Kung Foe specializes in helping women of every age protect themselves while engaging in a health-promoting program. Activities are adapted from the most effective martial arts techniques specially adapted to women's physique, psychology and needs.*
>
> *Classes are exclusively open to women. They learn to defend themselves in challenging situations, enjoy improved and physical well-being and develop confidence in their own ability to handle hostile or aggressive behavior. Classes are open exclusively to women because Jack found in working with people of all kinds that women have unique fears, a reluctance to hurt their attackers and a need to overcome their smaller stature and other physical limitations.*
>
> *Options include . . .*

This copy might work OK for a print brochure, but readers will lose patience with it online. For a **website home page**, the same material might read this way:

> ### Women: Learn Kung Foe and Stay Safe Anywhere!
>
> *It's a dangerous world.*
>
> *Whatever your age, whatever shape you're in, protect yourself with Kung Foe—the martial art designed for women.*

Your teacher: *Jake Lane, a black belter devoted to helping women defend themselves since 2010. Jack adapts killer martial arts techniques to women's special physique and psychology. Sign on for a women-only class!*

- Build your confidence.

- Turn the tables on attackers twice your size.

- Turn fear into action.

- Overcome your reluctance to fight back.

- Shape up—and have fun!

See what women like you say about the experience and results . . .
Choose your option . . .

To ensure a good impression on a mini-screen, the writer might tighten up the website version further and put the bullet list on an inside page.

The copywriter's goal for website writing: simple, concise, punchy, to the point. This demands cutting all wordiness and the discursive tone of traditional print materials. For a product or service, online content must relate directly to the target audience's problems and provide the solution. This framework leads naturally to crystallizing statements, short-burst paragraphs, short words and sentences, and easily grasped formats like bulleting.

Would this approach work better for a print vehicle as well? Often, yes. Reading online has accustomed us to brevity and graphic impact, so print media increasingly adopts these techniques. Notice how many ways today's newspapers try to attract reader attention and deliver information. They summarize content up front in a sentence and, more than ever, use images and strong captions, subheads and pullout quotes.

BLOGGING: KNOW WHY, KNOW HOW

One of the exciting things about the Internet is that anyone with a PC and a modem can publish whatever content they can create.

—Bill Gates, cofounder and CEO of Microsoft, in a 1996 essay

In the olden days, to reach a substantial audience with information and ideas you'd write an article. The process could take a year—to research, pitch, interact with an editor, draft, revise and so on.

While some publishing still works that way—notably newsstand magazines and many professional journals—today anyone can be a published author. There's no gatekeeper or editor to block your voice or demand that you meet her standards.

In 10 minutes, you can write and post a blog (or an article) on someone else's site or a discussion forum. If you want your own blog site, it is easy to set up at little or no cost. Then you become your own publisher as well.

There are two catches to taking the blogger route casually.

Catch 1: To succeed, you must perform most of the editorial functions yourself—choose a good topic; angle it right for the audience; and write, edit, proofread and market. That's a lot of responsibility! And it takes real time. Some consistency of output is needed to build and maintain an audience.

Catch 2: A lot has changed since Bill Gates's 1996 statement. Many people have taken advantage of the extraordinary opportunities of online publishing. One recent estimate says that 133 million people in the United States alone have blogs—but more than 90% of them have been abandoned. Both statistics are significant. Clearly, it is extremely difficult to find audiences and recognition today, and tomorrow looks harder.

If you want to blog for anyone other than yourself, family and friends, you need to be determined, anticipate a long haul and follow a plan based on your goals, target readership, and a subject to which you can contribute value. Rather than focusing solely on what *you* want to communicate—your ideas, opinions, experience—think like a marketer from the outset. Ask: Who is my ideal audience? How will I find and interest its members? What do I know that people need or want to read about? How can I help these readers? Can I identify a niche related to what I can share that is relatively unoccupied?

Inventory Your Strengths and Expertise

Wherever you are in life and career, you can potentially share useful information and insights about one or more subjects. Start by inventorying what you know. Then divide your expertise into narrow pieces.

Take an accountant, for example. She could break her expertise down into topics like how to prepare for an audit, choose an accountant or work with one, take advantage of tax loopholes, revamp a financial system and so on. Each of these subjects can be further broken down—for example, organizing your papers for an audit, what to say to the auditor, what not to say and whether you should bring your accountant with you.

She could also blog about

- how a movie presents an outdated view of the profession,

- how she solved a common problem that readers experience,

- a conference that covered the impact of new tax laws,

- a challenge the profession is facing,

- a professional view of a relevant court case or issue in the news,

- common mistakes people make on their tax returns, and

- how to evaluate your accountant's service.

And/or, if she has an established fan base, she can write about a passionate hobby, an interesting experience or an inspiring book. In fact, many bloggers-for-business choose to incorporate posts on a hobby or pastime, rather than the work itself, to build a more dimensioned persona and connect with other enthusiasts.

Notice that most of the ideas on the accountant's subject list translate to many professions. If you're a business student right now and define that as your profession, you can come up with a similar list of knowledge areas and viewpoints worth sharing—for example, the impact of a brand-new tax law that you learned about, an interesting celebrity lecture, an observation on effective teaching methods and so on.

Find Ideas in Your Current Experience

If are now a student in any field, you might have interesting ideas to share for studying better, saving money, finding social time and so on. Then your target audience is your fellow students and you can aim to expand beyond your immediate circles (like Mark Zuckerberg did with Facebook). Or you might aim for an audience outside school and share cutting-edge research, interesting statistics, trends, big-picture thinking and insights on current problems or legislation that will affect people already engaged in the field. You might interview professors and share their insights, cover trends in teaching strategies or a shift in textbooks. This type of blog could work because people in the workforce rarely have time to keep up with such subjects and might like to know about them.

And, of course, you can choose to blog about your passionate hobby, fitness program, travel, experience living on $30 per week, whatever. Don't assume that your own present world does not hold potential for sharing and conversation with others. But some structured thinking and brainstorming helps.

Here are two examples of inventive thinking.

Example 1

Assigned to come up with a blog for a writing course, one graduate student submitted a "what I think" idea with a list of topics that included a movie review, a book review, his opinion on the election and other ideas. The instructor was not impressed. She asked, "Do you have a hobby? Anything you really like doing?" The young man lit up: "Oh yes! I'm a part-time DJ and I earned my way through college doing gigs." Aha! "And is there anything you know about DJ-ing that would interest other people?" "Sure! How to liven up your party, how to get started as a DJ, what you need, how to get bookings, new ideas. . . . "

Can you show people how to do something? If you have a passion, or have accomplished something uncommon, find inspiration and audience there. Be especially alert to any two skills or experiences you can combine. For example, if you've learned classical French cooking and studied dieting, a blog could almost write itself.

Example 2

Assigned to plan a blog for a communication class project, three students decided to write about their personal opinions of new Apple products. The instructor observed that their potential blog posts had value. But what did they intend to do with them? Where would they post them, and who would find them? Forced to think about the marketing angle, the group came up with a niche. They scouted the Internet and found few reviews of Apple products written by people in their age group—Millennials. It was a short step to wonder:

Might Apple want to support a blog about their products, by Millennials for Millennials? They wrote a letter with a few sample blog posts. The company responded with interest; the foot was in the door.

If you need help with your own thinking, the Internet is crammed with information, ideas and advice on developing content. Here's a fun resource to generate ideas when you're out of steam: Portent (www.portent.com/tools/title-maker). Enter your general subject, and a generator instantly comes up with promising titles.

I entered "business writing," and Portent suggested "16 Unexpected Ways Business Writing Can Give You Better Hair." At another time, it offered "What Mom Never Told You About Business Writing," "Why Business Writing Should Be 1 of the 7 Deadly Sins," "20 Ways Business Writing Can Find You the Love of Your Life," "How Better Business Writing Changes How We Think About Death." Not all are workable, of course—but they are thought-provoking and suggest how popular bloggers think. The titles come with funny comments and, last I looked, a good freebie on following up a title with good content.

Hubspot (www.hubspot.com/blog-topic-generator) is another idea generator. Enter three nouns, and you get 10 ideas. Here I entered "blog," "goal" and "audience." The results included "5 Tools Everyone in the Blogger Industry Should Be Using," "10 Signs You Should Invest in Audience," "14 Common Misconceptions About Audience."

And one more: Linkbait (http://linkbaitgenerator.com/marketing/index.php). Entering the same subject produced "Guns don't kill people—business writing kills people," "8 ways business writing can be used as a weapon" and one that you might like best: "The rise of business writing and how to make it stop."

Take Trouble With Headlines

Notice that the idea generators favor headlines with numbers in them—these are "listicles," and they're not only endlessly popular with readers, but easy to write. Come up with the headline and you have an instant copy map, already organized. For example:

The 5 Biggest Reasons College Students Get Depressed

8 Incredibly Simple Ways to Get More People to Read Your Content

Six Ways to Change People's Minds—and Make Them Like It

17 Quick Wins to Boost Your Social Reach Today

Focusing on people's "pain"—what they fear or worry about—is also a great technique for choosing subjects and waving that headline flag:

How to Stifle That Noisy Roommate

Three Ways to Turn a Monster Boss Into a Booster

How to Say No to a Contractor and Keep the Door Open

Secrets of an IRS Insider: How to Prevent an Audit

Create your own list of headlines that prompt you to read the content. Here are a few online titles that intrigued me recently:

What to Do When You're Shtickless: How to Add Humor to Presentations

How the U.S. Army Uses Social Media

Why a Bad Memory's Not Such a Bad Thing

Notice that all the headlines get right to the point and promise a benefit. Many of these samples tend toward some drama or exaggeration and are heavy on the adjectives, something not recommended for most writing formats. For blogs, this language works better than understatement. Questions are good—and so is hinting that you will share "secrets," or something new or surprising.

But don't shortchange your readers: Give them what you promise—practical advice they can put to work or ideas to stimulate their thinking.

An overwhelming amount of research on what works on the Internet is readily available. For headlines, the general advice is to write up to 65 characters, including spaces. And use your keywords as early as you can.

Craft an Engaging Lead

Once you've hooked your readers with the headline, keep them with you by starting strong. One way is to start with a question. Or connect readers directly to the problem you're more or less solving for them. For example, a lead for "Three Ways to Turn a Monster Boss Into a Booster" might read:

Does your boss never stop carping and criticizing? Is he all too eager to pounce on your mistakes? Nothing makes work more miserable. But grin and bear it is not your only option. Try one of these three strategies and you might just turn the situation around almost overnight.

Another good tack is to use an anecdote, your own or someone else's, to make an instant connection. For example, "How to Say No to a Contractor and Keep the Door Open" could lead:

If you've ever rejected one of your contractors and lived to regret it, because the next guy really screwed up, you're not alone. I faced this situation last week. I thought I could save a few bucks by. . . .

Starting a Blog Q&A

Q: **How do I create a blogging plan?**

A: Use the ideas in this chapter to create your personal Blogging Guide like this:

1. Write down your goal—what you want to accomplish.

2. Define your audience—who you want to reach—and create a written persona that includes the group members' interests, problems, worries.

3. Choose a subject area that connects goal and audience with your own knowledge base.

4. Check your idea against marketing possibilities. How will you reach the audience you defined?

5. Create a one-paragraph statement based on your four answers to serve as your guiding light; include a brief plan for marketing the blog.

6. Brainstorm a list of 10 to 20+ headlines for topics you can look forward to writing about that align with the guiding light.

Q: **How long should a blog post be?**

A: It depends. Until recently, general advice was to write short-ish blog posts, in the 350- to 600-word range. But research shows that across most industries, long posts—2,500 words or more—gain more readership. It makes sense that with so much available, readers prefer in-depth treatments and tend to save and share them more. Still, some of the most popular bloggers choose to write short, at least sometimes. Choose lengths you're comfortable with and do justice to your subject and consider, realistically, your time constraints.

Q: **How often should I blog?**

A: It depends. Conventional advice recommends at least twice a week. But many leading bloggers worry that the pressure to produce so much yields lower quality, so some make a point of blogging less often but well. To build a following, though, it's best to publish new blog posts on a predictable schedule, at least twice a month.

Q: **But shouldn't you keep publishing timely blog posts so there's always something new to read?**

A: Blogging is a good way to keep a website fresh and attractive to both search engines and people. However, writing "evergreen" blog posts—in-depth pieces with information that doesn't change much—offers an excellent option for satisfying readers and delivering value on a website.

Q: **Can I blog without creating and maintaining my own site?**

A: Yes. You can be a guest blogger—ideally, research existing blogs on your subject, get familiar with them, contribute comments, then offer a guest post. Or use existing venues that welcome bloggers, such as LinkedIn and Medium. Try out your voice on Quora, a fascinating compendium of questions and answers from the sublime to the ridiculous, which draws numerous prominent people to write answers. Set the filter system to bring you questions in your interest areas, and then write answers to those you like. Another good starting point is to post comments on other people's blogs. Say something nice about the blog, contribute additional points respectfully, ask if a guest piece is welcome. Don't self-promote, but clearly state how readers can connect with you.

JOINING ONLINE COMMUNITIES

LinkedIn, and other professionally oriented sites that serve specific industries and associations, are best seen as communities rather than social media platforms. Since their members include recruiters and employers who use the site to fill a job or a contract, it's short-sighted not to put them high on your list of valuable media. When you approach an employer yourself, they are likely to check you out online—particularly LinkedIn and Twitter. And in turn you can check the company's people out by reviewing their profiles and then use what you learn to create effective messages. When you're hunting for jobs and gigs, these communities give you the chance to find key people and make direct contact or reach them via other people you already know.

VIEW FROM THE FIELD: HOW TO GENERATE AN ONLINE CONVERSATION

Search by keywords for people who are interested in what you're interested in, read them, see what they think, go in with a how-can-I-help-you attitude. A community is about a purpose, a shared passion, maybe a vision of a better future or something everyone can believe in and get on board with. Once you see what the culture is like, add value. Start conversations. Ask curiosity-based questions, which are often better conversation starters than statements. A question can relate to the topic or culture of the group; it can pique people's interest and beg for a response. It can help promote your interests, too.

For example, I asked on LinkedIn, "What comes up when you Google your name or brand?" A few people responded in ways that made it clear they were open to help that I was able to give without selling. I've asked, "What impact has SEO had on your business?" This is a much-misunderstood subject and the question opened up revealing dialogues. I've also asked, "What is the worst or funniest experience you've had on a website?" I heard from angry, frustrated people, and it helped my own knowledge base—and ability to deal with clients.

—Jerry Allocca, founder and CEO
of Connected Culture, digital marketer

Using LinkedIn

You are what you write on LinkedIn. Good writing can help you in several significant ways. It's a forum for blogs, comments, and information-sharing posts. Create them carefully. And post a well-crafted profile if your goal is to support and advance your career.

Craft Your LinkedIn Profile

Head shot. Use one of good quality that presents you as professional and friendly. Judge the degree of formality or informality by the industry that interests you.

Headline. If you're employed, use an honest, accurate title (and note that a current employer might be offended if you present yourself as independent). Or you can choose to create a generic title for yourself and even a mini elevator speech—like "Elementary school phys ed teacher and three-time winning coach of Sixth Grade Regional Basketball" (provided you want a relevant job). If you're not now employed, you can use the same tack or invent a title that positions you the way you want to be seen. For example, "Record-setting Fundraiser for Nonprofits." You're entitled to say "Engineer in Training" or something similar if you're in school or just "Graduating Senior at Cal Tech." The character-count limit for titles is 120.

Summary. Like a résumé, your online profile should tilt toward the future—where you want to go—using your past as the platform. But prospective employers expect to find more insight into your personality and way of looking at things than your official résumé affords.

Your own background gives you the best clues to presenting yourself with originality. In relation to your work, brainstorm:

- What energizes you, motivates you, gives you the biggest rewards?
- What makes you feel happiest and proudest?
- Why do you do the work you do (or want to do)?
- What do you envision accomplishing?
- What expertise or experience make you interesting, relevant, likable?
- Do you want to help people? If so, who, and why, and how?
- Any multiskill combinations? If you speak four languages, for example, or even two like a native, that's a plus in many kinds of jobs and makes you unusual.
- As with your résumé, find the achievement in what you do. Move past the jargon and generalizations to convey a sense of what you've actually done and what it says about your capabilities. Cite evidence of your value—like an honor or award, an anecdote about an achievement, a glamorous credential.

The character-count limit for summaries is 2,000.

Writing Tips for Online Profiles

Frame it in I. First person helps you share who you are with more genuine feeling and warmth and feels more authentic than talking about yourself in the third person.

Keep it short and active. Aim for three to five paragraphs. Use simple concrete language. Take trouble with your sentence rhythm; you want a fluid read. Check it with the reading-aloud method.

Smile when you write that! Aim for a warm and friendly tone—enthusiasm is contagious. Given a choice, we'd all rather work with people who clearly care about their work and enjoy it. Use high-energy verbs to demonstrate this.

Link to multimedia. As appropriate, link to articles, social media, video, your website. But be sure the material shows you off well.

Remember SEO. People must be able to find you, so identify your search terms and use them, but without disrupting or distorting your message.

Be consistent. Your profile must not contradict your résumé, nor anything else a seeker can find out about you online. Which is potentially everything.

Write endorsements and recommendations for other people judiciously. Ask for them, too, courteously and carefully. *Your overriding goal is to build relationships.*

VIEW FROM THE FIELD: PUT YOUR PROFILE TO WORK

My core message to clients is that an Internet presence gives small businesses and individuals the same tools that once would have been the playground of very large companies. One important way to use the power behind it is to flesh out your online profile. The more you can keep it pointing at your expertise and intelligence and can get recognized as an expert at what you do, someone who is a knowledgeable information resource, the better. So make a concerted effort to update your status. Link to blogs you've written, note if you're giving a speech or win an award, or tweet—everything counts.

—Adrian Miller, CEO of Adrian Miller Sales Training and founder of Adrian's Network

Success Tip: How to Be a Good Online Sharer

The New York Times Customer Insight Group carried out research on why people share on the Internet. The key findings provide a good orientation for individuals as well as companies who want to make a mark. The top reasons identified:

- To bring valuable and entertaining content to others; 49% said sharing allows them to inform others of products they care about and potentially change opinions or encourage action.

- To define ourselves to others; 68% share to give people a better sense of who they are and what they care about.

- To grow and nourish our relationships; 78% share information online because it lets them stay connected to people they may not otherwise stay in touch with.

- Self-fulfillment; 69% share information because it allows them to feel more involved in the world.

- To get the word out about causes or brands; 84% share because it is a way to support causes or issues they care about.

As reported by Garrett Moon, 2015. "Why People Share, The Psychology of Social Sharing." *CoSchedule*. Retrieved from https://coschedule.com/blog/why-people-share/.

Using Twitter's Micro Magic

When you work with 280 characters, it's hard to believe that you're using a highly effective business communication tool, let alone one that fosters political revolutions and might serve as a president's main communication platform—but, of course, you are. And by now most of us refrain from telling people what we're eating for lunch (except for famous chefs, whose lunch is riveting to followers).

You can tweet to solve problems, get help or advice, let people know where you are and much more. Often it feels like you're throwing information out into the world without expecting results. We all know stories about happy surprises: a reporter who won a plum assignment from an editor who noticed he was vacationing in a hot spot, a company that fixed a problem because it received a tweeted complaint, somebody who landed a dream job because an executive read her tweets and so on.

Rather than using Twitter in a random way, make it part of your strategic campaign to promote your goals. It's a unique chance to establish yourself as a subject expert, connect with people who have similar professional or personal interests, and reach people you'd ordinarily have no hope of accessing. It's also a principal means by which to direct people to more substantial online material, like your latest blog post.

All you have to do is be relevant, useful and interesting! Audiences expect from micromedia very much the same things they want from all media: substance, relevance and, ideally, entertainment.

Asked to explain his goal in tweeting, social media commenter Steve Rubel said, "To share my passion with the community and solicit ideas all with the intent of moving me toward my long-term goal of revolutionizing marketing communications through technology." Your own goal may be more modest than that, but identifying it empowers you to choose good subjects and target audiences. You can be a firsthand source of information or ideas and at other times, "curate" by monitoring your universe for interesting things other people are saying and link to or retweet that information.

Always write well. People will help you get the word out by favoriting or retweeting your message if it has value, helps them look on top of things or is interesting or funny. Including images increases the number of retweets exponentially.

Twitter gives you a formidable way to keep in contact with employers after an interview, build your acquaintance with someone you met at a meeting, introduce yourself to someone you want to know and keep your presence alive in the minds of clients or prospects, many of whom monitor the site or actively participate.

Some Twitter Writing Tips

- Use fewer than the allotted 280 characters to facilitate retweeting.

- Abbreviations are OK *if you're sure your audience will understand them*. If your readers may not understand texting shortcuts, find a different, tighter way to say what you mean.

VIEW FROM THE FIELD: CHOOSING YOUR SOCIAL MEDIA WORDS

Think twice before you speak once—that's incredibly important. Does it fit with your message, your image? Try to keep the message consistent, and stay in context of your online persona.

Your writing must be clear and concise so people don't misconstrue what you say—they'll read into it and interpret, which is a big problem online. So write unambiguously. Keep away from sarcasm; many people don't get it. Never write when you're angry or impassioned. No vulgarity: It damages your credibility completely.

Use terminology that promotes your expertise and makes your message searchable by interjecting keywords, like for SEO. I keep a list of the top words I want to include handy. Also, you can check out what you write with a word cloud [e.g., via www.wordle.net] so you can look at a visual of your message and see what words you used the most.

—Bill Corbett, president of Corbett
Public Relations

- Adopt an active tone. Use simple direct sentences—avoid *–ing, –ize* and similar kinds of words as well as cluttered constructions that need *is* and *are.* Good active verbs go a long way.

- Use short, basic words and only those that are essential to the message. Cut every unnecessary word and phrase.

- Make sure the finished message doesn't get so telegraphic that it's hard to understand.

- Ask for what you want. Saying "please retweet," for example, hugely increases the likelihood that people will.

- Check online sources (like Twitter itself) for up-to-date guidance on using the medium's conventions well.

- Don't send first drafts—review your message and work on simplicity, clarity and wording. All the editing guidelines in Chapter 5 apply. This limiting format is good practice for your editing skills.

- Don't blatantly self-promote. A general guideline is to tout your own article, blog, book or service once out of every four or five tweets.

- Write a snappy, concise profile in either a carefully honed paragraph or a telegraphic style. Many professionals like to cite a set of skills; for example, "Prettybook Prize Winning Writer, Editor, Communications Consultant"; "U.M. Senior, Nuclear Researcher-to-Be, Redwings SuperFan."

CHOOSE TO BRAND YOURSELF

Only a few of the current social channels can be covered here—and in any case, you need not and should not use them all. There's not enough time in the universe. How should you choose? Consider whether the platform is peopled by individuals you want to meet or connect with based on their industries, occupations, age, companies and other factors important to you. If you create something with a strong visual aspect, a site like Pinterest makes sense. Some channels offer features that add special value. Participating in Google+, for example, directly helps with search engine optimization because Google, the dominant search engine, favors it.

Remember to integrate your social media channels with each other and with whatever traditional print media you use. Repetition is good in this flicker-fast world, so posting the same items on multiple channels, multiple times, is standard practice. Many experienced social media users repeat the same tweet four or five times, because different people read their feeds at different times. If you're promoting a blog post or article, you might promote it half a dozen times with different headlines or information nuggets.

Add your most important social media platforms to your e-mail signature. Maximize your time through sites that aggregate your social media output so your new material is widely distributed.

Websites, blogging, social media and online communities give you the power to brand yourself, once solely the prerogative of giant enterprises. Why do this? Because you own the power to decide what you want to be known for and how you want to be seen. Then you can access all the tools of digital and traditional media to present a consistent, thoughtful, strategic "you"—a you that can make the most of opportunities and accomplish what you most want.

Of course, this is a lifetime enterprise. Your goals will change and so will the tools of communication. Plan to stay flexible and learn to use new channels that make sense for you as they materialize.

Exercise your writing skills, and you're equipped with the most important constant. Adapt them to your chosen platforms with imagination.

VIEW FROM THE FIELD: HOW TO LAUNCH A STRATEGIC SOCIAL CAMPAIGN

People start at the wrong end, with the tools—it's like asking, how do I use this hammer or screwdriver? They jump on the tools instead of what they're trying to accomplish. Before leaping into social media, conduct a social media marketing audit. Know your objective and who you want to connect with. Then ask, where do these people participate? First listen—people don't listen enough.

Start there; learn what this community you're building or joining is looking for. Next think about what you want to share and how and whether the content is in sharable form so you can go viral. If you can identify information gaps and fill those, you'll quickly and naturally gain a standing in that community and a following. It's good to work to a theme; chunk your content down. If your resources are limited, limit your scope so you can make a solid effort.

—Arthur Germain, principal and chief brandteller of Communication Strategy Group

THINK GLOBAL: THE INTERNET LIVES EVERYWHERE

Global thinking used to be less important when people communicated mostly in print and cared mostly about audiences that spoke the same language. But other than being limited by some governments, the Internet goes everywhere. It's a major force for globalization and demands that we consider the world outside our own borders, time zones and language.

One enormous advantage owned by native English speakers is that their language has become the language of business, the language of science and much more. Even Japan's business world—long resistant to using English—is moving toward intensive English instruction. However, the globalized marketplace poses growing challenges to the United States, United Kingdom and other English language countries.

All over the world, people move toward online buying, create websites, use social media, write blogs and all the rest. Your own competition may be international. People today have more opportunities to buy from sites in their own languages, for example, and naturally prefer doing so. Therefore if you want to reach an international audience or might benefit from doing so, consider nonnative English speakers in the early planning stage. Writing must be crafted to be easily read by nonnative speakers around the world, including those in our own workplaces. Here are some general guidelines to help internationalize your online writing.

Keep Wording Super Clear and Direct

Minimize slang, idioms, clichés and colloquial expressions. Use one- or two-syllable words. Try to avoid abstract words and words that can be misinterpreted. Contractions can confuse; *we have* is better than *we've*. Spell out even commonplace abbreviations like ASAP.

Use Simple Language Structure

Try to average 8 to 14 words per sentence. Avoid multiple clauses and *there is* and *that is* constructions. Also cut wordy phrasing with many prepositions—for example, *able* is better than *in a position to*, *justify* is better than *give a justification for*. Keep paragraphs short, one to three sentences; use space between paragraphs and substantial margins.

Keep Graphics Accessible and Uncluttered

Make navigation as clear and straightforward as you possibly can. Make all your headers unambiguous and don't get too clever; skip subtle graphic devices. Build in plenty of white space.

Stay Conscious of Cultural Differences

Observe basic differences in how various cultures cite dates, times, numbers and so on. But you must know another culture and its language well to understand its idioms, attitudes, sensitivities and inside jokes.

If you're aiming to reach a particular language-speaking group, it's wise to have someone from inside the culture review your copy. Remember that a widely used language such as Spanish has many cultures, and there are real differences between a Spanish, Cuban and Argentine audience, for example.

When it's important for the message to reach a global audience effectively, you may want to consult with specialists and use good translation services.

Note that if you're writing for a global institution with facilities in other parts of the world, you're automatically writing for a multiple-language workforce and need to consider cross-cultural guidelines.

Moreover, writing to be understood by nonnative English speakers is similar to writing for the diverse audience that characterizes many U.S. workplaces and the country as a whole.

In general, drill down to the core of your content and be specific and concrete. People with limited English skills will not invest time in finding your important points, so don't bury them in material that doesn't matter or is there just to entertain.

Globalized writing is admittedly less colorful and spontaneous-sounding. That's another reason why understanding your goals and audience is high priority. A website aimed at a world audience is necessarily a balancing act. If you aim for a domestic audience, you may be less concerned with appealing to diverse readers. If you want to reach specific communities, either geographically or online, there are good tools for pinpointing your audience. In this case, know and use its language.

PRACTICE OPPORTUNITIES

I. Create and Post a Comment

Identify at least three bloggers who write about a subject that interests you. Read at least five posts for each one. Write a paragraph or more saying why you like the blog, as specifically as you can, and also describe anything that doesn't work for you. Then choose a post that invites input and write a comment. Exchange the draft with a partner, make changes based on your partner's input if you wish, and post your comment.

II. Plan and Write a Blog

This series of activities can be done in pairs so each student receives ongoing feedback during the project's course.

1. Find a subject that relates to your current expertise or interest and that will contribute in some way to your professional image or career.

2. In writing, plan a blog, considering your goal and audience. Research online to locate bloggers in your area of interest, and review those with whom you'll compete.

3. Brainstorm content ideas and make a list of at least 15 topics for suitable blogs. Add additional topics already done by other bloggers if you like—some professionals look

for the most popular blogs and then write a better version, knowing the audience is hungry for this information.

4. Write the first blog post and use it to define your purpose, who you are, what you'll be writing and why—or just plunge right in and focus on one of your top subjects.

5. Plan a marketing program, in writing, to promote your blog and find readers you want.

6. Based on the plan, write promotional messages enticing people to subscribe to your blog that are suitable for e-mail, Twitter and other platforms favored by your chosen audience.

III. Group Debate: An Ethical Issue

Is it appropriate for people to blog in someone else's name? Tweet? Should authorship be explicit? Is it legitimate for CEOs and politicians to use staff members or outside PR people to blog in their name? Tweet? Divide into groups: Half the groups prepare to argue that hiring other people for this work is ethical, and the other half of the groups will argue against. Hold one debate or more. Evaluate results by comparing people's opinions before the debate with their opinions after the debate. The winning team is the one that changes the most minds.

IV. Tweet Practice

In a series of 10 tweets, distill the most useful information in this chapter as if you're sharing it with friends.

V. Build an Online Profile

If you have a LinkedIn profile, review and update it, taking into account the advice in this book. If you don't have one, create it now. Start by writing down your goals and describing the characteristics, interests and needs of your intended audiences.

VI. Q&A Practice

Identify an affinity group new to you on LinkedIn or another site, and review the Q&A. What self-interest can you identify for various contributors? Which questions provoked discussion, and which did not? Can you draw useful generalizations from this?

Can you offer answers to any of the questions? Do so.

Then think of five good questions to ask that would stir a conversation and give you something helpful—an idea, information, solution to a problem, connection and so on.

VII. Plan a Social Media Program

In the same groups, look at the website you created for a charitable cause in Chapter 9. Plot out a comprehensive social media strategy for that charity. In the context of goals and audience, what tools would you use, and how? How would you integrate with traditional marketing strategies (e.g., brochures, newsletters, marketing materials, mass-media campaigns, press releases) and cross-promote?

VIII. Plan a Reputation Management Program

Audit your own online image as objectively as possible. Consider all platforms you participate in. Do you like what you see? What do you want to change? What guidelines does this process suggest for the future? Some tools you may want to use: Tweet Eraser, TweetDelee, Delete.

SELECTED RESOURCES FOR SOCIAL MEDIA AND THE INTERNET

The best place to keep up with the fast-changing world of social media is . . . online. Here are some resources and a few personal favorites.

Website or Blog	Address	Description
For good general advice and to stay abreast of online trends:		
Mashable	http://mashable.com	Portal to a wide mix of social media news and information
Copyblogger	www.copyblogger.com	Online copywriting and content marketing strategies
HubSpot	https://blog.hubspot.com	"Inbound Internet Marketing Blog"
Mediabistro	www.mediabistro.com	Media news, blogs, job listings
Jeff Bullas	www.jeffbullas.com	Good in-depth blogging advice and ideas
Shel Holtz	http://holtz.com/blog	Social media commentary and advice from an established voice
Buffer	https://blog.bufferapp.com	Helpful information on content, building traffic and relevant research
For graphic presentation tools:		
Before & After	www.bamagazine.com	How to use design tools and sharpen your eye
Canva	www.canva.com	Easy-to-use design tool with templates for nondesigners
Gimp	www.gimp.org	Free image manipulation program resembling Photoshop
Easel.ly	www.easel.ly	Templates for creating infographics
Infogr.am	https://infogr.am	Helps you create charts and graphs

Website or Blog	Address	Description
For tech support, writing and SEO help:		
Internet Marketing Ninjas	https://internetmarketingninjas.com/seo-tools/free-optimization	Free on-page optimization tool
The Readability Test Tool	http://read-able.com	Tells you how readable your website copy is
Emotional Marketing Value Headline Analyzer	http://aminstitute.com/headline	Tells you how emotionally appealing your headline is
BuzzSumo	http://buzzsumo.com	Analyzes what blog content performs best in a particular niche
Keyword Planner	https://adwords.google.com/KeywordPlanner	Helps you figure out the best keywords
SavePublishing	http://savepublishing.com	Finds tweets on your website pages
For finding stories and facts:		
Digg	http://digg.com	What's happening on the Internet
Medium	https://medium.com	What's happening in the world
Contently	https://contently.com	Helps you tell great stories
Quora	www.quora.com	A super Q&A forum

11 PRESENT YOURSELF: WRITE WELL TO SPEAK WELL

He who fails to plan is planning to fail.

—Winston S. Churchill

Good writing is the secret ingredient of presenting yourself to advantage in all spoken and visual media. Here is the reasoning.

Effective speeches—no matter how informal—begin with writing. So do good introductions in business and professional settings. Whether a presentation is 30 minutes or 20 seconds long, experienced speakers use writing to think through and organize their content. Then they say it aloud, edit the written version to sound conversational and rehearse, often repeating the cycle a number of times.

The process for successful visual presentations via PowerPoint, Prezi and other alternatives is similar. They are best seen as illustrated talks driven by words rather than images. And even powerful images often originate with words—the challenge is to translate a fact, data or an idea into visual form that communicates and supports your message.

Then there's video. A good one usually starts with a written script that plans for spontaneous on-screen action along with the words. Even good interviews are scripted, based on good questions grounded in subject knowledge and project goals. Live video is not really an exception. It works best if you consider beforehand: Who is the audience? What do I want to communicate with this experience? What is my message and the question? Why should viewers care? How do I want them to react?

And writing gives you the best possible way to prepare for important conversations, confrontations and job interviews. This chapter shows you how to use writing for all these communication challenges. The principle: Preparation is key to success. Let's start with what might seem an easy channel: how you introduce yourself to colleagues at work and in outside business situations—meetings, events, professional groups. In fact, communicators and high-up executives work ceaselessly to improve their mini-speech content and delivery. It's a self-discovery process that will serve you well in many situations that matter. Working on it also prepares you to go about bigger oral presentation projects.

> **LEARN HOW TO...**
>
> - Introduce yourself with an elevator speech
> - Produce speeches and presentations
> - Prepare for face-to-face interactions
> - Create and use video
> - Translate ideas into visuals

THE ELEVATOR SPEECH: WHY AND HOW TO WRITE IT

If you're not familiar with the term *elevator speech,* also known as *elevator pitch,* it's what to say to someone you want to connect with when you're in the same elevator and you have about 15 to 20 seconds till he gets out.

It's the statement you make at a meeting when asked to introduce yourself—or any event where you meet new people and exchange business cards. Professionals of every kind who are networking, job hunting or looking for new customers try to develop elevator speeches that crystallize their marketing message. It's a primary tool for building new business connections and opening doors.

If you're not yet working in a career position, do you need an elevator speech? Absolutely. It's never too soon to connect with your industry of choice—and your peers. If you're studying for a degree, consider yourself a professional now, refer to yourself that way and use the professional's tools.

Like a speech or presentation, this brief pitch about yourself is, of course, spoken—but first it must be written. Planning to wing even a mini-speech won't do you justice. In earlier times it was assumed that a typical building had 50 floors and you had 60 seconds. But elevators, like the world, move much faster now, and most advisers would say 20 seconds is pushing it.

Everything you've learned about writing in terms of goal and audience applies to crafting an elevator speech. Honing a brief self-definition is tough. In some training approaches, participants are asked to deliver their mini-speeches while holding a lit match and must finish before burning their fingers.

So the effort is to distill what makes you special, what differentiates you, in that sliver of time. Communicators call this the value proposition or core value statement, and it usually applies to how an organization self-defines to distinguish itself from the competition. Similarly, put effort into seeing things from the audience viewpoint: What about you is relevant or interesting enough to hold listeners for 15 to 20 seconds and entice them to remember you or want to know more? It boils down to WIIFM—the tried and true what's-in-it-for-me factor.

It often works to start with your name and what you do, mentioning the company if you work for one. Then explain how you help, what problems you solve and how what you do can benefit your listener. Here are a few paired examples to demonstrate what works:

1. *"I'm a CPA, and for 15 years I've been practicing with Atlanta's largest accounting firm, ABC&D. We handle taxes and financial planning."*

2. *"I'm a CPA, and I help single women plan their finances so they save on taxes and can count on a secure future as independent people."*

1. *"I'm a nutritionist. I have a master's in biology from Cornell and wrote my thesis on how to be a locavore. Right now I work in the Major Medical Center and I'm also a consultant."*

2. *"I'm a nutritionist. I create personal food plans to help people with serious medical problems eat better and improve their health. I work with patients at the Major Medical Center and I also help private clients."*

1. *"I'm a personal trainer and work with a lot of different clients. Many are middle-aged women."*

2. *"I'm a personal trainer. I specialize in helping older women who feel they're out of shape get fit and healthy and look great."*

Notice the main differences between versions 1 and 2 in each case: The first versions, centered on process and generalities, are unlikely to spark interest. The second versions are calculated to pique the curiosity of possible clients and provoke questions. *They accomplish this by focusing on specifics rather than generalizations.* Granted, the speaker may not be introducing herself to a prospect. But the other person might know people who need the service or will remember the exchange should someone he knows need the service.

In each example, the speaker tailors the message to the audience. If the CPA also works with businesspeople, and is talking to them, for example, she adapts her introduction.

Note, too, how much information can be delivered in a short space. The longest intro in the group is 10 seconds. Thanks to specificness, each one might extend the conversation because it prompts a question. For example, "How much can you really transform someone by changing his diet?" "How long does it take?" "How is a workout program for an older woman different?"

Smart businesspeople always have answers ready in their mental pockets and, ideally, great examples of success. When you tell your story through the success of other people, you demonstrate your passion for the work and how good you are, rather than making vague claims.

When You're a New Career Builder

If you're just starting out in your career field, or moving into a new one, don't feel shy about identifying yourself as a professional. Your serious intent entitles you to feel part of the industry. Just as writers are told to present themselves as writers even if they've not yet published anything, you're an accountant or engineer or marketing specialist as soon as you have a few years of academics or training under your belt.

This is true if you're between jobs as well as when you're switching careers. If you're earning a living at something else until you complete a degree or land a career break, it's still legitimate to present yourself as what you want to be.

If this feels uncomfortable, identify yourself as a marketing specialist, or whatever, in training or in transition.

If you're at an interim or preliminary stage and find the setting hospitable, use your elevator speech to advantage. It's more than OK to ask for something. Here are three examples:

Hi, I'm Margaret James. I'm finishing my master's in public relations this spring, and my career goal is to help nonprofits communicate better. I'd love to contribute right now as an intern, and I'm looking for an opportunity. Can you suggest anyone for me to talk to?

Hi, I'm Jeremy Jones. I'm a business management major headed for a career in retail marketing. I love the program, but I'd really like to learn from professionals in the field, too, and it would be great know people in this group. Is there a way I might get involved and contribute to the association?

Hi. I'm Melanie Smith. I'm studying at Georgia Tech, and since I was little, I've wanted to build bridges. I'd love to be sure I'm on the right path with my courses and internships. Does anyone come to mind who might be willing talk to me about that?

Sayability is critical, so be sure your mini-speech is easy to say and sounds natural and conversational. It must be easy to remember and comfortable for you. This dictates short words and very short sentences. You do not need to use the same wording each time you deliver the intro. In fact, it's better to internalize it, then reinterpret it on the spot in response to the person you're talking to.

Still another advantage to a thoroughly prepared elevator speech is that it *frees you to listen*. You need not worry about what you'll say when your turn comes, and you can fully focus on the other person. You can adapt your own intro to mesh better with the other person's orientation. This truth applies to all situations where it's important to interact well face to face with an individual or a group of any size.

VIEW FROM THE FIELD: A SALES TRAINER'S TAKE ON THE ELEVATOR SPEECH

Here's what I taught people when I worked for a sales institute—and still teach people I work with. I have seen this approach work for so many people.

1. **Communication begins with listening.** Whether you have the opportunity to share your elevator speech in a brief introduction on the elevator or in the context of a conversation that will last more than a couple of minutes, begin by asking a question or two that helps you get to know the other person. When you start by listening to someone, you earn the right to be listened to.

2. **Differentiate yourself from your competition.** We're all accustomed to salespeople who quickly dive into all the wonderful things their product or service can do for us and why it's better than everyone else's—so much so that we become numb to it. Instead, formulate a brief description of what you do in a way that differentiates you without being self-promoting.

3. **Make it about them.** When you talk about features, it's all about you. Don't take it personally, but your listeners don't care about you—they care about their own issues, challenges and objectives. Get into their world and talk about how you solve the problems they may be experiencing. If you are able to ask good questions first, you may have a better idea of which problems to include.

So the elevator speech components are name, company, framing statement (very brief description of what you do) and two or three problems you solve (ideally tailored to the audience). If you do it right, they will want to learn more.

For example, here is my elevator speech for my current position:

I'm Catherine Gates with WorkMatters. We help people close the gap between faith and work. People come to our programs because they're struggling with chaos and uncertainty—they feel overwhelmed by a lack of balance and the demands of the workplace today. They want to figure out how their faith fits in. Our programs help them find peace, courage and workable solutions.

—Catherine Gates, director of outreach and engagement at WorkMatters

DEVELOPING SPEECHES AND PRESENTATIONS

Say what you mean, and mean what you say.

—General George S. Patton

Few things intimidate most people more than standing in front of an audience and giving a speech. Famously, it ties for first place with death as the most-feared human experience. While you may not need to address large audiences in your earlier career stages, you certainly might be asked to present at meetings or to share something in less formal circumstances. See such demands as opportunities. Watching staff members present is a key way that supervisors identify talent, fair or not as that may seem. To do yourself justice, prepare: plan, draft, speak it, revise it, practice it. And prepare for Q&A. Assembling Talking Points is a good way to do it, as explained in Ken Koprowski's View From the Field later in this chapter.

Don't aim to memorize even a short presentation. First, it's impossible; second, it focuses you inside your head instead of on the audience, with which you must connect; and third, it deprives you of the chance to come across spontaneously and maximize your engagement with listeners. Rather than memorizing a literary-style presentation, the goal is to feel confident with your content and remember some key "headlines" for topic areas in a logical progression. A PowerPoint-style visual backdrop can serve this purpose. You can also use index cards or some other notation that can quickly remind you of your key points with minimal attention.

Actors learn to make each performance individual and fresh by responding to each audience. This technique is a good one to keep in mind. Every audience creates a different atmosphere, even if people listen silently. Observe response. Are many people checking their e-mail? It might be time to move to a different point.

Should you use humor? A joke? It's great for rapport building, but handle with care! Be sure it can't possibly offend a single person in the universe. Try it out on a few people. Rehearse it well.

Build your confidence by using Marla Seiden's Presentation Planning Worksheet for just about any speech, from initial thinking through delivery. When you build with visuals, it adds another dimension—we'll catch up with that later in this chapter.

MARLA SEIDEN'S PRESENTATION PLANNING WORKSHEET

1. **Prepare to succeed.**

The better you prepare, the better you succeed.

Your goal is to develop the right presentation for the target audience and then practice, practice, practice so you can deliver it with passion and clarity. Follow these steps for a well-organized and polished presentation. In writing:

2. **Profile your audience.** Demographics. WIIFM? What do they want to know? Already know or believe? Need to know?

3. **Clarify and state your general purpose.** Demonstrate, inform, entertain, persuade, motivate, inspire? Aim to achieve one, some or all.

4. **Define your specific goals.** Your call to action—how do you want the audience to think, respond? Do you want them to improve their understanding or change an attitude or behavior? Buy something?

5. **Crystallize your message in 20 words or less.** For example:

First-quarter earnings are down and we need everyone to pitch in toward recovery.

Learn six simple presentation techniques to advance your career.

Donate to our anti-hunger campaign and help us save hundreds of children.

Exercise 90 minutes per week and reduce the risk of _____ by 35%.

6. **Write the lead.** Grab attention in less than 30 seconds. For example, tell them what

they'll gain. Use a story, rhetorical question, provocative statement, quote, statistic or visual.

7. **Develop the message.** Create a series of main points (three often works), each with supporting evidence in this pattern:

Main Point 1: Appropriate support (can include examples, stories, data, anecdotes and visuals).

8. **Craft clear and concise language.**

Use:
Short sentences, short words

Sound bites—memorable lines such as "Ask not what your country can do for you; ask what you can do for your country."

Transitions: Link all elements to establish a logical flow with wording such as *first, next, before, now, after we do that, here's an example, on the other hand* and so on.

Vivid images that paint pictures in words

Avoid:
Jargon and clichés

9. **Conclude.** Before inviting questions, summarize: Tell them what you told them. Restate the benefits. Explain action they should take. Remember that last words linger, so end on a high note: a memorable quote, compelling statement or story.

—Marla Seiden, founder and president
of Seiden Communications Inc.
and presentation skills specialist

Adapt Your Personal Story

In Chapter 6, you learned how to find and develop your personal story. This is one of the most powerful means to bring a spoken message alive and connect with your audience. If you've worked on your personal story, adapt it to the audience and occasion. It may call for a 30-second version or much more. If you haven't thought about your story and a presentation is at hand, consider what value you may add by developing it.

To adapt or create a story for a speech or other presentation:

Relate your story to the audience. What elements of your story can connect you to people's common experience? Life events that raise similar feelings are shared by everyone, though the details vary. Almost everyone has lost a job or an important person, handled a challenge over his head, felt lost and alone, experienced failure or a moment of triumph and so on. Connect to such shared feelings, and people engage with you emotionally.

Center on how you overcame challenges. That's the essence of the stories we love from movies, novels and biographies. Suspense is built in—how will "the hero" (that's you!) overcome those obstacles? How will she change? How does the experience motivate her? What's the big lesson? How does it relate to your audience?

Start strong. You can start in the middle, at the point of crisis, then go back to cover how-I-got-there and what you did to emerge successfully. Or tell it sequentially from the beginning. But unless you own a mesmerizing opener, be sure the audience knows early on *why* you're telling the story.

Focus on the specific and concrete. A story may lead to an abstract kind of conclusion—like "I learned to always give people a second chance"—but how you got there must be spelled out and feel real. Use simple, unassuming language that works orally. Bring people into the experience with graphic language that helps them see, hear and feel what it was like to be there.

Communicate how you felt. Rather than saying something directly, like "I was shocked," try for imagery that connects people with the experience more graphically. Someone might describe an unexpected job loss, for example, this way: *Suddenly I was Alice falling down that hole—I'd crashed into a whole new gray world with no warning. I just wanted to wake up and be back in my life . . . but there was no road.* Many expert storytellers prefer present tense for immediacy, experiment with that: *Suddenly I'm Alice. . . .*

End happily. Avoid stories that don't help you look good in the end. Certainly, depict how you started from a dark place, but you must eventually come out on top in a meaningful way. And you must bring home the relevance to your audience. You might pick up on a metaphor you used: *So that's how I found the road and left my cave. I love living in the light. Now I know how to . . . and can help you. . . .* This kind of close leads naturally to an "ask"—for example, I'm happy to talk with each of you personally about what this system can do for you—*if you leave me your card.* This can be a good way to close the Q&A.

PREPARE TALKING POINTS FOR IN-PERSON OCCASIONS

Today, audiences much prefer interactive experiences and expect presenters to answer questions. Encourage questions from your audience after you speak or at other points if the occasion is informal or the group small. Of course, have answers ready. As with many situations that call for you to think on your feet—job and media interviews, for example—add Talking Points to your toolkit. Coming from the PR arsenal, this is a one-page rundown of the most critical points to remember when you face a high-stakes situation on behalf of your organization or yourself. It's also a good way to remember what you want to communicate, in the wording of your choice.

Preparing these guides is a mainstay tactic in the corporate, political and government arenas. It will work for you too. Do not bring the written document with you into a meeting, interview or other situation. The point is to absorb it before the event. This equips you to supply the points you most want to make as opportunity allows, and prepares you to field every question that you (and your team) can imagine.

Here's how a communications pro uses the process.

VIEW FROM THE FIELD: HOW TO ASSEMBLE TALKING POINTS

In professional communications, Talking Points—usually a few brief sentences to address a key topic for your organization—are the basis for every public conversation about policy and important issues within the organization. They ensure that everyone is on the same page and in agreement, because the points have been debated and vetted by company experts, including the legal department, if necessary.

Assembling Talking Points is a key tool in preparing for an in-person presentation that may be controversial or hostile. As in government and politics, big companies depend hugely on Talking Points, especially when events open them to criticism. The approach is not often used by smaller businesses but offers an easy way for them to implement tactics and for individuals to present themselves optimally in interviews and public situations.

Compose Talking Points by asking the most logical questions you can ask about the subject matter—as many as you can—and then come up with good, clear, concise answers. Put yourself in the mind of the interested parties and think about the questions they are likely to raise. Act like an investigative reporter familiar with the subject and think of what he or she would ask, and write the answers. Remember that in the logic of an investigative interview, one question leads to another, a follow-up question. Often, the logic is the logic of "if-then" questions.

Begin by anticipating the questions that worry you most, especially the one you dread—it's the most important. Find out anything you need to know to develop an answer to that question. Other questions—and their answers—grow out of that process and

help bolster your key message. Combined, they result in a balanced communication.

When positioning is involved, frame the answers the way you want them perceived. The entire project should be based on a communications strategy with objectives, goals and tactics. You want to persuade and influence but with accurate, factual and verified data so no one can poke a hole in it.

Thus, an approach often used to tell a positive story about your organization, product or service is to take the offense. Draft your key messages in a conversational voice, prioritize these "selling points," and be sure to include them in your interview with your "defensive" Talking Points. Beware of the unintended interpretation of a statement. Be sure that what you say could not be misinterpreted in a pejorative way.

If you're going into a job interview, create Talking Points to present and position yourself so you share your strengths, the value you'll bring to the organization and the reason you should be hired. Limit yourself to one page with a sentence or two at the most for each point: just enough words to remind you of the point you want to make more fully in person. Do the same if you're selling something or introducing yourself with an elevator speech. Just as for press briefings, the Talking Points become a type of script.

Don't underestimate the time it takes to come up with thoughtful questions and phrase good answers.

—Ken Koprowski, communications consultant, writer and professor

WRITING TIPS FOR SPOKEN MEDIA

Effective writing for spoken media aligns with most principles of good writing, but oral delivery makes its own demands, too. Oral language must sound natural and closer to conversation. It's especially hard for people in listening mode to decipher complex sentences and strings of abstract words. Aim to create language that people instantly understand by ear and will keep them with you.

- Use short sentences throughout, but vary their length (short, a little longer, short, medium, a single word, etc.).

- Use short, basic one-syllable words (like you see in the Bible, the Gettysburg Address, Winston Churchill speeches).

- Edit out *all* unnecessary words and phrases.

- Build in pauses to emphasize important points.

- Say *you* often, and structure sentences that way.

- Say *we* and *us,* not *I* and *me* if at all appropriate.

- Use transitions to frame and underline logical flow and carry listeners along (e.g., *Our goal was to, We began by, Then we looked at, We also considered, So we decided, But we were surprised by, Here's what we concluded*).

- Repeat your main message periodically—absorbing information and ideas orally is tough.

The rhetorical tradition offers a number of time-polished devices to draw on, formally developed by the argumentative Romans (thus their Latin names). Here are a few examples. All are valuable for effective oral delivery.

- Rhetorical questions: a familiar device to vary pace and spark interest (*Why do we accept this as inevitable?*)

- Alliteration: a phrase or sentence with repeat initial consonants (*the market's dreary downward dive*)

- Anaphora: repetition of a word or phrase (*We believe that . . . We believe that . . . And in the end, we believe that . . .*)

- Oxymoron: a two-word paradox (*happily miserable*)

- Onomatopoeia: words that sound like what they mean (*splash, plop, whizzed, clunked, splotch*)

- Metaphors, similes, analogies: graphic comparisons of all types

- The rule of three, which resonates with us in many contexts: three main points, three examples, three-part statements (*We came, we saw, we conquered; We set out to identify the problem, find the solution and tell the world*). There is a Latin name for this, but it's so long, I won't impose it on you.

Studying rhetoric to any degree is a great way to improve all your writing. Train yourself to listen analytically to speeches, political and otherwise, and observe how good presentations achieve their impact.

Of course, don't focus on the trees and lose the forest (metaphor). Deliver your messages in a big-picture context that your listeners care about. Whether people hope for a helpful perspective, a better way to do something or general inspiration, make your message matter to them. Nearly always your audience wants you to help them improve their lives in some way. *Give people a vision of a better future, even in a small way, and your message becomes more compelling.*

And always, make it sayable and natural sounding *for you*. Your first imperative is to connect with your audience, and this happens when you're comfortable, confident and prepared. Always remind yourself that you're sharing something valuable and that the audience is on your side—by giving you time, they invest in you and root for your success.

SUCCESS TIP

How many words do you need?

On average, 130 words takes one minute to speak—unless you're from a part of the country where people speak faster or slower than average. So a two-minute speech is about 260 words, a 10-minute speech is about 1,300 words and so on.

Time your own speaking pace: If you find you speak fast, work at slowing down so people can absorb what you say more easily. Plan a long speech based on word count—for example, in the case of a 30-minute speech, 260 words/two minutes is the lead, 1,950 words/15 minutes is the middle, 390 words/three minutes is the conclusion.

Think about imaginative ways to keep people engaged: a live demonstration, an interactive experience, an invitation to ask questions in the middle. Keep an eye on your audience. If attention wanes, change the pace, speed up the section or move on to something else. You need not tell people everything you know about a subject, and if you leave material out, probably no one will suspect.

Delivery techniques are beyond the scope of this chapter, but here's the nano version: Breathe deeply and steadily; stand with good posture and hands at your sides when not gesturing; use natural gestures; make eye contact with specific people in the audience for three to five seconds each; maintain your energy and enthusiasm; avoid upward inflection at the end of sentences unless you're posing a question; and throughout, reflect your total conviction in your own message. Actors and experienced presenters routinely use warmup routines before presenting: five or ten minutes of routines like slow deep breathing, body relaxation, voice range and power exercises and more.

Audiences will forgive a great deal if you share something of value that you clearly believe in. But don't risk an impromptu performance when the stakes are high. Rehearse. You might video yourself or at least audio-record your full presentation and review that critically, then do it again. And/or practice with an audience; a single person is enough.

Always time what you plan to say so you don't undercut your message by jamming in important points or skipping your close. Almost always, it's better to say less, but say it well.

Be sincere; be brief; be seated.

—President Franklin D.
Roosevelt on speechmaking

SUCCESS TIP

How to prepare your own speaking notes

If you need to deliver a speech word for word because the occasion calls for it or you must not forget a thing, here's a simple trick for preparing your script.

Type it up to reflect how you'd read it with natural pauses. Start a new line at each pause. For example, here's how part of a memorable speech by President John F. Kennedy would look:

And so, my fellow Americans:
ask not what your country can do for you—
ask what you can do for your country.
My fellow citizens of the world:
ask not what America will do for you,
but what together we can do for the freedom of man.

Finally,
whether you are citizens of America
or citizens of the world,
ask of us the same high standards of strength and sacrifice
which we ask of you.

This method allows you to deliver the message much more powerfully. It also enables you to look up frequently and maintain almost steady eye contact with the audience. And if you use this approach, you won't need to hold long lines of copy in your head as you speak and will feel much more relaxed. Help an executive use this method and you'll be appreciated.

What rhetorical devices can you spot in this short excerpt?

CREATING BETTER POWERPOINTS

PowerPoint and its cousins have evolved into two different uses:

1. As a presentation aid, for which it was designed.

2. As a basic vehicle of communication in the business world, for which it was not designed.

Unfortunately, PowerPoint, Keynote, Prezi and the rest are rarely well used in either capacity, which has led to a lot of impassioned and dismissive criticism. But realistically, PowerPoint remains a core tool in many business situations and its use grows, especially given the appetite for online learning. So creating a good slide deck is a valuable skill.

Although you might regard PowerPoint as a visual experience, good writing strategies are key. Think of the presentations you hate and you'll find that in many cases, the presenters allowed the medium to master the message. They shaped their content based on a predetermined restrictive format rather than developing a solid presentation that uses visuals to support a message. If you spend all your time and energy turning information into visual materials that fit a limiting format, the message often gets lost and the information distorted.

PowerPoint is best seen as a way to add visual dimension to a speech and/or keep it clearly organized. If it distracts the audience from focusing on the speaker, success diminishes.

VIEW FROM THE FIELD: POWERPOINT PRO AND CON

PowerPoint conveys information very well—but it's horrible at persuasion. So knowing your objective is the first step. If you're doing a data dump, it can be very effective. But if you want to persuade and move an audience or change the way they think, it's actually counterproductive. Writing a speech is about constructing the arguments and synthesizing the ideas—a valuable process. PowerPoint can be like creating a cheat sheet rather than doing the hard work—like building a lean-to instead of a house, where the data points are second to the arguments.

—Dan Gerstein, CEO of Gotham Ghostwriters, political adviser and commentator

---

Rather than starting with images and finding ways to jam in your message, first plan and write your presentation as a speech. As covered in the preceding section, a speech needs an engaging opener, a central focus, a clearly presented sequence of ideas and facts (not too many of either, though), a strong close and, preferably, planned audience interaction at given points.

What role does that give PowerPoint? Use it as a visual backdrop to do the following:

- Interpret the meaning of information through relevant images and photographs as well as easily understood tables, charts and graphs that leverage the medium's ability to show change over time or helpful comparisons. Embed video clips to liven things up if relevant.

- Provide cues to keep yourself on track when speaking and guide the audience through. Slides can be as simple as a headline: "What we learned from this research" or "Moving into the future" or "Questions." Steve Jobs of Apple was famous for using a few simple words with splashy, imaginative graphics as a backdrop to himself.

- Reinforce important points you want the audience to focus on. Visual learning is very effective, provided the material is simple and quickly absorbed. Some experienced presenters use slides solely to reinforce points they want the audience to remember.

- Provide ready-made handouts, which gives you a chance to circulate your contact information if you want people to find you later. But avoid supplying handouts before or during the presentation because they will distract people from *you*.

As you develop content, note any ideas that arise for using the visual dimension to enhance and support your message. But complete every step of your speech, from idea to messages to support points to organization, before deciding what visuals to use.

Aim for simplicity in slide content and language. Note media guru Guy Kawasaki's widely accepted advice: *Use the 10/20/30 rule: Use only 10 slides, take 20 minutes maximum and use at least 30-point fonts.*

Pay close attention to transitions between slides and keep them visually consistent.

VIEW FROM THE FIELD: HOW TO WORK WITH POWERPOINT

I always start by profiling my audience, understanding their core needs and expectations. And if I want things from the audience, what are they?

My next step is to go with pen and paper. A lot of people start with a blank computer screen and the tools, PowerPoint or whatever they're using, but I believe that's limiting in building a story line and coming up with content organically.

So I develop a storyboard, thinking about it like a filmmaker. What's the overall plot line? The key messages or takeaways? What are the scenes that will build up to deliver that? I think about the logic of the ideas and how to translate them into visual representations. When that's well developed on paper, I go to the computer screen, and that's where some principles of slide design become more relevant.

I think audiences do one of two things: read what's on the slide or listen to your words. You want them to listen, which means using fewer words and more images to depict complex content graphically.

When I've written the presentation's initial draft, I spend most of my time preparing to deliver it—I present to a colleague or stand in front of the mirror. This leads me to simplify the slide content even more. If you learn your message, you rely less on the slides to remember your notes, and the audience focuses on you. The final step is to refine the content, which usually means simplifying, stripping what's unnecessary so the key messages speak louder than the detail.

Keep in mind that PowerPoint is not always the right tool, as opposed to spoken word alone or a written memo or video. People might not perceive there's an option, but I think they're actually hungry for innovation. They want to be communicated to in a way that suggests they are unique and understood, and that you're not just defaulting to what you've done with other audiences. I think people are hungry to move away from death by PowerPoint. But deal with expectations early on.

When you're preparing slides to distribute as a handout, the concepts are the same in that you want the audience to listen to you, so put less on the page and know your story really well. But if you're handing out a presentation without delivering context and it must stand alone, it's different. Then you're writing more of a document in slide format and people need time to sit down and read it. If it's then used for presentation, you must translate it to simplify content and deliver more verbally.

—Clint Nohavec, director of SwitchPoint

PLANNING AND USING VIDEO

New technology makes it easy to shoot, edit and disseminate video; the medium moves everywhere. It's an increasingly important force for websites, blogs, social media posts, crowd sourcing pitches, online résumés and many other venues. You can now easily create a six-second video on a smartphone to use on your blog or website and share online. You can also shoot your own two- or five- or 20-minute video explaining how to do something and show off your expertise. You can create videos that make you a personality.

Whether your video is a few seconds or 30 minutes long, if your goal goes beyond sharing your day with friends visually or showing off your kitten's antics, know your story before you shoot. It's popular to assume that production values no longer count.

In fact, some PR agencies have found, literally, that video shot by the mailroom clerk draws more viewers than expensively produced "traditional" video. People often do seem to find unfocused video with shaky movement more "authentic" than the carefully created kind, at least on YouTube.

But generally, such video needs to be short or highly entertaining, lest we lose patience with it. More important: When you're using video for business purposes, be cautious. No matter where you show it, your clips speak for the enterprise. Having huge numbers of viewers doesn't necessarily provide a benefit you want.

Video Dos And Don'ts

Whether you're a job seeker using video to introduce yourself, a specialist who wants to share your how-to expertise or an entrepreneur on the hunt for funding, start with a clear idea of your goal and your audience. For a substantial video you need a script.

This applies even if the whole video consists of you as seen by an unmoving camera. It helps to view such a video as a speech. And a speech needs a good lead, an informational middle and an effective end. It needs to be smoothly and convincingly delivered, so you must know exactly what you will say and rehearse. You can't read the script on camera, but you can use written cues.

Or if you're a confident speaker, just as for a speech, use Talking Points to help you partly wing it. The advantage of video versus a live performance is that you can do the "bad" parts over and edit the best takes together.

If you're creating an ambitious video, you need a storyboard to represent the main points and how they connect. This tells you what to shoot. It can be done simply, as described for PowerPoint. In addition to video clips, you can include stills and graphics. You'll need to marshal what's available to work with and decide what else you can feasibly add to the mix.

Practical online apps are available to make professional-style storyboarding techniques surprisingly accessible. In particular, check out the free software Storyboarder (https://wonderunit.com/storyboarder/). It enables you to visualize your story in comfortable ways.

Another simple planning method is to create a two-column script with a line down the middle. The visuals go on the left side, which reminds you of their primary importance in this medium, and the words go on the right. For example:

Visuals	V/O (Voiceover)
C/U (close-up) of JB	Hi. I'm John Brown, and I'd like to show you how my team won this year's debating conference in Miami.
WS (wide shot) of team giving presentation	We took a long road getting there and learned a lot. Here's how we got ready.
Pan: Stills/team practicing	Live sound
Cutaways of notes, papers, faces C/U of Ellen	I can't believe how much work it took. Every day we spent three hours . . .

The core concept is that with video, you don't just script words: You also must script the visuals—"picture"—in tandem. You need something on the screen for every second of voiceover or natural sound. Your two-column script enables you to list all the shots you need to tell your story, which is essential to planning the logistics. Shooting in sequence is rarely possible. You need to plan for efficiency, optimize your time and minimize expense. Of course, later you'll have to edit all the pieces together neatly, but these days, if you don't want to hire an editor, the software is there and the skills can be learned.

Unless you're creating the kind of simple, straight-on video where the camera stays on you and you talk through it, perhaps demonstrating something, words and images must be juggled to tell the story. Video specialists aim to use few words and let what's on the screen say as much as possible. For informational material, narration helps bridge between scenes and ideas and explains what can't be represented visually.

However, those few words must be carefully chosen. Try for highly accessible language—short, sayable sentences with good cadence. Fragments work fine, since in spoken language, formal sentences can sound unnatural and jarring. *Don't fill the script with wall-to-wall words. Silence is the videographer's version of white space.* It allows viewers to focus on the action and hear the ambient sound—for example, the team members rehearsing—or absorb the music if there is any. Music is one more dimension for developing effective video. A soundtrack can trigger and underscore emotions and unify the presentation.

The very smallest video cameras, or even your smartphone, can work increasingly well for many purposes. But they carry some important limitations.

One is sound quality. With tiny machines, sound quality has lagged far behind the level achieved for visual recording. Research says that people have far less patience for bad audio than for bad picture. Especially if you're selling something, or delivering any message that people don't need or that doesn't entertain, *pay attention to the sound quality.* You may need to use auxiliary equipment for this. And you may need to use a camera that allows you to plug in a microphone.

A second limitation of using small devices is lighting. If you watch a professional video crew at a shoot, you'll notice that excruciating time is spent setting up the lights. It's the critical factor in getting good, real-looking, interesting pictures. You are unlikely to have a lighting specialist, but know that simple front-on lighting gives you a flat (and unflattering) image. Worse, though, is backlighting—where the source comes from behind the subject. This obliterates all detail and produces, at worst, a silhouette. So (a) watch for where you position your subject and the angle you shoot from, in relation to the light, and (b) consider a supplementary light when your video is important.

A third limitation is the shakiness of tiny cameras. This is easily solved by attaching a suitably sized tripod, but you won't be able to move it to change angles without stopping the shoot.

A content caveat: Try to not rely solely on what the industry calls "talking heads" to deliver your message. Use imagination to come up with visual ideas so the camera doesn't just stay focused on one person. When you can't do this or don't have the resources, keep it short. That generally means less than two minutes.

Another way to use video is to assemble your "show" from still images, drawings and other existing materials. This can be done without shooting any new footage at all. Create movement by panning across a photo, or zooming from the full image to a detail, and vice versa. Assemble the images carefully using special effects like fade-out and fade-in. If you have a good trove of material to work with, this can be quite an effective approach— especially if you add music or narration.

Planning, shooting and editing video takes hands-on practice. So if you want to use it, spend some time experimenting and see what works.

Introducing Yourself With Video

One of your primary reasons to produce a good video may be to introduce yourself, on your website, social channel or as part of a job query or application. Where to start? What to include? Use Janet Beckers's seven-steps approach outlined in her View From the Field.

VIEW FROM THE FIELD: SEVEN STEPS TO YOUR VIDEO SCRIPT

Video is fast becoming one of the most effective communication tools for marketing and for internal communication in business. In fact, it is so popular that many employers now expect job applicants to include an introductory video as part of the application process. With phone technology, it is simply so easy to create and upload video, yet with this ease comes a problem. It is also easy to create boring, rambling videos that damage your reputation, and if you are using video to impress a potential employer, "boring" loses you the job!

To help you stand out from the crowd, I've adapted the seven-step script I use to create marketing videos to market you. Important: You *must* follow the script in the order given. There is psychology behind the inclusion of each step and the order they follow.

The Absolutely-Everything Script Process

Welcome the viewer. In the case of an application video, create a new one for each position and mention the name of the employer personally if you can. For example: "Hello and welcome, Ms. Beckers (or the Niche Partners Team). Thanks for this opportunity to introduce myself."

Establish credibility. Keep it short and sweet. For example: "My name is _____ and I have over five years' experience in the xx industry" Or "I'm a grade-A graduate with recent intern experience in your industry." Don't list your résumé material here; just let them know you are relevant.

Hook your viewers. Why should they keep on listening? Here's a suggestion: "In the next three minutes I'll cover three important reasons why I am perfect for this position."

Your story. Now they'll want to know a bit about you. Why are you passionate about this opportunity? What's unique about you? Keep it short but let them know what type of person you are. Here's a starting idea to adapt: "I'm a city/country girl who grew up in x town. I've always had a passion for xyz/people always told me I was a natural at xyz, so I've spent the last few years studying/working to master my craft. I'm interested in xx position because. . . ."

The problem. Let them know you understand the problem they are trying to solve by advertising this position. If you can explain the problem well enough, they'll assume you know how to solve it! For example, "I appreciate that one of the biggest problems in xyz industry/position is finding a person who not only knows how to do the job, but also can work with minimal supervision and save you time, instead of creating more work."

The solution. Give three reasons why you are great for this position. Choose which three to cover according to the job advertisement or your knowledge of what the employer is looking for. Make sure to include an example that demonstrates you can actually deliver the solution. You don't have to go into a lot of detail—that's in your résumé. The video's purpose is for them to see your body language, hear your voice and hear your conviction. For example, if they are looking for an organizer, you can joke here that you are a compulsive list writer and get great satisfaction from delegating tasks and, as a team, checking them off.

Call to action. Let them know what happens next. It may be as simple as "I look forward to receiving your e-mail to set an interview time" or "I will follow up with a phone call within the week to get your feedback." End on a positive note.

The most important thing to remember: Be yourself! Record numerous takes until you can relax, and then imagine you are talking to someone whom you respect and you know respects and likes you. Good luck!

—Janet Beckers, author, speaker and mentor who "helps business owners build a tribe of loyal fans online"

More Ways to Use Video

Some of these ideas are best suited to substantial organizations that have video support—always nice if you can get it. But many can be done by nonprofessionals. An increasing number of ready-made templates that can be customized to your business message are available online. Some stock video is available free, and short clips can be purchased from stock photography companies.

If you're in business or plan to be, consider video for purposes such as these:

- how-to demonstrations of a product or process
- behind-the-scenes looks at your company or team at work
- a "meet the staff" video for your website
- customer and client testimonials
- case histories of how client problems were solved
- examples of employee involvement in the community
- commercials or public service announcements

If you do invest in good video production, recycle the results imaginatively to recover the cost. Use components on the website home page, "About Us" page, or product or service pages; for presentations, meetings, e-mails, internal communications; to liven up your social media posts; and perhaps to distribute on YouTube, if appropriate for wide sharing.

TRANSLATING VERBAL INTO VISUAL

Like oral storytelling, communicating through images predates written language. Think caveman drawings. Today we're newly in love with the power of visuals in the form of photos, illustrations, data-driven graphics, videos, virtual reality and much more. It's long been observed that a picture is worth—well, not always a thousand words—and that images make communication more effective, entertaining and memorable. Groups that research media issue startling statistics about how much more successful blogs, tweets and even e-mails are when visuals are built in. Online posts are far more likely to be opened, and material from tweets to white papers are much more often shared when they include visual interest.

One reason visuals have come to seem so dominant is the scanning factor. When we look at online media, the eye decides what we should read. There's always more than we can handle. Images scream for our attention and we fasten on them. Pure text, on the other hand, feels passive and requires more effort to engage with.

Images also hold the power to

- move immediately past our mental defenses and analytic thinking;

- symbolize ideas or facts more interestingly and memorably;

- translate complex ideas, trends, patterns and comparisons into easily grasped form;

- demonstrate a process: how to do something;

- cross borders—cultural, geographic, language, beliefs;

- trigger emotional response—anger, excitement, amusement, sadness, happiness;

- provide evidence of a situation, event, need or accomplishment;

- act as an emblem of a brand or identity.

But never believe that words don't count. Unless a platform bases on visuals for the pure joy, or you use it to share your day with friends, *the job of an image is usually to attract attention to the writing, complement it, or amplify understanding and emotional response.* You might stop to read a blog that draws you in with a photo or drawing, but if the content doesn't prove out, you'll probably stop and move on. Then your effort and the viewer's time are wasted. You might like how an infographic looks, but if the substance isn't well thought out—which requires research, analysis and writing—you're disappointed.

Visuals should not be treated as eye candy. They are best used in partnership with the written word. Technical sophistication may not even matter. One favorite blogger, for example, illustrates his ideas with stick figure drawings right out of first grade. His content is so good, and the drawings so well integrated, that it works beautifully. Another popular blogger emphasizes his major points with photographs of himself holding up simple signs.

That said, digital technology makes it ever easier to produce effective visuals that align with your purpose. Today's smartphones take high-resolution images technically sufficient for most uses. There are apps for creating graphs and charts with dynamic appeal, infographics, picture-and-word superimpositions, special effects and of course video. And all these possibilities can be integrated for presentations, websites, blogs, Twitter, social media, marketing materials and even e-mails.

Free or inexpensive photographs, illustrations, icons, vectors (primitive-style abstract illustration) and video clips are readily available with a little research. Even (some) clip art is better than it used to be and more easily customized. The only limits are your imagination and skill with technologies that every day become easier to use.

Creating Your Own Visuals

To come up with an image, whatever the subject and medium, first clarify:

1. What you want to communicate

2. How you want the audience to respond

3. What kind of visual connects the two

In addition to photographs, illustrations, icons and maybe animated GIFs, remember that your potential toolbox includes typeface choices, color and layout. The guiding principle always: simplicity. Most designers advise picking one style consistently—photographs or cartoons, for example—and not mixing them.

If you're using photographs or video to show something concrete, like what a garbage dump looks like or how to make a paper airplane, logic suggests the visuals you need and their order. It's harder to translate abstract ideas into visual form. You may need to do this for a blog, promotional piece or other media. Here are a few ways to go about that.

1. **Articulate your content theme.** Is it a concept like "streamlining" or "improving," for example, or "confusion" or "profitability"? Look for an image that conveys the concept. The image banks offer excellent opportunities to do this. For example, I looked for a way to visualize the subject "Try not to bore people." I entered "boredom" in the search box of one image bank and 349 pages came up—each with 40 or more images: bored people from babies to grandparents, classrooms and meeting rooms full of glassy-eyed people, yawning kittens and so on and so on. I saw photographs, cartoony illustrations, vectors. Beyond yielding fruitful ways to illustrate the theme in your head, browsing time in these resources can lead you to generate ideas for new topics to write about.

2. **Think about what the central idea resembles or feels like.** A post that talks about how hard it is to meet self-imposed deadlines might be visualized as a person pushing a rock up a hill, a group of kids scrambling after a moving target, a trapeze artist reaching for a set of hands, three coffee cups and a pile of crumpled papers. Once you've identified some possible ways to visualize your idea, you can almost certainly find it in a stock image bank, free and cleared for use. Some will help you customize it.

3. **Build your own image library.** Journalists these days are encouraged to take their own photos in the course of their day, and this is a good habit, especially if you're covering an event or place or experience that won't repeat. You may be practicing

this camera-ready approach for social platforms. It is also valuable for your more formal communication. Build your library as you go, keep it reasonably organized and you'll develop a personal and more individual resource to draw on. Given today's technology, you may find it's also easy to create your own simple sketches.

4. **Juggle your chosen or potential image against your headline words.** Integrating the two dimensions reinforces the message and makes it more fun. For example, choose a trapeze image for the blog post about meeting deadlines and you might write, "Reaching Those Deadlines: 10 Ways to Avoid Missing the Target." Or a photo of running kids, one of them heading the other way, might suggest "Deadlines: How to Run in the Right Direction." The image of someone pushing a rock uphill: "Deadlines: Why So Hard? Five Ways to Lighten Up."

One caveat: Be ethical. Many sources of free, copyright-cleared images are available online, so don't steal. Copyright law is fuzzy on digital media because it hasn't been updated in decades. But you can still get in trouble. Play fair.

PRACTICE OPPORTUNITIES

I. Write Your Elevator Speech

Create your own 15- to 20-second elevator speech based on the ideas in this chapter. Write and practice it so you can deliver it without referring to notes. Present it to the class and collect feedback; then revise it.

Do one version as if you are preparing for a professional meeting in your target profession.

Do a second version introducing yourself to your classmates, and include at least one thing they don't know about you.

II. Group Activity: Develop Guidelines for Elevator Speeches

Together, listen to all the class's elevator speeches and pay attention to language, memorability, general impact and delivery style. When all have been presented, collaborate as a class, or in smaller groups, to develop a set of guidelines for developing effective elevator speeches based on the practical experience.

III. Analyze a Speech

Identify a speech you like by a politician, a historical figure, a business leader or someone you personally admire. (Find it in one of the resources at the end of the chapter). Print it out and mark it up to identify the rhetorical devices and other tactics used, as described in this chapter and additional reading. Write a review 400 words or longer summarizing what you see as the most important takeaways about writing for oral delivery, illustrated by the specific speech you chose.

IV. Plan a Presentation Slide Deck

Drawing on methods suggested in this chapter, create a storyboard for a presentation your group will deliver to raise funds for a good cause you select—either an existing one or one you make up. Use either paper and pen or computer, but fully develop your plan and content and describe the visuals.

V. Present the Plan

Each group presents the plan to the class—which represents the management team—to request funding to further develop the ideas and create the actual presentation. Each class member evaluates the plans and votes on which to fund. The class discusses what worked best.

VI. Graphic Interpretation: Nonprofit Example

Pick a cause you personally believe in, and come up with a practical visual idea to express the severity of the problem or need in a way that will connect with a specific audience.

VII. Graphic Interpretation: Corporate Example

Read the annual report of a company that interests you, or Warren Buffett's most recent one for Berkshire Hathaway, and develop a set of visual ideas to support the information for a slide show of five to 10 slides.

VIII. Evaluate Speech-Making Advice

Here is a statement made by Winston Churchill:

> *If you have an important point to make, don't try to be subtle or clever. Use a pile driver. Hit the point once. Then come back and hit it again. Then hit it a third time—a tremendous whack.*

Do you agree or disagree with this approach in regard to speeches? Is this advice you would take? Do you think audiences have changed in the 75 or so years since Churchill made the statement? Have techniques of persuasion changed? Write your opinion, and be as specific as you can about your reasoning.

IX. Group Project: Plan a Video

Your subject: How to write a good proposal. Review the guidelines in Chapter 9 and decide on the most important points to make. Then use a storyboard or the two-column script approach to plan the audio and visual segments together. Pretend you have a substantial budget. Brainstorm at each step about what visuals can be created or drawn on to explain, illustrate and engage (e.g., still photos, documents, original footage). Write the script, including a strong lead and close, and minimize the words.

Also, try developing a script on the same subject with a budget of $25.

X. Group Discussion

Create a set of guiding principles for deciding when video, PowerPoint or a speech without visuals is the best vehicle.

XI. Illustrate Your Own Post

Pick a blog post you've written or would like to. Figure out one or more ways to articulate the theme, considering the idea, problem, feeling or emotion you want to communicate. Find 10 ways to express it visually using one or more stock image banks, shooting your own photo or video, creating a drawing or any other way.

SELECTED RESOURCES

Speechwriting

10 Steps to Writing a Vital Speech, by Fletcher Dean: Excellent readable and doable ideas from a top speech ghostwriter

On Speaking Well: How to Give a Speech With Style, Substance, and Clarity, by Peggy Noonan: Personal advice and ideas from a great political speechwriter

How to Write and Give a Speech, by Joan Detz: A practical and down-to-earth how-to

American Rhetoric (http://americanrhetoric.com): Online speech bank with hundreds of speeches relating to current events, movies, historical figures and more

Cicero Speechwriting Awards (www.vsotd.com/cicero-awards): Presents best speeches of the year

The Genard Method (www.genardmethod.com/blog): Gary Genard's blog on "performance-based public speaking"

Julie Hansen (http://performancesalesandtraining.com/resources/): A sales trainer's useful guidelines for creating presentations and free tools for delivering well, especially "The 7 Minute Power-Presenter Warm-up"

Public Speaking Skills

Public speaking is best learned live, with the benefit of constructive criticism and practice. Consider Toastmasters International (www.toastmasters.org), where many business leaders started. Courses are also available in professional education programs at colleges and universities. Trainers are often people with theatrical, voice or media experience. Learning to use your voice and feel comfortable in front of audiences is one of the best investments for anyone.

Presentations

TED (www.ted.com): Great examples of presentation techniques by specialists of every kind, many with good use of visuals

Presentation Zen, by Garr Reynolds (www.presentationzen.com): Advice on creating better PowerPoints based on planning, simplicity, use of stories and more—and what not to do.

Video

For helpful advice, try the websites of journalism schools. Many colleges offer hands-on video training courses in their continuing and professional education departments.

INTO THE FUTURE

12 WIN YOUR OPPORTUNITIES: WRITING FOR THE HUNT

There is nothing to writing. All you do is sit down at a typewriter and bleed.

—Ernest Hemingway

You may be surprised to know that employers and placement specialists view writing as a core skill in almost every industry. No matter how good your technical credentials, how well you present yourself in writing can be make-or-break when you apply for prize internships and career positions. Application materials must demonstrate your good judgment, connect with the employer's perspective and evidence outstanding writing skills. If your networking messages, résumés and cover letters don't score well on these scales, fewer doors will open and they may not be the ones you prefer.

For employers this is dollars and cents. More and more organizations have discovered the high cost of bad writing: not just mistakes and misunderstandings, but poor reports, failed proposals, unread newsletters, random social media campaigns and unmotivating websites. Poor written communication alienates employees, customers, clients, donors, the public. Many employers cite a shortage of good writers as the biggest gap in their ranks. They find that both new recruits and existing employees fall short on both writing and speaking skills. And as always, shortage spells "opportunity."

Writing, communication skills, and organizational skills are scarce everywhere. These skills are in demand across nearly every occupation—and in nearly every occupation they're being requested far more than you'd expect based on standard job profiles. Even fields like IT and Engineering want people who can write.

—Burning Glass Technologies research report, *Baseline Skills: The Human Factor*, 2015

This chapter focuses the principles you've learned from this book on gaining you the opportunities you want. Good applications are your career tickets, your chance to gain the edge no matter how competitive the field of your dreams. Today there are more dimensions to the application process. Job candidates still find prospective employers by responding to ads or through intermediaries like employment agencies. But now employers and job seekers can directly connect on the Internet. One way of looking at it: The whole World Wide Web is your résumé. Consider it totally public. So beyond presenting carefully wrought résumés and letters, understand that your profiles and posts are read by those who want to know who you are. Whether you're just entering the career place or already possess solid credentials and experience, all your writing including online must be your best.

Let's start with the document you probably least enjoy creating: the résumé.

PLAN A RÉSUMÉ BASED ON STRENGTHS

You will probably hold a number of jobs during your career and will therefore need résumés at many points. So accept that it's part of your life to craft a strong résumé and keep it alive. If you hope to run your own business, you still need a résumé at times and certainly the variants, like profiles and bios.

I don't recall ever knowing anyone who liked writing résumés. Why is the process so hard?

A good résumé demands that you truly understand where you've been, what you're ready for and how to prove it. This requires you to think analytically about your life thus far and generalize about your experiences and skills. If you're going for a specific opportunity, everything you've done must fit into that perspective: how it prepares you for this role.

It's all relevant: work, education, specific training, part-time jobs, internships, sport and hobby interests, accomplishments, volunteer work, personal qualities and what you did on your summer vacations. Also, be aware of the kind of people you relate to best, the work atmosphere you prefer, the assignments that make you happiest and the ones that make you miserable. (Why put all that effort into getting an opportunity you'll hate?)

Consider all the elements of your personal history that have made you who you are.

Equally helpful: Have an idea of where you want to be next year—and in five years—even knowing that your direction may shift radically.

None of this means that you can't toss off an OK résumé in a day or two and score some hits or win the job you want. But there's a big bonus to crafting an outstanding résumé: The process sharpens your career planning, helps you recognize good opportunities and enables you to see yourself in a realistic perspective. It also convinces you that you're equipped for the job—which gives you what you need to ace the interviews.

VIEW FROM THE FIELD: TAKE A WIDE PERSPECTIVE ON JOB HUNTING

Communication has always been one of the top skills employers say they look for, and now it is much easier for them to get a sense of someone's abilities before reading a cover letter or meeting for an interview. Leverage various social media platforms to give people a sense of your capabilities before they even see your résumé.

Your LinkedIn profile, Facebook page, Twitter posts or blog must give employers a real sense of your communication skills and style. You are evaluated by what you put "out there" on the Internet, so build your brand by connecting with industry and sharing, posting or tweeting about topics you are passionate about and relevant to the field you want to go into. Be mindful of what you put out there, as it can be easier to get discounted, but even more importantly it helps you to connect with industry.

It's a lot easier to build relationships with industry and vice versa today. You need to have a clear idea of your personal brand and what you want prospective employers to know about you. This doesn't mean you necessarily have to know what you'll do the rest of your life, but know your values, interests, motivators: What are you passionate about?

Be really aware that the relationships you build today will be very important in developing your career. Whatever the industry, you must be able to maintain your relationships even when there's no job attached to the conversation. Be a keeper-in-touch rather than a job seeker. Ask yourself: How can I achieve multiple touch points so people know who I am and what I offer? How do I get on people's radar so they can reach out to me if opportunities arise?

Don't worry about building relationships with important senior people. Engage with people who've been in your shoes recently, know what it's like and

will think of you when the opportunities come up. Reach out to individuals. Choose the social media platforms that make sense to you, use your alumni network and find common denominators to build relationships. Let people know what you're involved in reading, attending and writing about. People often connect based on personal interests—nothing to do with the job—so don't be too narrowly focused.

It's predicted that those now beginning their careers will hold over 20 different jobs in various industries throughout their professional life. Keep growing by doing an outstanding job wherever you are. Identify internal opportunities, take risks and volunteer for projects and take on additional responsibilities that will give you more visibility in your own organization. Your hard work and dedication will pay off: Most people follow their managers, bosses, colleagues from organization to organization, so even though you might be in a role for a few years, your reputation and professional brand will be remembered as others in your network learn of opportunities or look to hire.

—Jeannie Liakaris, director of the NYU Wasserman Center for Career Development, School of Professional Studies

Apply the Goal and Audience Structure

Start your thinking process with the same strategy you practiced for e-mail and more formal materials.

Consider your goal. Do you think it's to win you a job? Actually not—the goal is more modest: to earn you an interview so you can make your case in person. That may not change the content of your résumé, but it may suggest giving it a different slant. It needs to work as a self-contained message and position you as worth interviewing so you survive the initial filtering process.

Consider your audience. Defining those who will view your résumé as "audience" reminds you of the following needs:

- Bring to bear everything you know or can ferret out about the organization and, sometimes, the specific person you're targeting. As always, the more you understand the reader, the better you can gauge your message.

- Expect that the résumé may be read by a series of reviewers on different levels who have different specializations, and probably a computer filtering program, too. Your message of qualification must be clear to both people and machine.

● Understand that the typical reader sees the review assignment as tedious and perhaps overwhelming; he will happily trash your effort on the least provocation—a typo, poor organization, dull language, unwelcoming appearance, off-target content, maybe even because it's boring.

Expect to get less than six seconds of a reader's time to make the cut.

How Traditional Must Résumés Be?

When an employer requests a résumé, whether e-mailed, snail-mailed or delivered in person, assume a traditional format is in order. That means presenting your skills, experience, education and related background in a standard order on a piece of paper—real or virtual—using a reverse chronology (most recent first). Do you think demonstrating creativity puts you in front of the pack?

It may, but not by taking major liberties with the format. When you're hiring and must plow through half a ton of résumés, a standard format makes comparisons among candidates easier and you know where to look for the information you want.

The ground rule applies even if you're trying for a creative position. Someone hiring a staff art director, for example, or a violinist wants to see a great portfolio but still needs to know about each candidate's experience, track record, education, reliability and so on. The trick for creative people is to demonstrate their originality within the restrictive standard format: a writer, for example, through terrific use of language and a designer by making the document look great. For most others, creativity is best applied to expressing yourself well and adapting the presentation to best serve you.

The biggest exception to this "think standard" rule of thumb is the virtual résumé, which exploits online capabilities to deliver a multidimensional impression of the person. This usually involves creating a website and using video, podcasts and social media links to showcase multiple aspects of your abilities and personality. When is this a good idea? It depends on your skills, the type of job involved, the company, who will review your qualifications and many other factors.

VIEW FROM THE FIELD: A RECRUITER'S DOS AND DON'TS

A great résumé has flow, a presence. It captures the targeted industry. Its purpose is not to get the job but the interview, giving you the opportunity to sell yourself. So see it as a teaser and keep it down to one to two pages. Aim to speak about yourself with subtle confidence.

Based on my own peeves and what I hear from colleagues and employers, my advice is:

1. Don't change the standard format: Keep it simple and chronological.

2. Put it in an easy-to-e-mail format like Word.

3. No typos! That's the biggest complaint we get from employers, and it amazes me.

4. Don't clutter the layout, change fonts and vary the type size—keep it clean and easy

for that 15-second capture, which is the most time you have to make an impression.

5. Use the industry's keywords throughout but omit words that aren't searchable, like abbreviations.

If you have time gaps, definitely mention and address them—otherwise it's a red flag. And everything is so easy to check on now by Googling someone's name. Remember that the Internet is also your résumé and an employer can immediately find out if you're part of any dark side of the world. Use the Internet to your benefit, and build a sub-résumé on sites like LinkedIn or Spoke.com, which people look at when hiring.

—Tina Ruark-Baker, senior vice president of strategic staffing at Access Staffing

Tweak the Format to Advantage

Even with traditional résumés, you can take some liberties. The point is to present you at your best, so look for ways to adapt the format to what works. For example:

- If you jumped around a lot in a short period of time or your work history reveals big gaps, soften the chronology by putting employment dates at the end of job descriptions rather than more prominently in a column on the left.

- If you've held a number of brief or minor jobs, group them and create generalizations so they don't clutter up your landscape and make you look scattershot. Part-time or summer jobs, for example, can be grouped as such with a clear heading rather than listed separately:

Retail Sales Experience, Summers of 2015, 2016 and 2017

Salesperson for Macy's, Ben & Jerry Ice Cream, March Gift Shop

Intensive customer interaction and problem-solving experiences. On-the-job training in customer relations, inventory management, large and small store operations.

- If a personal interest or pastime is relevant to the job and helps you stand out, find a way to cover it early on and/or use it in a cover letter.

- If you're jumping careers or don't have a relevant job history for any reason, focus on skills up front and make it clear why you can transfer them from whatever experience you do have.

Your goal is to present your information in a way that looks simple and accessible and is easy to absorb. Use fonts, layout and white space to produce an inviting document. Start with a standard format, such as the one on the next page, and adapt it to your own assets and the relevant industry.

This also applies to choosing the categories to include.

The usual essentials after your masthead, contact information and "summary of qual-ifications" overview (covered later) are work experience, education, professional organiza-tions and awards. Skills is another useful category. If you're at an early career stage, you may want to lead with this section. If you're experienced, you may want to put "Skills" at the bottom if not already covered—factors such as technical capabilities, software expertise, public speaking, foreign languages and so on. Avoid repeating, however; if you've cited a skill as part of a job description, don't waste space and your reader's time by saying it again.

But exercise some imagination to incorporate sections that let you include your strong points. Here are some to consider:

- awards and recognition

- strengths

- social networks

- technical training

- clubs and associations

- certifications

- pro bono work

- community service (better than calling it "volunteer activities")

- catchall categories such as additional data, related experience, special qualifications or career highlights

Another good category is "Favorite Accomplishments" or something similar. If you've jumped around a lot, or want to highlight points of pride in a former job because it's more relevant to the one you want now than your current position, this is a good way to do that.

Do not waste space on the obvious, such as "References available on request" or "Available for interviews." Vary the sample format based on your career status and industry. If you will be entering the job market with an MBA and a few years or more of work experi-ence, then put the experience first because it will be of more interest to employers. If you're a business school student looking for a first or second job, or an internship, list education first.

Industries vary in their content and format expectations so check around with people who work in the one you want to join. Definitely provide a summary of experience if you are changing careers or need to explain a break from the workforce. Guidelines for creating these are given later in this chapter.

WRITE TO OUTSHINE THE COMPETITION

A résumé must be crystal clear, concise, instantly understood and fast to read. It should be concrete, built on short words and sentences, and scrupulously edited. In other words, follow all the guidelines you've already learned for business writing in general. Don't shortchange

CLASSIC RÉSUMÉS FORMAT

Name

Address

Contact: telephone, e-mail, website if you have one—perhaps LinkedIn profile or personal blog

Summary of Qualifications (or Experience)

Three to five lines putting your qualifications/experience in perspective. (You need not label it since this is your lead paragraph.)

Employment

Dates, job title, name of company, location of current or most recent job

Big-picture overview of your role and capsule description of the company

Bullet points representing accomplishments (up to six)

For previous jobs, most recent first: same format as current one but less detail (unless an earlier job shows especially relevant experience)

Career Highlights

Community service, special training, capabilities not covered by job descriptions, publications, speaking

Education

Starting with most recent:

Degree, name of school, location

For graduate work and college, any honors and strong focus

Any technical or professional training that relates to your career path

Dates (unless you don't want to indicate age)

Distinctions

All awards, honors, recognition—including any given for character or time given to a good cause as well as academic achievement (if not covered under Education)

Skills

Technical, language, social media, certifications

Interests

Hobbies, community service (if not already covered), activities the proofing process; borrow another set of eyes to double-check because one bad typo and poof! There goes your credibility no matter what kind of job you're applying for.

Use Concise and Energetic Language

Do you need full sentences? No—you don't have room for that. Résumé real estate is at a premium. You can reduce some of the *I*'s and *a*'s and *the*'s, for example. But don't distill statements to fragments that may mislead or make you look illiterate.

For example, you needn't say,

I completed all the requirements for my Executive MBA in 18 months.

Nor should you say,

Exec. MBA, completed 18 mos.

Better:

Completed Executive MBA in 18 months

Do you need keywords? Yes! Many employers assign the preliminary review to people who have no idea what your experience means and depend on keywords, scanned for by eye or machine. Professional recruiters do the same. So build in the terms that characterize the industry and that denote required skills. Glean these from the job posting and some online research, backed by your knowledge of the industry. Make a list of the search terms to include and as you write the résumé, work them in appropriately, keeping the language natural. Once the draft is complete, check it against the list.

Do you need action verbs? Absolutely. Good résumés hinge on action verbs. If you want to come across as an active rather than passive person, someone who is outstanding rather than just capable and brings initiative and spark, make every verb zing. This is also how to take credit for your accomplishments. To find hundreds of great possibilities, just Google "action verbs" and scout out those that will work for you. (You might find this a good way to jump-start your résumé-think.)

For example, here are some strong verbs for describing management capabilities.

- accelerated
- consolidated
- generated
- renewed
- led
- initiated
- piloted

- secured
- reorganized
- steered
- streamlined
- strengthened
- originated
- launched
- oversaw
- instituted
- rejuvenated
- shepherded
- mobilized
- navigated
- systematized
- redirected
- designed

You are entitled to use such words to convey a big-picture view of your work product. For example, "I entered information into the database" is blah. Better: "I managed and upgraded the customer database system."

Notice the different tone action verbs set, as opposed to when you depend on overused and unconvincing words like experienced, dynamic and enthusiastic. Adopt the "show don't tell" mantra and your résumé will take you a lot further.

Do you need bullets? Yes, bullets are an excellent way to list skills or achievements in a short amount of space. But depending entirely on bullets is usually a lazy route and may not serve you well. Good narrative statements make sense of what otherwise come across as laundry lists, a disconnected collection of statements. This kind of disjointed rundown violates a fundamental principle—that it's the writer's responsibility to interpret the message, rather than letting readers draw their own conclusions.

However much you use bullets, be sure to compose strong statements that are easily absorbed. They must be uniform in style, starting with the same part of speech—preferably an action verb. Remember that more than about six bullets makes readers sleepy.

How much to include? Aim to give the reader a solid grasp of what you've done, what you've accomplished and what you're equipped to do now, and connect your strong points to the job. *But don't provide so much detail that the basic message gets buried and don't trivialize your experience with routine responsibilities.* For example, if you managed an ice cream shop, you may have supervised and trained other people, been in charge of the cash register and learned to handle customers. Why also say that you mopped the floor and took out the trash? The same holds for office jobs: drafting memos for your boss is more meaningful than filing, unless you invented a new filing system.

Do you need to customize your résumé for every job application? Yes. Always.

Writing successful cover letters is addressed later in this chapter. Review that section for more ideas on presenting yourself in writing.

Create a Summary of Qualifications

It's very helpful to write a summary of experience even if you don't include it on your résumé, because it forces you to articulate who you are and what you're ready for.

You can begin by defining yourself professionally. At an early career stage, you have less to work with, so keep it simple. For example, if you're a recent graduate applying to a leadership training program at a multinational organization:

> *Business Honor Society graduate with BS focused on marketing and leadership.*
> *Related internship experiences with three global organizations. Four years*
> *part-time work in retail sales with progressive responsibility, leading to role of*
> *Team Coordinator. Excellent writing and in-person communication skills,*
> *proven analytic abilities, fluent Chinese.*

This statement puts the writer's assets right up front and establishes a set of competitive advantages. Scour your own background: If your degree is from a prestigious school, work that in. If you edited the newspaper, graduated in the top 10%, were honored as a volunteer, helped a professor with an impressive project, won three scholarships, earned your way through college, created a business while still in school, lived part of your life in another country—all such factors set you apart.

If you're hunting for your first career job and a summary just doesn't work for you, try starting with the job objective—what you want. Be as specific as possible. Instead of saying "A position that enables me to utilize my skills and helps me grow," for example, write something more like "A position that expands my knowledge of the utility industry and enables me to further build my skills in big data analysis." Such a statement shows you already possess a direction, which makes you much more attractive than candidates who seem to want any job at all. And it suggests you may actually be useful!

A Business Communications Summary Statement

In her original résumé draft, this writer began with an objective:

> *To obtain a challenging position in internal corporate communications that utilizes*
> *my prior experience in employee communications, internal web writing/editing and*
> *executive communications/correspondence*

Persuaded to begin with a summary of experience instead, she developed the following:

Employee Communications Specialist: Strong track record originating and directing programs to engage employees, build morale and generate a positive work environment. Four years multinational Fortune 500 experience producing publications, video features, online material and executive speeches. Adept in balancing print, digital and social media channels to achieve company goals. Written and oral communication skills enhanced by advanced training.

Notice that with more experience to work with, this writer is able to follow up the "who I am" first statement with a very broad view of what her work achieves, *not* her specific job responsibilities. Then she moves to her major credentials and some specific work products and ends up referencing some differentiating skills. This is a useful pattern to try, but shape your summary so it shows off *your* best selling points.

Here's an alternative format you may prefer for your summary. It combines a short opening overview statement with a bulleted list of skills.

Profile

Hands-on, collaborative communications leader. Strategic thinker with a passion for helping organizations shape customer and employee perception to grow a healthy business. Recognized for:

- *Exceptional communications skills: Can effectively simplify the complex to deliver clear, concise and compelling communications*

- *Trusted communications counsel to executives: Have helped CEOs effectively develop and deliver their messages to multiple audiences*

- *Equally strong left brain/right brain: Ability to think creatively and execute effectively; strong project management and analytical skills*

- *High-performance team-builder: Track record of execution through teams, driven by a genuine desire to help others succeed*

Your goal with the summary profile is to bridge between what you have done in the past and what you can do for a new employer. To simply list responsibilities qualifies you for the job you already have, and what's the point of that? *In the summary statement, and the rest of the résumé too, try to avoid phrases like* responsible for *and* duties include. *Think about proving your capabilities instead.*

An opening profile gives you a writing advantage: It tells you what content to focus on in the rest of the résumé. Everything you include should back up the summary with convincing detail. So draft the summary first—but after writing the rest, review this intro statement carefully to see if in fact the full résumé backs up your claims. Or perhaps you've developed other points worth including in the summary. Touch up all sections to strengthen and clarify your message.

Showcase Your Work Experience

Start with your most recent job, and follow with the rest in reverse chronological order. Logically, a current job merits the most description—but what if it's a diversion from your career path or you've only held it briefly? Then say as much as it's worth, and use fuller descriptions for one or more of your earlier jobs.

Try for a short narrative paragraph generalizing about the position and/or employer. For example:

Associate Social Media Marketing Director, JFL Inc., Seattle, WA, 2015–Present

Increasingly responsible marketing role for Fortune 1000 firm, second-largest distributor of home repair supplies on West Coast, employing 7,000 people. Strategize, create and direct social media campaigns to support all company marketing.

The company is described for a reason: The reader may not readily know what it is or may recognize the firm's name but not its scope. In both cases, positioning the company—especially if significant in some way in size or standing—makes your experience look all the better.

Amplify the job overview statement with bulleted specifics:

- *Built and nurture Facebook community of 27,000, producing a 29% fan base increase*
- *Initiated campaigns for Snapchat and Instagram, attracting 5,500 new followers in six months*
- *Develop user-generated content, currently supplying 58% of all posts*
- *Generate research analytics monthly and report to Leadership Team*
- *Train staff in use of social platforms to support mission*
- *Coordinate social campaigns with marketing, public relations and customer relations managers*

VIEW FROM THE FIELD: WHAT A HUMAN RESOURCES MANAGER WANTS

When I hire for a position like marketing, I get easily 700 or 800 résumés. Realistically, you have five or 10 seconds. So don't tell me—sell me.

You don't have to include everything you've done, but put it in a way that makes sense. For example, one résumé I reviewed said, "Managed a variety of integrated marketing programs." I asked her to explain and she redefined it to, "Launched 1.5-million-person direct mail piece with a response rate exceeding 20%." Similarly, a line that read "Managed creative and production processes to ensure budget delivery" is better as "Created new internal budgeting process that kept more than $700,000 worth of production under budget."

So write less, be more accurate and to the point. Try using the STAR approach: situation-task-action-result—to make a sentence or brief paragraph.

—Doug Silverman, general manager of human resources at Nikon Inc. and former president of Society of Human Resource Managers/Long Island

Following up in the same pattern, name each position in reverse chronological order with a short narrative and three to six bullet points for each.

For each job, cite accomplishments as possible. A list of responsibilities you've carried out is a lot less interesting than evidence that you performed this work in an outstanding way. Employers want to know how you made a difference to the organization.

To understand how to do this, note the contrast between A and B in each of the following.

Statement A

Manage, write and budget enterprise-wide employee contest for two company intranet sites.

Statement B

Invent ideas for employee pop culture contests to engage a diverse workforce, regularly drawing 2,000 to 3,000 entries per month and contributing to a positive culture aligned with the entertainment industry.

Statement A

Responsible for managing and improving inventory process and supplying regular reports to team leaders.

Statement B

Revamped company's inventory process and introduced new controls that reduced shrinkage 17% and saved 24% in staff costs, earning a department commendation.

Statement A

Redesigned a warehouse.

Statement B

Transformed a disorganized warehouse into an efficient operation by totally redesigning the layout, saving an estimated $50,000 annually in recovered stock.

Notice in particular that the B statements do the following:

1. Use the industries' power words and action verbs to frame the work and energize the writing.

2. Relate either to major ongoing aspects of the position or to a project. Because project work has a beginning and an end, think through projects you've handled to identify accomplishments worth citing.

3. Quantify accomplishments in terms of time or money saved, efficiency achieved or other contribution to company goals—all music to every prospective employer's ears.

Numbers are magical and talk the bottom-line language of all enterprises, so quantify everything you possibly can. This is challenging but well worth the effort.

When you can't quantify, think about a way to suggest a positive outcome in other terms. For example:

Introduced knowledge management program to promote better use of resources company-wide, creating new tools such as orientation toolkits and e-newsletters.

Invented new process to streamline online purchasing, adopted organization-wide.

Another good technique for bringing your résumé alive is to look past the glib-type generalizations we tend to produce and find the concrete facts behind them—what we do can be much more interesting than the generalizations. For example, I recently questioned a young woman whose résumé contained lines like this:

I monitor executive e-mail shadowboxes and manage the executive correspondence processes.

What did she mean? On a weekly basis, she scans about 300 e-mails in the Fortune 100 company's general inbox, assesses their importance, responds according to her judgment and prepares a trend report.

This might be phrased something like this:

Monitor public input: Review hundreds of e-mails weekly, evaluate their importance, frame answers and report on trends to top management.

Employ Stand-Out-From-the-Crowd Techniques

Here are some ideas to give you the edge. Choose those that best show you off and relate most directly to the job you're after. When you customize your résumé to an opportunity, review your content to see if different elements would strengthen your chances.

Highlight promotions. Does your work history overall, or with a major job, demonstrate a steady advance in title or responsibility? Or fast progress? Make the most of it up front in your overview profile and in the way you detail the job. Recruiters will assume that impressing one employer means you're a good bet for their firms.

Cover personal attributes. Your "soft skills" can be very important to an employer: for example, leadership or facilitation abilities, good teaming, fast learning, consistent willingness to go above and beyond, ability to inspire others and so on. Are you unflappable under pressure? Good at training new staff members or mentoring? Able to handle multiple projects and deliver on tight deadlines? Play your strong suits but be specific and cite evidence as possible.

Use endorsements. Let others say it for you. This can be terrific if you're switching careers or are relatively new to the job market. Have a former boss or even coworker state how valuable you were to the team, how hard you worked and took initiative, what a good problem solver you were.

Endorsements need not come from employers. Your mother's word might not hold much weight, but a professor's might, or a colleague's, or the head of an organization for which you've done volunteer work. When including an endorsement, use quotation marks, italics, and a full attribution—the person's name, title and affiliation. Put it at the top of your résumé or, better, the bottom.

Include pro bono and community work. Especially in tough times when organizations shrink, people on every level find themselves out of work. Many choose to give time on a non-paid basis to a worthy cause or an organization they can learn from. Don't shrink from saying so—it demonstrates a mind-set that many recruiters will appreciate.

Include teaching and presenting. If you've taught anything that's career related—even remotely—use it. If you've given lectures, mentored others, coached a team or taught a course even at your local high school, say so. Being able to teach shows mastery of the subject or at the least a great sharing attitude. Presentation skills are highly valued in most fields.

Include your own business. Even if you didn't succeed with it, starting and running a business testifies to your initiative, courage and big-picture thinking. Include it, and say what you learned from the experience. But be prepared to convince the recruiter that you're not looking for an opportunity to go back to entrepreneurial life anytime soon.

Create better job titles. If your official title is inaccurate, vague or unimpressive, take the liberty of generic titling, but keep it lowercase to be honest. For example, if you are Third Assistant Manager for Procurement Support, use a more descriptive title to set the stage—such as procurement specialist for recycled metals.

Play the social media card. In most industries, the people in charge recognize that social media is critical to their marketing, customer relations and employee communications. If you are adept with social media and your online presence bears this out, say so. But don't overplay your hand. Remember that to businesses and nonprofits, social media is one more toolset to accomplish their goals and ties tightly to their marketing. If you've used your online presence to achieve something beyond making friends, this may be more significant.

Mention other skills and talents that are interesting, relevant or both. If you raised championship bulldogs, grew up on a farm, lived in another country, won dance contests or chess tournaments, play in the community orchestra, captained the college soccer team—whatever: It may or may not be worth mentioning in your résumé. A growing number of employers value social consciousness, so evidence of your commitment to something bigger than yourself may give you a plus. You must judge the value according to the job you're targeting. Always be aware of other people's sensibilities: Mentioning that you work for a particular political party or collect guns will probably not help your cause in some circles.

Consider length. This is not as big an issue now that most résumés are delivered digitally, but as a general rule, when you apply for your first career job, one page is probably enough.

But if you feel justified in saying more, don't try to cram it into a single page and sacrifice readability. More experienced people with five or more years of experience can certainly use up to two pages, but more is not usually necessary unless you apply for an academic job. In any case, draft your document based on what you believe is important, then work to tighten and sharpen the language. Check total content to be sure you're not diluting your central message with overkill.

Make it look great.   Take trouble with your layout; enlist the help of an artistic friend if you need to. Stick to one highly readable typeface and make it at least 11 point. Resist the temptation to make margins narrower than one inch. Make judicious use of bold, capitals and italics. Build in enough white space, even if this means cutting a bullet or two.

Use good paper if supplying hard copies. Head a second page with your name, as it may get detached. When you deliver a résumé online, don't depend on color for appearance or emphasis. The document will probably be printed out in stark black on white. And don't rely on special effects. Recruiters warn that when they print out some résumés, graphic techniques like a shadowed font may not show up at all—and if it's used for the heading, there goes your name.

Remember, too, that your résumé will be viewed on various platforms and that spacing, fonts and even punctuation marks can change. For safety's sake, send it to a few friends to see if it holds up.

Create and deliver as a PDF?   No! Use Microsoft Word, which is essentially universal. A PDF raises barriers to evaluating your credentials, which is the last thing you want to do. Probably 90% of the time, hiring managers and recruiters use an applicant tracking system, which doesn't work well with PDFs. Adding PDFs to their database is complicated and errors may creep in, to your disadvantage. So create your résumé to look good in Word, or use Google Docs to create a Word doc.

VIEW FROM THE FIELD: AN EXECUTIVE RECRUITER'S TIPS FOR FIRST-JOB SEEKERS

Aim to craft a résumé that is clear, concise and targeted. A résumé is your advertisement and must entice an employer to notice you. It tells hiring managers enough about you so that they'll want to meet you and find out more.

Writing your own résumé can be difficult. Ask people in your network what they think about it. Use your alumni association to find people who work in the field you want to enter, and see if they suggest adding or changing anything. Just remember that your résumé represents you. When you go for that interview you want to feel absolutely comfortable with it. Some tips to help:

Experience. You may not have a great deal of experience or any in the area where you're looking, but you still have experience. Use at least one or two bullet points for each job. Use active verbs to start your sentences; for example, Created new work schedules; Developed new menu ideas.

Also worth including: any research you've done, study abroad and volunteer experience, if it shows skills development. Include as many keywords as possible. Scan the ad and use the words the company used if they fit your background.

Keywords for online submission. When submitting your résumé for a position through a company's website, you will need to make the résumé very specific. It will be scanned by their applicant tracking system and the information the company is looking for will be pulled from your résumé and put into their format. So what you are submitting is not what they will see. Make sure to include any skills/keywords listed in the ad in your résumé.

Keep it simple. Research has shown that sans serif fonts make a résumé easier to read. Keep in mind that the typical résumé is scanned by a hiring manager for six seconds, so give them white space.

Length. Most people will tell you that a one-pager is a must for an entry-level résumé. If you have prior experience through jobs or internships, you can go to two pages. The experience you list must be relevant and match the job advertisement/description. Otherwise, stick to a one-pager.

Education. If you have had a full-time job for over one year, put your education on the bottom of the résumé. Put it first if you have only had internships or part-time jobs.

If your GPA is above 3.0 (on a 4.0 scale), definitely put it on your résumé. Academic achievements definitely belong on your résumé because they show how hard you worked and your determination to excel.

Provide your address. If you are still in school while job hunting, include both your school and home information. After graduation, just use your home address.

References. Make sure you have a current list of references in case you are asked. However, the phase "References provided on request" is considered old-fashioned, so don't state it on your résumé.

More than one résumé? You may be looking in several areas, and tailoring your résumé for each industry is essential.

—Marie Raperto, owner of
Cantor Integrated Marketing Staffing Inc.

The Social Media Résumé Option

Is a social media résumé right for you? It may be a great way to showcase who you are and what you can do. It presents you as a multidimensional individual who can be seen and heard. But, to pull it off, you need the creative skills to produce a website or blog (preferably with HTML know-how and some design talent), produce your own videos and/or podcasts and, preferably, blog regularly. And need I mention, this all takes good writing skills. As with all online media, you must be committed to constantly updating your material so it doesn't grow stale.

A social media résumé also can instantly connect your audience with some or all of your online "lives," such as Facebook, LinkedIn, YouTube, Twitter and so on. But be sure these sites show you to good advantage. Understand and exercise your privacy options, but don't count on them to protect you. Assume that if you put it online—they will come.

DEVELOP STRONG COVER LETTERS

The eternal question: Do you need to write cover letters when you submit a résumé? The short answer is *yes.* In many instances the letter may be ignored, but in others, without a cover letter that passes muster, your résumé will not be read. It's often hard to judge which will be the case. Many executive recruiters encourage job seekers to put their energy into the résumé and provide a perfunctory cover note at most. But when live human beings do the screening, and are invested in finding the very best candidate for their time and money, the cover letter can open the door or close it.

When you're applying to a small organization or department, a culture and personality fit is high priority, so write the cover letter. If people skills are critical to the role, expect that the cover letter matters. When the hiring process has a personal feel to it, write a cover letter. If you anticipate stiff competition, write the letter.

In practical terms, writing an effective cover letter is challenging, and there's little economy of scale—one size definitely doesn't fit all. A useful rule of thumb: If the opportunity is one you'll be heartbroken to miss, whether because it aligns with your highest aspiration or you really need the money or the opportunity, take the trouble. Write a great letter.

An acquaintance was hired to direct and expand a nonprofit institute that supports basic education in war-torn countries. She advertised for an assistant, new graduates eligible. This drew several hundred résumés. Filling the role with the right person—who'd be her sole staffer—was so important that the director sorted through all the applications herself and soon decided to read only those résumés that arrived with outstanding cover letters.

Her rationale is important to note even if you're applying to a monster corporation. *A large percentage of applicants cite excellent qualifications that are nearly equivalent*: high class standing, impressive internships and activities, relevant skills already developed. How to distinguish between candidates? The cover letter was the answer for the nonprofit director, because excellent ones require good writing and good thinking. More than a résumé, which is fact-based, a letter shows how well the person understands the job and connects with it, and illuminates the applicant's individual personality.

Also, you will find occasions when the letter alone must speak for you. Employers might screen them without even asking for a résumé. And if you need to write a "cold call" letter offering yourself to a chosen organization, asking whether they have an unadvertised opening or might create one for you, the letter must be good.

Options for Strengthening Your Letters

Here are some of the patterns taken by letters that made the cut for the nonprofit director. Even if your industry of choice is far removed from hers in nature, the format, language and approach to content suggest some useful strategies.

Salutation: Variations on "Dear Hiring Committee" and "Dear Ms. White."
Unequivocally, addressing a letter to a specific person is best. Take the time to track down a name and avoid "To whom it may concern."

Close: A few alternatives:

I hope to speak with you soon and can be reached by phone at _____ or by e-mail at _____. Thank you for your consideration. Sincerely,

I would be delighted to support the important work of _____ and hope to hear from you. Respectfully,

I would love the opportunity to provide _____. If you'd like to get in touch, please e-mail me at _____ or call _____. Thank you,

Message Patterns

You can start by introducing yourself. Here are four beginnings:

1. *I'm writing to apply for the _____ position at _____. I recently finished an internship at _____ and now seek . . .*

2. *It is with great pleasure that I submit my résumé for _____. I am a recent graduate of _____. I am passionate about this position because . . .*

3. *I am an exceptionally detail-oriented program manager interested in the position of _____. I would be a valuable addition to the staff because . . .*

4. *Three years ago, in a roofless classroom in Afghanistan, my dedication to improving the lives of young war victims was born. I was teaching as an international scholar sponsored by . . . (two-sentence anecdote)*

Which do you like best?

All four earned an interview, but when you're able to relate an on-target personal experience as in #4, it's magnetic. If you're entering an arena other than nonprofit, you may still have a strong reason for wanting to do this particular work. Are you training to be an engineer because you grew up next to a magnificent bridge? Was your idea of fun as a child playing with numbers, leading you to want a career as an actuary? Is working at the cutting-edge of digital technology your driving force?

There are no wrong answers! But the *why* of your life choice is worth some thought and is probably central to what makes you an individual. If this tack doesn't work for you, matter of fact is fine—but show some enthusiasm! A nonprofit application may call for "passion" or "dedication," as in the example, but whatever the industry, take the trouble to sound like an interested, high-energy, proactive prospect. Few organizations prefer to hire someone who comes across as a passive, unengaged plodder, unless perhaps she's an exceptional atomic scientist. Strive for a consistently positive upbeat tone—a quiet confidence.

In the above examples, each of the leads is followed by three or four paragraphs that cover

- what the applicant values about the job or why he was drawn to it, not "this looks like a good opportunity and I will really appreciate it and work hard at it," but specific facts about how the organization's mission resonates with the writer, why in his view it's important;

- what she brings to the mission, putting her education, internships and relevant job experience into perspective;

- special qualifications such as recognition for previous work well done, integrated with describing the job responsibilities;

- summary at the end: why it's a good fit.

Tips for Connecting With Reviewers

Never dash off a cover letter at the last minute. Most of your competitors spend excruciating weeks on polishing their résumés and then write sloppy, ill-crafted, thought-free cover letters that may close the door up fast. Invest the necessary time to plan, brainstorm, draft and revise a strong letter.

Absorb the organization's philosophy and priorities. If you're answering a posting, read it 20 times; it's full of clues to what the advertiser wants and believes is important to the company. Read between the lines for hints about a problem the organization needs to solve. Look at the company's website and whatever other materials you can access—talk to people who know the industry or, better, the specific firm. Read online sources where current and past employees offer insights on culture and values. Especially if you're sending a cold-call query, try to figure out "what keeps them up at night." But you need not directly mention your discoveries—as in, "I know your business volume went down 9% last quarter." More often just use what you learn as background information to help your content.

Remember your goal. A cover letter should introduce you in a more personal, targeted way than a résumé. It need not give a comprehensive overview of your career and qualifications—that's what the résumé is for—but should aim to

- present an insight about you that the résumé format doesn't accommodate;

- put a relevant perspective on your experience and credentials;

- highlight the most significant qualifications for the job;

- suggest some personality, or personal attributes, relevant to the job;

- set the stage for the reader to review your résumé as you would like;

- show why you are the most qualified person for the job.

A strong application demands that you know why you are the person that the company should hire. Have a good answer to "why me," and the cover letter will reflect your conviction and include the facts to back it up. And so will the interview.

Name that connection. If you have a personal link of any kind to the recipient or organization, say so up front. Name-dropping can work wonders: Who wouldn't rather hire somebody who comes vouched for, even a little bit? So don't be shy if you can come up with anything relevant—for example, that someone the person knows suggested you write—a colleague, former employer, professor, friend; you saw the person speak at a conference; you went to the same school.

Say why you want to work there.   For example, "As someone who follows the business press, I know that Y is the leading company in its market"; "I admire the company's strategic marketing tactics"; "I'm impressed by how Y Inc. has created breakthrough products in only five years"; "Z told me that working for you was the best experience he ever had." But don't follow this advice without doing your homework. If you want to compliment an organization's ethics, make sure the leaders haven't been indicted lately. One applicant I heard about ruined his chances by complimenting a nonprofit's recognized authority in its field. But the organization was less than six months old. Take the time to know what you're talking about, and find a truly good reason why you want to work in that place and that role.

Use the language, style and keywords of your audience.   Cover letters, like résumés, are partial exceptions to the "no buzzwords" rule. Aim to reflect the company's style, and focus and get your message across in terms these readers will relate to. This is especially important because many reviewers will scan your letter mechanically and look for their keywords. That said, people often don't like to read the way they write themselves or don't like the biz speak that job ads provoke. So a conversational (but courteous) style is still best. And be wary of adding any jargon of your own, from a different industry, to theirs.

Use the space to communicate more personal factors.   In addition to using the letter to say why you're an enthusiastic fit for the job, this is a good place to tell your "inside" story. For example, if you're leaving a bank job to follow a career with nonprofits, share your reasons for doing that. If your résumé isn't linear and one or more gaps are evident, explain to the degree that seems called for.

Consider using a testimonial.   It can be incorporated into the body of your letter or added as a pullout, carefully placed on the page with the name, position and affiliation of the person you're quoting. A testimonial can speak to your technical qualifications but at least equally well to your personal qualities—for example, perseverance, hard-work habits, fast learning, taking initiative and so on. This is particularly effective if you don't yet have a lot of work experience to your credit. A professor who likes you is a great source.

Good news: An error-free letter is now so freakin' rare that the minimal care required to send a letter with zero defects, combined with a few crisply written simple declarative sentences, will, alone, guarantee a respectful reading of a résumé. Maybe even secure an interview.

—From Bob Killian's "Cover Letters From Hell"
feature at www.killianbranding.com

Adopt an Upbeat Tone

Your cover letter should feel totally positive and upbeat. Worth repeating: Whatever the field, show enthusiasm, even passion, for the work you want to do, the profession and the specific job opening, as appropriate. These days, few employers look solely for technical skills, unless they intend to plant you in some hidden back office. The soft skills—relating to people, teaming, leading—are almost universally valued.

Communications is graduating from being considered a soft skill to a baseline skill—one that's needed everywhere. The key to citing these skills is to be specific: Rather than stating, "I am good with people," go for something like "chosen as Intern Representative to communicate on behalf of cohort." Find evidence of your claims.

Remember that the people you're writing to are focused on their own problems and challenges. They work hard to explain what they want. It's your job to match yourself to those needs. If you're doing a cold job hunt—writing letters in the hope of unearthing an unadvertised opportunity—you need to figure out what problem the firm might have, and present yourself as a solution. This is how independent contractors of every variety grow their businesses.

Write with a quiet conviction. Résumés and cover letters are at heart sales pitches, and first and foremost, you must believe the message yourself. Forging your own individual message step by step and discovering how to articulate it well is the best path to your future. So never begrudge the time these materials take.

Meet the Technical Specs

1. Keep the letter to one-page maximum. Less is better. If you're writing a cover letter that will be e-mailed, keep it even shorter—like three brief paragraphs. The need for brevity is one reason not to waste space on stock phrases, stilted language and obvious statements (like "It is herewith my pleasure to provide you with . . . in response to your recent posting for . . ."). A nice way to save space, which lets you invent a more interesting lead, is to write "In application for the X position" at the top of the letter, or as a subject line under the salutation.

2. Don't send letters that look mass-produced. If you're mailing an inquiry to 500 prospective employers, personalize and tailor each and every one and include at least something that demonstrates your interest in that specific company.

3. Instead of erudite language, use concrete language based on short words; uncomplicated sentences that alternate between long and short and; and, especially, short paragraphs that build in lots of white space. Better to say less and get it read. Check your transitions, polish up the conciseness, energize your verbs, try for a strong lead. You're writing for a very impatient audience.

4. Remember the serial audience. Expect your cover letter to be screened by somebody in the hiring office, a department head, the CFO's assistant or the new intern—or the CEO. Fortunately, the letters this process prepares you to write will work for every level.

5. Make it look good—like a letter, not a casual e-mail: proper salutation, wide margins, white space for breathing, respectful sign-off. Ideally it should match your résumé's appearance for a uniform impression. As with the résumé, keep in mind that when you e-mail your application, fancy formatting and fonts may get lost in cyberspace.

6. Execute it perfectly. There is no margin whatever for spelling errors, sloppy writing or anything that can be interpreted as a mistake in either a cover letter or a résumé.

In many cases, a simple, straightforward, correct letter introducing your résumé may be enough. Many of the ideas in this section are geared to those special jobs that you really want, which may be highly competitive and may represent a reach. In such cases, excellent communication helps you stand out. And while, yes, each letter must be customized, when you forge a way to articulate something well, stockpile it into your resource kit. Draw on these strong statements when they're appropriate—but always be sure to integrate them with the whole message and take care that everything you include helps make the match.

Many, many opportunities today are discovered via personal and professional networking. In addition to the networking advice in this chapter, check out the section on networking messages in Chapter 8. Also helpful: techniques for presenting yourself well, covered in Chapter 11. The Talking Points strategy outlined there gives you a good way to start brainstorming your message and selling points.

PRACTICE OPPORTUNITIES

I. Plan for a Job Hunt

Expect to look for a new job, internship or summer associate position this year? If so, do the following:

1. Define—in writing—your set of goals, with detail. In addition to stating the job you'd like to have, specify what you want to gain from it.

2. Write the most complete profile you can of your audience—the people who'll review your application at the organization where you want to work.

3. In the framework of your answers to the first two tasks, brainstorm the content of your résumé. What should you include about your experience and personal qualifications?

II. Write an Ad for the Job You Want

Put yourself in your prospective employer's shoes and figure out how she would advertise your ideal job. Write a detailed posting that covers all relevant aspects. Then evaluate your qualifications against the posting. How well prepared are you? If you believe you are qualified, does your résumé demonstrate that? Does this perspective give you any ideas about how to improve your résumé? And any experience or learning opportunities to pursue?

III. Question for Discussion: How Is Applying for a Career Job Different?

How would the content of a résumé for a summer job or an internship differ from one for your next career job? Write your analysis. Then exchange it with your classmates' observations and discuss as a group. Keep track of ideas you hadn't thought of, and consider how to use them in your next job search.

IV. Write Your Summary of Experience

Draft your strongest summary of experience and qualifications with a specific job goal in mind.

V. Review Your Current Résumé

Evaluate how well it works in terms of what you've learned in this chapter and the book as a whole, and decide how to improve it. Turn at least three of the responsibilities you describe into accomplishments and try to quantify them or cite other proof of accomplishment.

VI. Write a Letter for Your Dream Job

Find a posting that at this point represents your dream job. Though you may not be ready to apply, draft the best cover letter you can develop to make your case. Try this process:

- Brainstorm your history, experience and every qualification that might relate.

- Analyze and interpret the job description and other employer material.

- Figure out what you'd bring to the job beyond the bare essentials.

- Figure out why you are the best possible candidate and why the organization should hire you.

- Come up with some imaginative leads and evaluate whether they are appropriate.

VII. Compare Job Application and Personal Ads

Scan entries on a dating site such as OkCupid or Match.com, or any app where people describe themselves in order to connect with other people. Review what they say about themselves, how they describe the person they want to meet and how they say it. What insights do some individuals provide (often inadvertently) about who they are through their writing? What do you discern about their values and priorities? Are they presenting the right information—the content—to engage the kind of person they say they want to know? What ideas does your analysis suggest that relate to presenting yourself as a job candidate? Write 500 words or more about what you learned, citing examples. (Can be used as a basis for class discussion.)

VIII. Role-Play Job Interview Scenarios

This set of activities centers on role-playing, a helpful technique for understanding other people. It can be hard to see past our own perspective, but we always gain immeasurably from seeing situations (and ourselves) through someone else's eyes. You'll find that, done seriously, these exercises activate your imagination for how other people think and feel. You can even practice a form of role-playing by yourself, by staging a two-way conversation in your head. This taps into your intuitive powers.

However, when one or more other people are involved, even constructive criticism can be intimidating or hurtful when voiced. To sidestep this risk, the class should agree to refrain from all negative comments and focus entirely on providing positive input. Remark on what worked, what each person did well, new ideas generated by the role-play scenarios and so on. You will find results to be at least as illuminating as critical commentary, and at the same time, participants learn how to improve their own presentation more naturally and happily.

1. Partner Activity: Interview for Your Dream Job

Exchange your résumé and dream job cover letter with a classmate. One partner assumes the role of hiring manager. From that perspective, she takes some time to understand the job requirements and perhaps the industry. Then she decides how as hiring manager she would conduct the interview and what she would want to know. She develops the best and most probing questions relevant to the job in question that she can come up with. Together, candidate and hiring manager carry out the role-play and stage the interview. Then they reverse roles. At the end, they give each other constructive criticism.

2. Class Activity: Develop Interviewing Guidelines

In this version, two volunteers or randomly chosen members of the class can assume the roles and carry out the interview session in front of the whole class, which then comments on both performances. A series of such demonstrations might be conducted. Ultimately, the class collaborates on drafting 10 guidelines for handling interviews well. Include recommendations for the content of answers and also delivery: the candidate's voice, bearing, body language and anything else that contributes to creating an overall impression.

3. Explore the Interviewer's Perspective

Analyze: What did you learn about how someone responsible for conducting interviews thinks? Did you find it took effort to frame good questions? Was it hard to lead the conversation? What differences did you observe in how various classmates handled the role of interviewer: Did some try to make the candidate comfortable? Did some take charge more aggressively than others? How well did they listen and respond? Can you make any observations about the characteristics of effective interviewing? Collaborate in groups or as a class to draft 10 guidelines for being a good interviewer. And discuss how this gives you insights into being a better interviewee.

APPENDIX

Activities, Practice, Planning

Love words, agonize over sentences. And pay attention to the world.

—Susan Sontag, philosopher and author

It's time to pull it all together! This "extra" chapter provides more ways to practice what you've learned. It also helps you develop your own tools to support your continuing improvement as a writer. You'll find the following:

- sentence rewrite exercises drawn from this book's first draft

- some real-world examples to dissect and remedy

- conversational starters about the ethics of persuasion and outsourcing services

- group projects and assignments that show you how to tackle new subjects and media

- a primer on interviewing and the art of developing good questions

- a set of assignments chosen by teachers

- an action method to solve your own writing problems and create a personal improvement plan

SENTENCE REWRITE PRACTICE (NOBODY'S PERFECT)

Here are some terrible sentences—quite a few, actually—that I wrote for this book. You will be happy I rewrote them in the editing stage, but now it's your turn. Figure out how you would express the thoughts better. I like to think sharing these first draft examples gives you a quick overview of the book's content and encourages you to edit your own drafts. Remember: A professional is a writer who edits.

1. Even if writers could restrict themselves to writing only for traditional print form, they'd have to take account of fundamental ways in which on-screen reading (whether computer, etc.) has changed reader expectations.

2. The Flesch Index is a box that appears immediately after spell check.

3. All the approaches are excellent, and you can find one that works for you to supplement the practical strategy we'll pursue here.

4. Have you considered any sensitivities your audience may have?

5. All the graphic tools are even more important because many people are resistant to on-screen reading.

6. Note that the longer sentences give the writer the ability to make connections between actions.

7. Giving the audience the responsibility generates either misinterpretation or indifference. You never want your readers to wonder "why is she telling me that?" or substituting their own reasoning for your own, even nonconsciously. Ambiguous connections generate misinterpretation or indifference.

8. Nevertheless, if you write better sentences, combine them effectively and use the structured thinking principles covered in the last two chapters, you're on the way to a powerful, flexible writing capability that will serve you well.

9. Improving the way you use verbs gives you one of the best tools for improving all your writing.

10. Try to improve your use of words, create better sentences and use verbs more effectively.

11. Did you fully articulate your goals?

12. Our assumption was that better writing results from having practiced more.

13. The amount of interaction in contemporary office contexts is continually diminishing, because of technology.

14. This method will demonstrate the need for clarity.

15. The subject line of an e-mail is the biggest factor in determining whether the message gets read or not.

16. Is there anything that can be interpreted as being against the writer's interest?

17. E-mail can be critical in scoring opportunities and in building and maintaining relationships, so examples of messages to support networking are included in some of the preceding chapters.

18. Even a significant e-mail should be stashed for a few hours.

19. Passages to which writers are especially attached are suspect—they probably are distracting to readers.

20. Almost always, you can glean good ideas from writers you admire.

21. A proposal is successful when it reads like a story.

22. People are likely to underestimate the value of reports they are required to write.

23. Use online systems to share documents, such as Google Docs, which makes sharing easy for collaborative purposes.

24. It's not a good idea to tell the boss something like, I was absolutely decimated not to be awarded the assignment.

25. Here's a tactic that is almost universally fail-safe: Define your goal and your audience before writing.

26. Think about whether you want to make course adjustments.

27. It may at times seem easiest to send a written message of some kind, rather than talking, especially when what you want to get across is hard to deliver.

28. Often you can use a combination of techniques to edit.

29. It will be very rewarding for you to see how your goals can be achieved.

30. Think about a way to solve the problem that is less costly in terms of time.

31. If you're a supervisor, it's smart to hold a training session on creating relevant reports and explain how they will be used in decision making.

32. Get out of the habit of thinking you need to memorize grammar rules to edit your work.

33. Your intuition may be to write a shorter memo without technical detail to the boss.

34. It's a mistake to make a decision to leave a job without speaking up to your supervisor.

35. The purpose of an editing cheat sheet is to help you remediate your personal writing problems.

36. One of the big benefits of storytelling is that it leads you to look more closely at your life experience.

37. There is nothing that needs to be done further.

38. It's important to consider how your tone affects readers.

39. An important message is a letter, even when you're using e-mail to deliver it.

40. Yesterday, there were sharp distinctions between e-mails and letters.

41. Immersion in the audience's perspective is a must.

42. If you've allowed enough time for a project, you'll end up able to edit well.

43. If you want to promote your career with online media, you'll find that the field is crowded and competitive.

44. Think about how the strategies can be adapted to your own writing.

45. Learning to plan and edit your writing does not mean you should not have fun writing.

46. If you want to ask people to risk making an investment in you, write well.

47. We don't know what is the reason for that.

48. If you would like to get a glimpse of the process, start here.

49. You may be surprised to know that to most employers and placement specialists, writing is considered a baseline skill rather than a soft skill.

50. Open your message in a way that directly makes the connection with your audience.

51. If there are many gaps in your work history, deal with it honestly.

52. From a 15-second elevator speech that introduces you to people you want to know, to a PowerPoint-style presentation, to giving a webinar, the rule is plan, write, rehearse, deliver.

53. Your ability to understand other people better will give you the ability to build better relationships and achieve what you want more often.

54. You may have been having trouble finalizing your word list.

55. The lead of any message should really be aimed at telling readers something they might be interested in knowing.

56. A single composite document is created and distributed to the class.

57. Create a Talking Points cheat sheet to guide class members through the job interview process by brainstorming and researching the commonly asked questions that may be asked and developing good answers.

58. More and more goods and services are now purchased online and this produces an escalating amount of correspondence—questions and complaints.

59. Today identifying material that relates to our own interests is a challenge. There's just so much of everything vying for our attention!

60. What content does the group think will both serve your purposes and be found interesting and relevant to your primary audiences?

UNFORTUNATE REAL-WORLD EXAMPLES TO DIAGNOSE

Collect your own file of material that leads you to wonder, "What were they thinking?" This collection gives you a start. The clips demonstrate, by negative example, why writing well matters and some of the pitfalls to avoid. Read through each example to diagnose where the writer—or in some cases, a whole department, division or company—went wrong. The problems range from plain old bad grammar to radical errors in tone and content. What's the impact on the audience in each case? Figure out how you would fix each example.

A. From a corporate announcement

The Area Vice President, Enterprise Customers will develop and manage a sustainable strategic relationship that transforms the current commercial model by creating joint value that results in the ongoing reduction of costs, continuous process improvement, growth and profitability for both partners with the ability to export key learnings.

B. From a news article

"I am absolutely devastated if this caused offense to anyone," Hollywood posted on Twitter. "The picture was taken 14 years ago on our way to a Comedy TV Shows Themed New Year's Eve Party and a group of us dressed up as characters from the classic TV show "'Allo 'Allo."

C. From an apartment building manager

Residents, around 6pm today a pipe burst on the 2nd floor cause a major amount of water damage to 2nd floor and water to enter lobby. Emergency elevator teams and clean up companies are on their way. We are doing everything. We can to mitigate damages and will send further correspondence as we know more. At this time the elevators are down and we are hoping to have them resorted as soon as possible. Please be patient as the staff and arrives teams do their best to restore the building back to normal operations.

Thank you. Residents

D. The lead of a company statement following news coverage of exploding batteries

Samsung is committed to producing the highest quality products and we take every incident report from our valued customers very seriously. In response to recently reported cases of the new Galaxy Note7, we conducted a thorough investigation and found a battery cell issue.

E. A statement by the Bank of England chief (which produced a change in the pound's value)

Some removal of monetary stimulus is likely to become necessary if the trade-off facing [policy makers] continues to lessen and the policy decision accordingly becomes more conventional.

F. Congratulations! You've been accepted to Columbia University . . . only it turned out 276 students received this letter in error and were not, in fact, admitted. Other universities have made the same mistake—the University of California, San Diego, once sent a letter of acceptance to 28,000 students in error. What would you write to inform these candidates that they are not, in fact, joining the student body?

G. A memo announcing the layoff of 12,500 Microsoft employees by a VP

Hello there, Microsoft's strategy is focused on productivity and our desire to help people "do more." As the Microsoft Devices Group, our role is to light up this strategy for people. We are the team creating the hardware that showcases the finest of Microsoft's digital work and digital life experiences, and we will be the confluence of the best of Microsoft's applications, operating systems and cloud services.

To align with Microsoft's strategy, we plan to focus our efforts. . . .

Seven l-o-n-g paragraphs follow about the company's plans for product development and marketing strategies. Around paragraph 9 comes this statement:

We plan to right-size our manufacturing operations to align to the new strategy and take advantage of integration opportunities.

And finally, in paragraph 11:

We plan that this would result in an estimated reduction of 12,500 factory direct and professional employees over the next year. These decisions are difficult for the team, and we plan to support departing team members' with severance benefits.

Three more paragraphs ramble on about where the company will focus with hints about which segments are affected. Here's the close:

Collectively, the clarity, focus and alignment across the company, and the opportunity to deliver the results of that work into the hands of people, will allow us to increase our success in the future.

Regards,

Stephen

H. A response by Amazon to a customer complaint. An urgently needed medical device had not arrived after a week, although Amazon had promised a two-day delivery.

Hello, I have checked your order and understand your concern regarding the order.

Please don't worry, I will be glad to assist you on this.

On priority I have contacted the carrier and provided special instructions for them to deliver the package at the earliest.

Please rest assured you will receive the package by the end of the day. In this situation I will personally follow up with you to see if you receive the package.

I understand the inconvenience this situation may cause.

If in case the package doesn't arrive by the end of the day, please let us know whether you would prefer a replacement or refund.

I appreciate your patience in this regard.

It was a pleasure assisting you today! Hope you have a great day!

We'll appreciate your feedback. Please use the buttons below to vote about your experience today.

Best regards,

Xx

Amazon.com

Your feedback is helping us build Earth's Most Customer-Centric Company.

WRITING AND ETHICS: CONVERSATION AND DEBATE

Using Techniques of Persuasion

Here's a statement by Warren Buffett, part of a cover letter to his company's directors. It accompanied his letter to stockholders.

The priority is that all of us continue to zealously guard Berkshire's reputation. We can't be perfect but we can try to be. As I've said in these memos for more than 25 years: "We can afford to lose money—even a lot of money. But we can't afford to lose reputation—even a shred of reputation." We *must* continue to measure every act against not only what is legal but also what we would be happy to have written about on the front page of a national newspaper in an article written by an unfriendly but intelligent reporter.

Sometimes your associates will say, "Everybody else is doing it." This rationale is almost always a bad one if it is the main justification for a business action. It is totally unacceptable when evaluating a moral decision. Whenever somebody offers that phrase as a rationale, in effect they are saying that they can't come up with a *good* reason. If anyone gives this explanation, tell them to try using it with a reporter or a judge and see how far it gets them.

If you see anything whose propriety or legality causes you to hesitate, be sure to give me a call. However, it's very likely that if a given course of action evokes such hesitation, it's too close to the line and should be abandoned. There's plenty of money to be made in the center of the court.

1. Analyze: What do you think of Buffett's position? How would you feel if you received this message from your CEO? Does it feel like Buffett believes in what he's saying, rather than just giving lip service to a moral directive? How does the way he writes carry sincerity (or fail to)?

2. Note that not long after Buffett wrote this letter, one of his top executives (and expected successor), David Sokol, was accused of unethical behavior (buying substantial stock in a company that Berkshire Hathaway was about to acquire). Sokol resigned, but Buffett's initial response, which didn't express much outrage, was widely criticized. He later called the violation of the rules and company ethics "inexcusable." Does this set of events alter your view of Buffett's letter? What does it suggest about the relationship between written ideals and actions in business? Other spheres? Research the events and statements this situation generated, including Buffett's account of the situation (https://www.forbes.com/sites/ steveschaefer/2011/03/30/potential-buffett-successor-david-sokol-resigns-from- berkshire-hathaway/3/#71e54c6621e7). Digest the information and write an opinion piece, in blog or op-ed style, about what the episode means or how it should be seen.

3. Do you see any dangers in using persuasive techniques to accomplish business purposes? What examples of unethical use come to mind in what you have observed or read about?

4. Identify a specific example of unethical use of persuasion strategies you find interesting in any realm. Analyze why you believe the tactics were unethical. Then present your thinking to the class or group in three to five minutes. After hearing from all participants, collaborate with the group to draft a set of guidelines for the ethical use of persuasive techniques.

Take a Position: Hiring Essay Writers

You may have noticed that essay writing services are proliferating and that students can buy customized papers on demand, including dissertations for advanced degrees. These services are sometimes publicized covertly—for example, by presenting them as "editorial support" in articles that purport to offer writing advice.

What do you think of outsourcing your writing assignments? Consider it from your personal perspective and what you've learned about the role of writing in this book. Think about the effect outsourcing would have on your future career and hopes as well as your college experience. Write a letter to the editor of a publication that ran an article like the one described above that recommended several outsourcing companies. Explain why hiring other people to write your papers is unethical, unproductive, counter to a student's self-interest and so on. (I like to assume you feel that way! If not, write the letter anyway and see if you end up persuading yourself that it's a bad practice—or not.)

HANDLE UNFAMILIAR MEDIA: A NEWSLETTER PROJECT

As you know, the media landscape changes rapidly and as new venues rise, old ones slide into the sea, sometimes almost overnight. How to approach a new platform or one that's unfamiliar to you? The principles of understanding goal and audience will never fail you. All else follows. As an example, suppose you are asked to create a newsletter for a nonprofit. How to go about it? This project draws on strategies you practiced in many of the book's chapters.

Work on this in groups of about five people, if practical. Together you are the new newsletter's editorial board. As a group, choose a good cause for the newsletter to represent. It can be a real cause, perhaps the local chapter of a national charity. Or you can invent your own worthy cause.

Brainstorm to plan the newsletter. Explore and decide:

A. What are our goals for this publication? What is our central message? What specifically do we want the newsletter to accomplish?

B. Who are the audiences, both primary and secondary? List *all* of them (a proper breakdown may include dozens of groups; "women 17 to 20" is different from "women 35 to 45," for example). Decide which are the primary, most important audiences and profile them in detail.

C.   What content will serve our purposes and engage the audiences we want? Block out major content areas and then specific subjects for each (similar to the process for generating blog ideas in Chapter 10).

D.   What format and presentation style will best serve the audience and support our message and content? How many pages? Online or print?

Each group produces a written plan to share with the whole class. And each presents the plan orally to explain the thinking behind the ideas and decisions. If desired, the presentations can incorporate a PowerPoint-type presentation or video.

If course time allows, the groups can proceed to write, edit and design prototype issues. At this stage the editorial board members take on suitable roles such as editor-in-chief, managing editor, feature editor, copy editor, designer and so on. When finished newsletters are shared, interesting conversations are sure to result.

MAKE YOUR OWN CHEAT SHEETS

Guidelines for Finding the Lead

How to write a good lead (or lede) endlessly challenges journalists and editors. It's just as important to business writing. Today, so much vies for our attention that we're challenged to identify what's valuable to us. How you begin an e-mail, proposal, blog post or résumé determines whether it is read or trashed. Good leads are well worth the time required to craft them.

For this assignment, each student scouts for three leads she likes, in a favorite source: print or online media—magazine, newspaper, blog. Reproduce these in written form, one per page, and print them out. Create a single composite document and distribute it to everyone for review, in preparation for a class discussion. Each person should rate each lead's effectiveness on a 1 to 5 scale or other system.

Hold the discussion:

A.   To what degree do class members agree about which leads work best? Are there universal favorites, or close to it?

B.   Can you see reasons for the differences in opinion?

C.   What do the favorite-by-consensus leads have in common?

D.   Together, create a set of guidelines for developing strong leads. The ideas should be concrete and answer basic questions such as these: How does a good lead pull readers in? Signal the reader to care about the subject? Reflect content? Include a few examples for each guideline.

E.   Discuss: What does the "Find the Lead" cheat sheet tell you about writing strong leads for e-mails and other everyday media? How should the rules be applied to them? Does this project illuminate the reporter's mantra, "Don't bury the lede"? How can you keep that from happening?

A follow-up angle: Organize the one-lead-per-page printout by type of media—all the blog leads, news article leads, magazine leads and any other grouping that reflects what the class collected. Review and compare: In what ways are the lead strategies for each platform different from the others?

Cheat Sheets and Templates for Solving Problems

Adapt the find-the-lead model to develop cheat sheets for any aspects of business writing that the class finds challenging. In some cases, the cheat sheet can be developed as a template to use when needed. Some possibilities:

- Profile: Develop a step-by-step template for profiling a new supervisor or a difficult coworker. The goal is to guide the user through analyzing that person's perspective, reason out how to communicate and interact with him effectively, and develop a better relationship.

- How-to-communicate guidelines: List as many work situations as you can think of (resolving a problem with a colleague, asking your boss for something major or minor, etc.). Discuss and decide which form of communication (in-person, e-mail, social media, etc.) to use in each type of situation.

- Website guidelines: Review websites, identify individual favorites and create a cheat sheet of characteristics to aim for in creating personal sites.

- Blogging criteria: Share a shortlist of your favorite blogs for class members to review. In class, explore the characteristics of successful blogs that apply to every subject. Prepare the cheat sheet.

- Interview tactics: Create a Talking Points cheat sheet to guide class members through the job interview process. Brainstorm and research commonly asked questions and, together, develop good answers.

- Headlines and subject lines: Collect good headlines from a range of media, discuss what makes them successful and build a cheat sheet with a checklist of guidelines and ideas. Do the same for e-mail subject lines.

- Interviewer tactics: Create a Talking Points cheat sheet of good questions to ask the interviewer when you're applying for a job.

- Grammar problems: Identify the five (or 10) most important grammar and language problems common to members of the class, and build a two-column template that states the problem on the left and the solution(s) on the right. Research as necessary, and state solutions in practical commonsense terms as much as possible rather than formal grammar terms. Include one or more examples for each.

- Source reliability: Explore what makes resource materials credible, authoritative and trustworthy. What are the clues that an online source can be trusted? What reliable resources are available for specific needs (statistics, facts, information about people and employers, etc.)? Assemble an annotated list.

DEVELOP YOUR INTERVIEWING SKILLS

The ability to draw information from other people—a hiring manager, your boss, a client, a technical specialist, a coworker with expertise—is an invaluable career asset. Practice this skillset now and take it wherever you go. Developing good questions is the key. Here are some activities to kickstart your thinking. An active curiosity is always rewarded. It gives you not only a business environment you can engage with more successfully, but a world full of people who are more interesting than you expected. And because you listen, people will magically find *you* more interesting.

Interview a Relative for a Magazine Portrait

Pick a relative you don't know very well or someone familiar to you who has not shared much about his personal history with you. This is commonly the case with older relatives. We're accustomed to taking for granted their interest in us but often don't express interest in them as individuals. Alternatively, choose a friend or acquaintance, preferably from a different generation than your own.

Your goal is to interview the person and obtain interesting information to write a blog post or an article for publication in whatever medium you'd like. It can be a community newspaper or a newsletter rather than *Wired*. It's best to pick out a target platform right at the beginning. Then follow these steps:

1. Prepare: Do your homework and find out about the person from any available source—online if relevant, or by asking a few polite questions of other people. For example, if you're interviewing your grandfather, you might ask your parents what is interesting about him and what might prompt him to tell you about whatever that is.

2. Brainstorm a list of questions: They must be open-ended rather that answered with a yes or no. For example:

    - What happened when . . .

    - Do you have a favorite story about . . .

    - What do you recall as a hard (or happy, etc.) part of your life?

    - How did that affect you?

    - Why did you make that major decision to . . .

Or be specific:

- What was your first date like?

- Where did you meet Grandma?

- What are you most happy to have achieved?

- What are you most grateful for?

Of course, follow your own curiosity in regard to the person. Produce a list of written questions that begins with big-picture queries that give the other person a chance to suggest what *he* thinks is important. Try not to orient the conversation in a predetermined way that narrows the field down.

3. Carry out the interview: Ideally, make an appointment in advance, explaining the reason. Open with your open-minded lead question, which should be comfortable for the interviewee. Take notes as you wish: fast writing, recording if OK with your conversation partner, video. Be a good conversationalist—listen for clues to an interesting path and follow it. Especially be alert to emotional signals: things that make your subject contemplative, sad, perhaps angry. Follow up to get detail, but with sensitivity. At the end you can refer back to your question list to see if you forgot to cover anything important.

4. Write your story: Draw on the advice on blogging in Chapter 10. Note that it's much easier to frame an article by studying your target publication. Check out how articles like the one you're writing are handled there and in other publications you like. Take care with your lead and the rest may follow: What was the most interesting or surprising thing your subject said?

5. Debrief yourself: Was your relative, or other subject, more interesting than you expected? What was the effect of expressing deep personal interest in the other person? Which questions were most effective? Does the experience have any impact on your general understanding of your fellow human beings?

Interview a Classmate

1. Partner up with a classmate you don't know and interview each other. Try to find out at least one surprising or interesting fact about the other person without saying "Tell me something interesting." Look also for something in common (an experience, interest, hobby, etc.) and any special experience or expertise.

2. Take five minutes to write an introduction for your partner that you'll deliver orally. Aim for a one- to two-minute speech.

3. Introduce your "subject" to the class.

4. Once all the intros have been made, discuss as a group what intro approaches worked well, what was surprising, what was learned. If oral delivery is covered in the course, also talk about effective delivery techniques. Restrict comments to positive only!

Frame Good Questions for Business Situations

Reflect and discuss in class: How does what you learned about interviewing apply to work situations?

Identify various times which call for drawing information from another person; for example, a computer software expert, your supervisor, a researcher, a long-term coworker, a leader in your field with whom you have a chance to spend time, an HR specialist. Then the class divides into small groups, and each is assigned to focus on one of the listed situations. Share results and discuss: What did you learn about the nature of questions? Are some almost universally useful for different situations? How hard is it to think of good questions? Does group brainstorming make a difference?

FIVE FAVORITE ASSIGNMENTS

As part of its annual conference, the Association of Business Communicators (ABC) invites business communication teachers to participate in a session called "My Favorite Assignment." The results are published in ABC's journal, *Business and Professional Communication Quarterly*. Here are five of the contributions shared at a recent conference, described in abbreviated form.

Teach Your Grandparents to Use Their Mobile Device
Xiaoli Li, University of Dayton

Create a one-page tip sheet for specific older adults, people in their late 50s or above. Aim to teach this person how to use a specific function of her cell phone, or an app she's not familiar with. This requires conducting research to understand the target user's needs, attitudes and knowledge; writing clear, step-by-step instructions for nontechnical users; and applying design principles to create clear and user-friendly documents.

"How Do I Sound to You?" First Impressions on the Phone
Catherine Smith McDermott, St. Edwards University

A student volunteers to hold three conversations with the teacher, who plays the role of a potential employer trying to arrange an interview with the student, who is seeking an internship. The "candidate" leaves the classroom room with his cell phone and the phone is put on speaker so the other students can listen in.

Round 1: The "employer's" call reaches voice mail: The class assesses the greeting for content, professionalism and tone.

Round 2: The candidate returns the call, hears a recorded message and leaves one of his own. The class assess the message for clarity, professionalism and succinctness.

Round 3: Employer and applicant engage in a live conversation. The class assesses the professionalism of the call and, if criteria for effective telephone communication were not previously discussed, may do so now.

Round 4: Students partner with classmates to practice their own voice greetings, voice messages and phone conversations.

Progress Report: Self-Assessment of Your Online Presence

William Christopher Brown, University of Minnesota Crookston

Business faculty are concerned that students' online presence may hamper their career opportunities. An online search of two equally qualified candidates often decides who gets the job. An immature and unprofessional online presence could tip the favor to a candidate with a "cleaner," more professional social media presentation.

"Progress Report" allows students to examine their online image and consider the importance of a professional presence. The three stages of research:

1. Find articles that discuss the importance of having a good online presence.

2. Assess their own online presence.

3. Collect professional advice designed to improve their online presence.

Students then compose a report with headings and concise professional-style paragraphs covering:

- what I am doing well

- what I need to control

- what I can do to improve: a plan of action

- the importance of a good online presence

References, quotes and citations should be incorporated.

Shark Tank: Business Proposal Project

Kathleen Ditewig-Morris, University of Illinois-Champaign

Team project: Like the popular TV show, teams create an innovative product. They pitch their idea to prospective investors.

Each team develops a target market, creates an audience analysis, investigates the idea's feasibility, crafts a rhetorical strategy to persuade potential investors, writes an Executive Summary and presents the idea as a team to the "company." The goal is to obtain funding and/or support.

The class—the "sharks"—decide if the idea is feasible and presented effectively. (This is not an advertising or marketing campaign to reach consumers. Focus is on communications tools and strategies for pitching an idea to a business audience that has a clear stake in the outcome.)

Online Posting Complaint and Adjustment Statements

Susanna Shelton Clason, University of Cincinnati

Students choose a product or service that has disappointed or injured them. They write a letter of complaint for posting on a selected online venue. Message factors include the

Internet's wide viewership, description of the problem and any resolution or compensation desired. Students also write a cover memo explaining their venue choice and goals, including what they hope the post will achieve. Both pieces of writing are exchanged in class and students discuss the solution strategies.

CREATE YOUR PERSONAL WRITING RX

As mentioned throughout this book, particularly in Part II, every one of us writes with specific problems and shortcomings. Being conscious of your own is the best possible shortcut to improving everything you write. Use the magic wand of writing itself to chart and document the writing habits you want to change. Try it with pen and paper, which activates our analytic brain more deeply than typing.

On a sheet of paper, draw a line for a column about one third of the way in from the left. In the narrower left-hand column, list the problems you see in your writing—all the things that you have trouble with or that instructors, past and present, consistently correct. You might scout previous papers from other courses and note the reviewers' remarks. Do you begin to see any patterns?

Next, write down a solution to the problem in the second column. If you don't immediately know one, figure out how to find out. Suppose you identify a grammar problem—like a frequent mismatch between a subject and pronoun (e.g., him, their). If you're fuzzy on how to do this, first check this book to see if it's been dealt with. If not, or you need a more specific guideline, consult one of the grammar resources at the end of Chapter 5 or any other you like. Then write the rule down in any way that makes sense to you.

When problems are more general, like too many lengthy sentences or wordiness, the solution might be "read aloud and fix" or "look for and count the little words" (conjunctions and prepositions) and cut them back (see Chapter 5). And/or "start new sentence."

In case you think this is childish, I'll mention that I use such a cheat sheet myself, even though I've invested a lifetime in professional writing experience, endless learning opportunities and teaching. My cheat sheet keeps evolving. Here's part of a current version:

PROBLEM	SOLUTION
Too many "you shoulds," "you musts" (e.g., You should know your core message)	Use the plain imperative (Know your core message)
Too many hedgy words—can, might (e.g., You can learn this easily)	Cut them; use positive framing (This is easy to learn)
Too many dashes to hold sentences together	Start a new sentence; substitute commas
Awkward repeat wording (e.g., You'll be able to figure out a way to . . .)	Find another way to say it (Figure out how to . . .)

This personal cheat sheet is best done over time as you notice your own pitfalls. It will assume different dimensions depending on the nature of your job, the kind of writing involved or the project you're working on. Much of my list cited here relates to the particular challenges of writing a self-help book, which *Business Writing Today* is designed to be, as well as a textbook.

A problem diagnosed is a problem with a solution. Try creating your own Writing Rx. Working to analyze your own writing helps you write every message and document more effectively, which in turn supports your thinking and people skills. What could be more valuable?

INDEX